Recognizing the Latino Resurgence in U.S. Religion

EXPLORATIONS
Contemporary Perspectives on Religion

Recognizing the Latino Resurgence in U.S. Religion

THE EMMAUS PARADIGM

Ana María Díaz-Stevens
Union Theological Seminary

Anthony M. Stevens-Arroyo
Brooklyn College

WestviewPress
A Division of HarperCollins*Publishers*

Explorations: Contemporary Perspectives on Religion

Published in 1998 in the United States of America by Westview Press, 5500 Central Avenue, Boulder, Colorado 80301-2877, and in the United Kingdom by Westview Press, 12 Hid's Copse Road, Cumnor Hill, Oxford OX2 9JJ

A CIP catalog record for this book is available from the Library of Congress.
ISBN 0-8133-2509-9 (hc)   ISBN 0-8133-2510-2 (pb)

10   9   8   7   6   5   4   3   2   1

To the 14th of December in our lives.

To
William Loperena, O.P.
Teacher, muse, brother in religion

The Misa Jíbara
God's voice to our people, from the peaks of
island mountains and into the depths of patriotic conscience

Adán Esteban
Our one son, in the image and likeness of our union,
alchemy of legacy and hope

Contents

Figures and Tables

Figures

Tables

Acknowledgments

This book reflects scholarly research during the better part of twenty years, and our most heartfelt gratitude is to the Latinas and Latinos of faith who made the commitments and sacrifices we report her. Assuredly, many of the key ideas developed in this book were first published in other sources. The demographic patterns explained in the first chapter were first presented in a keynote address by Ana María Díaz-Stevens at an important 1997 meeting in Washington. Analysis of past sociological approaches to Latino religion reflects the thrust of a European publication by Anthony M. Stevens-Arroyo. The second chapter uses material from an encyclopedia article published under both our names. "The matriarchal core" and "pious colonialism" were terms defined by each of us in separate articles published in the *Latino Studies Journal*. The final chapters incorporate materials that were part of our contributions to the Notre Dame historical series. Despite this repetition of some key ideas, this book represents a unique publication that places these notions into a coherent narrative.

We are grateful to the Program for the Analysis of Religion Among Latinos/as (PARAL), a true community of scholars who have supported us in the view that Latinos and Latinas are essential contributors to contemporary religion in the United States. In particular, the participants at the April 1996 PARAL conference at the University of California, Santa Barbara were helpful in clarifying how to present the resurgence as a social movement. We are indebted to Justo González and Rubén Amendáriz for insightful comments on the resurgence among Protestants and to Barry Kosmin for his invaluable guidance on matters statistical. Support from our colleagues at Union Theological Seminary and Brooklyn College was timely, and the sabbatical years we spent as Fellows at Princeton University's Center for the Study of American Religion provided us with time and critical input during the preparation of the manuscript. Those weekly seminars at Princeton led by Professor Bob Wuthnow convinced us that non-Latinos were eager to learn more about the Latino experience. At Westview Press, Mary Kay Scott and Spencer Carr were the first to have faith in us. In the production process, we say "gracias" to Laura Parsons, Gabriella Zoller, and Scott Horst. The copy editing by Michele Wynn was not only efficient, but she was so diplomatic in her comments that we felt good about most of the changes she suggested. Finally, we have to thank our son Adán, who had to learn during the writing of the book that there were times when his parents were "unavailable." He has matured enough to be able to make these sacrifices gracefully. We thank him, and hope that this book offers him not only a description of a legacy he has received but also the outlines of a commitment he should make.

Ana María Díaz-Stevens
Anthony M. Stevens-Arroyo
February 2, 1997
Our Lady of Candelaria

Introduction

THE GOSPEL ACCORDING TO LUKE contains one of our favorite passages (Luke 26:13–35). Two disciples are leaving Jerusalem after the Passion and Death of Jesus, with heads held low as they walk on the road leading out of the city. They meet a stranger, with whom they strike up a conversation as they go along. He seems not to know anything of the events of the past three days, and the disciples spin out their tale. They admit they had hoped that Jesus would restore the Kingdom of Israel to its past glory, which discloses their political views; they relate that they do not believe the account of "some women" that Jesus had risen from the dead, which says mountains about a gender bias. But the stranger proceeds to cite the prophets and the scripture to convince them that they should have anticipated these events rather than be discouraged about them. As the trio approaches the small town of Emmaus, the two disciples excitedly plead with the stranger to dine with them now that evening has fallen. And when he breaks bread at table with them, they recognize that the stranger is Jesus. He vanishes from their sight before they can recover, and they are left with emotion: Their hearts, they feel, were "burning inside them" as they walked on the road with a man they did not recognize, speaking of events they had not understood.

This book spells out our Emmaus experience. We lived through the tumultuous 1960s and 1970s. We were a part of most of the events we describe herein, and we know as personal friends many of the persons who helped make the history told in these pages. But like the disciples, when we were on that road, we did not fully recognize that we were engaged with important events. Moreover, we were sometimes discouraged and downcast at seeing how many of our hopes were dashed. Now, thirty years later, we have come to see a pattern and a reason not only for the successes that inspired us but also for the failures that often discouraged us. It is the "Emmaus paradigm" that has enabled us to revisit the path and recognize that we were in the generation that produced the Latino Religious Resurgence.

We have attempted here to provide a thematic description of how religion among Latinos and Latinas has assumed a major role in the United States. Others have told the tale in personal, theological, and historical works; we would not have been able to complete our story without reference to these valuable efforts. But by using a social science framework in this book, we think we can address a particular need today. We have tried to supply to the social science literature a comprehensive and systematic analysis of religion among Latinos and Latinas, with special emphasis on the last thirty years. With some bold comparisons and detailed exploration of events and circumstances, of individuals and institutions, we think we offer here an insightful overview of one of the most important developments in U.S. religion in the last one-third of the twentieth century. It has been a resurgence not entirely unlike that which has occurred in other parts of the world (Robertson and Chirico, 1985), though with its own unique characteristics. Perhaps more important, the trends we describe point to directions for religion into the next Christian millennium.

Much in this book resembles the growing number of autobiographical books on the Latino movements of the 1960s. But while there is certainly a similarity of genre, ours is not merely a story of the struggle. We adopt here a reverence for our subject because the movement was as much religious as it was social. Matching these two characteristics to the same events sets a minefield in social science. "Religion" is often easier to experience than to describe. People know what has touched their hearts, breathed inspiration into their souls, radiated light into their despair, crowned their joy, and made more bearable their sorrow and suffering. But these experiences, which are found in almost all religions, no matter the denomination and at times in spite of it, defy description. One need not believe with us in order to recognize that our people—Latinos and Latinas—have been animated by belief. As familiar as the journey will seem to those focused upon secular militancy, we cannot describe the trek without acknowledging the destination: Emmaus and the table of faith.

A social science emphasis brings an obligation for measurement. We hope the theologians and pastoral ministers among our readers will not view our questions about religion as an attack on belief. Legitimate scientific inquiry into religion's dimensions is no more hostile than examination by X ray to corroborate a doctor's diagnosis of a patient's state of health. Our analysis will do nothing to rob religion of its organic life. "When?" "How often?" "How low or how intense?" "How many or how few?" are some of the questions that ought to be asked of religious people in order to better understand their testimony. In this way, we set a standard frame of reference so that we can move from study of each individual's experience toward knowledge that permits reasonable generalizations that benefit everyone.

These caveats are probably unnecessary for readers who are familiar with the social sciences. But we think that sociologists, anthropologists, political scientists, and others in related fields like urban studies will profit from this book because it provides new perspectives on a subject of grow-ing importance to the field of religious studies. Much of U.S. social science has been limited, if not also regressive, when it comes to incorporating the Latino experience as part of religion in the United States. In preparing for this book, we discovered a big gap between the quality and number of spe-cialized publications on Latino religion and the standard textbooks in the field. Although the 1995 PARAL (Program for the Analysis of Religion Among Latinos/as) publication *Discovering Latino Religion* cataloged var-ious and significant social science studies of religion, the majority of these works focused on particular groups like Mexican Americans and Puerto Ricans and were published in specialized journals or presses. Although this scholarship is often of high quality, few authors of general studies of reli-gion have included it in their works, with some exceptions (McGuire, 1992). We have attempted to synthesize the most significant of the special-ized studies and to place them in the context of U.S. religion.

Our initial purpose was to provide a compendium of reliable previous studies and highlight the challenges these data present to current concep-tions in the field. This has been a daunting task because there is no previ-ously published "masterwork" on Latino religion that could serve as a guide. We therefore had to find our own way of building a bridge between specialized studies of Latino religion and the general field of U.S. religion. Of course, we rely heavily on our own publications over the past twenty-five years. Many of the chapters are built around previously published arti-cles that have been rethought and retooled here. The anthology *Prophets Denied Honor* (Stevens-Arroyo, 1980) broke new ground by assembling key documents from Latino leadership and sketching out a framework to grasp the importance of the movement, which at that time was still ex-panding. *Prophets Denied Honor* won an international prize for its schol-arly vision. In a somewhat different way, *Oxcart Catholicism on Fifth Avenue* (Díaz-Stevens), published in 1993 from a prize-winning manu-script, also prepared the way for this book. *Oxcart Catholicism* dealt with the already well-documented theme of Puerto Ricans in New York City and the Catholic Church, radically altering the perspective by examining what the Puerto Ricans had done for the Catholic Church rather than just describing what the Catholic Church had done for Puerto Ricans. We hope that the broad national vision of *Prophets Denied Honor* is repeated in this book and that the healthy perspective established by *Oxcart Catholicism* carries over to these pages as well. In fact, since both previous books ended their narrations with events in the early 1980s, our volume here may be considered a sort of sequel to these earlier works.

We have not been afraid to mix into this book comparisons with mili-tant cultural and social movements. In fact, it is our opinion that the reli-gious effort would not have succeeded without the combination of other circumstances. We describe the convergence of religious and social forces with the word "syzygy." "Syzygy" is not an everyday word, but then syzygy is not an everyday occurrence. Syzygy of the moon, planets, and stars produces effects through the simultaneous alignment of these bodies, for instance, gravitational pulls or enhanced visibility, that individually would not be possible. We have applied this term to religion among Latinos in the United States. In this analogy, our celestial bodies include the natural course of denominational development, congregational formation, religious education, conversion, and devotional practice of Latinos in the United States. These are forces that course through the religious orbits. But social forces simultaneously pursue their own paths, thus religion finds itself in the gravitational pull, so to speak, of demographic growth, upward mobility, educational achievements, socioeconomic class, and political power. At least one scholar (Blasi, 1988) has viewed Early Christianity as a social movement in its time.

Finally, we want to note how crucial the support of the Program for the Analysis of Religion Among Latinos/as has been. Over the past five years, PARAL has offered us manifold opportunities to explore most of the issues raised here. Our colleagues have been knowledgeable, critical, and encouraging, in a just about perfect mix. Moreover, in the company of PARAL, we have been supported with research funds from the Lilly Endowment, the Pew Charitable Trusts, and the Louisville Institute. To each and every one, we say, *"Muchas gracias."*

Of course, no publication ever meets all of its expectations. We see some things in this one that are likely to cause puzzlement. For instance, our book does not follow a strictly chronological order: Our pursuit of themes required us to analyze the same events from several different perspectives. We constantly strove to include discussion of both Puerto Rico, the island, and Puerto Ricans in the United States as part of the story, even though this was difficult at times. But a central premise of our study was that each of the movements—Chicano, Puerto Rican, Cuban, Mexican American—influenced each other through the prism of the church. Perhaps more than in the secular sphere, the religious experience is a "Latino" one, a synthesis of the regional and the particular. Some will no doubt consider our constant inclusion of the Puerto Rican status question as somewhat partisan. We would respond that it is impossible to understand Puerto Rican identity or the public role of religious institutions without reference to the perennial debate over status: statehood, autonomy, or independence.

We also faced several dilemmas of a very pedestrian sort. For instance, some works use terms like "Hispanic" or "Mexican American," while others prefer "Latino" and "Chicano." We have used "Latino" in most cases and have made "Mexican American" and "Chicano" into almost interchangeable terms. We know that some scholars use "Latinos/as" to avoid gender bias: we find that cumbersome and have tried using the two words "Latinos and Latinas" when there was special reason to emphasize that both men and women were involved. Similarly, "United States" is preferred to "America." For us, "American" includes the people of two continents, and we have tried to avoid using it as a synonym for citizens of the United States. We see problems with "white" as a racial term that excludes Latinos and prefer "Euro-Americans." We put accents where they belong for those who use them with their names, omitting them if the authors do.

We have used "Latino religion" at times to avoid repeating the longer (but more precise) formulation, "religion among Latinos and Latinas"; but we do not suggest that Latino religion is a substitute for or a heretical form of Christianity. We include an extensive bibliography with ample citations. We wrote the book with theory—but not about theory. If we have misinterpreted the meaning intended by any of the theoreticians, we apologize. But our focus has been on the reality rather than on the neat theories from books. Throughout the text, we have attempted to relate theories that seldom mentioned Latinos to our experiences, showing both points of agreement and disagreement. We have stretched and pulled these theories into contexts in which they have heretofore been unfamiliar. We will take no umbrage if some of the authors wish to clarify that their "universal" theories do not apply to Latinos and Latinas.

Finally, we hope that this book helps explain that Latinos and Latinas have been a part of religion in the United States for a long time. The Latino presence is not new. What is special to our time is the recognition on our part of our particularities and a newfound pride in asserting them. Hence, the subtitle "Emmaus Paradigm" is meant to suggest that our journey was under way before we or others realized its importance. The Emmaus paradigm also belongs to scholars of religion in the United States, who have perhaps not yet viewed Latino experiences as integral parts of their generalized study. We hope this book will make that responsibility easier to meet. One does not have to be Latino or to practice religion to feel that for those who experienced the Latino Religious Resurgence, "hearts were set burning." That is the message when one views the Latino past through the prism of the Emmaus paradigm.

A. M. D-S.
A. M. S-A.

Recognizing the Latino Resurgence in U.S. Religion

1

Questions

No te metas en camisa de once varas is a bit of hinterland wisdom we learned from our families: "Don't try to wear a shirt that's too big for you." This is a proverb that suggests minding your own business and not picking up someone else's unfinished project. But unfortunately, social science depends upon accumulated knowledge. The field requires that each scholar must pay attention to, if not always agree with, the research conclusions of colleagues. Moreover, our chosen subtitle "The Emmaus Paradigm" suggests that the data required for understanding Latino religion have been among us for some time. What is missing is an interpretive framework that satisfies the particularities of Latino and Latina experiences (see Stevens-Arroyo, 1995a).

Certainly, many of the scholars previously engaged in study of Latinos and religion are better known than ourselves, and challenging their work is neither a joyous task nor one taken lightly. But we have a responsibility to "put on the shirts of others," if only to satisfy ourselves that the old does not fit. This is not an empty exercise, since many of the mistakes in earlier studies have been helpful in fashioning the new response; in other words, we owe a debt even to those with whom we disagree. Before we begin to offer our paradigm, therefore, we have a responsibility to critique previous scholarship and explain why we find it deficient in the task of explaining religion among Latinos and Latinas. Most often, our focus is on an inappropriate interpretation, not on the effort; we critique the scholarship and not the scholar. This first chapter, then, poses several questions about the premises of previous work in the field.

Survey Analysis of Latino Religion

Shallow conceptions of Latino religion have been common in past sociological survey analysis. In the 1950s, research data on Latino religion were most frequently concerned with how many Latinos considered themselves Catholics, how often they went to church, and how "important" religion was to them. C. Wright Mills and Clarence Senior, for instance, asked these types of questions in *The Puerto Rican Journey*, their 1950 study of New York City Puerto Ricans (Mills, Senior, and Goldsen, 1950:110–114). Forty years later, a 1990 political survey conducted nationwide by the Inter-University Program for Latino Social Research asked almost the same questions (de la Garza et al., 1992). Quantification scales for the frequency of attendance and recording the distribution of church affiliation are important, of course, but they do not capture the motivations behind behavior, nor do they explore the ways in which religion shapes culture and social interaction.

These deficiencies should not be attributed to the numerical dominance of Euro-Americans in social science fields, as if the problem were created solely by the ethnicity of the researchers. Latino descent is no guarantee of expertise in analysis of religion. Although we admire the many university-based Latino and Latina scholars engaged in Chicano, Puerto Rican, and Cuban American Studies who have greatly enriched the knowledge of Latino experiences, we note with disappointment that most of them have afforded only limited and superficial importance to religion. Often, publications in these fields demonstrate either lamentable bias toward or negligent omission of religion's role in shaping Latino experience; a few have attacked belief in general and Catholicism in particular.[1] Fortunately, the religious experience of Latinos is so much in evidence among the people that the better anthologies on Latino Studies (e.g., Rodríguez and Sánchez-Korrol, 1980/1996; Haslip-Viera and Baver, 1996) include religion as an integral part of Latino experiences. In addition to the work of PARAL, which has high visibility in the area of comparative study of different Latino groups and institutional responses, several quality works explore related issues.[2]

Perhaps one could excuse C. Wright Mills for a certain touch of myopia about Latino religion because he did not specialize in the study of religion. Likewise, we can be generous with our pardon to professors of Latino Studies who find other issues to examine within a community beset with myriad social problems. But it is harder to explain why, until recently, so few works in the sociology of religion have treated Latino experiences as integral parts of the U.S. experience. As late as 1977, Andrew Greeley, the priest-sociologist-fiction writer, published a book entitled *The American Catholic*, in which Latinos (called "the Spanish-speaking") were practically excluded from consideration. Although he stated at the outset that his work was a "social portrait" of U.S. Catholicism and the culmination of fifteen years of research on "Catholic ethnic groups," Greeley did not include Latinos in any of the statistical data throughout the book, even though Latinos constituted as much as one-fifth of the U.S. Catholic population in 1977. Greeley stated bluntly: "Spanish-speaking Catholics and blacks are excluded from the analysis because better data on them are available from the census and because one wishes to exclude the cross-cutting influence of race from any attempt to measure stratification and mobility of religious denominations" (1977:52–53).

We always thought a sensible response to "better data" was to use it, and it is puzzling for an author to knowingly publish a book that is essentially incomplete. Although he was correct when he recognized the enormous influence of racial differences in the United States, Greeley's 1977 exclusion of Latinos allowed him to avoid the hard work of rethinking categories that he had used in previous studies of Euro-American groups. In our opinion, Greeley's *The American Catholic*, like many sociological studies of Catholicism published in the first three-fourths of the twentieth century, represents a kind of "ethnic studies" approach to Euro-American Catholics and does not constitute an analysis of U.S. Catholicism as a whole. Sadly, this approach is often repeated in journals and among ambitious junior scholars (Budde, 1992a, 1992b) who mistake the visibility of published authors such as Greeley for reliability in understanding Latinos.

Most of the general literature in the sociology of U.S. religion appears to employ the premise of eventual Latino assimilation into the "mainstream" (Stevens-Arroyo, 1995d). That reasoning provides an excuse to avoid further analysis: If Latinos are going to melt into U.S. society eventually, why bother studying them, except perhaps to find out why the assimilation is so slow? Equally pernicious are questionable notions like "folk religion," "syncretism with pagan beliefs," and (even!) "survivals of superstition." Suspect as scientific categories, these terms often accompany an effort to dismiss and denigrate the experiences that contribute to the special character of Latino religion. The subject of Latino religion has received the same kind of welcome from some sociologists of religion as did the guests of the mythical Procrustes. When this chap had an overnight visitor who did not fit into the bed, his remedy was to chop off the legs of those who were too tall or to stretch by means of torture on the rack those who were too short.

Both of us recall during our university years a frequent perplexity among our mentors and fellow students: Why did we want to study religion or Latino religion? Some understood our interest in Latinos but questioned the relevance of religion; others saw religion as acceptable but considered a focus on Latinos as an academic dead end. While respecting the right of others to their opinions, it seems to us that those who gave such advice viewed Latino religion with a jaundiced eye, in a Latino version of "Orientalism," to apply Said's term (1978). Latino religion could be excluded from general study of U.S. religion because by definition things Latino were not "American" and were therefore unimportant (Said, 1978:3–4). Researchers into Latino experience have often had to attack this Latino version of Orientalism before they can begin to make their arguments (Stevens-Arroyo and Díaz-Stevens, 1994:17, 24; Stevens-Arroyo and Pérez y Mena, 1995:24, 55, 116). But in keeping with what Said argued (1978:12), we believe that such attitudes toward Latino religion say little about the real world and convey more about the imagined world of those who refuse to acknowledge the importance of Latinos and Latinas. The ability of various fields to ignore either religion or Latino religion is "a reminder of the seductive degradation of knowledge, of any knowledge, anywhere, at any time" (Said, 1978:328).

The exclusion of Latino religion as a topic integral to the study of U.S. religion or U.S. Latinos has left an unfortunate legacy. Bearers of the message that there are special characteristics of Latino religion offered information many in the academy did not want to hear, lest it complicate the reigning theories and methods. The more they were ignored, the louder the Latino spokespersons protested, which served to further inflate the notion that their work was more "politics" than scholarship (Stevens-Arroyo, 1995d: 27), particularly in fields where non-Latino scholars held hegemony. The general stream of the sociology of religion before 1977 sets an unhealthy climate for integrating Latinos within the general study of U.S. religion. Thus, even pioneers in the study of Latino religion like the late Father Joseph P. Fitzpatrick, S.J. (1971) and Patrick McNamara (1970) were forced to use vocabulary and approaches eventually recognized as ill-fitting for Latino experiences (McNamara, 1995:24–27). Yet, as we have stated in the introduction and hope to underline throughout this book, Latino Christianity is the oldest form of Christianity in the present-day United States. Latinos and Latinas have been journeying alongside many of the later-arriving Euro-American groups, although we have not often been recognized as fellow pilgrims. That helps underscore the need to study Latino religion with a new paradigm drawn on the model of the Emmaus pericope.

Positive Contributions

The impropriety of omitting Latinos from a sociological study of U.S. Catholicism was obvious to reviewers of *The American Catholic* (Blasi, 1978:174) if not to the book's author,[3] thus 1977 represented a turning point in the sociology of American Catholicism. Happily, most serious studies of American religion since then, particularly those on Catholicism, have recognized that exclusion of Latinos threatens credibility. Moreover, part of the slack was picked up by important contributions that focused on Latinos alone. Two pioneering surveys deserve special recognition: the Gallup report to *Our Sunday Visitor* (1978) and *The Hispanic Catholic in the United States,* by Roberto O. González and Michael La Velle (1985). Among general surveys of U.S. Catholics, the studies of Catholic laity

(D'Antonio et al., 1989, 1996) are characteristic of today's felt need to in-corporate a Latino sample.

But including Latinos in a survey sample (D'Antonio et al., 1989, 1996) is not a guarantee that the data will faithfully reflect Latino experiences (see Stevens-Arroyo, 1995a): The penchant of Procrustes dies slowly. Nor have the professional publications of scholarly associations provided a fo-rum for exchange within the field about how to conduct research on issues unique to Latinos (Stevens-Arroyo, 1995d). From 1986–1996, one of these publications, the journal *Sociology of Religion*, has published more articles on the fans of Star Trek than on Latinos!

We have concluded that using standard research approaches to survey Latino religion is no longer defensible in contemporary social science. For this reason, Gerardo Marín and Barbara Van Oss Marín argue (1991:82 ff.) that inclusion of items in social science surveys requires a rethinking for "a cultural equivalent" and not just a literal translation into Spanish. Likewise inadequate are works that justify previously held ideas with a disturbing re-liance on non–social science publications about Latinos and religion (O'Brien, 1990; Budde, 1992a, 1992b; see Stevens-Arroyo, 1995d). The Latino presence demands that we question the status quo. Simply repeating in the 1990s what was acceptable in the 1970s may impede rather than aid an understanding of the particular contours of Latino religion.

We think there are enough data on Latino religion now to require any general overview of religion in the United States to be on the lookout for the Latino exception. Although we do not think that everything or even most of everything is different among Latinos in the practice of religion, the differences that do exist are crucial. If one proposes to study attitudes toward religion among U.S. youth, for instance, definitions of "adult" and "youth" may not correspond when comparing Latinos and Euro-Americans. At a 1995 meeting of Catholic leaders in Washington attended by Anthony M. Stevens-Arroyo, an upper-middle-class Euro-American stated that "adult" life does not begin until age twenty-five when the par-ents have helped make the down payment on a condominium apartment. Until then, it was suggested, Catholic youth do not make serious decisions about life. Although this view of what constitutes an adult is not scientific, it does dramatize social and cultural differences. For a Latino, reliable so-cial science data tell us that lifetime decisions about marriage, children, and career choice may begin much earlier. In the example just given, the two populations are at different stages of the life cycle, even if their chronological age of twenty-five is the same. No good researcher can ig-nore the fact that age and life cycle introduce variables into attitudes to-ward religion (Roof and Walsh, 1993; Stolzenberg et al., 1995). When these considerations are added to social class factors, the need to note Latino differences becomes essential to the interpretation of survey data.[4]

In some instances, reading Latino reality with defective concepts may be worse than giving it no attention at all. We think social science needs to put social class data and similar measures into sharper focus in order to properly study religion among Latinos. That is the task we set for this book. In an attempt to answer this need, we have highlighted the points of similarity or difference between our interpretations and those of other authors. Our telling of the "story" of Latino religion in the United States also includes theoretical explanations based on social science. We hope that we have provided the reader with "handles" that can be used to grasp not only descriptive variations but also more deeply rooted religious differences that distinguish Latino religion from the rest of U.S. religion. We invite those who might disagree with our interpretations to utilize the extensive bibliography here to illustrate an alternate understanding that might improve upon our efforts.

Inclusion of Theology

Our book is organized around events that are described in chronological order, although we felt it necessary to overlap historical periods to better develop certain themes of analysis. We have attempted here to examine the phenomenon of Latino religion, striking a balance between perspectives both synchronic and diachronic so as to avoid reductionism (Hanegraaf, 1995; Merkur, 1994). As pointed out by Brian Malley (1995) in a prize-winning essay, analysis of religion requires examination from two perspectives: The first treats its dependence on the underlying social context, and the second involves the dynamics of its continual reinterpretation of that social order. In other words, while we review how religion is shaped by its social environment, we also need to recognize that through its precepts, charisma, and virtuoso expression, religion challenges its social context. Often the best window on religion's challenges to society is theology. On these premises, we have taken theology as a serious actor on the stage of religious experience.

Theology as well as social science tags and labels religious experience. Theology provides a systematic way of knowing and interpreting the religion of most believers in the United States. Its role in constructing or disassembling denominational boundaries of orthodoxy is particularly instructive in the Latino experience. Because theology provides the vocabulary for the interaction of religious institutions with the people's experiences, it influences perceptions on both sides. Institutions view a particular group of members through the prism of theology, legitimizing certain policies in the name of the faith; a similar process colors the people's expectation of the religious institution. Because of these functions alone, theology deserves inclusion in any scientific study of religion.

Unfortunately, like much of the current sociology of religion, mainstream theology in the United States has been developed largely without a focus on Latino experience. In rebuttal, for more than one decade Latino theologians have emphasized popular religion as a key concept for Latino religious experience (Espín, 1994:308), reinventing aspects of U.S. religion that were sometimes supposed to be inimical to modernization. We have dedicated an entire chapter and much in other segments of this book to a social science discussion of these matters. But although we cannot conceive of analyzing Latino religion without including Latino theology, we recognize that not all the concepts in that discipline translate into social science categories.

The temptation is to leave theology alone. Gustavo Benavides, for example, provides a commentary on the ambiguous meaning of *"mestizaje,"* a term used extensively in current Latino theology (1995:20–21, n. 4). During the pre–World War II period in Latin America, *mestizaje* was invoked in promoting various forms of populist nationalism. Derived from a concept first described in a 1925 book by the Mexican political philosopher José Vasconcelos, *mestizaje* described a national culture based on genetic or biological factors, much as articulated by the Italian philosopher Benedetto Croce (Stevens-Arroyo, 1980:32–34, 58–59). *Mestizaje* is *not* a Latin American equivalent of the Aryan doctrines of German Nazism because, unlike Fascist usage, the concept was used to extol the "impure" racial mixtures, not the "pure" ones. Still, it is playing with fire to entertain a link between genetics and culture, and a term like *"mestizaje,"* though common in the vocabulary of Latino theologians, presents problems to social science analysis by mixing the cultural and the behavioral on a priori premises of ethnic identity.

Even more troublesome is the disciplinary divide that separates social science from theology and religious studies. We apply Dan Merkur's analysis (1995) to theology because the rules of evidence within the discipline allow theology to make assertions that social science could not. What social science considers "empirical" is not usually the basis of theological discourse. Meanwhile, because there is so much attention paid to measures of frequency and distribution, theologians often conclude that social science analyzes only what is already known. As remarked in another description of this rapprochement, "the rough edges . . . reflect the need for continued mutual learning and collaboration for both theologians and social scientists" (Stevens-Arroyo and Cadena, 1995:17–19).

Tradition and the Diachronic-Synchronic Dilemma

The disciplinary dilemma posed by mixing social science analysis with theological concepts constantly challenged us, as, for instance, when using terms such as "syncretism" and "popular religiosity." We solved that here

by reexamining the concept of "tradition," which has been somewhat neglected by current social science. By adding a social science dimension to
the concept of "tradition" in order to embrace theology, we think we have
erected a road sign pointing to an intersection between these disciplines.

The traditions of Latino religion have become a source of "symbolic
repertories" (Benavides, 1995:20, 1994:40) that are connected in complex
ways with social and economic forces. Whereas theologians and sociologists might argue over which force is *primary,* we are content to observe
here that all have importance. Where reliable research suggests, we trace
how one or other influence assumes a greater role at a particular juncture
in history or impacts upon a specific religious organization. We hold fast to
the belief, however, that Latino religion should not be viewed as a warped
or unevolved form of Euro-American experience. Religion grows in many
varieties, and Latino experience has bred a distinct species in the genus of
"American religion." To appreciate the flowering of religion on the U.S.
landscape, we need to recognize each of the different types.

We would like to pose again the question explored by PARAL scholar
Gustavo Benavides in his provocative article (1995:20): "What is the core
and what is the surface of religion?" Benavides answers his own question
by suggesting that a theologian sees theology as the "core" because popular practices are considered by elites to flow from theological dogma,
something not apparent to a social scientist. The assertion that theology is
not the core of religious practice is validated by an analogy from everyday
experience: Do we not recognize our friends most frequently by looking at
their faces and not by examining their skeletal structures or inner organs?
Surely, the skeletal structure of religion—dogma and theology—is important; but precisely because they lie on the "surface" of religion, people's experiences better define their religiosity. Benavides is right: Lived experiences—not the arcane and intellectualized discourse of formal theology
and canon law—provide the best social science perspective for what is and
what is not religion. We part company with Benavides, however, when he
adds: "One will have to consider whether religions can be regarded not as
systems with cores and boundaries, but rather as networks of representa-
tions, as symbolic repertories, whose margins—and possibly centers as
well—are ultimately nowhere to be found" (Benavides, 1995:20).

The cores and boundaries of religion do exist; they are just hard to define. Although we disagree with Benavides's suggestion that boundaries
"are ultimately nowhere to be found," we think he paradoxically has
pointed to a crucial need to include theology in a social science analysis of
religion. As suggested above, theology sets the boundaries of belief by imposing orthodoxy. Although social science does not cede this power of
defining religious practice to theology without critical examination of motives and of social and political purposes and the like, the effects of orthodoxy need to be considered.

In this book, we have tried to redefine theology in a way that examines how it is produced by a particular social climate without denying its role in modifying the society that produced it. Perhaps it is enough to say that neither theology nor religion are static. Both defy easy categorization as "core or periphery" without losing the ability to set boundaries. An analogy based on Benavides's term "networks" may be helpful here. Almost everyone who has strung together flashing Christmas tree lights knows that one loose connection can shut down the entire string. One has to test each bulb to find the one that has disrupted the current. The faulty bulb is not the "core" of the string because it is not essentially different from the others on the string: But without it, the rest do not function. Religion, we think, often behaves in this way when a particular theological belief or ritual practice becomes essential to illuminating the networks of that religion. Theology can help explain why the practice of religion by one group can be classified as either authentic or heretical by another, even when social science can identify no significant material or situational differences.

The Term "Latino"

Spanish-speaking Catholics brought Christianity to the Americas, and some of their settlements were located in parts of what is now the United States. The oldest Christian institution under the U.S. flag today is the (Arch)Diocese of San Juan, Puerto Rico, which was constituted in 1511, and Saint Augustine in Florida was the site of the first Christian church in the present-day United States nearly half a century before the Pilgrims landed at Plymouth Rock. Descendants of these Iberian colonizers, including some with mixed racial origins, can be called "Latinos." Their settlements were located in areas now parts of the United States. The nineteenth-century expansion by the United States incorporated these societies by military force and juridical decrees. The conquered lands were opened to people from the United States, who immediately benefited from hegemonic advantages such as the establishment of the English language in commerce and education. But these conquered additions to the United States remained the homelands of the original Spanish-speaking population. They had not come from Latin America as immigrants: The United States had "migrated" to them, depriving them of political and economic influence in the process. Subsequent waves of Spanish-speaking immigrants to the United States from Latin America joined these core Latino communities, and new ones have been created, especially in the twentieth century. Thus, ours is a layered reality, interpreted best through a historical and generational examination, much as archaeology relies on analysis of strata to identify cultures that emerged in succession, one upon another.

We recognize differences between Latinos born into families that have been in the United States for generations and Latin American immigrants to the United States. However, the U.S. census counts both as the same, and the reliability of these enumerations inclined us to use the census figures. But we view "Latino" as a term of cultural identity that differs from the official government census category of "Spanish/Hispanic origin." By "Latino" we mean *people of Latin American heritage born or raised in the United States.* Because it is a key predictor of linguistic ability and cultural expression, we think that socialization before the age of eleven is often more important to Latino identity than place of birth. In our experience, many young people brought to the United States from Latin America while still small children grow up to be almost indistinguishable in cultural traits from people of similar heritage born in the United States. In contrast, people who immigrate to the United States at an older age seem to retain a Latin American cultural distinctiveness from the Latinos and Latinas. These Latin Americans who immigrated when older often consider themselves different from Latinos, even if their children (or brothers and sisters) do not. However, as we hope to point out, there are strong forces at work to eliminate these differences based on immigrant experiences, and both Spaniards and Latin Americans may identify themselves as "Latino" from time to time.

Our reluctance to merge Latino identity with immigrant status may seem strange in light of our frequent emphasis on the differences Latinos exhibit in culture and language from the rest of the United States population. We recognize that Latinos are generally viewed as "foreigners." But as will be shown with more detail in Chapter 3, the "foreignness" comes not from immigration but from military conquest. An "American" dimension is easily understood for Latinos in places like Texas, New Mexico, and California, but it is also true for Puerto Ricans. "Foreign birth" on the island of Puerto Rico is not quite so "foreign." Puerto Rico is a U.S. colony, and in 1917, the federal government imposed U.S. citizenship on all people born in Puerto Rico. Consequently, Puerto Ricans can freely enter the United States without a passport, with no more legal difficulty than people driving across the Walt Whitman Bridge from New Jersey to Pennsylvania. Technically speaking, Puerto Ricans can never be immigrants because all of them share the right of U.S. citizenship. However, as long as Puerto Ricans reside on their island, they cannot vote in federal elections and have no voting representative in either the House or Senate. And despite nearly one century of U.S. rule over the island and domination of almost every social institution, most Puerto Ricans on the island do not speak English. Thus, Puerto Ricans look and act "foreign" even if one could argue on technicalities that they are not. One survey found that although Puerto Rico was a U.S. colony, it served the same identity formation functions as *la patria* ("motherland") for Puerto Ricans in the United States as Mexico (a foreign country) did for Mexican Americans (de la Garza et al., 1992:12 and throughout). Throughout this book, we consider Puerto Ricans born and living on the island of Puerto Rico to be "Latinos," although Puerto Rico is convincingly described as a foreign nation that is under U.S. political jurisdiction, and official U.S. census counts generally omit Puerto Ricans on the island.

The term "Latino" as a definition for all the people of Latin American ancestry in the United States has a tortured history (Moore, 1990; Stevens-Arroyo, 1994). Rather than enter into a description of the political and ideological arguments for and against this designation, a few major points will suffice here. Within the concept "Latino" are several different nationalities, much as "Spaniard" is a general term for Gallego, Castilian, Catalan, Andalusian, and even Basque. Moreover, not only are people of Mexican, Puerto Rican, Cuban, and Central and South American heritages different from each other, Mexican-origin people in Texas may view themselves as distinct from their compatriots in California: Both may find the New Mexicans dissimilar. The same regional experiences affect Latinos with Puerto Rican, Cuban, and other Latin American roots. Rudolfo De la Garza and his colleagues (1992) found that most respondents in their survey did not identify as "Latinos," preferring "Spanish American" as a general term. In fact, most often it was the specific identity such as "Mexican American" or "Puerto Rican" that was adopted by those surveyed.

The intra-Latino differences are not merely matters of subjective choice. For example, there can be significant variations in racial heritage, in the pronunciation of Spanish words, and in the use of a different lexicon. A Mexican American might look more "Indian" than a Puerto Rican, who in the eyes of some might be considered a mulatto, that is, a person of a mixed black and white racial origin; the Puerto Rican is likely to speak Spanish faster, aspirating the "s" at the end of words, whereas the Mexican American will intone sentences in a distinctive pattern; the Mexican American will say "*mande*" where the Puerto Rican says "*por favor*" for "please." Attending a championship bout between Mexican American and Puerto Rican boxers, the two might well feel these differences and root for opposing favorites.

In calculating these differences, it becomes impossible to talk of a single Latino experience as the "core." Benavides's suggestion to replace such static notions with that of relational "networks" seems a better direction. That does not mean that we should avoid using "Latino" or other such concepts—only that we should take care to use them properly. In a noteworthy treatment of Latino identity, Joan Moore (1990) points out that one conceptualizes identity within the group (endogenous), but one may also have an identity imposed by others (exogenous). Outsiders' opinions of the group and its own self-conception are interactive. They may alternately reinforce or undermine each other. These are parts of a relational dimension. They combine with an objective or "material dimension" that consists of measurable categories such as language, customs, and socioeconomic status. Moreover, when the material dimension changes—as a person gets more economically successful, for example—the relational dimensions of identity are likely to be altered. Social science can ask questions that relate identity with observable behavior.

Language use provides an example of the interaction among these factors that is particularly relevant to religious practice. Like an icon on a computer screen, clicking it open offers a checklist of survey questions. How often is the use of Spanish motivated by personal preference (endogenous) and how often are Latinos shunted into Spanish-language services by an English-speaking majority population (exogenous)? Do these purposes, endogenous and exogenous, correlate with other factors such as age and years of residence in the United States or with socioeconomic status? To what extent do individuals from different nationality backgrounds accommodate their regional pronunciations or local lexicon to include other Spanish speakers? This book reports that such processes are common under the aegis of religion, although survey data as proof are limited.

The Mexican American and the Puerto Rican cited in our previous example may not always behave differently. They might find themselves sharing a dance floor together swaying to a merengue beat; they might shop at the same store for rice and beans and join the same Latino caucus within a teachers' professional association. In such contexts, they might choose to emphasize their similarities rather than their differences. Moreover, as film and television frequently demonstrate, there is such as thing as a "Latino look" that characterizes large numbers of Mexican Americans, Puerto Ricans, and Cuban Americans who are virtually indistinguishable from each other. This is particularly important among younger Latinos who speak English more often than Spanish. Many of the old nationality differences have been blurred for them, and intermarriage among the diverse Latino groups has become more common. The children of these intra-Latino unions may identify themselves more readily as "Latinos" than as members the specific nationality group of either of their parents.

People can describe themselves in different terms, and the circumstances for using ethnic, racial, or gender tags are constantly in flux. Accordingly, usage tends to develop as responses to social context. Thus, people may call themselves Catholics or Christians, Mexican Americans or Chicanos, members or women members in different situations in which one or the other identity calls for adherence to a group. Nothing prevents a person from claiming or reclaiming each identity as the circumstances dictate. In sum, Latino identity is not a hard and fixed reality. We have concluded that Latinos often use multiple identities rather than investing completely in one or another term, and this pattern may well constitute a characteristic particular to the experiences in the United States.

Moore reminds us that multiple identities can be distinguished as "primary" or "secondary." Primary identities such as race tend to be fixed by relatively stable criteria. Secondary identities, in contrast, sometimes are easily assumed or discarded. A New Yorker, for instance, may not make much out of being from Brooklyn or the Bronx because little is at stake (except in terms of loyalty to either the Mets or the Yankees!). Normally, people control their secondary identities, much as they decide daily what to wear for a day in the office or for leisure at home. However, when a society is burdened with discrimination or group conflicts, identity becomes a more serious project. A person may even face rejection or persecution for holding to a particular cultural or religious identity. In such circumstances, the use of one or another identity assumes the dimension of a major choice in one's lifetime. A secondary identity may in fact become a primary one.

As complex as the issue may be, we feel examination of the Latino reality cannot ignore multiple identities. Admittedly, there may be an inability to manage multiple identities when a person is unable to decide which are primary identities and which are secondary. When a group fails to logically identify itself, either internally to its own members or to the larger society, it becomes caught in collective cultural schizophrenia, wherein the same word is simultaneously complimentary or derogatory. In our own time, popular usage has fostered a series of terms: "Negro," "Black," and "African American," any one of which can be considered either appropriate or insulting among various publics. This experience has its parallels within Latino experience. For example, as a result of the controversies in 1992 as to whether Columbus "discovered" America, a Native American identity was claimed by some Latinos, perhaps as a means of distancing themselves from Spanish imperialism. This occurred even in instances when as phenotypes, these Latinos looked more white and Spanish than Native American. For another set of reasons, within some families there are contradictory tendencies wherein a few members identify as "Spanish" while others emphasize an African heritage.

The search for a name—Hispanics, Chicanos, Ricans, Boricuas, and Latinos—is part of a social process. In making decisions about which term is most appropriate, one should not expect strict logic to dictate popular preference. Rather, social and cultural trends become crucial in determining usage. This book reflects our perception that the use of "Latino" seems to be increasing dramatically, especially among youth. In a study begun some years ago by Alejandro Portes, Lisando Pérez, and Ruben Rumbaut (Aguilar, 1997), nearly five thousand youth of Latin American heritage averaging fourteen years of age and living in either San Diego or South Florida were polled for their choice of a tag of ethnic identity. In that first poll, 20.9 percent of the youth chose "American" and only 14.7 percent opted for either "Hispanic" or "Latino." The more popular terms were their parents' country of origin (33.9 percent) or a hyphenated identity (29 percent). Four years later, when the respondents averaged eighteen years of age, the responses were strikingly different. Those choosing identity as "American" had plummeted to only 5 percent of the respondents, whereas "Latino/Hispanic" had more than doubled to 31 percent. The foreign country designation had dropped to 21.8 percent, whereas the hyphenated choice had grown slightly to 33.6 percent.

It would be premature to draw general conclusions about the reasons for this rapid growth in popularity for "Latino/Hispanic" as a term of identity scarcely five years after the general poll nationwide by de la Garza and his colleagues (1992) reported considerably less popularity for these terms. It does seem, however, that frequent use of "Latino" in the media and in academic discourse over the past decade has helped determine usage. Our use of "Latino" throughout most of this book is not intended to prejudice the terms "Hispanic" or "Hispano," for it is possible that someday "Latino" will be superseded. In fact, some argue that it has already been rendered obsolete unless it is used with both gendered endings "Latina/o."

Census Data on Latinos

With these caveats, we can turn to census data collected on the Latino (and Latin American) population in the United States to see what information they provide that will be useful to examining Latino religion (see Moore, 1994). In 1950, for the first time in the U.S. census,[5] Spanish-speaking people were counted in an ethnic category. Previously, the manner of counting Latinos in the census was through the classification entry "foreign born." In other words, those Latinos born in Mexico (and before 1900, those born in Puerto Rico), Cuba, or any other Latin American country were distinguished by place of birth. But for those Mexican Americans born in the United States and for all Puerto Ricans after 1917, there was no census category different from the general population.

In a significant advance, the 1950 census issued reports on the Spanish surnamed in five states of the Southwest. However, any Latino with a non-Spanish last name was omitted from the listing, even though individuals with Spanish surnames—who may not have considered themselves Latinos—were included. Puerto Ricans in the New York metropolitan area were counted through the use of a sample of 5 percent of that population. These numbers were extrapolated to profile the entire Puerto Rican population. For the 1960 census, two other categories were added to the Spanish surname as identifiers. Entries on "birth or parentage" and "mother tongue" were included. At best, these were imperfect conceptualizations of Latino identity, and the census data from the 1950s and 1960s suffer from these limitations. Lacking was a direct question to the respondent for self-identification as "Mexican American," "Puerto Rican," or even as "Hispanic" or "Latino."

Between 1960 and 1970, several political changes had revolutionary effects on Latinos. President Lyndon Johnson announced an ambitious War on Poverty in 1964. The plan opened up direct federal grants to the poor—now classified racially as "minorities"—and used census data to proportion funds. In 1965, the Civil Rights Bill was passed. This legislation used census data to regulate and, when necessary, to penalize electoral districts where discrimination took place. Although the bill centered on African Americans and their struggle for justice, it addressed discrimination against Latinos, especially where states imposed language requirements as a condition for voting rights. Also in 1965, the immigration laws were changed and new legislation allowed for dramatic increases in legal migration, not only of Mexicans but also of other Latin Americans who had not previously established significant communities within the United States.

The immigration provisions dramatically increased the numbers of Spanish speakers in the United States. Latinos, who in other contexts might have resented Latin American newcomers as threats to scarce jobs, were quick to learn the advantages of an increased Spanish-speaking population. Federal funds increased in proportion to the census numbers. The new use of the term "minority groups" as a racial category also thrust Latino identity into a context wherein, along with affirmative action and hiring preferences, there was a direct advantage in *not* being white (Hurtado, 1976; López, 1973).

Soon after these landmark legislative initiatives, in 1967 the first bilingual education program was funded in Dade County, Florida. Bilingualism, always a reality within Latino communities, was now elevated to a desirable social goal in education. In seeking federal funds for this kind of education, school districts across the United States employed bilingual teachers, generally Latinos. Breaking with a long tradition of linking the learning of English with the abandonment of Spanish, the funding of bilingual education was intended to establish a mode of instruction that preserved the language spoken at home while simultaneously adding English as a second language. Bilingualism might be seen as the logical extension of parental prerogatives to the schoolroom. Indeed, many anti-Castro Cuban immigrants who generally voted Republican welcomed bilingual education when Florida was chosen as the site for the first program. Rather than being considered a "liberal" cause, bilingualism may be considered an essentially conservative policy, since it bends the public school system toward family values.

In sum, the 1960s federal legislation had radically reversed the policies of more than a century toward Latinos. Latinos, now considered a "minority group," were recipients of new attentions that extended to them treatment as a racial group that had suffered from prejudice. Accordingly, government set itself the task of providing special opportunities to Latinos as a remedy for past injustices (Haveman, 1997). The new policy set in motion an unprecedented mobilization of political energies within Latino communities nationwide.

Soon the need for bilingualism extended beyond the classroom and included civil servants, social workers, and agency and personnel directors. Moreover, bilingualism was wedded to biculturalism, meaning that in addition to cultivating the Spanish language, policy was also intended to reinforce favorable conception of the culture, history, and heroes of the native homeland. In Texas, for instance, the hoary tradition of the Alamo as the victory of the English-speaking immigrants was challenged by a Latino view that stressed the role played by the Spanish-speaking natives of San Antonio (Matovina, 1995b). The improved self-conception of Mexican Americans eventually provided the political climate for Mexican American elected officials and for a popular mayor, Henry Cisneros. Similar results cropped up wherever there were significant numbers of Latinos.

A more detailed description of this new awareness and its effects upon religion is found in subsequent chapters, but in terms of the politics of ethnic/racial counting, the results were clear. Latinos, who had been grateful recipients of the new attention from government, soon became activists, demanding still more change. For instance, when the 1970 census was taken, a list of racial and ethnic groups was included as a self-identification item. But in this list of blacks, American Indians, Chinese, Japanese, Filipinos, Hawaiians, Koreans, and whites, there was no Latino label. Calculation of the number of Mexican Americans, Puerto Ricans, and so forth, or even of cumulative categories such as "Hispanic," still needed to be derived from the questionnaires sent to random samples of the total population. Ironically, because the place-of-birth question was retained, the census had more accurate counts of "Central and South Americans" than of native-born Latinos.

The decision by the Bureau of the Census not to extend to Latinos the self-identification question that had been granted to the other groups in 1970 was seen as a serious matter. The U.S. Commission on Civil Rights (1974) documented that the sampling methodology had resulted in an undercount of the Latino population nationwide. The census undercount became a matter for civil rights investigation because the funding formulas of most federal laws used census statistics and if the numbers were wrong, citizens would be denied money legally appropriated for their needs. Anthony M. Stevens-Arroyo was a member of the New York State Advisory Committee to the U.S. Civil Rights Commission that negotiated with the Bureau of the Census for inclusion of a self-identification question in the 1980 census. At the meetings he attended, it became clear that not every

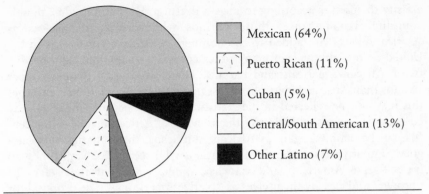

FIGURE 1.1   Ethnic Composition of Latino Population in the Fifty States. *Source:* U.S. Bureau of the Census, 1994.

term popular with a segment of the Latino population could be used. For instance, among people of Mexican descent, there were three major terms: "Mexican American," "Mexican," and "Chicano." Pretesting showed that respondents sometimes gave a positive answer to two or even all three of these categories, which made for statistical nightmares. The Census Bureau eventually agreed to ask whether respondents were "of Spanish/Hispanic origin or descent" and if the response was "yes," then further questions determined whether this origin or descent was Mexican, Cuban, Puerto Rican, or some other type of Spanish/Hispanic.

Because social science data usually follow the practice of the census, this decision for the 1980 census has set a pattern for how to classify Latinos. Accordingly, most studies divide the Latino population into four major ethnicities or nationalities: "Mexican," "Puerto Rican," "Cuban," and "Other." The relative share each of these groups has of the total Latino population is represented in Figure 1.1. Mexican Americans are the largest group (64 percent), followed by Central/South Americans (13 percent), Puerto Ricans (11 percent), and Cubans (5 percent). A catchall category of "Other Latino," including Dominicans and those who answered with "Hispanic" as their ethnicity and listed no specific country, accounts for the remaining 7 percent. It should be noted, however, that due to Puerto Rico's colonial status, most statistics on Latino population in the United States (including this chart) omit the 3.8 million Puerto Ricans who live on the island.

But is Latino identity both a racial and an ethnic category? The census data and surveys are based on classifications that separate Hispanic ethnic identity from that of race. In this formula, Hispanics/Latinos may be of any race, and Euro-Americans become "non-Hispanic whites." However, the census allowed those who responded to the ethnic category "Latino" to classify themselves according to race, a decision that permits some double counting. For instance, those Latinos who identify themselves as "African/black" are added to the numbers of African Americans in the United States, although in many other contexts, society distinguishes between African Americans and Latinos. Therefore, even if there are more Latinos than African Americans in a segment of the population, sometimes this may not be reflected in the statistics gathered because those already counted as Latinos who classify themselves as "African/black" in the census will be counted again as African Americans, thus inflating this category. Similarly (if less commonly), Latinos who see themselves as mestizo (i.e., Native American and Caucasian) may think of themselves as "brown" and classify themselves as "Native Americans." The proposal for the census for the year 2000 to allow multiple racial entries for multiracial individuals does not seem entirely satisfactory. Would a Latino who checks both "white" and "Native American" be counted twice?

The use by the U.S. government of dichotomous racial terms produces confusion among Latinos whose culture has long supported racial mixture (Rodríguez, 1989). Moore (1994:8) explains that in the 1990 census, only 55 percent of Mexican Americans identified themselves as "white," while 38 percent sought a mixed-race category. By contrast, 84 percent of Cubans chose the "white" category, a suspiciously high figure that may have more to do with Cuban racial attitudes than actual racial composition (Moore, 1994:8, nn. 8, 9). An estimated 10 million people skipped the Hispanic-origin question on the 1990 census, which had been placed after the racial identification question. In 1996, the Bureau of Labor Statistics experimented by changing the order of the questions. In two versions where origin *preceded* the racial question, 10.79 percent and 10.41 percent of respondents listed themselves as "Hispanics." But in the instruments where the origin question came *after* the item on race, the percentage of people identifying themselves as Hispanics dropped to either 7.53 percent or 8.58 percent (Torres, 1996).

Thus, although the census formulations of 1980 and 1990 were better suited to counting Latinos than earlier versions, there is still room for improvement. More distressing, however, was the open contempt by the Census Bureau when ordered by a federal court to adjust the 1990 census because of an undercounting of Latinos. Despite the court order and direct congressional action mandating the rectification of the official census numbers with a correction certified by the Census Bureau, its director during the Bush administration refused to authorize any change. Accordingly, states redrew electoral districts, and the federal government distributed funds using population statistics for Latinos *that were known to be false*. During preparations for the census of 2000, the Department of Commerce (which sponsors the census) was challenged by Republican members of

Congress to demonstrate the usefulness of continuing to use any item on ethnic or racial identity. At one point, legislation was suggested to drastically reduce the forthcoming census and ask only six questions in total (Salvo, 1996).

The suggestion to eliminate all government statistics on racial or ethnic origin is part of a political trend and is not to be dismissed as absurd. The ideology behind such efforts views attention to racial or ethnic difference as weakening national unity. Such thinking is not confined to reactionary Euro-Americans. Latino neoconservatives have attacked the landmark legislation of the 1960s, using the word "liberal" as a derogatory description (Chavez, 1991). They denounce the federal government for funding Latino needs, on the premise that this stifles independence and old-fashioned pluck. Sometimes, the neoconservatives describe the racial and ethnic antagonisms directed against Latinos as caused by liberalism, arguing that "special treatment" for Latinos angers the rest of the population.

The neoconservative arguments are based on the speculative, unproven assumption that something better would have happened if the status quo of the 1960s had been preserved. Linda Chavez (1991) argues that if no preference had been given to Latinos through bilingual education, affirmative action, or minority hiring preferences, the assimilation of Latinos into the "mainstream" would have been hastened. Even self-described chroniclers of the Latino experience (Rodriguez, 1982; Stavans, 1995) express disdain for affirmative action as an impediment to Latino advancement since, it is said, professional Latinos face their peers under suspicion that they have achieved success only on the basis of preferential treatment.[6]

While we do not share these neoconservative interpretations of the federal legislation of the 1960s, such views are a part of the competition to define Latino identity. These conservative trends are also found in church circles, as will be described later in this book. Taken as a healthy difference of opinion, such critiques are useful for reevaluating programs.

We should point out, however, that the antipoverty legislation has ameliorated suffering in the United States (Haveman, 1977). We consider it undeniable that the legislation of the 1960s had a generally positive effect for Latinos on a broad range of fronts. This is the conclusion in a 1996 report of the Center on Budget and Policy Priorities: "Based on analysis of recently released Census Bureau data, . . . Federal and state anti-poverty programs have lifted millions of children and disabled and elderly out of poverty. Many of those who remained poor were significantly less poor than they would have been without government assistance" (Primus et al., 1996:1).

Educational achievement, material improvement of housing conditions, entrepreneurial opportunity, and the employment opportunities for Latinas are basic elements of this progress (Primus et al., 1996:1–24). However, we hasten to add that the pace of these advances for Latinos have lagged be-

hind those of the general population and African Americans, and, ultimately, the principal beneficiaries have been a small number of recent en-
trants into the middle class (Carnoy, Daley, and Hinojosa, 1990:62–64). In
fact, we are alarmed that in September of 1996, the U.S. Census Bureau reported that in 1995 Latinos had dropped below African Americans in most
social indicators of poverty (Baugher and Lamison-White, 1996). This is
an ominous development because it occurs at a time when Latino immigration has become a whipping boy in U.S. politics. Cutting benefits and programs to Latin Americans when they are most in need will impact negatively on them and probably on Latinos as well.

Population Facts and Figures

Latino population growth comes from two factors: new births and immigration. Latino birthrates are higher than in the general U.S. population
and are the principal reason for yearly increases in the number of Latinos.
When island Puerto Ricans are included, nearly 70 percent of Latinos in
1990 were born as U.S. citizens: The majority of us are not "immigrants"
(Enchautegui, 1995:6; Moore, 1994:9). This statement is sometimes met
with incredulity by those who perceive themselves as surrounded by people
only recently arrived in the United States. But the native Latino (U.S.-born)
population, while more than twice as large as the immigrant (foreign-born)
population, is not evenly distributed. Some areas, such as New York City,
have higher concentrations of the foreign born than native born. Elsewhere, the conditions may be reversed. Alvin Sunseri reports that nearly 95
percent of New Mexican respondents to his questionnaire came from families that were living in New Mexico between 1840 and 1865 (Sunseri,
1979:44–46).

The combination of the two—new births and immigration—has produced a rapid expansion of Latino presence in the United States (Moore,
1994). In assessing these numbers, it should be remembered that percentage increases are most dramatic when the base numbers are small. Thus,
for instance, when there are only 2,000 individuals in a census tract, an increase of 2,000 more represents a 100 percent growth rate. But if there are
200,000 individuals, the same increase of 2,000 indicates only a 1 percent
growth rate. One should be wary of demographic projections because high
rates of growth are hardly ever sustainable over a long period. In the
Latino case of the past twenty years, however, the rates have remained remarkably high. From 1970 to 1980, there was a 60 percent increase in the
number of Latinos in the United States; the decade 1980–1990 saw a 47
percent increase. Growth in Latino population can be estimated by calculating the difference between projected immigration entries over departures

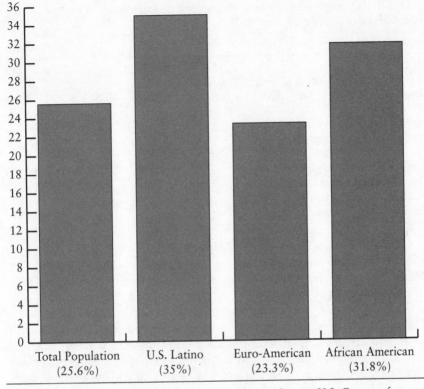

FIGURE 1.2   Percent of Population Under Eighteen. *Source:* U.S. Census of Population and Housing, 1990.

and natural births over deaths. The most recent report of the U.S. Bureau of the Census states that by 2010, Latinos will be more numerous in the United States than African Americans. By 2020, there are expected to be 47 million Latinos, or nearly 15 percent of the total U.S. population; by 2050, 95 million Latinos will make one out of every four persons in the country Latino (U.S. Bureau of the Census, 1996; Seelye, 1997; also see González, 1988). Moreover, as the Latino population grows larger, its relatively high birthrates and lower median age indicate that future growth will come mostly from natural demographic increase, not from immigration. In other words, even if tomorrow the borders with Latin American were closed, Latino population growth would still outstrip Euro-American and African American rates of increase, although not by as much. The difference in the percentages of the population under the age of eighteen is striking: only 23.3 percent of Euro-Americans (whites), as compared to 35 percent of Latinos (Figure 1.2). Using 1990 census data, one can review other significant contrasts between the Latino and non-Latino populations

TABLE 1.1   Comparison of Selected Population Characteristics of Latinos and
Non-Latinos in the Fifty States, 1990

Characteristic	Latino	Non-Latino
Total persons	21,848,903	226,275,115
Share of total population	8.8%	91.2%
Population growth (1980–1990)	53.0%	7.0%
Median age	25.0 yrs	32.6 yrs
Proportion children (under 18)	35.0%	24.7%
Proportion elderly (over 65)	4.9%	13.3%
Proportion foreign born[a]	35.8%	5.3%
Proportion with only high school	52.7%	23.6%
Proportion college graduates	7.5%	19.3%
Male labor force participation	78.6%	74.0%
Female labor force participation	10.3%	5.8%

[a]Excludes Puerto Rico.

Sources: U.S. Bureau of the Census, 1/100 Public Use Microdata Sample, 1990
and 1993; *Hispanic Americans Today,* Current Population Reports, series P-23:
María E. Enchautegui, *Policy Implications of Latino Poverty* (Washington, D.C.:
The Urban Institute, 1995).

(Table 1.1). Latino families are larger; they are younger, have more children, and are growing at a dramatically faster rate (53 percent) than the
non-Latino population (7 percent). Among this population, most people
have only a high-school education. Thus levels of college education are
lower (7.5 percent) than the non-Latino level (19.3 percent).

Poverty is growing rapidly among Latinos. Between 1979 and 1990,
poverty within Latino families grew by 6 percentage points, while the
African American and Euro-American increase was less than 1 percent
each. More recently, between 1993 and 1995 there was a 3.6 percent *increase* in income for African American households and a 5.1 percent *drop*
in income for Latinos. In 1996, the Census Bureau reported that 28.5 percent of African American households were poor, a smaller figure than for
Latinos, who with 29.2 percent are now the poorer of the two groups
(Figure 1.3). The number of Latino and Latina families living in poverty
grew during the period 1974–1995 by 222.24 percent; for all African
Americans, the growth rate for families in poverty was 43.81 percent,
smaller even than the growth rate (49.02 percent) among all Euro-
American families in poverty (Table 1.2).

Generally, high rates of poverty are attributable to the increase in fe-
male-headed households. Although most U.S. families today have more
than one wage earner, single parents depend on one salary or government
assistance, or both, to support their family. But it is alarming that even
among families with both parents living under the same roof, the poverty

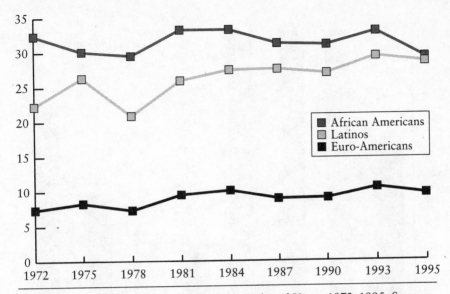

FIGURE 1.3 Poverty Rates in U.S. Families, Selected Years, 1972–1995. *Source:*
U.S. Bureau of the Census, 1996; Eleanor Baugher and Leatha Lamison-White,
Poverty in the United States: 1995, Current Population Reports, P60-194
(Washington, D.C.: U.S. Department of Commerce, Bureau of the Census, 1996).

TABLE 1.2 Poverty Status of U.S. Families

	Number (in thousands)		
Race	1974	1995	Percentage Growth
Euro-American			
All	3,352	4,995	49.02
Married couples	1,877	2,443	30.15
Female-headed	1,289	2,220	72.23
African American			
All	1,479	2,127	43.81
Married couples	435	314	−27.82
Female-headed	1,010	1,701	68.42
Latina			
All	526	1,695	222.24
Married couples	278	803	188.85
Female-headed	229	792	245.85

Source: U.S. Bureau of the Census, 1996; Eleanor Baugher and Leatha Lamison-
White, *Poverty in the United States: 1995,* Current Population Reports, P60-194
(Washington, D.C.: U.S. Department of Commerce, Bureau of the Census, 1996).

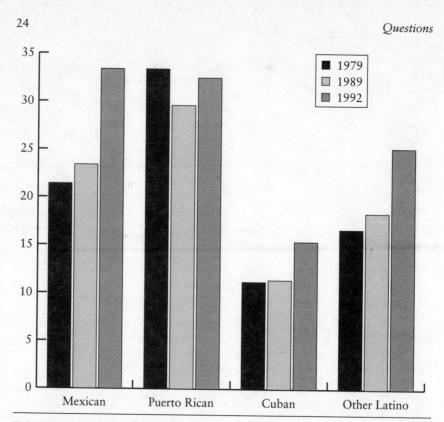

FIGURE 1.4 Latino Family Poverty Rates by Subgroup, Selected Years. *Source:* Frank D. Bean and Marta Tienda, *Hispanic Population of the U.S.* (New York: Russell Sage, 1987); *The Hispanic Population in the United States:* March 1993, Current Population Reports, series P-20, no. 475 (Washington, D.C.: U.S. Bureau of the Census, 1994); María E. Enchavtegi, *Policy Implications of Latino Poverty* (Washington, D.C.: The Urban Institute, 1995).

growth rate of Latino families increased 188.85 percent between 1974 and 1995, whereas that of Euro-American families with two parents increased by only 30.15 percent. Strikingly, African American families with both parents present had a drop in total numbers of those in poverty between 1974 and 1995, making for a negative rate (-27.82 percent). Apparently, the civil rights struggles have benefited African American families.

The group of married people worst off in the United States in 1992 were the Mexican Americans, having overtaken the endemic poverty levels of Puerto Rican families (Figure 1.4). Mexican family poverty has dramatically increased between 1989 and 1992, as has that of the category "Other Latinos," which includes many recent immigrants from Central America. Cubans in the United States remain the best off of all Latino groups, although they also experienced an increase in poverty from 1980 to 1993,

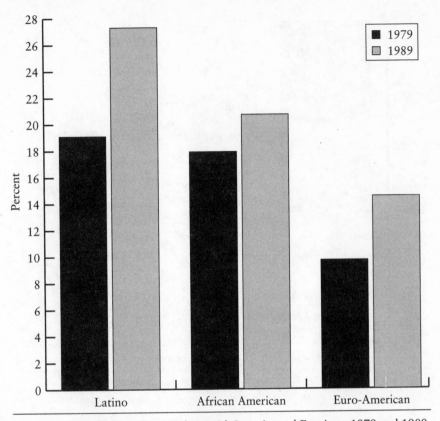

FIGURE 1.5   Full-Time U.S. Workers with Low Annual Earnings, 1979 and 1989.
Full-time workers are employed a minimum of 35 hours per week for no fewer
than 50 weeks of the year. *Source:* U.S. Bureau of the Census, 1992.

probably because of the Mariel immigration. María Enchautegui (1995:13)
points out that even with comparable levels of unemployment, Latinos have
a proportionally lower participation in welfare and food-stamp programs
than either Euro-Americans or African Americans. Not only do many
Latinos fail to collect benefits legally theirs, but they also work in worse
jobs than any other major group. Whereas in 1979 in the category "full-
time with low annual earnings," Latinos (19.1 percent) and African
Americans (17.9 percent) were almost equal, by 1989 Latinos (27.3 percent) were worse off than African Americans (20.7 percent) (Figure 1.5).
But even when employed in professional positions, the average income for
Latinos is less than for Euro-Americans or African Americans with the same
jobs. Whether the Latino or Latina is a manager or engineer, secretary or
bus driver, their pay is generally less than that of people who call themselves
"white" or "black" (Goldberg, 1997). In 1995, whereas the weekly salary

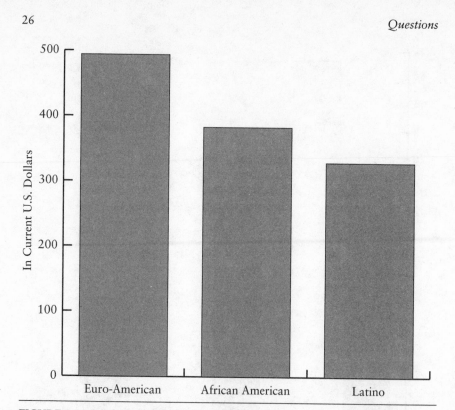

FIGURE 1.6   Median Weekly Earnings for Full-Time Workers, 1995. *Source:*
Bureau of Labor Statistics, 1995; Queens College Department of Sociology.

for Euro-Americans working full time stood at $494—more than $100
more than the weekly salary for African Americans who held full-time jobs
($383)—Latinos trailed African Americans by more than $50 less pay per
week (Figure 1.6). In contrast to other groups, the Latino wage earner receives less pay, has more children to feed, is more likely to expect to have
more children, is less likely to have a spouse who brings home an additional
paycheck, and tends to have a third worker in the household (Table 1.3).
As Joan Moore has pointed out (1994; Moore and Pinderhughes, 1993),
poverty in the Latino barrio is long-standing.

   Education has been a traditional path out of poverty, and the 1996
Census Bureau report found that the proportion of young African
Americans who had completed high school had risen to 87 percent; for the
first time in the nation's history, African Americans attained relative parity
with white youth (91 percent). The comparable statistics for Latino youth
stood at 57 percent. And although the attainments of Euro-Americans and
African Americans have lowered the percentage of the total U.S. population without a high-school education, among Latinos today one out of

TABLE 1.3   Comparison of Selected Characteristics of Latino and Non-Latino Families, 1990

Characteristic	Latino	Non-Latino
Mean household size	4.6	3.4
Mean family size	3.9	3.1
Mean number of births to women	2.1	1.8
Households with children (%)	58.1	31.4
Households with elderly (%)	14.3	22.6
Households with subfamilies (%)	6.9	2.1
Households speaking only English (%)	16.1	79.6
Number of workers per household		
One worker (%)	31.6	27.9
Two workers (%)	39.6	45.7
Three or more workers (%)	17.4	12.9

Source: U.S. Bureau of the Census, 1/100 Public Use Microdata Sample, 1990, 1993; *Hispanic Americans Today,* Current Population Reports, series P-23, no. 183; María E. Enchautegi, *Policy Implications of Latino Poverty* (Washington, D.C.: The Urban Institute, 1995).

every three persons still lacks a high-school diploma (34.7 percent). This is slightly better than 1974 (37.1 percent) but worse than 1984, when the lowest rates were recorded at 34.2 percent (Figure 1.7). To better understand these statistics, one must take into consideration that, for example, graduation rates rise from the first to the second generation of Mexican Americans but stagnate in the third generation. This trend undermines the argument that Latino poverty can be attributed to immigrant status and, therefore, will be eliminated as Latinos assimilate in subsequent generations. None of these trends augurs well for the future. While two-thirds of U.S. families in poverty escape that classification within two years (Enchautegui, 1995:12), some 80 percent of Latino families stay in poverty over the same period of time. In fact, the group of Latinos who are not immigrants—the Puerto Ricans—is among the worst off of ethnic/racial communities in the United States. Puerto Ricans are born citizens of the United States. In Puerto Rico's local elections, they have 100 percent Puerto Rican representation among their elected officials. They live under U.S. law, are familiar with government programs such as food stamps, and are taught English in all the public schools on the island. If citizenship, political prowess, knowledge of U.S. law, familiarity with social programs, and instruction in the English language were conditions for socioeconomic achievement, Puerto Ricans would be the Latin American or Latino group most likely to succeed. Yet instead of ranking first, Puerto Ricans in the United States rank next to last—behind even many new immigrants from Latin America. Our interpretation stresses the colonial condition as the ex-

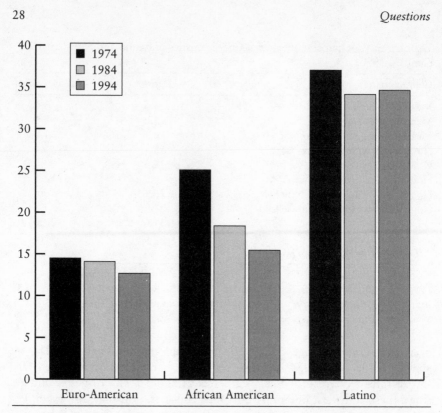

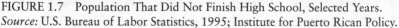

FIGURE 1.7   Population That Did Not Finish High School, Selected Years.
Source: U.S. Bureau of Labor Statistics, 1995; Institute for Puerto Rican Policy.

planation for socioeconomic underachievement. In our opinion, because Puerto Rico is the place where the colonial contradictions of U.S. rule are most evident, Puerto Ricans are the most unlikely to derive benefit from Americanization or to believe that they could.

We question those who blame lack of knowledge of English for Latino poverty. The third-generation Latinos who know English drop out of school more often than the first-generation immigrants from Latin America. As noted, Puerto Ricans (who even in their native island study English from the second grade on) are next to the poorest of Latino groups in the United States. Despite such facts, many commentators such as Wayne Cornelius, the director of the Center for U.S.-Mexican Studies at the University of California at San Diego, insist that "limited English proficiency is the single most important obstacle to upward mobility" (Goldberg, 1997).[7] Such a statement may seem true from the perspective of immigration studies, in which Dr. Cornelius is a recognized expert, but from a wider, comparative look at Latinos nationwide, the Puerto Rican and Chicano experience indicates that English proficiency is not a cure-all for poverty.

Latinos are also highly segregated within U.S. society. A Latino neighborhood, or barrio, is defined by the census as a tract with 50 percent or more Latino population. In 1990, 36 percent of all Latinos and 46 percent of all poor Latinos lived in such barrios. Moreover, the barrios themselves are poor. The census has a precise definition of a poor neighborhood: A poor neighborhood is one where 40 percent or more of the families have incomes below the poverty line. In 1980, 15 percent of all Latino neighborhoods were poor; in 1990, that percentage had risen to 21 percent (Moore, 1994). The barrios are also increasingly multi-Hispanic, that is, they are places where Latinos are a majority, but no one national Latino group accounts for more than 50 percent of the population. In 1980, 29 percent of Latino neighborhoods were multi-Hispanic; in 1990, the rate had risen to 35 percent, more than one-third of all Latino barrios.

In sum, although demographic projections suggest growing numbers of Latinos in the United States, the indicators of poverty point in the direction of a widening gap between Latinos and the general population. Overall, U.S. median incomes are lower in current dollars today than in 1989 for all groups (Figure 1.8). The median income of $22,860 for all Latinos is slightly more than that of all African Americans ($22,393), about $10 more per week. But the future prospects for Latinos are worse than for African Americans. Examining the rise in the median family income in the 1990s reveals that the fastest growth was among African Americans, who showed an increase of almost 10 percent in the three years 1992–1995, rising to $22,393 in constant 1995 dollars. Although this is still considerably below the Euro-American median income of $35,766, the African American growth rate of 10 percent was proportionately greater than that of Euro-Americans (2.2 percent). But whereas the other groups prospered, Latino families lost ground. From 1992 to 1995, the median income for Latinos *dropped* 6.9 percent (Goldberg, 1997). In other words, while other groups are moving ahead during the 1990s, either slowly (Euro-Americans) or rapidly (African Americans), Latinos are going in the opposite direction.

In saying this, we do not want to lose sight of the fact that an argument about who is poorer and why is a sad discussion that distracts attention from the pernicious effects of poverty on all of society. The growing distance between economic classes and the sharpening of ethnic and racial differences increases social conflicts in the United States. After all, when groups are pitted against each other in seeking a piece of the social pie, they are less likely to get along. This affects everyone, regardless of race or ethnicity, sharpening differences about policies from those affecting education and social spending to law enforcement and immigration. Indeed, anti-immigrant and racist

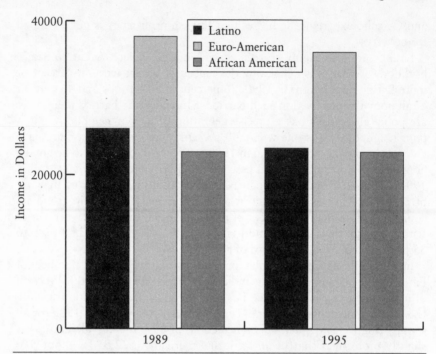

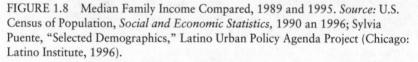

FIGURE 1.8   Median Family Income Compared, 1989 and 1995. *Source:* U.S. Census of Population, *Social and Economic Statistics,* 1990 an 1996; Sylvia Puente, "Selected Demographics," Latino Urban Policy Agenda Project (Chicago: Latino Institute, 1996).

movements in U.S. history have generally occurred at times of economic hardship for the working class, and the 1990s are no exception. It is to be hoped that some of the energies that have improved the social conditions of African Americans who suffered from slavery can now be focused on Latinos, who continue to suffer from colonialism.

Yet, a silver lining in this gloomy horizon may be the *potential* for intergroup alliances. Different Latino nationalities are in more frequent contact with each other and with African and Asian Americans; these conditions make possible intergroup cooperation in specific issues. And those alliances among racial and ethnic groups may be cemented because of the inability to assimilate in other ways with Euro-Americans. When you are told that you are unwanted in "America," the likelihood of replying that you do not want to be "American" increases—especially if that term implies a surrender of language and cultural distinctiveness. Thus, constructed identities such as "Latino," "people of color," and "Third World peoples" may be considered pragmatic terms (Maldonado, 1991; Padilla, 1985). Each stresses some aspect of intergroup cohesiveness and becomes a replacement for a nonfunctional description as "American." Recently, scholars in Latino Studies have employed a term used by anthropologist Renato Rosaldo—"cultural citizenship"—as a mode of describing Latino identity (Rosaldo, 1989; Benmayor, Torruella, and Jurabe, 1992). Because holding on to language and certain traditional values are the ordinary ways people express their identity, people can be considered "Latino" even if they do not go into the streets in political demonstrations or consciously resist certain aspects of Americanization.

This depoliticized understanding of Latino resistance to Americanization is useful in our analysis. Family values, while under assault by socioeconomic factors, are a major factor in Latino identity. Ironically, although the Mexican American family is the poorest in the United States, it is also the ethnic group most likely in the entire nation to preserve the traditional family unit of father, mother, and children living under the same roof. Does the Latino family stick together because of poverty or in spite of it? Would prosperity and upward mobility lead to assimilation and a loss of Latino identity? These are important questions for which there are no simple answers as yet.

Latinos and the American Prospect

Common wisdom holds that the direction of assimilation in the United States has always been affected by the rhythms of upward mobility. In the U.S. economy of the 1990s, are the structural changes that have increased Latino poverty merely cyclical variations? Or is there a radical and irreversible shift under way toward globalization that spells rigid divisions in U.S. society? Without adopting a dogmatic position, we think that the changes occurring now in the U.S. economy are more than temporary downturns: They are structural changes (Carnoy, Daley, and Hinojosa, 1990). And if the current trends are not reversed, poverty is a menace that broods over the Latino future. Poverty means low birth weights for Latino infants, lower-quality medical care, hunger, malnutrition, and violence in the neighborhoods. These conditions delay a child's physical, cognitive, language, and emotional development. How will the Latino family structure negotiate these suffocating conditions?

Our concern is not only for Latinos. We wonder if increased poverty and social inequalities that segregate Latinos from the Euro-American population pose an eventual threat to the nation-state. In the past, the U.S. federal government in Washington, D.C., had assumed leadership in countering dangers arising from national economic disparities. Often, funding for programs to aid the disadvantaged played a crucial role in diminishing conflicts generated by social inequality. However, this is not a likely scenario for the twenty-first century because Washington no longer seems capable of summoning the political will to enact the major federal programs that would be necessary to bring Latinos into equality within U.S. society. What will be the result?

Certainly, the centripetal force that centralized much of government in Washington since the early nineteenth century has run its course. Or as President Clinton proclaimed in the 1996 State of the Union Address, "The age of big government is over." But the idea of turning back responsibility to the states and localities is not a panacea. Once unleashed, centrifugal forces cannot easily be limited merely to tax and welfare matters. If one believes the political cant that "regional groups should stop looking to the national government as the answer for their problems," why would the regions continue to look to a federal government for anything at all?

Puerto Ricans inhabit a peculiar political and social environment where the possibility of separation from the United States is debated daily, and they may therefore be more ready than other Latinos to think the unthinkable. But economics is a powerful factor in the making and unmaking of national links. If Latino cultural identity grows stronger than the ability of the U.S. economy to provide advancement, then valuable lessons might be learned from the experience of other nation-states that have struggled to accommodate multiculturalism and multilingualism (Glazer, 1983). For instance, during the Mulrooney administration in Canada, the federal government in Ottawa cut back drastically on national programs. This devolution of power and responsibility to the provinces exacerbated the disparities between French-speaking and English-speaking citizens to the point that separation into different nations now seems likely. Similarly, the decentralizing perestroika of the Gorbachev years was followed by the dissolution of the Soviet Union. The strife in the former Yugoslavia provides still another example of the collapse of a nation-state after a reduction of the role of the central government. Thus, the correlation between a weaker central government and the fragmentation of a nation-state into multiethnic entities is more than a hypothesis (Huntington, 1996).

These observations are not meant to prophesy the end of the United States as a country but only to note that government programs play a crucial role in cultural and political unity when a nation's economy begins to move in a centrifugal direction. If we used the example of Switzerland, it could be suggested that multicultural communities live in relative harmony when the economy provides prosperity to all, a notion Robert D. Putnam (1993) applied to the United States of the Reagan years. In the case of Europe, transnational integration of the economy has generated more cultural regionalism. Because of its size, the best example for the future of the United States may not be nations like Yugoslavia or Switzerland in Europe (Barrera, 1988) but rather all of Western Europe itself. The European Union has eroded most of the trade and political boundaries between age-old rivals such as France, Germany, and England. But simultaneously with an economic system that is integrating, there has been a rebirth in many re- gions of once-suppressed cultural differences. Thus, for instance, the Welsh and Scots in Great Britain are reviving their cultural identities at a time of economic integration into larger Europe, and in Italy, the Northern League advocates a secessionist state of Padania.

There is special urgency to resolving issues of identity because of the de- mographic projections for the United States into the next century. Although most future scenarios have a habit of disappointing the pundits, the Euro-American and Latino populations are headed in such radically different directions that it merits repeating some of the probable results spelled out by the U.S. Census Bureau (1996; 1997). Latinos will replace African Americans as the largest "minority" in the United States by 2010. By 2020, more Latinos will be added each year to the general population than African Americans, Asian Americans, or Native Americans, or all of them combined. The most rapidly growing segment of the Euro-American population is of those over the age of eighty-five, and by 2050, there will be nearly 18 million of them. The aging of the Euro-American (not Latino, Asian, Native American, or African American) population also points to the year 2034, when more of them will die each year than will be born or enter the United States as immigrants. Not only will the percentage of Euro-Americans in the total U.S. population drop from the 1995 level of 73.1 percent to a bare majority of 52.8 percent, but their total numbers will be less in 2050 than in 2035. When the Euro-American population is further divided by class, religious, and ethnic lines so as to register Catholics, Protestants, Jews, Anglo-Irish, Eastern and Southern Europeans, it will not be easy to identify who is "majority" and who is "minority" in the United States of the next century.

As the U.S. population is becoming more diverse, its economy is simulta- neously being integrated into a world community. In the face of these trends toward diversity and internationalism, will there be a paradoxical need for a sharper U.S. cultural identity? The connection between the econ- omy and cultural unity has been explored in a series of thoughtful essays by Harvard scholar Robert Putnam. By focusing on the demise of bowling leagues and other communal activities in the United States, Putnam sug- gests that because citizens are preoccupied with maintaining economic sta- tus, they spend less time with others. As a result, society is losing a valu- able source of cohesiveness. He states that in America, the decline of bowling indicates a loss of social capital, that is, the resources necessary to be invested in preserving a common good (Putnam, 1995a; 1995b).

We believe that religion is an increasingly important source of social cap- ital in the United States, especially because so many other reservoirs have gone dry. Religion is a particularly powerful wellspring of Latino identity, cultural cohesiveness, and social organization. Latino religion will play a key role in the unfolding of the twenty-first century for both Latinos and for the larger society, in part because religion offers both meaning and moral order to society (Wuthnow, 1987). Our positive understanding of religion should not be interpreted as a Pollyanna view that all ills can be swept away by a return to the church. We would not argue that religion can substitute for government programs of assistance to the poor, educational reform, or the building of more low-cost housing. We view religion more as a resource for communities and individuals that can often strengthen and enrich social programs.

Moving beyond Putnam's thesis about social capital, we are intrigued by its connections with larger themes, such as those elaborated by Samuel Huntington (1996). Although we hesitate to embrace all of his principles and conclusions, the premise that religion gives genesis to a particularized worldview or civilization seems valid. If one gives more weight to Ibero-American culture as a civilization than does Professor Huntington, the distinctiveness of Latinos stands in sharper relief. In fact, the idea that Latinos share a civilization distinct from Euro-Americans partially explains why Latino cultural differences stubbornly remain, even though Latinos have been in the United States longer than most other ethnic groups. In several chapters of this book, we will offer historical and contemporary examples to suggest that Latino religion belongs to a different civilization than much of Euro-America, specifically in terms of the following: (1) language; (2) religious faith; (3) shared traditions, values, and symbols; (4) literature, folklore, and music; and (5) concept of government and social responsibilities, particularly those that address neighborhood and family preservation. In addition to being hallmarks of civilization, all these experiences produce social capital. Of course, that production varies from one denomination to another because each of the churches has different ritual and theological traditions. But even if the social capital comes from different sources, it enriches the Latino experience of religion.

The Contours of Latino Religious Belonging

Statistics on religious membership are somewhat difficult to verify because the census of the United States does not ask any religious identification question. Church estimates about Latino members, however, frequently use census and other statistics for a total number and then apply the percentage of estimated adherents to their denomination in order to approximate the number of believers (Saldigloria, in Stevens-Arroyo, 1980: 166–169). In seeking to improve on these estimates, the summary that follows of Latino participation in U.S. religion is taken from the important National Survey of Religious Identification (NSRI) of 1991, from the prize-

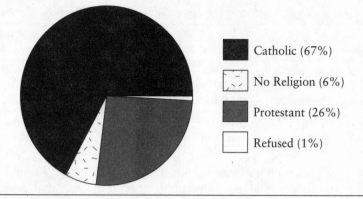

FIGURE 1.9   Religious Affiliation of Latinos, 1990. *Source:* Barry A. Kosmin, *The National Survey of Religious Identification. 1989–1990* (New York: City University of New York, March 1991); Barry A. Kosmin and Seymour P. Lachman, *One Nation Under God: Religion in Contemporary American Society* (New York: Harmony Books, 1993).

winning book *One Nation Under God*, by Barry A. Kosmin and Seymour P. Lachman.

As in other recent surveys, the NSRI reported that two out of three Latinos identify themselves as Catholics (65.8 percent) and roughly one out of four as Protestant (24.6 percent [or 25.4 percent, including Mormons as Protestants]). These percentages, along with the percentages for those with no religion and those who did not respond, appear as rounded off in the chart in Figure 1.9. The findings of Kosmin and Lachman can be compared with a similar identification item in the Latino National Political Survey (LNPS) of 1989–1990 (Table 1.4). Protestantism is highest among Puerto Ricans and lowest among Cubans—except for those in Texas. The NSRI sample was large enough to provide numbers for the distribution among Protestants of the different denominations (Table 1.5). Baptist is the largest of these denominations (7.4 percent), followed by Christian, meaning Evangelical churches (5.2 percent). Other denominations had very few respondents, and many used generic rather than denominationally specific terms. Moreover, for purposes of accuracy, the NSRI employed weighting in translating the raw numbers to percentages. With all of these limitations, however, the results are illuminating. Overall, this survey found only 2 percent of Latinos identified as Pentecostals. But since the categories supplied in this survey depended on classifications that came from the respondents, it may be asked whether those who answered that they belonged to the Christian Church, Assembly of God, or Jehovah's Witnesses might be Evangelicals or Pentecostals in other classification systems. Likewise, the generic term "Protestant" was used by 2.5 percent of

TABLE 1.4   Religious Affiliation by National Origin (in percent)

Religious Affiliation	Mexican	Puerto Rican	Cuban	Euro-American
Catholic	73.7	65.1	74.8	21.2
Protestant	15.0	22.3	14.4	54.2
Other/no preference	11.3	12.5	10.9	24.5

Source: Rudolpho O. de la Garza et al., *Latino Voices: Mexican, Puerto Rican, and Cuban Perspectives on American Politics* (Boulder: Westview Press, 1992).

the respondents, with no more specific denominational tag. Without more research, it is impossible to resolve ambiguities of this sort that arise from most general surveys. But it can be stated rather clearly that among Latinos, Catholics are two and one-half times more numerous than all Protestants and that Latinos identify themselves as "Catholics" twenty times more frequently than as "Pentecostals."

With characteristic thoroughness, Kosmin and Lachman also provide a cross-check on their findings by including a comparison with other sources. The Scholastic Aptitude Test (SAT) is one of the few general sources that allow for both ethnic and religious identification. Or course, this is a test only for youth seeking to enter college. It does not represent the older generations, which tend to be more religious than eighteen-year-olds, nor does it account for young people who do not aspire to a college education—which is most Latinos. Yet the results from the SAT show a religious affiliation pattern among Mexican, Puerto Rican, and Latin American youth that conforms generally to the percentages from the national survey. It is worth noting that among youth identifying themselves as Pentecostal, Puerto Ricans responded nearly three times as often (6 percent) as Mexican Americans (2.1 percent) (Kosmin and Lachman, 1993:139–140). The principal drawback in conducting the NSRI among Latinos was limiting age to individuals eighteen years old or older. This eliminated Latino children and reduced overall percentages of Latinos vis-à-vis other groups with older populations. Thus, for instance, according to the NSRI, Euro-Americans account for 80 percent of the Catholic population (Kosmin and Lachman, 1993:117), a percentage that undercounts the Latino proportion. But there is a higher percentage of Latinos under age eighteen than Euro-Americans, so the methodology of the NSRI disproportionately reduced the number of Latino Catholics. Moreover, the NSRI used a telephone survey and did not have bilingual interviewers, further inclining it toward an undercount of Latinos.

The 1984 telephone survey by Robert González and Michael La Velle, while useful, is less reliable than the NSRI. First, it is now outdated; second, it interviewed only Latino Catholics. Using 1980 census numbers, 40

TABLE 1.5   Religious Affiliation of Latinos and Latinas

Denomination	Respondents	Percent*
Catholic	6,421	65.8
Protestant	240	2.5
Jewish	59	0.6
Buddhist	27	0.3
Moslem	25	0.3
Hindu	6	0.1
Taoist	5	0.0
Rastafarian	3	0.0
Bahai	2	0.0
Assembly of God	39	0.4
Baptist	720	7.4
Christian	507	5.2
Church of Christ	24	0.2
Church of God/Worldwide	9	0.1
Congregational	7	0.1
Disciples of Christ	2	0.0
Episcopalian/Anglican	39	0.4
Evangelical	29	0.3
Greek Orthodox	5	0.1
Holiness/Charismatic	42	0.4
Jehovah's Witness	163	1.7
Lutheran	78	0.8
Methodist	167	1.7
Mormon/Latter-day Saints	74	0.8
Nazarene	1	0.0
New Apostolic	8	0.1
Pentecostal	199	2.0
Presbyterian	66	0.7
Quaker/Mennonite	1	0.0
Seventh-Day Adventist	27	0.3
Nondenominational/Independent	6	0.0
Agnostic	40	0.4
Total	9,754	

*Weighted to sample. Total includes "No Religion," which is not listed here.
Source: Barry A. Kosmin, *The National Survey of Religious Identification,
1989–1990* (New York: City University of New York, 1991).

metropolitan sites were identified for random sampling. But when it became difficult to find Latinos according to this sampling method, lists of
Latinos were purchased for the survey. It can be argued that this methodology skews the results, finding more Catholics than a strictly random survey
might have (Stevens-Arroyo, 1995a:39–40). Notwithstanding these draw-

backs to its accuracy for describing denominational affiliation, the survey offers valuable insights into the religious attitudes and practices of Catholics, the largest religious group of Latinos. More than one-half of Latino Catholics say they go to mass once a week or more. When this is added to those who attend at least once a month, three out of four (77 percent) Latino Catholics can be considered to be at least as fervent as most Protestants in the United States (González and La Velle, 1985:74, table 131). The close links between cultural and religious identity for Latinos are affirmed. The respondents who said religion was very important to them were more likely to say that Latino culture was important in church services (84.7 percent). Those who said religion was less important were less concerned about Latino culture in religious expression (57.1 percent) (González and La Velle, 1985:163). Although more analysis is required, these results suggest that religious commitment strengthens cultural citizenship among Latinos.

The González and La Velle survey found religion was more important to the Latino poor (86 percent) than to those earning more than $40,000 a year, of whom only 61 percent said that religion was important to them. Significantly, neither age nor education was a predictor of increased or diminished importance for culture in religious expression (1985:163, see their tables 256–257). The data also showed that up until the sixth generation in the United States, a majority of Latinos felt it was very important to use the Hispanic culture and language in worship (1985:162–163). Finally, although English gained in usage proportionately to its being preferred over Spanish (1985:165), it would be more accurate to label this preference as "bilingual" rather than as a rejection of Spanish.

In general, then, the data from such research establish the demographic importance of Latinos within the United States and indicate areas of religious practice that distinguish Latinos from Euro-American groups. To conclude this chapter, we analyze four areas in which we believe the current wisdom of the social scientific study of religion needs to be reexamined. These are: (1) Americanization and assimilation, (2) race and ethnicity, (3) upward mobility and denominational affiliation, and (4) civil religion.

Americanization and Assimilation

Social science studies of religion among particular ethnic groups have usually focused on discussion of Americanization, that is, assimilation into U.S. society. In most instances, use of the term "Americanization" is equivalent to "modernization" or "secularization," as is summarized by Milton Gordon in his important and much-cited work *Assimilation in American Life* (1974). As is suggested by the subtitle of his book, *The Role of Race,*

TABLE 1.6   Gordon's Assimilation Variables

Subprocess or Condition	Type of Assimilation	Special Term
Change of cultural patterns to those of host society	Cultural or behavioral assimilation	Acculturation
Large-scale entrance into cliques, clubs, and institutions of host society, on primary group level	Structural assimilation	None
Large-scale intermarriage	Marital assimilation	Amalgamation
Development of sense of peoplehood based exclusively on host society	Identificational assimilation	None
Absence of prejudice	Attitude-receptional assimilation	None
Absence of discrimination	Behavior-receptional assimilation	None
Absence of value and power conflict	Civic assimilation	None

Source: Milton Gordon, *Assimilation in American Life: The Role of Race, Religion, and National Origins* (New York: Oxford University Press, 1974).

Religion, and National Origins, Gordon was interested in the persistence of distinguishing traits that kept groups "ethnic" in the face of general trends of Americanization. Acknowledging a debt to Oscar Handlin, Gordon developed a set of types or stages of assimilation that have seeped into much of the subsequent literature on assimilation (Table 1.6). Although Gordon has been criticized for viewing assimilation as inevitable (Flores, 1993:185), the lasting contribution of his analysis is his relating the notion of assimilation—becoming "like" the dominant society—to a set of relatively distinct measures. In his study, Gordon divided the process into categories like "structural," "marital," "cultural," and "civic." He gave names to some of these so that one could point to "acculturation" in one sphere and distinguish that from intermarriage or "amalgamation."

Subsequent authors have often developed scales of assimilation that reflect Gordon's basic outline. Thus, for instance, Edward Shils provides a list of how traditions "assimilate" each other: addition, amalgamation, absorption, and fusion (1981:275–279). Carsten Colpe (1975/1980:166–176) and Kurt Rudolf (1979) have been interpreted by Benavides (1995:21–22) in a spectrum of behaviors that resonates with Gordon's 1964 contribution: symbiosis, amalgamation, identification, metamorphosis, and isolation (although the Europeans add an emphasis upon conscious and unconscious formations of belief and do not specifically examine ethnicity).

We agree with Gustavo Benavides, David Carrasco, Otto Maduro, and Andrés Pérez y Mena in *Enigmatic Powers* (1995) that all such processes

are impacted by social and religious power. Although it is theoretically possible to have a "pure" encounter in which different cultural groups mutually enrich each other without damage, in actuality such exchanges seldom
take place because almost every encounter is freighted by power relations.
Only when such encounters are viewed as drawn-out historical processes
may the power relations be overcome and a tertium quid emerge from the
opposing forces. Benavides uses the analogy of the creation of pidgin or
creole dialects that replace a classical grammar over the course of generations and become new languages (Benavides, 1995:36). Although Spanish
and Italian are derived from Latin, they are languages in their own right,
and neither is Latin anymore. In somewhat the same way, the encounter
between the Normans and the Saxons in medieval England began with
clear class differences between the two groups and the languages they used.
However, the social relations of the groups shifted, allowing the Saxon language to absorb elements of Norman speech. Eventually, the process of
centuries produced not two separate groups, one out of power and the
other with the hegemonic role, but one people.

Could something like this process take place between Latinos and the
Euro-American populations in the United States? Certainly, the present
state of power relations impedes a kind of "mutual" assimilation on both
sides. But with enough time, might such a merging without exploitation
occur? We would call this the process of "transculturation." First developed through the collaboration of don Fernando Ortíz, the Cuban *homme
de belles-lettres,* and the anthropologist Bronislaw Malinowski, it is our
preferred way to speak of a symmetrical exchange between groups.
Transculturation describes acquisition of new cultural traits as mutual enrichment, independently of power relations. From the transculturation perspective, common property is common gain. As Malinowski defines it in
his introduction to Ortíz's *Cuban Counterpoint*, rather than a "mosaic" or
a "conglomeration," it is "an original and independent phenomenon"
(Malinowski, in Ortíz, 1947).

Recognizing the valuable critiques of this term, especially among Cuban
scholars, we think that transculturation can be best understood as a historical reality only over a considerable stretch of time. Examples of transculturation over centuries would be the processes that syncretized the Saxons
and Normans in England or the Celts, Visigoths, and Arabs in Spain
(Rouse, 1992:25, 103). But ascribing transculturation to one or another
aspect of social exchange requires a distinction between diachronic analysis and synchronic perception. The recipients of the transculturated reality
are not likely to understand the different origins of various elements in
their culture. In our opinion, we only enter a blind alley when we argue
that this Latino custom is "really" Aztec and another custom Spanish,
African, or American. Such a perspective fragments the sum and recognizes

only the parts and noninteractive pieces. On the contrary, we think transculturation modifies and reconstructs each separate piece of another culture into a new synthesized totality (Díaz-Stevens, 1994c). Like a person tasting a soup, the first step is to savor the results; only later might the curious ask about the ingredients, when they were added, and in what quantities as they were cooked.

Transculturation is not an uncommon phenomenon. It occurs in daily experiences like eating and listening to music, and the multicultural, multiracial reality of the United States has its share of good examples. For instance, the frankfurter has been so transculturated from its German origin as a sausage that it is viewed as the quintessential American "hot dog." Of course—pardon the pun—food is easily assimilated: Culture and religion are more complicated. But there are instances of U.S. transculturation on these more difficult terrains. One might suggest that the considerable body of sociological literature on a U.S. civil religion reflects the conviction that religious symbols can be transculturated across denominational boundaries so as to become common property, a topic explored further on.

The best way to understand transculturation among Latinos, we think, is to examine migration to urban areas. Transculturation is linked to several stages of sociologically measurable phenomena. First comes the experience of relocation, with the direct effects on material culture. Food, clothing, and living arrangements of the immigrants are the most directly affected. Next, there seems to be the lag time or anomie, in which most people experience the inconsistencies between their expectations and the reality of their new circumstances but no new substitute has yet been found to supply the guiding traditions of the past. It is during this stage of lag time or anomie that new arrivals are expected to be most vulnerable to radical change, such as by religious conversion or—in a negative sense—by addiction, crime, and family disintegration (Poblete and O'Dea, 1960). Lastly, the stage of acculturation arrives, wherein people devise strategies of assimilation and resistance to incorporate what they find useful in the new circumstances and to resist those elements that would undermine group identity (Flores, 1993:182–195). Transculturation helps us understand why certain of the traditional practices and conceptions endure through this process, while others are cast aside. It is the transculturated reality that is the substratum of identity and the constituent basis for a Latino difference.

Individual assimilation is not the focus of this analysis, however. There have always been individuals who, for any number of reasons, exchange identification with another nationality in order to assimilate as completely as possible the culture of the United States. For such people, the myriad characteristics that serve as association with culture[8] are surrendered in order for them to become indistinguishable within United States society.

Assimilation at this personal level has always occurred within ethnic groups and is often a conscious, individualized choice meriting respect.

Our focus, however, is upon religious expressions of Latino identity as they are expressed in communities and congregations across the spectrum of individual experiences. There are those who only partially surrender their Latino characteristics, those who refuse to surrender at all, and those who have surrendered but who now attempt to recover and reclaim certain Latino characteristics. With a Latino identity come common values, established customs, and behavioral patterns, which, although never rigid, are measured by observation or survey. In almost all cases, religious expression has a component corresponding to each of these categories. In fact, the preservation or rediscovery of identity is often tied to religious experience. Religious conversion or commitment may be a more reliable indicator of cultural behavior than political voting patterns.

Race and Ethnicity

Race and ethnicity are concepts that are not as clearly applied to Latinos as to other groups in the United States. For instance, Greeley (1977) lumped together "black and Spanish-speaking Catholics" as racial groups. This is counterintuitive, since—unlike "black"—"Spanish-speaking" has an ethnic application (language) rather than a racial one. Yet Greeley not only held to his strange terminology but ridiculed the notion that Latinos were an ethnic group. On page fifteen of *The American Catholic*, he comments: "In the Northeast, for example, there is a deliberate attempt to create a Spanish-speaking ethnic group (an attempt that is not supported, incidentally, in the Southwest)." This trivializes the Chicano struggles, which were very real. Consequently, in the absence of any empirical proof to substantiate his opinion, Greeley's distinction between Latinos being an ethnic group in the Northeast and not in the Southwest may be discarded.

That does not mean that the issues of race and ethnicity have an easy resolution. Unlike most Euro-American groups, Latinos are multiracial, encompassing not only white but also black, Native American, and mixed-race phenotypes. One could plausibly make the case that "Italian, Irish, Slavic, and so forth" are racial and not ethnic terms because they generally exclude people who are not Caucasian. However, "Latino/Hispanic" is a more completely ethnic, that is, cultural, term because it transcends racial limitations.[9] Greeley (1982) has subsequently adopted a better analytical perspective on Latinos, but the application to Latinos of standard, dichotomous social science definitions of race and ethnicity remains a slippery slope.

We think that these are areas where a group's multiple identities are at work. Not unreasonably, Latinos will alternate between a racial identity and an ethnic one where each is advantageous. It would be useful if social scientists in the United States paid more attention to Latin American experiences wherein mixed-race categories are frequent. We think there is too much reliance on the black-or-white racial dichotomy in U.S. social science. It affords too few categories adequate for describing the Latino experience. Unless social science finds new and more flexible categories for race and ethnicity in the United States, analysis might remain as barren as Greeley's misfired interpretation.

Social Mobility and Denominational Affiliation

Upward mobility has long been a facet of U.S. denominational experience, particularly in Protestantism (Wuthnow, 1988; Roof and McKinney, 1987). The pattern has been for individuals to switch denominations as they become more prosperous. Thus, Pentecostals, Baptists, and Methodists are at or below the middle-level income groups, whereas Presbyterians and Episcopalians are closer to the top. There have always been exceptions to such patterns, of course, and in the case of Latinos, we believe that denominational membership is not a reliable predictor of social class. For instance, in Puerto Rico's middle class, Pentecostalism is sometimes the religion of choice. By not moving to mainline Protestant denominations in the march toward upward social mobility, island Puerto Rican Pentecostals offer their churches financial resources and social standing that was not common a generation ago (Silva Gotay, 1994:164–167). This example finds its parallels among other groups of Latino Pentecostals, and we await better survey data to provide the extent of this trend in the fifty states.

But mainline Protestantism is undergoing a significant shift away from certain of its long-established patterns (Roof, 1994). Some Protestant congregations have not been passive in the effort to hold on to their Latino members. In the continental U.S. context, many urban Protestant churches have adopted policies of sharing the building among various ethnic congregations. This is viewed as preferable to closing the church because the English-speaking members are too few to maintain the congregation. Thus, Korean, Chinese, or Latino congregations are formed under the guidance of separate ministers and use one building. In some ways, this approximates the Catholic multiethnic parish that has been described in detail (Díaz-Stevens, 1993a). It spells a new twist to the study of denominationalism in the United States, and a recent trend toward congregational studies is a welcome development that will aid in understanding Latinos (Warner, 1996).

Civil Religion

Finally, Latinos provide a challenge to the study of civil religion, as suggested in the published exchange between Philip Hammond and Spencer Bennett after a National Endowment for the Humanities conference held at the University of California in Santa Barbara. Hammond, an esteemed sociologist and collaborator with the legendary Robert Bellah, cautioned Bennett against including the struggle of César Chávez as part of U.S. civil religion (Benavides and Daly, 1993). Following Bellah (1975), Hammond establishes criteria for what he believes belongs within civil religion and what does not. Without denying the centrality of Chávez's role in summoning a religious feeling among Chicanos and other Latinos, Hammond opines that a direct appeal to a particular ethnic experience disqualifies that experience from inclusion within U.S. civil religion. He reasons that precisely because that appeal is "ethnic," it cannot be the property of a generalized civil religion, which by definition appeals to identity as "American." Hammond says, "The point can be put crudely: César Chávez would have no hope of winning the moral support of Americans generally by offering a particularistic ideology, a creed so peculiar to farmworkers that, in motivating them, it leaves everyone else unmoved" (Hammond, 1993:171).

But from a Latino perspective, it is possible to critique the view that civil religion has been all-inclusive in the past. History provides examples of an appeal to "a particularistic ideology, a creed so peculiar . . . that . . . it leaves everyone else unmoved," the "everyone else" including Latinos. For instance, civil religion in the nineteenth century was based on conceptions of U.S. Manifest Destiny. This was a creed historically prejudicial of Latino culture, nationality, and religion, so much so that it encouraged invasion, subjugation, and colonialism. It most definitely left Latinos "unmoved" in Hammond's sense; yet, it was U.S. civil religion. We do agree with Hammond, however, when he states: "But whether the judgment is good or bad is not the issue; the issue is whether a course of action is urged or justified in the name of an ideology having the nation-state as the principal actor in a drama believed to be written and directed by transcendent forces" (Hammond, 1993:170).

By this definition, Manifest Destiny was a major part of U.S. civil religion. But if something as evil as Manifest Destiny belonged in civil religion even though it directly excluded the experiences and gifts of Latinos and Latin Americans (at the same time that it sanctioned U.S. intervention into their lands and affairs), then we have to question Hammond's disqualification of Latino symbols as "so peculiar, that in motivating them [Latinos] it leaves everyone else unmoved." The issue of who is the majority (and by inference, hegemonic) population and who is the minority (subaltern) needs to be considered. Much as we observe in terms of syncretism and popular religiosity, the definition of what does and what does not fit into civil religion as "American" is a judgment that implicitly reflects social power. With Latinos' demographic growth, it is conceivable in one scenario that symbols that are not compatible with civil religion *now* might become so in the future. But in a second scenario, it is also conceivable that Latinos may view civil religion as the denial of the differences that ought to be respected rather than diluted. In other words, reject a sterile religious–politically correct melting pot and celebrate differences. A third possibility is that the Latino presence may impact upon civil religion in such a way as to remake it into something other than what up to now social scientists have understood and defined for this phenomenon. If civil religion is a dynamic social construct rather than a static notion, then the third possibility has to be given serious consideration.

It is in this light that we review Hammond's commentary on the symbols of the Virgin of Guadalupe and the cross. These are alien to U.S. civil religion, he says, because "while non-Catholics may tolerate her, they will not resonate to her. Nor can the symbol be the cross, because the American civil religion is not Christian" (1993:172). He suggests instead the notion of "sacrifice," which finds echoes in general religious experience and may be better represented by the symbols of "fasting and penitential marching." But in the Mexican context, devotion to the Virgin of Guadalupe gained its importance as a national symbol even among Protestants and nonbelievers because it emphasized the racial and social factors of one segment of the Mexican population—poor, Indian, mestizo, or criollo—against another sector, the rich Spanish (Lafaye, 1974/1976). Thus, in setting limits of civil religion based on the U.S. experience alone, Hammond may be underestimating the scope of the phenomenon. The comparative perspectives supplied by Putnam on the issue seem more compelling (Putnam, 1995c). Of importance, we believe, is his assertion that some nations (or peoples) function quite well without recourse to civil religion. Moreover, it seems artificial to cut and paste a multifaceted reality like Marian devotion onto any of its constituent parts, as Hammond seems to imply. Can "fasting and penitential marching" be separated from the banners, songs, and images of the Virgin of Guadalupe and the Passion of Jesus Christ, in whose name they are celebrated?

We are not sure how to answer these questions. But we hope the chapter that follows will provide some insights into these issues from a Latino perspective. We think that when related to shifts in demographic predominance and social power, civil religion is another area where Latino religion is producing new configurations that impact on all religion in the United States. As we hope to make clear in the following chapters in this book, Latino religion has a past, present, and future that merit extensive analysis.

Notes

1. Three examples of this unfortunate tendency, each in a different field, are Ramón Gutiérrez, *When Jesus Came, the Corn Flower Mothers Went Away* (his-

tory), Olga Rodríguez, ed., *The Politics of Chicano Liberation* (political science), and Ilan Stavans, *The Hispanic Condition: Reflections on Culture and Identity in America* (literature).

2. Among the earliest studies notable for their reference to Latino religion are the following: Felix Padilla, *Latino Ethnic Consciousness*; David Abalos, *Latinos in the United States: The Sacred and the Political*; David F. Gómez, *Somos Chicanos: Strangers in Our Own Land*; the work on Mexican American Catholicism by Patrick McNamara should be highlighted and is cited extensively throughout this book, particularly his "Dynamics of the Catholic Church from Pastoral to Social Concerns" in Grebler, Moore, and Guzmán's *The Mexican American People*. Charles A. Tatum in his "Geographic Displacement as Spiritual Desolation in Puerto Rican and Chicano Prose Fiction" offers a literary perspective on religious themes in *Images and Identities: The Puerto Rican in Two World Contexts*. On Puerto Ricans within U.S. Catholicism, the late Joseph P. Fitzpatrick, S.J., of Fordham University offered valuable insights, especially in his *Puerto Rican Americans: The Meaning of Migration to the Mainland*, although this work has been superseded by the work of Ana María Díaz-Stevens, *Oxcart Catholicism on Fifth Avenue*. For Cubans in this country, see the essay by Marcos Antonio Ramos and Agustín Román in *Cuban Exiles in Florida: Their Presence and Contribution*; and José Llanes, *Cuban Americans: Masters of Survival*, which offers insights not based strictly on religion. We consider our coauthored overview, "Religious Faith and Institutions in the Forging of Latino Identities" in the volume edited by Felix Padilla for the *Handbook for Hispanic Cultures in the United States*, to carry merit for a general reader.

3. When Greeley's conception of race and ethnicity in a 1976 article was critiqued, Greeley responded in his nationally syndicated column with what must be categorized as the classic ad hominem argument: "Who is this Stevens-Arroyo? Who ever elected him to anything?" (Greeley, syndicated column of January 6, 1977). See the letters to the editor in *Priest* 33 (5) (May 1977):3–5 and the similar experience of Samuel A. Mueller (*Journal for the Scientific Study of Religion* 13 (4) (November 1974):503–504.

4. D'Antonio et al. (1996:158 and throughout) confirmed the vast differences in socioeconomic and educational achievements between Euro-American (called "First Wave") and Latino Catholics but nonetheless asserted that Latinos "will come to resemble first-wave Catholics even more as time goes on." Since the authors offer no data to substantiate their premise of assimilation, it can be safely interpreted as their brand of wishful thinking. See Chapter 7 for a more detailed examination of this issue.

5. The 1930 census used the term "Mexican?" as a racial category alongside "white, Negro, Indian, Chinese or Japanese," but this racial classification was discarded by 1940 (United States Commission on Civil Rights, 1974:5–6).

6. For critiques, see Flores (1993:209–216) on Rodríguez and Stevens-Arroyo's review of Stavans's *The Hispanic Condition* in *Commonweal* 122 (15) (September 8, 1996):22–23.

7. Carey Goldberg, "Hispanic Households Struggle as Poorest of the Poor in U.S.," *New York Times,* January 30, 1997.

8. The *Harvard Encyclopedia of American Ethnic Groups* (Thernstrom, 1980:vi) provides the basis for fifteen characteristics: common geographic origins; migratory

status; race; language or dialect; religious faith or faiths; ties that transcend kinship; neighborhood or community barriers; shared traditions, values, and symbols; literature, folklore, and music; food preferences; settlement and employment patterns; special interests in regard to politics in the homeland and in the United States; institutions that specifically serve and maintain the group; an internal sense of distinctiveness; and an external sense of distinctiveness (see Maldonado, 1991).

9. The dogged exclusion of Latino Catholics by *The American Catholic* passes over to the index, which does not have a single entry for "Spanish-speaking," "Hispanic/Latino," or "Mexican American." Cubans (p. 22) and Puerto Ricans (pp. 22, 225) are mentioned in passing by name; there is a listing for Spanish-speaking on p. 172 and a footnote with anecdotal information on p. 18.

2

Tradition

$\mathcal{A}$LONG WITH MANY OTHER GROUPS in the United States, Latinos have a rich heritage of religious traditions. But to understand how such traditions influence U.S. religion today, we have to avoid interpretations that either reduce traditions to celebratory "folklore" or suppose that they reflect an inability to "modernize." This chapter delves into the dynamics of tradition: We seek to analyze what makes traditions expand or contract, perdure or wither, renew or retard religious experience. We have waded into the salty waters of theory because a positive appreciation of tradition and its role in U.S. religion is not always reflected in the general sociological literature. Edward Shils's treatment of tradition in his book *Tradition* (1981) is our starting point, which seems more suited to our application to religion than a book on the same topic edited by Eric Hobsbawm and Terence Ranger (1983).

Noting the disrepute tradition held for Max Weber and Karl Marx, Shils offers a brief description of tradition that includes both material and ideational aspects: "It includes all that a society of a given time possesses and which already existed when its present possessors came upon it and which is not solely the product of physical processes in the external world or exclusively the result of ecological and physiological necessity" (Shils, 1981:12).

Shils stresses that tradition offers "normative models of action and belief" (1981:3), an aspect denigrated by both Marx and Weber (1981:9). The segment of Shils's definition of tradition that is most relevant to Latino religion is found in his explanation of how tradition transmits itself to human actions: "The transmissible parts of them [human actions] are the patterns or images of actions which they imply or present and the beliefs requiring, recommending, regulating, permitting or prohibiting the reenactment of those patterns" (1981:12).

We want to focus on the normative character of tradition that Shils has described because that is the intersection with Latino religion. Although we recognize that almost every religion is connected to some tradition, we think that among Latinos and Latinas, tradition is more frequently invoked than in most types of U.S. religion.

The irony of religion traditions is that not all of them are essentially sacred according to theology. The traditions of Christmas, for instance, have acquired many aspects that are not based on Christian scripture. But we should not be too hasty in dismissing the secular elements that are incorporated into religious traditions as if they were alien to the study of religion. If we recall the theoretical issue of cores and surfaces that was discussed in the first chapter, we can assume it would be a mistake to presume that theology or doctrine drives all traditional religious celebrations. More to the point, Leigh Eric Schmidt (1995) of Princeton University suggests that in the United States, commercialism has made a contribution to the longevity of religious traditions. The need to send Christmas cards, to buy toys for children, to exchange store-bought gifts, says Schmidt, reinforce the importance of the religious events in popular culture. Although a theologian might consider these social preoccupations as negative influences on religious meaning, social scientists view the convergence of secular and religious meanings as an integral part of the tradition.

The Burden of Temporality

A normative function helps make a tradition dynamic rather than static. In other words, when people say they feel it is important to repeat customs for themselves, their families, and communities, we know that the tradition is alive. We would like to call the obligation to repeat tradition "the burden of temporality." Repetition of traditions helps form a community and holds it together. Observing a tradition honors the past whence it came, the present for which it has importance, and the future in which it will again be repeated. Or as Shils puts it, tradition creates a "sense of filiation, i.e., connectedness to other generations" (1981:14). Traditions always require a community: If there is no group that holds a common understanding of the tradition, it will cease to exist. Obviously, this premise can be applied to almost every group, as Ann Taves (1986) has traced in nineteenth-century U.S. Catholicism in general and as Robert Orsi has described for past and present-day Italian Americans in New York (1985) and Chicago (1996).

Social Location

The "burden" of temporality contributes to a second dynamic. Tradition not only recognizes past, present, and future, but it also surfaces as awareness of social location. Admittedly, the terminology, "awareness of social location" requires elaboration. We examine Latino religious traditions broadly enough here to allow room for theoretical concepts like collective memory (Kammen, 1991), *mentalité* (mind-set) (Vovelle, 1990), Jungian archetypes (Abalos, 1986; Stevens-Arroyo, 1995b), class (Maduro, 1982), organic intellectuality (Fulton, 1987; Cadena, 1992; Williams, 1996), and historical consciousness (Mészáros, 1972), all of which can be utilized to interpret cultural identity. We have found some of these useful in other writings (Díaz-Stevens, 1990, 1993a, 1993b, 1993c, 1996b, 1996c, 1996d; and Stevens-Arroyo, 1994, 1995b, 1997b), and we believe the subject merits continued exploration. However defined, tradition rests upon relationships built upon class, race, gender, and other such social determinations. We do not intend to imply that religious traditions always function in the same ways. Surely, there are instances where tradition can be linked to liberation; but there are others where traditions are empty observances, or even worse, where they are sterile and contain only imitations of real religious commitment.

The writings of Georg Lukacs, the Hungarian Marxist theoretician of culture, can be interpreted in such a way as to shed light on the function of tradition in a religious context (Díaz-Stevens, 1996b). In the first one-third of the twentieth century, Lukacs explained that art is related to class consciousness, even when the creator of the art is not directly concerned with political issues. Lukacs suggested that the artistic imagination challenges the inevitability of historical forces. When art creates a might-have-been alternative to the status quo, says Lukacs, a step is taken toward liberation (Mészáros, 1972:173–190). Although Lukacs himself strongly criticized as alienating the type of art and literature that romanticized reality, his insights into artistic production can be applied to religious tradition.

If the reader of a novel can be moved from treating history as a thing—reification—to historical consciousness wherein events are seen as the results of human actions, cannot the reader of the scriptures also acquire consciousness? Novels often portray lower-class heroes who successfully humble the proud and mighty; so does scripture. If one can learn from literature that the struggle between social classes is not always predetermined in favor of the dominant elites, it is not too far a stretch to view scripture as having the same potential. It has been shown, for instance, how sermons on the Good Samaritan take on specific details that reflect the social location of the listeners (Wuthnow, 1991).

To borrow a phrase from another important Marxist theorist of culture, Antonio Gramsci, the scriptures and popular religiosity can be "counterhegemonic" (Fulton, 1987). Through religious traditions, scripture is relived and retold for a community, interpreting the biblical narrative in contemporary terms. Functions like those described by Lukacs and Gramsci have been elaborated by Frederic Jameson (1981), who considers narration "a socially symbolic act" that is the basis for the "political unconscious." We think contact with such a defining narrative comes to most people through religious experience (although clearly not every religious experience). Special events such as conversion, joy, or consolation at traumatic times of life and the like often elevate people to a philosophical view of their human existence. Tradition serves as a vehicle to sustain and amplify such life-defining experiences.

Although it has been misused to dull sensitivities, there is a potential in religious tradition to move believers away from the sterility of reification and toward the dynamism of liberation. Religion can spur a group to challenge its current social location in a society, or as Justo González describes it, one can read the Bible "in Spanish" (González, 1990:75–85). At that point, tradition serves as collective memory, binding together members of a community more closely (Kammen, 1991). The group acquires a *mentalité* that dialectically helps group members distinguish between the world as it is and the world as it should be (Vovelle, 1990), part of the "we-they" that is reinforced by a religious belief in eventual vindication. Tradition in this dynamic sense is continually reinventing itself (Maravall, 1975/1986:138–139). Factual or historical accuracy is clouded by tradition because it is not history but rather the memory of a collective history that contains an emotionally charged meaning for the present. As Shils observes: "A rule of conduct, explicitly articulated or implied in a pattern or conduct, or a belief about the soul, or a philosophical idea about the common good does not remain identical through its career of transmissions over generations" (Shils, 1981:13).

Inherent in this notion of tradition as a religious dynamic is its protean nature as it interacts with changing social conditions in successive generations. Sometimes the changes produced in one generation are rejected in another, says Shils (1981:212). In fact, this shifting pattern has entered sociology as "Hansen's Law." Our colleague in PARAL, Gilbert Cadena, has interpreted this generational transmission with his concept of "*abuelita* (grandma) theology," showing that members of the younger generation rebel against their parents by readopting elements of religion taken from their grandparents (Cadena, 1987). As stated above, the element of social location can be explained by various theories: collective memory, *mentalité*, and historical consciousness. But in our view, all of them allow religious tradition to become a dynamic force. Without this dynamism, the critics would be right: Tradition would degenerate into merely "folkloric customs," doomed to disappear with modernization.

Awareness that a group holds an inferior social status is not in itself a revolutionary call to arms. Intriguingly, the same phenomenon may be a dynamic tradition for one segment of the population and quaint folklore for another. Awareness of social location in tradition is not to be automatically identified with "popular liberation" because the "political" part of these traditions is usually "unconscious," as Jameson (1981) reminds us. In our view, religious traditions deserve to be studied for their religious meaning and not as much because of their political potential for the causes of either the Right or the Left. In the study of religion in Latin America, there has been a lamentable tendency to reduce movements like Liberation Theology; *comunidades de base* (grassroots Christian communities), the preferential option for the poor; and Pentecostalism to the role of surrogates for ideological politics. There is no doubt that religious change has political effects, but to be properly understood, this change must be analyzed in terms of religion. This concern is part of our effort here.

Despite the academic premise in certain sectors to the contrary, for an enormous majority of Latinos, religion is more important than politics. Latinos are not alone in this. At a time when the rapid disintegration of important social institutions has shaken public confidence in the future, religion in the United States has become a last refuge of social trust. Even if church institutions suffer in public opinion, religion as the personal and communitarian encounter with God continues to hold high esteem.

Social Location and the Political Process

In the process of refashioning religious traditions to fit new social circumstances, the dynamics of tradition are increasingly important for everyone in the United States. These dynamics come into play as social groups juggle the changing demands on their social, cultural, and religious identities. But although the demands are new, religion delivers its response in terms of the past. It is an essential requirement for religion—as contrasted with political movements—to possess eternal truth. New religious solutions must be based on old wisdom. The new course of action is usually not presented as a departure from tradition but as a return to some aspect of belief that has either been neglected or forgotten. The important role of theologians and charismatic leaders of religious reform has been to juggle and reinterpret tradition to fit the new circumstances. Often, theologians and reformers appeal to the populace, offering their ideas in language that can be understood and repeated. To the extent that this process identifies religion with preoccupations about the social forces that have generated the new conditions, religion creates what Gramsci calls "organic intellectuals" (Entwistle, 1979:112–129; Sassoon, 1980:137–141; Fulton, 1987; Williams, 1996). In other cases, opposing theological camps are created among elites to argue their cases without involving the majority of believers. Most often the two opinions are reconciled by some moderate middle way that evolves from mutual compromise; but if not, then the group in power considers itself "orthodox" and declares the others "heretics."

Religious change has often accompanied history's major social changes: In the United States, the turn-of-the-century Protestant Social Gospel movement that confronted the emergence of an urbanized, industrialized nation is a splendid example of the engagement of theology with religious tradition at a time of social change. We will describe a similar movement for Latino religion in the social changes since the 1960s and discuss how theology and religious tradition were drawn into the process.

However, although religious changes accompany, influence, or even spark social changes, the two are not exactly the same. To explain our understanding of the relationship between religious movements and social changes, we present an extended analogy in the passage that follows. In order for people to tell time, the numbers on a clock dial must remain constant; if they do not, then there is no meaning to the position of the hands of the clock. In this analogy, religion is the constant of the numbers on the dial. When social and political change adjusts the position of the hands, telling us in effect that we are in a different time, reference is made to religion because the face of the dial is necessary to define the hour. But religion cannot support a change that denies the constancy of the numbers on the dial. Assuredly, that dial may have more legible numbers or may substitute symbols such as dots to mark the intervals or switch to Arabic numerals from Roman ones, but the distancing and meaning of the symbols must remain the same. The role the hands play must also remain constant in order for the clock to be useful and for the message it conveys to be intelligible. Alterations that do not conform to these prescriptions will result in chaos and total confusion for anyone trying to determine the time of day. So it is for believers when social and political changes are presented with no reference to religion's eternal meanings. These changes may result in being as unintelligible to believers as a clock whose hands have been broken or whose numerical sequencing has been disrupted. Religion can contribute to political change by agreeing that "the hands of the clock" need to be adjusted from time to time as they become too loose or rusty. But when political movements deny the validity of the face of the clock, that is, if they deny that there are metaphysical or transcendent values in society, they proclaim a material utopia. To date, political movements that have attempted to usurp religious meaning by proclaiming material utopias have not outlasted religion.

In a sense, religion is humankind's collective memory, par excellence. Long before the Enlightenment separated culture from religion, all societies expressed their collective memory as religion. From the inspiring drawings on the caves of Altamira through the building of the pyramids in Egypt to the composition of the Upanishads and the construction of Europe's great cathedrals, to talk about culture is to describe religion. We are optimistic about the permanency of religion as a major factor in culture formation. In addition to the communitarian aspects of life's meaning, which it shares with culture, religion also has a normative dimension. In ways that culture cannot, religion holds individuals to a standard, a standard that integrates public behavior and individual morality. To return to the example of the clock, we can tell time because one of the hands points to the hour and the other to the minutes. In a similar way, religion not only refers the individual to the community and its culture but also indicates where the individual's personal behavior stands. For a religious believer, the communitarian or cultural standard requires a second, or personal, morality for intelligibility. A clock with only one hand does keep accurate time, and a religion that is either only cultural or only personal lacks integrity.

Ironically, the United States, a nation created after the Enlightenment, often holds its public officials to standards of communitarian culture and individual morality. It celebrates a civil religion composed of traditions of Protestantism, Catholicism, and Judaism. In contrast to politicians in European societies, U.S. politicians are far more likely to invoke God and appeal to religious beliefs in their speeches. Collective memory in this country is almost impossible without the scent of the religious, despite the frequency with which its expectations are contradicted (Bellah, 1975).

Communities are capable of creating a religious tradition when collective memory lacks that dimension. Thus, for instance, American Jews have reshaped the religious feast of Hanukkah into family remembrance that has much in common with the Christian Christmas. An even more recent example of creating a tradition is the African American Kwanza, which began in 1965 when Ron Karenga, a political scientist, saw a need for an African American collective memory at Christmastime. Borrowing elements from religious traditions like the candle lighting of Hanukkah, the figure of Santa Claus from Christmas, and the Muslim custom of naming days for virtues, Kwanza unites these in its reference to an African winter harvest festival (Early, 1997).

Kwanza may be considered a new holiday in the U.S. religious calendar. Kwanza is afforded equal time with Hanukkah and Christmas in many public-school celebrations, although it is ostensibly a "nonreligious" observance. In fact, it might be better described as a "nondenominational" tradition, since it provides an Afrocentric celebration both for African Americans who are Christian and for those who are Muslim. Ironically, the success of Kwanza in merging with civil religion in the United States has generated the problem of commercialization. Because of a multimillion dollar business of greeting cards and store-bought gifts among African Americans, Kwanza now faces a set of problems that have beset the celebration of Christmas. Moreover, at least one commentator believes that Kwanza has resulted in a "delusional dogma" that has fed the beast of racial exclusiveness among African Americans (Early, 1997). None of these observations are meant to disparage Kwanza or similar "inventions" of traditions that interpret social location for groups in the United States. On the contrary, the ability to create new religious celebrations that are clothed in the mantle of historical tradition is a sign of vitality, and controversy is a sign of connectedness to people's most deeply held beliefs. In fact, the dynamic of the Emmaus paradigm we propose depends largely upon this capacity to rediscover contemporary meaning for familiar traditions.

The Religious Imagination

Recognizing that even today a new tradition like Kwanza assumes the guise of long-standing customs, we should not be surprised if traditions that began centuries ago were generated out of a similar process. This is the position of María Jesús Buxó i Rey, professor at the University of Barcelona and coeditor of a multivolume study of popular religiosity in Spain (1989). Interpreting the convincing body of studies included in the second volume of the series brings us to consider what Buxó i Rey calls "the religious imagination." This imagination is the power of a social group to match symbols and religious meaning in ways that elude the direct control of clergy or theologians. We consider it to be the third key dynamic crucial to the formation of a religious tradition, along with the burden of temporality and awareness of social location. Professor Buxó i Rey (1989:7) indicates three effects of the religious imagination: (1) It adds embellishments to doctrine and ritual that legitimate the origins and substance of devotion; (2) it links life, death, and other such experiences to cognitive and emotional strategies for survival in a changing world; and (3) it creates legends and miracles for popular devotion so that the attendant fervor and piety thus produced sustain belief in religion.

The religious imagination does not operate in a vacuum: When it bestows religious power upon a people, it does so in a specifically defined social circumstance. Devotions, such as the Mexican dedication to Our Lady of Guadalupe, will forever be Mexican, because this cult can never be completely transferred out of the specific society that created it. Whereas the Mary to whom Mexicans pray is identified with Mary of Nazareth in the Gospels and the Madonna of European devotion, she is different from other apparitions because she is Mexican. Guadalupe, or La Morenita, as she is affectionately called, is rooted on a hill in Mexico and in the legends, miracles, and piety over centuries that have made that a holy ground (Rodríguez, 1994; Vidal, 1994b).

Religious imagination is an excellent context in which to examine a recent academic debate about the historical authenticity of certain aspects of the history of the devotion to Our Lady of Guadalupe at the beginning of the seventeenth century. The Vincentian historian Father Stafford Poole (1995b) criticized theologians such as Father Virgil Elizondo and Jeanette Rodríguez for their lack of historical accuracy in describing the origins of the contemporary devotion to Our Lady of Guadalupe among Chicanos and Mexican Americans. With convincing logic and impressive research on the historical sources, Poole refuted several claims about the dates for the devotion, the numbers of converts produced, and the reliability of many texts. His critique was not about the use of the devotion as a source for theological reflection, but rather, he questioned the advisability of structuring this reflection on an uncritical use of historical texts as if every legend and miracle were factual.

Reviewing Poole's book (1995a) in the pages of *America*, Jesuit Allan Figueroa Deck (1995b) accepted the need for greater historical accuracy in theologizing about devotion to Our Lady of Guadalupe. But he raised a question about which part of the cult is more important in a religious sense: the historical fact or the contemporary devotion, the factual events or the people's mythos that envelops their faith? This questioning by Figueroa Deck of Poole's presumption in favor of history implicitly recognizes the dynamic of religious imagination. Precisely because it is not the same as history, "tradition is invented" (Hobsbawm and Ranger, 1983). But in religious tradition, the "invention" takes place in a climate of faith. When a people generates vital religious meaning out of symbols and events that by themselves are merely curious, an important religious event has taken place. In fact, one could argue that precisely because the historical origins are less than convincing, a devotion as powerful as that of Our Lady of Guadalupe among the Mexican peoples is all the more religiously significant. The creativity of the religious imagination of the people has made something greater than a history without belief could have provided. Recalling from the first chapter the example of the string of Christmas tree lights, religion is misunderstood unless we see that when faith flows through religious behavior like an electric current, it radically transforms each of the individual parts, much as a lighted bulb is different from a dead one.

Thus, if the focus is on religious observance, historical facts are not the most important aspects of religious tradition. The interplay between temporality, social location, and the religious imagination discloses the dynamism of belief. Even people who deny the existence of the supernatural or of a particular miracle that explains the origins of a religious tradition ought to admit that belief is a social fact, even if its transpersonal grounding remains unprovable. Returning to the Emmaus narrative, the hearts of the disciples were set burning because of faith: The rediscovery of Jesus was connected to his explanations of the scriptures and the mission of the Messiah—but these remained merely cerebral without the passion of faith.

The study of religious tradition can be compared to the use of paper currency instead of precious metals. Few people today worry if there is enough silver in some treasury vault that amounts to a dollar at an exchange market; it is more common to take the greenbacks at their face value when making calculations. Similarly, scholars analyzing religion try to avoid getting sidetracked into issues of metaphysical proof for the validity of belief; it is truer to the sociological task to accept religion for what the people say it means to them. Such an approach is scarcely novel. When surveys reveal the public attitudes toward political parties, the popularity of presidents and policies, they simply report what people believe and do not comment on whether the attitudes are based on the cold facts. We think that consideration of religious traditions ought to follow the same methodological rules.

The Dynamics of Tradition

In sum, we view tradition within these three dynamics: temporality, awareness of social location, and religious imagination. If analysis remains satisfied with only the description of customs, rites, and rituals that form the content of traditions, it will miss the inherent dynamism that keeps traditions relevant to the study of Latino religion. Returning to the normative function for tradition described by Shils, we view religious tradition as a constituent element of Latino identity because it has provided the organization and the institutions upon which a sense of peoplehood was built.

> These institutions provide the internal spine and the outer frame of the culture which maintains a society. Where they fail to do so, the society is in danger of losing its character as a society. . . . But if the internal spine and the outer frame of moral and intellectual traditions are so corrected that they lose their transmissive efficacy, parts of the society are in danger of becoming a horde, other parts are in danger of lapsing into the state of *bellum omnium contra omnes*. (Shils, 1981:185)

We are aware that in theology the word "tradition" has acquired a specialized meaning in terms of Christian revelation. The common wisdom says that the Reformation rejected tradition as revelation, insisting on the primacy of the Bible as the only source for revealed knowledge about God, while Catholics took the contrary position at the Council of Trent. However, the French historian Jean Delumeau (1971/1977) has shown that this is a too-simplistic interpretation of a complex theological stance. Following Delumeau, we suspect that the contrasting attitudes of Catholics as compared with Protestants and Evangelicals toward religious traditions have more to do with culture and history than with dogma and theology. Protestants and Evangelicals may reject traditional devotions to Mary and the saints because the public cultures of northern Europe did not privilege these expressions the way Mediterranean cultures did (Stevens-Arroyo, 1997b). Devotion to the apparitions of Mary such as those in Mexico or at Lourdes and Fatima are essentially Catholic. Most Protestants, however, do accommodate traditions such as the Nativity crèche, Christmas trees, holly and mistletoe, which are derived from popular culture and not from a biblical text.

Because they are centuries old, religious traditions resist sudden and profound change, even change as sweeping as the Reformation. The Protestant parts of Europe that retained the agricultural economy—Germany and Scandinavia in particular—had to create new traditions for protection and blessing that fit the expectations of farm society while sidestepping Catholic devotions to the saints. Out of this religious dynamic came the Pietist movement of the seventeenth and eighteenth centuries that fashioned traditions for the agricultural cycle within a Protestant context. We are not experts on this process, but driving through Pennsylvania Dutch country we noticed that almost every barn displays hex signs intended to ward off spirits capable of threatening the crops or livestock. Certainly, the origin of this custom does not lie in the scriptures but in tradition. Less visible than these multicolored designs are the host of simpler, home-centered, and family focused traditions that have maintained the faith for generations. Like the Jewish American Hanukkah and the African American Kwanza, religious imagination among these German American Protestant groups has preserved collective memory. And Latino Protestants share in the dynamics of a religious imagination that may contribute traditions to the U.S. future as striking as those of the Pennsylvania Dutch. The challenge of Protestantism (and Pentecostalism) among Latinos has always been to make the believers more religious without simultaneously making them less Latino (Silva Gotay, 1994:164–167; González, 1990:22–26). As we hope to show in subsequent chapters, Latino Protestants have begun to develop alternative forms of religious expression that have removed their denominations from easy categorization as "Americanizing."

In fact, U.S. Catholicism has also threatened to Americanize Latino religion. No doubt U.S. Catholicism has a theological framework more receptive to Latino Marian devotion than that of Protestantism. Yet there has been a significant preference in U.S. Catholicism to foster devotions among Latinos that more closely approximate the traditions still preserved among Euro-American Catholics. Latino Marian devotions are generally preserved by equating them to European devotions. Thus, in U.S. Catholic circles, the devotion to Our Lady of Guadalupe among Mexicans is often compared to French devotion to Our Lady of Lourdes or Polish devotion to Our Lady of Czestochowa. But when Latinos begin to introduce aspects of their devotions that have few if any parallels in the Euro-American experience, Catholicism in the United States no less than Protestantism becomes resistant to Latino tradition. Thus, for instance, processions to Our Lady of Guadalupe or Our Lady of Charity usually find more acceptance than placing food on graves or bowls of water and herbs under beds or before statues and icons. Nor are Latinos the only Catholics in the United States to suffer from an Americanizing prejudice. The work of Robert Orsi (1985) on Italian American popular religiosity describes the rejection suffered by traditional Italian piety as it encountered U.S. Catholicism, derived from Irish and English traditions.

But religious tradition has proven resilient, especially in the last decade of the twentieth century. The recent study by the same Professor Orsi on devotion to Saint Jude among women (1996) provides some evidence that temporality, social location, and religious imagination continue to create new and powerful devotions in the United States. Among Protestants, scholars like Robert Wuthnow (1988) have sensed a new importance for traditional piety among the mainline churches. Professor Clark Roof (1994) observed a similar trend among the baby boomers who reached middle age during the 1990s. Calling them "the seekers," Roof found some of the former "flower children" of the 1960s were returning to the religious traditions of their childhood. Lynn Davidman (1991) is among the several scholars who have recorded for social science a return to tradition among American Jews. Colleen McDannell (1995) has interpreted these tendencies as a form of "material Christianity" that connects religion and popular culture. Institutions are likely to satisfy these yearnings for ritual and symbols from their members. Thus, for instance, in 1995 the Presbyterian Church in the United States restored the distribution of ashes as part of its Lenten liturgical observance. The reappearance of religious tradition may be viewed as representing a move away from secularization. However, "less secular" does not mean "antimodern," "antiscientific," "medieval," or "obscurantist." Such dichotomies are so freighted with ideology as to prejudice a clear understanding of tradition.

The restoration today of certain religious traditions is not merely an imitation of the past, nor is it a call to chimerical longing. The authors cited earlier provide a social context for the trends. The fragmentation of the U.S. family, the pressures of consumerism, the collapse of civility, the ubiquity of violence, the insecurities of the marketplace, and the invasion of privacy in the contemporary communications explosion are just some factors that have propelled today's religious imagination. Old traditions are being asked to operate in new circumstances, and that means that traditions are undergoing changes that will likely impact on all U.S. religion.

The particular configurations of persistence and disruption [of traditions] are not matters of indifference to the societies in which they occur. The patterns of traditionality make a genuine difference to all who experience them. They are not epiphenomena which always exist in the same proportion. If they were, they could not give ground for concern because they would have no effect and because nothing could be done about them. But this is not really so. Every one of our actions and every one of our beliefs affects the fortunes of one or another tradition. (Shils, 1981:322)

The refashioned meanings often correspond to social location. The socioeconomic class of believers may be more important to how restored traditions operate among them than denominational ties. For instance, Catholic, Episcopalian, Presbyterian, and Jewish professionals in a high-rent district of Manhattan may be inclined to incorporate ecological concerns and health awareness into their religious mind-set, while working-class adherents of the same denominations in the enclaves of Brooklyn may view antiabortion legislation and a stricter code for sexual behavior as the principal purpose for their renewed religious commitment. Both sets of believers appeal to traditional religious values as a touchstone, although with different purposes.

Restoring tradition often results in "cultural wars," to use a term now in fashion (Hunter, 1991), although frequently the cause of the friction is political, rather than religious. And because Latinos are a rapidly growing segment of not only U.S. Catholicism but of some Protestant denominations as well, it is relevant to ask how the Latino presence might affect the political sides of some religious traditions. Do Latino members make a parish more conservative in political outlook? Or more liberal and in favor of programs to achieve social justice? It is tempting to claim that Latinos are polar opposites to Euro-Americans in every aspect, but this clearly exaggerates the issue of difference and trivializes the really important variations among groups. As Said (1978:328) has observed, the antidote to the negative effects of Orientalism that ridicules real differences among Asian peoples is not to do the same to "Westerners" in a kind of Occidentalism. We have tried to employ empirical data from history, the social sciences, and the limited survey data to trace the contours of the differences, which are often more like musical variations on an old theme than brand-new compositions.

The Sociohistoric Context

A way of analyzing the dynamics of religious traditions is to place them in a sociohistoric context. The most salient change in social circumstances surrounding the practice of religious tradition has been the rapid disappearance of the agricultural society in the United States. Almost all of Christianity's grand rituals use poetic references to the agricultural cycle. The Resurrection of the Lord is "Easter," a springtime feast about the rebirth of fertility in the Northern Hemisphere: Bunnies and colored eggs remind us of the Celtic imagery for renewed nature. The Nativity of Jesus Christ is celebrated after the winter solstice, when the days finally begin to lengthen, a cycle important to people who live close to nature. In pre-Reformation Christianity, saints were considered mediators with heaven in securing abundance of rain and good weather and as protectors against elements harmful to the crops. Many of these traditions were forged by the syncretism of Christianity with agricultural symbols and customs from ancient European religions through a process that Valerie Flint (1991) views as competition for belief between Christianity and the previous religions. Christianity developed miraculous shrines and holy wonder workers to rival those found in the competing religions. Thus, archetypes of feminine rain and masculine winds have entered into Christian traditions behind the visages of Mary and the saints (Benko, 1993). The dynamics of these traditions were well suited to the relatively closed cycles of an agricultural society. So powerful were these paradigms that as medieval Europe urbanized, the new guilds of tradesmen and merchants imitated the agriculture model of invoking specific saints as protectors and mediators. Saint Cecilia was patroness of music, just as Saints Abdon and Senen protected the fields against too much rain.

Returning to the analogy of religion as the two hands on a clock, the agricultural-liturgical cycle provided a third, or sweep, hand that reminded believers at every moment of how their personal and communitarian behavior was linked to seasonal temporality and cosmic events. This process of "confusion" of Christianity with long-standing beliefs among those to be converted continued in the Americas (Stevens-Arroyo, 1989; Foster, 1960). In Puerto Rico, for instance, hurricanes were named after saints and were often viewed as warnings or punishments from heaven just as in the Taíno religion of the Caribbean people before Columbus. In Mexico, All Saints' and All Souls' Days absorbed equivalent Aztec celebrations of dead ancestors. The Enlightenment and rationalism attacked this connection of religion to nature, viewing syncretism as evidence of an inferior conception of the world. And although the Enlightenment was not completely successful in rationalizing belief, it undermined the liturgical cycle. The great feasts of Christianity were compelled to exchange the simplicity of the agricultural world with more complex psychological and social meanings. Christmas as an occasion for family reunions became more important than as a marker for the onset of winter. Catholicism, no less than Protestantism, has made such adjustments (Stevens-Arroyo, 1997b). In our own time, perhaps as vengeance, New Age religions, Wica, or revived religions of witchcraft, and the Afro-Latin Santería have restored nature's cycles to center stage in ritual.

The Latino Religious Tradition

How has religious imagination functioned among Latinos? Before examining contemporary circumstances, a sketch of historically established patterns of the products from Latino religious imagination is useful. Adopting the stress on continuity suggested above, we need to examine here the religious traditions of only two epochs: from Charlemagne to Franklin D. Roosevelt; and everything since. As outlandish as this formulation may sound, it dramatizes the dependency of Latino religion on agricultural cycles. Our argument is that because the agricultural cycles scarcely changed, neither did the liturgical cycles. One Anglo, entering New Mexico in the 1840s, said that agriculture was "in about the same condition as when the Spaniards first settled the country" (cited in Sunseri, 1979:20, n. 23). Another pushed the analogy even further back than we have, claiming the tools used among Latinos in New Mexico were "the . . . same that Cain used six thousand years ago" (Sunseri, 1979:21, n. 25). The mass migration of Latinos to U.S. cities since the 1950s can make those with short memories forget that until relatively recently, most Latinos worked in agriculture. With the Great Depression and the ensuing New Deal, however, the agricultural niche that Latinos had occupied in the United States was destroyed. Thus, the landscape of Latino religion has changed more rapidly in the past seventy years than during the previous millennium. It may seem strange to tie Latino religious tradition as late as 1950 to the ninth century, but tradition has this kind of power, especially when seen as a form of transculturation taking place over centuries.

The ties of Iberian Christianity to the agricultural cycle were managed in a pace of development that was slow enough to allow religion to provide transition from one generation to the next, even when that required an incorporation of American societies. The history of Latino traditions after 1950 will be examined in detail in subsequent chapters, but the body of Latino traditions that reigned from the sixteenth through the early twentieth century demonstrates a significant continuity with the religion of medieval Europe. These traditions, which vary somewhat from group to group, are nonetheless remarkably similar in their overall dynamics, just as they derive from a common Iberian past. Margaret Clark (1970) offers a list of the most important feasts celebrated during the 1950s in Our Lady of Guadalupe Church in San José (cited in Burns, 1994:183). It might well have come from the 1590s.

The first Christianity among the American peoples was brought from Iberia, a European meeting place for Visigoth, Muslim, Jewish, and Christian religious traditions. In the Caribbean where the initial evangelization took place, a medieval pattern was followed (Stevens-Arroyo, 1993). A local lord who accepted Christianity was incorporated into the feudal structure, and his vassals were expected to follow the path of Christian fealty, much as if he were a Visigoth chief. Thus, the first evangelization under Spain sought not so much to convert individuals but rather "peoples." Fray Bartolomé de las Casas sought to maintain the structures of traditional authority among the native peoples during this process of evangelization. He argued that the Americans were not "savages" who could be denied social rights, but peoples with religious and political traditions that although different from those of Europe, were nonetheless legitimate (Stevens-Arroyo, 1996b). Official Spain turned a deaf ear, partly because the natives of the Caribbean seldom departed from their kinship relationships to the Roman "law of the peoples" that permitted the practice of certain local legal and religious traditions even after a people's being conquered (Stevens-Arroyo, 1993).

The failure of the medieval model in the Caribbean led to changes in the evangelization of Mexico, Peru, and much of the continent (Stevens-Arroyo, 1989, 1993). But what remained as a constant was the effort to fuse Christianity with the local religion. Spanish evangelizers built Christianity upon the foundations of the native religion—quite literally in some cases, for there are churches in Mexico City that have been erected on top of a temple. The notion of cultural *mestizaje* depends upon an interpretation in which native customs and rites were incorporated into a newly Catholic culture, and only elements that were seen as incompatible with the new faith were attacked (Elizondo, 1992; Rodríguez, 1994).

As the eminent historian of the Southwest David Weber (1992:359) has stated, we still walk about without an adequate paradigm to balance off the opposing extremes that everything sixteenth- and seventeenth-century Spaniards did was right or that everything they did was wrong. We can be more sure about the transculturated result at the dawn of the twenty-first century. Because the Iberian missionary effort at least until the eighteenth century was to transform rather than extirpate the existing religious sentiment, Christian feasts that had been tied to agricultural and pastoral cycles in Europe were essentially preserved by making them the labels for similar cycles found in the religions of the natives of America (Cahill, 1996). As it had done in the Europe of Franks, Goths, and Celts, the local economy shaped the way these "adopted" celebrations became Christian. And just as the popularity of medieval Christian feast days usually depended upon how well they fit the regional culture, Catholicism in Spanish America produced local variations to the religious matrix.

The Christian tradition of incorporating local religion had always depended upon religious imagination to fuse together different traditions. The evangelization of Latin America by Iberian Catholics cannot be understood without recognizing that this strategy was still operative. For example, a devotion like that of Our Lady of Guadalupe in Mexico took the name of a shrine in Spain (bearing an Arabic name) and reimaged the Marian cult as one typically Mexican (Poole, 1995a; Stevens-Arroyo, 1997b). In similar ways, the traditional feasts of European Christianity that marked the seasons were brought to the New World, creating religious traditions that reflected both Christian and native beliefs. The economies of the Latino homelands are different: Puerto Rico cultivated sugarcane and coffee; in Texas, New Mexico, and California, most people were engaged in cattle raising, sheepherding, and farming. But taking these differences into account, it is possible to offer an outline of the cycles that govern a broad range of social interactions (Stevens-Arroyo and Díaz-Stevens, 1993a).

The Agricultural Cycle

The cycle for planting and pasturage usually began in early February and was initiated by the Feasts of the Purification of Mary (Nuestra Señora de Candelaria) and Saint Blaise. These two feasts coincided with the clearing of the land for planting and the spring mating of the herds. As in Spain and much of Europe, fire and light are associated with Candlemas and blessing with candles for Saint Blaise, but they coincided with the old Roman feast of Lupercalia, which celebrated fertility for flocks of sheep (Maldonado, 1975:30–31, 331–332). These layers of meaning, both Christian and pre-Christian, were carried over to the Americas, as in New Mexico, for instance, where sheep raising was a major industry.

Easter brought springtime feasts, with special attention paid to vicarious identification with the sufferings of Christ. Good Friday, with its emphasis upon fasting and pain, sometimes supplanted Easter Sunday in the focus of Christian celebration. The Penitentes of New Mexico scourged themselves publicly on Good Friday in reparation for sins (Deutsch, 1987:50–51), much as in Seville, the hooded members of pious *cofradías* (confraternities) employed similar penances to show contrition. The May Feast of the Finding of the Holy Cross (May 3) coincides with the month dedicated to the Blessed Virgin Mary, and both feasts allow for the introduction of femininity[1] into festivals of the spring (Maldonado, 1975:33–38). These include various processions and other religious gatherings, often with young women assuming important roles, in which a statue of Mary is elaborately adorned and crowned with flowers or a prominent cross on a home altar is similarly decorated.

Summertime feasts included those for Saint John the Baptist (June 24) and Our Lady of Mount Carmel (July 16), which were of relevance to maritime settlements and include various forms of bathing and blessing of waters. The Feast of Saint James the Apostle (July 25) has rich roots in Iberian practice, where this feast reenacted symbolically the centuries-long wars between Christians and Moors (Foster, 1960: Benavides, 1995). In the New World, the Feast of Saint James is likewise celebrated by donning costumes reminiscent of a Spanish past and contrasting that with local pre-Christian dress.

The harvest season was marked by celebrations of prominent feasts such as those of Saint Michael the Archangel (September 29), Saint Francis of

Assisi (October 4), Our Lady of the Rosary (October 7), and Saint Rafael Archangel (October 24) (Maldonado, 1975:42–48). These liturgical feasts would often be matched with particular harvest or other autumn agricultural practices. The Feasts of All Saints' (November 1) and All Souls' (November 2) carry resonances of pre-Christian rites that communicated with the dead, particularly in Mexican-influenced areas.

In addition, each town has its patron saint, so that the village would often add the *fiestas patronales*, a week of festivities not unlike medieval feasts that symbolically united the different classes in a common Christian belief and practice (Díaz-Stevens, 1990). Civic, religious, and even ribald elements were put into stark conjuncture with parades, processions, and carousing to celebrate both the community and the saint's life and works. In the Americas, these fiestas preserved their popular character, adding Native American or African traditions to the Iberian matrix, much as had occurred in Europe's ancient religions. Stimulated by the Tridentine Reforms, such expressions of popular religiosity not only occupied public space in the town plaza but were afforded placement within the church as well. The instruction of the Vatican Congregation de Propaganda Fide in 1659 fostered the inclusion of local traditions from every part of the world into the Catholic faith:

> Make no effort, advance no argument to persuade these peoples to change their rites or customs unless they are patently contrary to religion and morals. What could be more absurd than to transport France, Spain or Italy or some other European country to China? Offer the people not our countries, but the faith. (Cited in Delumeau, 1971/1977:91)

The baroque epoch in which Latin American popular religiosity was established fixed a pattern of simultaneous interiority and public display for religion that has survived until the present (Stevens-Arroyo, 1997b). As a result, Latino traditions demonstrate a constellation of public and communitarian characteristics that are inseparable from an interiorized devotionalism. Such expressions defy easy categorization with the Durkheimian dichotomy of sacred-profane (Cahill, 1996:72–75). We prefer the term "communitarian spirituality" (Díaz-Stevens, 1995, 1996c) for this function of tradition, a notion we shall explain in subsequent chapters.

The special mixture of public and personal is perhaps most clear in the important cycle of Christmas. In Puerto Rico, Christmas begins at the end of November and in Mexican culture areas, with the Feast of Our Lady of Guadalupe (December 12). The cycle climaxes on the second Sunday of January, called "Bethlehem's Octave," which revolves around the Feast of the Three Kings, or Epiphany. The Christmas cycle features distinctive music and special foods, making it the richest segment of Latino popular religiosity. In the aftermath of the Council of Trent, the sixteenth-century Spanish missionary use of miracle plays, or *auto-sacramentales,* has significantly enriched many of these celebrations (Maldonado, 1975:341–343). Perhaps the most well-known of these traditional Christmas plays is *La Pastorela,* which has been celebrated in San Antonio, Texas, since the beginning of the twentieth century. Revised over the years, the play is based on a text brought to San Antonio by an immigrant from Mexico. Luis Valdés filmed an English version of *La Pastorela* for public television, inviting well-known Chicano artists like Linda Ronstadt, Paul Rodríguez, Cheech Marín, and Robert Beltrán to play some of the roles. The authentic performance of *La Pastorela* continues to be performed in Spanish each year in San Antonio. Anthropologist Richard Flores studied *La Pastorela,* actually joining the cast for two years. His studies, particularly his book published by the Smithsonian Institution (1995), describe with anthropological precision the dynamics of this tradition. His book provides reconstruction of sixteenth-century texts and rhyme schemes in order to demonstrate the fidelity to tradition of San Antonio's performance. Flores's impressive scholarship merits examination on its own right and provides specific examples of our general statement that Latino religious traditions are connected to Iberian sources.

Less formal celebrations of Christmas also involve elements of performance, although without the structures of the miracle play. In places of Mexican influence, *las posadas* (stops) are observed both for religious ritual and musical expression. The entire village is involved in a dramatic reenactment of the journey of Joseph and Mary to Bethlehem where Jesus was born. In the days before Christmas, those dressed as the holy couple go from one house to another, accompanied by the villagers bearing lighted candles and, sometimes, the statues of Joseph and Mary. After being ritually refused entry, they finally enter the last selected house, where pastries and hot chocolate are consumed amid communal singing. In the Mexican culture, the liturgical celebration of the formal liturgy is sandwiched between the more elaborate celebration of *las posadas* and the subsequent public party that includes the breaking of the *piñata* in a public place so that children receive their first Christmas gifts from the community, rather than from "Santa Claus."

But not every Latino tradition follows the Mexican pattern. In Puerto Rico, the processions from house to house are centered on a tradition of celebrating the journey of the Three Kings, or Magi. The Puerto Rican verb for this custom *"reyar"* is now included in the dictionary of the Royal Academy of Language in Madrid. Promises, or *promesas,* are made to carry rustic statues of the Three Kings in jovial processions, or *parrandas,* going house to house singing *aguinaldos* (hoc-in-anno songs) and asking for a gift (which is also called an *aguinaldo*), which, if in the form of money, is used for a big communal celebration and for offerings to the church. In the mountain towns, the *parrandas* were organized well beforehand and often announced so that people would prepare both the offering as well as refreshments (including alcoholic beverages, pastries, chocolate, and coffee) for the *parranderos*. As the *parranda* went about improvising songs, members of the different households would join in so that by the end of the evening members of the whole community had gathered together in singing and merrymaking. The *parrandas de promesa a los Santos Reyes* (processions of promise to the Holy Kings) often ended in the early hours of the morning in the town church for *las misas de alba o de aguinaldo* (the masses at dawn or the masses of aguinaldo), celebrated eight consecutive days before Christmas Eve. In areas within walking distance from the town square and church, for *las parrandas*, as for *las posadas*, the final stop on Christmas Eve is the parish church for the midnight mass, when *la misa de gallo* (literally, the mass of the rooster, or at the crack of dawn) gathered the whole Christian community in worship for the celebration of the birth of Christ.

In Puerto Rico, the *aguinaldo* has become a musical form of particular creativity, allowing native instruments and improvised versification in a popular style. More spontaneous and secular were the *asaltos,* which are unannounced visits to family members and neighbors and involved singing and sharing of food but had no connection to *promesas* or other religious practice, save general references to the season. Both in Puerto Rico and in Mexican-influenced areas, Christmas Day itself is marked by a meal for the extended family rather than by gifts for children. That Christmas meal often takes several days to prepare. Along with a main serving of pork (*lechón*) or other extravagantly prepared fare, families include either *tamales de maiz* or *pasteles de plátanos* or *yuca*, delicacies prepared by most of the females in the household. Among the Mexican and Central Americans, meat is diced and spiced in a stew, added to corn meal, whereas among Puerto Ricans and other people of Caribbean heritage, the meat is added to mixtures of ground plantain and green bananas or yuca. Wrapped in leaves of *tamale* (corn) or *pasteles* (banana), these individual servings are cooked for hours in a common pot. The preparation segregates men from women. The females honor a hierarchy of age by affording the most importance to the oldest recipe, bond together as family through "woman talk," and instruct the youngest women in age-old family culinary arts. Thus, popular religion often depends upon food offered in ritual cuisine. Men use rum or some other liquor to induce a happy frame of mind for male bonding (Díaz-Stevens, 1996c). As Richard Flores observes (1996), although these elements are ludic and seemingly divorced from sacred celebration, they are essential to the communitarian nature of the religious celebration.

The Feast of the Holy Innocents (December 28) comes from the Canary Islands but bears many similarities to the medieval Feast of Fools and the Roman Saturnalia (Maldonado, 1975:27–29, 217–221). Although this feast has lost popularity, in places where it is still observed, children carry mock spears imitating the soldiers of King Herod whom the Bible says mercilessly slaughtered all children under the age of two in a fruitless attempt to kill Jesus. In the past, when paint was a rare and often expensive commodity, these spears were decorated with white chalk, red dye taken from *achiote* (annatto), and black charcoal symmetrical designs and circles reminiscent of Taíno drawings. If this seems an unlikely theme of sport, one must remember that it depends upon the inversion of social status for its popularity. The children are provided with the power of political authority in a ludic representation of how the poor view the government's police. The children are followed by the infamous *mojiganga*, an adult wearing a grotesque mask in pursuit of children, much as Herod's soldiers pursued the Innocents. People naive enough to lend items to revelers on the Feast of the Holy Innocents may never have them returned.

The Feast of the Epiphany, or Three Kings' Day, on January 6, is the traditional time of gift giving to children. Today, Santa Claus has replaced the Three Kings in many households as giver of children's toys, but the Kings still bring gifts, often of a more personal kind. Puerto Rico has preserved a special dimension to this feast. Freshly cut grass is placed in a box underneath the bed. While the children are asleep they are told the kings pay their visit, the horses eat the grass, and in the morning, gifts will be found in the boxes, left to the children by the grateful kings. This attention to the horses of the kings reflects the kind of behavior expected from children on the visit to the house of their *padrinos,* or godparents. It was most often the children's responsibility to care for their godparents' horses while the godparents visited with the family. Thus, there is an extended kinship relation projected onto the kings. Moreover, the three visitors are depicted as combining the three major racial groups in Puerto Rican history: white (European), yellow (Taíno), and black (African), which contributes to a social meaning for the feast.

The Life Cycle

Our description of Latino traditions shows many similarities with the rest of the Catholic world. The agricultural products may change the kind of food eaten and substitute one saint for another, but the structure of the cycles remains essentially the same, whether the country is Poland, Italy, Spain, or Mexico. But the variations are important. The particular touches of local experience added to the cycle of liturgical and agricultural time helped create community, affording space and imparting purpose to social exchange. A second cycle was composed of personal and familial experiences that accompanied it. The rites of passages usually involve reception of the sacraments of Baptism, Confirmation, Matrimony, the Anointing of the Sick, and Christian Burial.

In the Catholic world, most of these rites of passage are accompanied by the recitation of the rosary. The rosary has been a privileged form of Catholic prayer since the sixteenth century. It requires knowledge of only a few formal prayers, easily memorized. But the rosary owes much to its biblical orientation and the profession of faith. The rosary asks those praying to meditate on thirteen biblical events and two traditional devotions in Christianity, each of which is called a "mystery" and is viewed from the familial perspective of the love between Jesus the Son and Mary His Mother. Often, each of the mysteries are parts of a spiritual bouquet of roses (hence the name) offered to Mary (Elizondo, 1975:192–193). Moreover, the public recitation of the rosary usually begins with imaginative introductions, or glosses, that use poetry to connect biblical events to individual needs. Unlike the droning recitation of the same prayers often caricatured as the example of lame Catholic devotionalism, the communitarian expression of the *rosario cantao*, or sung rosary, is a lively and animated event (Seda Bonilla, 1967/1973:55–64), stubbornly resisting rationalism, urbanization, and the Second Vatican Council.

Christians generally believe Baptism is required to enter Heaven. But in Catholic rural areas where priests historically have been scarce and the church distant, the ever-present danger of infant mortality before Baptism created a need for popular alternatives. Immediately upon birth, the midwife commonly sprinkled holy water on the child, sometimes reciting the Latin formula for the sacrament. This Baptism is called *bautismo de agua* and the practice is referred to as *echar el agua*. In the countryside the midwife, called *comadrona* or *partera*, often was godmother to all the children of the town on account of this "unofficial" baptism. A child frequently had two sets of baptismal godparents, one *de agua* and one *de iglesia o pila*.

Because the child had been initiated into the Christian life through *bautismo de agua*, the parents sometimes postponed the church Baptism until the *compadres* (co-parents) had enough money to throw a party. Baptism offered the family an opportunity to gain in social prestige, if the party was big enough and impressed family and friends. Influential patrons could be incorporated into a family as a *compadre* or *comadre* by serving as godparents in a Baptism. The common saying *El que no tiene padrino no se bautiza* ("You don't get baptized without a godfather") refers to the importance of social contacts to gain favors. Latinos have preserved this relationship from the Catholic tradition, calling it *compadrazgo* (Elizondo, 1975:158–164). The obligation upon the adults makes them the equivalent of brothers and sisters, barring them from marrying each other, even if

their respective spouses die. Birthdays and holidays such as Christmas ne-
cessitate gift giving between those spiritually related by Baptism as if they
were blood relatives.

The celebration of the sacrament now known as Reconciliation was less
spectacular than Baptism, but it was important because it was required before a child could receive the first Holy Communion (and most certainly,
when death was eminent). The child was usually taught the main points of
the Catholic faith by a local catechist. Most often, the children of the barrio were brought together for instruction on a schedule that prepared them
for a grand parish celebration, usually in May. The child was presented to
the priest for examination and first confession. In some places, a child
would have to make three confessions before approaching the altar for the
reception of the Eucharist. Confession meant for the child that as an individual he or she had entered the "age of reason" and therefore was held accountable before God and the community for his or her actions. Children
were told that they were no longer innocent and that every transgression
henceforth was punishable. Fear of offending the Supreme Being, parents,
and elders was very real, as was that of provoking their anger. Nonetheless,
there was always the assurance that through a good confession things
could be set right once again.

The first Holy Communion was another occasion for family social celebration, adopting some of the trappings of a wedding. Traditionally, the
use of white for both boys and girls was all-important. The dress and veil,
the white shirt and tie symbolized many things, from the innocence of the
child to the cleanliness of the mother. Reception of the sacrament marked
achievement of the "use of reason." After the child had received Holy
Communion, he or she was afforded participation in other communitarian
religious events and could become a member of guilds and pious societies
established for children.

Confirmation in the clergy-poor peripheries of Mexico or the Spanish
Caribbean was imparted to the very young, sometimes at the time of
Baptism. Since the bishop's visits were very rare, it became customary to
confirm all those who had been baptized, young and old alike. The selection of godparents for Confirmation afforded the parents another opportunity to expand familial relationships outside the blood ties or reaffirm them
among family.

The function of Christian maturity, fulfilled by Confirmation in other,
more settled places, was supplemented for female children through *la
quinceañera*. This custom of formally presenting or introducing young
daughters to society comes from a custom formerly limited to the middle
and upper classes, often inviting excesses of consumerism and ostentation.
But although it remains a very elaborate affair susceptible to exaggeration,
it has become common among Latinos, particularly those from Mexico

and Central America. It is customary for the young woman to dress in a formal white gown, not unlike a wedding dress, to be escorted by a male friend, and to be accompanied by "a court" of her best friends. The religious significance for this celebration requires that a church service precede the secular celebration. In the presence of the priest, her family, and her friends, the young woman formally pledges to remain chaste until her marriage. The Catholic Church has recently approved a Spanish language ritual for use by Latinas in the United States that was composed by a liturgical institute of Latinos, which is described more completely in subsequent chapters. The *quinceañera* is a notable example of a custom introduced into American religion by Latinos.

Consanguineous ties within the third degree of relationship were common in Latino agricultural societies. Many postponed marriage in the church until the first child was born, because it was usually easier to secure the necessary dispensation once there was proof that the union had been consummated—and what better proof than the birth of a child. Church marriage usually meant that the bride's parents had to provide her with proper attire (a white dress), a *desposorio* (a small celebration for the intimate family the day before the wedding), and the *bodas,* or big celebration on the day of the wedding. The groom had to provide an offering for the priest for the celebration of the ceremony and dispensations (if they were required). In many places, the ceremony includes the ancient Iberian custom of *las arras*, usually twenty silver pieces given to the bride. Itself a borrowing from an ancient Visigoth religious custom of bride price, the coins symbolize the groom's ability and willingness to support the household. As with almost every culture in the world, marriages are accompanied by huge family parties with food, music, dancing, and other ways of integrating the two families.

The first pregnancy of a young married woman was always a joyous occasion. The mother-to-be was rewarded by being pampered by family members, but most especially by the husband. Perhaps this was the one occasion on which she was so treated, since life in the countryside offered very little luxury to anyone. But during pregnancy, women could indulge themselves a bit more by appealing to others' sympathies and guilt through the yearnings of pregnancy, or *antojos*. Invoking *antojos* can be interpreted as very subtle manipulation by the woman not only to seek sanction for giving in to cravings, desires, whims but to procure other peoples' assistance in doing so. Most often the *antojos* were related to food, and often a husband was awakened in the middle of the night to be told his wife wanted some difficult-to-acquire "delicacy." Everyone would give in to a pregnant woman's *antojos*, because it was believed that to do otherwise would create undue anxiety and harm not only to the woman but to the unborn child. People went as far as believing that an unfulfilled *antojo* could even result in a miscarriage or the deformation of the fetus. This custom has been so pervasive that it has found its way into the literature of Puerto Rican women in the United States (Ortíz Cofer, 1990).

The *comadrona,* or *partera,* was called upon not only at the birth of the child but also during the pregnancy. Although lacking formal education, these *comadronas* were experts in home-based health remedies. From the expectant mother's behavior and appearance, the best among them learned to diagnose how well she was carrying the baby, whether it was going to be a difficult pregnancy and birth, how to prevent or minimize risks, and even what the gender of the child was. The social standing of these *comadronas* was very special and added religious status in most rural societies (Deutsch, 1987:46–54; Díaz-Stevens, 1993b).

When the hour for delivery finally came, the midwife would usually ask for very little assistance from others. Usually the husband, children, and other members of the household would be asked to wait in another room. An older child, grandmother, or aunt was asked to prepare a broth, which was usually made from an old hen that had been kept especially for that occasion. This broth was both ritualistic and pragmatic, providing nourishment for the two women. After all, they were both engaged in very painful labor, for hours or even days. Some *comadronas* would enjoy a hearty cup of sugary black coffee or a few swallows of homemade rum or tequila to ward off the early morning chill.

Often, the *comadrona* was also the town healer, or *curandera.* As a healer, she employed more than her expertise in confecting herbal remedies. In order to insure the medicine's effectiveness, a wide repertoire of prayers, *pases* (ritualistic gestures including the sign of the cross), sprinkling of holy water, anointing and massages with oils and the extract of herbs were added. This became the ritual called *santigüos y despojos,* (sprinkling and cleansing). If both the *curandera*'s medicine and that of the town physician failed, then it was time for the *rezador/a* to appear. This person (male or female) would be sought to pray over the ill person, asking divine intercession for his or her cure, and if this was not possible, then *la gracia de morir bien* (resignation and a good death). There were special prayers for the dying. Sometimes people would make it known that they would not die until a specific matter was settled between themselves and another person. If not present, the person was sought and brought before the dying person at which time differences were reconciled. There were times when what the dying person wanted was simply to ask a favor from a special someone—perhaps requesting that the person fulfill a commitment that could not be otherwise kept now that death was near or to care for loved ones after death.

When it became apparent that death was inevitable, the family and friends would be asked to gather around the bedside to help the dying person take leave of temporal existence. The prayers were initiated by the *rezador/a* and followed by everyone present, at times even the dying person, if still conscious. Someone would go for the priest for what then was known as Extreme Unction and today referred to as the Anointing of the Sick.

At death, special attire called *la mortaja* was prepared. The corpse would remain in the home overnight, and during that time, people would be permitted to come and pay their respects. This was called *velar al muerto*, or *velorio*. As with most wakes, the sorrow of loss was accompanied by reminiscence of past good times. There would be some eating and drinking to relieve tensions. But this was principally a time for prayers for the repose of the soul of the person who had died and for all the departed souls. For special *velorios*, the *rezador/a* would be asked for a *velorio cantado*, where the *decenario de difuntos,* or ten decades of the holy rosary with special prayers for the dead, were sung. The wakes of children were treated differently. Considering the child to be an innocent, which guaranteed immediate entry into Heaven without dalliance in Purgatory, the wake of a child was more festive with special use of flowers and songs reserved for these innocents. In some places, a child's wake was not called *velorio* but *florón*, referring to the customary flowers.

For burial, a simple wooden box was sought, and the closest of kin would carry the remains of the dear one to the town church and cemetery, where the priest would officiate the last ceremonies and a close relative or friend would be asked to give the final farewell or eulogy, known as *despedir el duelo*. The *dolientes* (mourners) would return home to comfort one another over a family meal, and for an octave, or an additional eight days, they would come together again to pray for the repose of the soul, thus completing *la novena*, or nine days of prayers. Every year, this day would be commemorated by an anniversary *velorio*, when a *rezador/a* and the friends and family would be invited back.

Death was not seen as the end, but as a new beginning. The closest members of the family, however, would be expected to mourn the person's departure by wearing black clothes and abstaining from dancing and other such festivities for a period of time in accordance with the traditions of that family and community. This was done out of respect and love for the departed one and for the benefit of his or her soul. Sometimes widows, orphans, mothers, or other relatives would vow to clothe themselves in black or not to cut their hair for the rest of their lives. These are called *promesas,* the Spanish word for "promise."

But *promesas* need not be connected to death and often they are not. A *promesa* (or a *manda*, among Mexican Americans) may be made in order to ask for any special blessing or in thanksgiving for one received. It may include wearing special attire such as the habit of a saint, not cutting one's hair, or doing special works of mercy or penance. The *promesa* may be temporary or for life, although priests generally took care to indicate that these *promesas* were not the same as vows that were binding under pain of sin. There are times when one person makes a *promesa* that another person is asked to fulfill. In this instance, the second person is not bound by it and can either disregard it or substitute something else for it. Once a *promesa* is made, however, people feel a need to comply, no matter who made the original commitment. Connected to *promesas* is yet another custom—the wearing of a necklace with medals of saints. An alternate devotion is to put on a shortened version of the cloth scapulars of religious orders or an abbreviated form of the religious habit itself.

Other Religions Within the Latino Tradition

This brief description of the traditions of Latino Catholicism is not exhaustive, nor is the emphasis upon Catholicism here meant to disparage other religions, particularly Protestantism and Pentecostalism. But Catholicism provides the base, or most common experience, against which more particularized experiences can be compared. In the imaginary period from Charlemagne to Roosevelt that we are considering, Catholic tradition gave these accretions a place in the devotions of popular Catholicism (Espín, 1994). Although the Tridentine Reforms asserted clerical control over the sacraments and celebrations within the church building, they also fostered a golden age of devotionalism in a baroque style (Stevens-Arroyo, 1997b). Jansenism disparaged the spontaneous joy of communitarian celebration, but the Latino religious imagination had been poured into this communitarian mold and continues as the pillar upon which Latino religious traditions have been erected.

Our description of Latino tradition as it evolved over centuries until the 1950s includes the process of transculturation between local, native religiosity and Iberian Catholicism. We do not overlook the dislocation and repression Catholicism regularly brought to the indigenous faith. As stated before, exchanges between religions almost never occur symmetrically: Imperial power, technological advantage, military force, and the like constantly intervene and contaminate religious experiences. Thus, even the best of intentions, such as those expressed by the Vatican's Congregation de Propaganda Fide cited above, were almost impossible to sustain over three centuries. However, although power inevitably influences transculturation, we do not believe it vitiates all religious exchanges. Conversion by individuals is too complicated a process to be reduced to an abuse of sociopolitical power alone (Besalga, 1970; Pantoja, 1996).

The premise that all conversion to Christianity is coerced is found in many works that simultaneously attack Spain and its explorers, colonizers, and missionaries in order to defend America's indigenous peoples. Such a polemic is certainly a powerful antidote to the triumphalism that has been enthroned in much of older historiography. In fact, the disputes spilled over into public view during the quincentennial commemorations of Columbus's journey to the Americas. History became a weapon in the battles between today's multiculturalists and back-to-the-basics conservatives. But in our opinion, vilification does not fit well with academic purpose. We consider religious exchange, syncretism, and transculturation as the normal results of contact among peoples, much as Eugene Bolton viewed the Southwest as "borderlands" where cultures merged rather than as "frontier" where there was always a loser and a single winner (Weber, 1992: 350–360). It would be antihistorical to expect symmetrical exchange in religion—à la Prime Directive in the fictional *Star Trek*. It makes no sense to distort the historical record to score debating points. There are enough mistakes in the past to satisfy any crusade for correction, just as heroes and heroines abound to serve as inspiration for every cause.

Thus, for example, while we admire the fine historical research into the evangelization of New Mexico by Ramón Gutiérrez (1991) in his tantalizing *When Jesus Came, the Corn Flower Mothers Went Away*, we think many of his interpretations do not ring true. New Mexican Catholicism today is replete with indigenous religious symbols and customs antedating evangelization. These are so woven into the whole cloth of Christianity that pulling on this or that loose thread would undo the garment. Much as the old-fashioned Christmas uses holly from the Roman Saturnalia, an evergreen tree reminiscent of Germanic religion, and mistletoe from Celtic fertility rites as parts of a whole, Latino Christianity knows how to transculturate belief (Stevens-Arroyo, 1995c). Thus, we would say that the Corn Flower Mothers did not "go away" or disappear when Jesus came—they simply altered their attire or changed their location. The process continues when people move. Migration to U.S. cities by indigenous peoples from Latin America, like the Mayans studied by Nancy Wellmeier (1995) in the city of Los Angeles, suggests that syncretized Christianity continues to produce new contemporary models. Nor is the process of syncretism with indigenous religion restricted to Catholicism. For example, Kathleen Sullivan (1997) reports that native converts to Evangelical Protestantism in Chiapas still participate in the centuries-old Chamulan rite of the Monkey Dance. She concludes that in Chiapas today there is a new form of "popular religion as cultural identity and communitarian spirituality" that competes not only with Catholicism but with U.S. Protestantism and Pentecostalism.

African Transculturation

Also absorbed into Catholic ritual were African-derived religious symbols and rites, although the process was less favorably viewed by missionaries. As slaves, the Africans brought to the Americas were not legally entitled to the protections Spanish law afforded, if reluctantly, to the indigenous peoples. The Spanish Empire under Philip II held to the legal premise that with the acceptance of Christianity, each of the American peoples were formed into a *natio,* or nationality. As a *natio,* each people had nonrevocable rights to preserve their local language and legal customs such as inheritance and land tenure (Stevens-Arroyo, 1997b; Stevens-Arroyo, 1996a:13–137; Lockhart and Schwartz, 1983:127–132). In fact, the Spanish emperor was king over other kings, co-inheriting the crowns of still separate nationalities such as in Catalonia and Portugal. The Americas had no kings other than the Spanish ruler; but they had national languages such as Nahuatl in Mexico and preserved the *cabildos* (municipal governments) and local laws just as was done throughout Iberia (Lockhart and Schwartz, 1983:167–169).

Africans were not protected by such laws, although in places like Cuba, slaves had the right to rule themselves in *cabildos,* a practice dating back to medieval Castile (Cros Sandoval, 1995:83–84), and to elect the chairperson, or *alcalde,* of these councils. These institutions tendered justice in petty civil cases and supervised the participation of the people and the expenditure of funds in religious celebrations like the *fiestas patronales* (Cros Sandoval, 1995). Spanish law permitted a certain cultural and social space for Africans in Spanish America, allowing for the transmission of linguistic, musical, and other cultural expressions. These were incorporated into the slave's celebration of Catholic devotions. We do not wish to suggest that slavery under Catholicism was "benign," only that these self-governing institutions fostered the inclusion of African tradition in the Catholic practice. Along with our PARAL colleague Andrés Pérez y Mena, we think it no longer tenable to hold the once-hegemonic opinion that the survival of African religious beliefs in the Americas was the result of the slaves' inability to understand Christian teachings (Pérez y Mena, 1995b). The syncretism of Yoruba spirits with Catholic saints is a marvelous achievement that testifies to the creative powers of religious imagination for the African heritage of Latinos.

But it bears repeating that syncretism opens the way to transculturation. No less than indigenous *curanderismo* (the celebration of the Mexican Day of the Dead), African-derived customs and symbols do not automatically constitute anti-Christian religious resistance. "Both/and" are better categories than "either/or" to explain these relationships, because the notion that "the same thing can be and not be at the same time" is key to an Aristotelian worldview but not an African one. We embrace Pérez y Mena's judgment (1995a:149–150) that the Civil Rights movement of the 1960s and the resulting Black Pride and Afrocentrism have given Afro-Latin religion the potential to oppose Christian beliefs *today;* however, our focus is upon these religions before the urban migrations. We see syncretism between Catholicism and Afro-Latin religions as the general rule during the period we are considering here.

Freethinkers and Spiritism

There were, however, outside forces that attacked the religious traditions based on Iberian Christianity rather than seeking accommodation. The mid-nineteenth-century movements of anticlericalism in Mexico and Spain distanced the upper classes from the traditional expressions of Catholicism. Rationalism and Positivism frequently substituted for Catholicism among the elites. These beliefs were packaged for delivery to the Americas by writers like Allan Kardec (pen name for Louis Denizarth Hippolyte Rivail, 1804–1869), who mixed the Positivist philosophy with Masonry and a mélange of beliefs and practices, including reincarnation and seances that had religious overtones (Pérez y Mena, 1991:39–42; González-Wippler, 1995:108–109). These became the foundations for Spiritism, which was popular because its emphasis upon clandestine rituals allowed it to serve as a cult rather than as a substitute for Catholicism (Koss, 1972). The official church found it easy to condemn the Freethinkers for these "heresies"—which they were—but conveniently, the church's official pronouncements also repudiated the liberal ideals of republican government that the Freethinkers espoused. With such antagonism toward the church, especially among those agitating for governmental reforms, the traditions of the common people were sometimes targeted for attack and eradication as vestiges of an obscurantist allegiance with Spain. To truly liberate Puerto Rico or Texas from imperial domination and make them into modern republics, it was said, the confidence of the people in Spanish Catholicism had to be destroyed because these religious traditions chained the populace to colonialism. At the turn of the century, Protestant leaders joined in this endeavor to de-Hispanicize and to Americanize Puerto Ricans through the use of a formal education system that would impose the English language as the medium of instruction, as well as through proselytizing efforts that went as far as the public destruction of centuries-old carvings of *santos*, or wooden statues, and the revocation of national holidays such as the Epiphany. But in a delicious irony, this anti-Catholic tenor allowed for an unexpected syncretism of Caribbean Spiritism with Afro-Latin religion, a phenomenon that will be further explained in Chapter 3.

The U.S. Conquest

Conquest of the Latino homelands by the United States permitted a turnabout in the elite's nationalistic antagonism toward Catholicism. In the transition to U.S. rule, the traditions of Catholicism acquired political significance for Latinos as resistance. Thus, in a rather short time, Catholicism was resurrected by criollo leaders as something better than U.S. Protestantism because it was a vehicle for tradition. For instance, in New Mexico, Father Antonio José Martínez (1793–1867), who had vigorously opposed the Mexican regime, articulated a prophetic form of Catholic practice identified with the common people once the territory had passed to U.S. rule. In Puerto Rico, leaders like José de Diego (1866–1918) and Pedro Albizu Campos (1891–1965) advocated independence from the United States, just as a previous generation had opposed Spain. The Mexican philosopher José Vasconcelos, mentioned in Chapter 1, developed the notion that Catholicism was the religion of the *raza cósmica* (cosmic race). For these leaders, Catholicism became the touchstone for a fundamental difference between the Catholic country and the Protestant United States. This line of thought eventually acquired a sophisticated philosophical argumentation redolent with the ideas of Jaime Balmes, Henri Bergson, and Jacques Maritain (Stevens-Arroyo, 1980, 1992, 1996a). The unfolding of these dynamics in response to the U.S. conquest and to the Protestant missionary efforts that accompanied annexation will be discussed in Chapter 3.

The Impact of Migration

The political turmoil and the Protestant challenges did not change the corpus of Catholic traditions among Latinos as much as the socioeconomic transformations set in motion by the New Deal. These changes of the 1930s created the circumstances for the rapid urbanization of Latinos after World War II. Once divorced from their agricultural roots, Latinos had the great burden of adapting their religious traditions to a new social setting. Later in this book, we examine the development of this process, in which some traditions endured, others withered, and some new ones were created out of the religious imagination.

Migration after the end of World War II considerably altered traditions by strengthening some and neutralizing or eliminating others. Most obviously, nature and agricultural cycles lose importance in the city environment, where the clang of garbage cans and the grind of truck motors replace the crowing of roosters and the creak of wooden wheels. Adaptation to these new circumstances is always necessary, but there is a time lag between perception of the need for change and the discovery of the most effective measures to provide transition. Sometimes people "get lost" in the city and never adapt.

For these and other reasons, it is useful to examine urbanization as a process with several phases, or as a journey with several stops (Portes and

Bach, 1985). As already noted in Chapter 1, first comes the experience of relocation, with the direct effects on material culture, including food, clothing, and living arrangements. Next, people experience the inconsistencies between their expectations and the reality of their new circumstances. But no new substitute has yet been found to supply the guiding traditions of the past. Last, there comes a period of acculturation. Of great importance in this last process are intergroup contacts. The city's ghettos provide the setting for oppressed groups to learn from each other—in ways that bring them closer to each other and distance them all from the hegemonic ethnic and racial groups. As J. M. Blaut (1983) suggests, this intergroup contact stimulates "the healthy interfertilization of cultures, the efflorescence of new creative forms . . . and the linking up of struggles" (cited in Flores, 1993:192, n. 13). Religion is often the meeting ground for such groups (Wakefield, 1959; Vidal, 1988).

The Matriarchal Core

Many Latinos and Latinas today believe that religion has only served to instill in women a sense of inferiority, docility, and servitude, especially in traditional Latin American societies. These assertions leave little room for differentiating between the institutionalized form of religion, or the official church with its male clergy and dogmas, on the one hand, and popular religiosity with its roots in the beliefs and traditions of the people, on the other. Religion is patriarchy, pure and simple, it is said, because the power to govern the institution resides chiefly with men (see Hamington, 1995:161–164). What must be understood, however, is that the religious imagination plays a major role in the last stage of acculturation, referred to in the previous paragraph. Unfortunately, a neglected aspect of Latino religion in migration has been the role that women have played and the influence they have had in this respect. Signified as the "the matriarchal core" and believed to be "the saving grace" of popular religiosity (Díaz-Stevens, 1993b), in many instances it is what has kept religion alive among Latinos and what has helped them to identify as individuals and as a group.

The Latina's role in religion is more complex, particularly in acculturation after migration, than those who deny its positive effects would have us believe. In patriarchy, men appropriate to themselves positions they consider to be dominant and allow lesser functions for women. But as social conditions change, social roles may invert. In such circumstances, the segregation of woman's influence to religion may become a function more powerful than male roles. For instance, the farmer who was the male head of a household moves to the city and secures only a low-paying factory job with little social prestige. But his wife goes to the new church and becomes an officer in one of the parish societies or congregational organizations.

The Latino neighbors and family never see the husband in an influential social role, but the wife becomes the mediator of family standing because of her prominent church activities. Thus, when Latino men are placed in an inferior position by migration into U.S. society, the old divide between men and women's roles leaves the matriarchal dominance in the home untouched. In migration, Latinas often acquire more social power within the community than Latinos (Stevens-Arroyo and Cadena, 1995:19–20).

Contrary to some current stereotypes, women have always had a religious role for autonomous decisionmaking, especially in clergy-controlled Catholicism. This is the inescapable message that comes from studies of religious women such as *Untold Sisters: Hispanic Nuns in Their Own Works* (Arenal and Schlau, 1989) and *Hispanic Women: Prophetic Voice in the Church* (Isasi-Díaz and Tarango, 1988). In its own historical framework, each of these books uses the words of the women themselves to shatter the stereotype of passive Catholic Latinas and Hispanic women. These books on Latinas in Catholicism strengthen the perception of a matriarchal core of Latina religion past and present that empowers women—mothers and wives, field and factory workers, *campesinas* (farmers and sharecroppers) and urban dwellers (Díaz-Stevens, 1993b; see Peña, 1996). Ordinary people in the rural areas took on some of the roles of the clergy, for example, calling the people to prayer and presiding over Christian gatherings on special occasions such as Fiestas de Santos, Aniversarios de Difuntos, *velorios, novenas, oraciones para morir bien*, and so on. In these circumstances, women, more often than men, assumed autonomous leadership, distanced from clerical control (Díaz-Stevens, 1993b; see Burns, 1994:147). They were not only leaders within the home but also community leaders because of these religious roles. Frequently, women were the faith healers and the *rezadoras* were more important in the rural areas than seldom-seen doctors or distant clergy. Furthermore, in a world afflicted with a high frequency of infant mortality, the *comadrona* also assumed the role of baptizer. Through closer relationships with an ever-increasing number of people as their *comadre* or *madrina*, her religious role was strengthened and her sphere of influence expanded. Although the local midwives perhaps baptized more babies than the parish priest in town and the additional roles were also more frequently present as *rezadora* and *curandera* than the priest at the bedside of a dying person, their ministry went unrecognized by officialdom; many have remained nameless to our day (Díaz-Stevens, 1993b).

It is our opinion that these rural women exercised an autonomous role analogous to the nuns of institutional Catholicism. From Teresa of Avila and Catherine of Sienna—two women Catholicism declared "Doctors of the Church"—to the lowly *rezadora* of the hinterlands, women are capable of understanding, analyzing, and producing a genuine religious expression. Among these peasant women, moreover, some were able to assume significant historical roles as preachers and founders of religious movements, just as did Saints Teresa and Catherine. For these tasks, official approval was a secondary consideration. The matriarchal core allowed women to mesh their perspectives with Christian doctrine; claiming an infusion of power by the Holy Spirit was sufficient for their calling (Díaz-Stevens, 1993b). Thus, the recall of the past implicit in the Emmaus paradigm has a feminizing future.

In the separation of Latinos from agricultural economies that accelerated dramatically with the New Deal, a new epoch for religious traditions began. These changes are the subject of subsequent chapters. But the reaffirmation of women's role in religion was one of the most remarkable effects upon religious traditions caused by the shift from rural agricultural to urban manufacturing proletariat after 1930. With mass migration to U.S. cities by Latinos after World War II, the traditions of women's religious leadership did not disappear. Rising economic needs in the cities thrust Latinas into the labor market, thus limiting the amount of time spent at home with the children. The new demands and expectations of the migration experience are often at odds with the Latinas' traditional role. With all of the whirlwind changes spawned by modern technology and mass migration, Latinas preserved traditions of the home and local community, shaping the transmission of social values. As in the past, the sustaining sources of popular religiosity are not the priests, or even lay male leaders, but women. In fact, one could cogently argue that with the inevitability of fewer clergy in the Catholicism of America's future, the autonomous power of Latinas in religion will grow, not diminish. When the institutional church fails to mediate the vital relationship between home and heaven, Latinas can summon a tradition of prophetess and priestess of popular religiosity to bridge the gap (Díaz-Stevens, 1993b).

The religious imagination is also spurred to create substitutes for traditional family intimacies. For agriculturally based societies, relationships were usually circumscribed by kin relations; in most barrios, or rural settlements of a few hundred inhabitants, almost everyone was interrelated. In the city, however, it is difficult to sustain these kinship relations, although the initial settlement patterns usually evidence the effort to keep kin together. Family ties help preserve cultural awareness, class consciousness, and collective memory. While the yearning for family is also present, mutatis mutandis, among most ethnic groups in the United States, the Latino experience provides a special window upon this aspect of religion in the United States.

The collective memory of Latinas and Latinos born and raised in the United States is refurbished by the religious imagination, although in different ways from the Latin Americans just arriving. When the immigrants arrive in the United States, they often settle near Latino enclaves. The mutual contact acculturates the Latin Americans to the Latino norms, making the new arrivals more like the Latinos who have been born in the United States. But the process also works in the opposite direction: That is, Latinos acculturate to some aspects of a Latin American identity. These exchanges usually occur in the symbolic language created by Iberian Christianity, and the American experience and religion's role is crucial to the process.

The juxtaposition of such groups stimulates a complex process of asserting differences and searching for similarities, of cooperation and competition, of recreating the setting of the home country and adapting to the urban circumstance. The same dynamic takes place when the groups are Nicaraguans in a Cuban American parish, Salvadoreans in a Mexican American community, or Dominicans among Puerto Ricans. In these dynamics, new configurations are created among the groups and cultural identity is sharpened. Ironically, tradition becomes not only a vehicle for preserving the past but also one that acts to facilitate constant adaptations to new circumstances, stimulating the religious imagination. In ways that seem unique to Latinos, religion in the barrios nurtures the revitalization of old traditions and the creation of new ones. It is a dynamic aspect of religion in America that needs to be included in any comprehensive assessment of the future of U.S. religion. How this religious imagination has adapted to contemporary society is the subject of the following chapters.

Notes

1. The Spanish language uses the feminine gender for the word "*la cruz*," which means that texts celebrating the cross would read in English: "*She* saved us from our sins."

3

Invasions

COLONIALISM DOES NOT OCCUPY the attention of people in the U.S. as much as racism does. In current political culture, U.S. racism is more commonly denounced as a sociopolitical evil than U.S. imperialism is. Although few historians or sociologists would deny that "racism" is one of the nation's ills, they are less likely to accept the imperialist indictment of the country. This disinclination to admit imperialism into U.S. history vis-à-vis the Latino homelands has presented obstacles to a clear articulation of the differences between Latinos and the African American population. Too often Latino social woes are described as "racism," a term taken from U.S. parlance and better suited to trace the effects of slavery. The unfortunate consequence of this tendency is to reduce the Latino history as a "brown" version of the "black" experience, with the implication that Latinos "suffer less" because their color is lighter.

One of the reasons colonialism is so often avoided in most generalized studies of U.S. history is because referring to it would indict the United States as the "American Empire." Descriptions in U.S. military history of colonialism as "wars of conquest" or "imperialism" are often considered shrill and exaggerated. When colonialism toward Latinos is treated in standard textbooks, it is usually Spanish colonialism that is denounced, not the U.S.-inflicted subjugation. We do not use the term "colonialism" as an invented catch-all epithet or an overinflated bumper-sticker insult. We intend its legal meaning: the denial of the right of self-determination, or sovereignty, to the people of a region where foreign rule has been imposed by force (Maldonado Denis, 1969/1972:68–72).

The modern world has repudiated colonialism. The European empires of Great Britain, France, the Netherlands, and Belgium granted sovereignty to almost all their remaining colonies, or "mandates," in the fifteen years after the founding of the United Nations. Following the same trend, in 1986 the United States surrendered its claims over the Mariana Islands. The Soviet

Union, legally a federation of sovereign republics, is now dissolved and its member states have become independent. Today, only a handful of nations on the planet remain colonies according to the definition established in the 1960 U.N. Resolution 1514 (XV). Yet when Resolution 43 (XLVII) was passed in 1988 to end all colonialism in the world by the year 2000, the United States was the only nation of 133 voting members to declare itself against the measure.

Puerto Rico is the issue: The United States does not want international law to challenge its control over the island, even if 132 other nations say it is time to end colonialism (Stevens-Arroyo, 1990). But the blindness is not limited to international politics. When a majority of the Puerto Rican people voted against statehood and in favor of sovereignty in a 1993 referendum on the island, Washington ignored the democratic expression of the people and in 1995 instead considered a measure sponsored by Congressman Young of Alaska for a referendum that would eliminate the formula of sovereignty chosen in 1993!

Colonialism and Religion

It is important to our paradigm to establish this inability to recognize the colonial character of U.S. treatment of most Latinos, Puerto Ricans in particular. It is not only Spain but also the United States that is guilty of colonialism. The facticity of imperial injustice toward Latinos is not at issue here, only the extent of its effects. Without a clear understanding of how colonialism produced the Latino presence in the United States, the functions of religion cannot be placed in context. This chapter is based on the premise that colonialism has plagued Latinos and that the institutional churches reinforced this colonialism and its negative effects because of their relationship to government. Nevertheless, Latinos fashioned religion into a refuge from some of the forces of Americanization.

As was suggested in the first chapter, viewing Latinos as "new immigrants" on the way toward assimilation is not a useful paradigm for social science. Invasions of Texas, the Southwest, California, and Puerto Rico are essentially connected to the religious history of Latinos in these homelands. Fortunately, a growing literature after more than twenty years of university-based scholarship in Chicano and Puerto Rican Studies has incorporated colonialism and its effects into a corpus of research that explains the Latino identity, culture, and history. We hope to connect this intellectual production to the examination of Latino religion.

We believe that a sober assessment of colonialism is a long-overdue step toward a better understanding of Latino religious expression. The analysis offered here is not intended as a political diatribe against the United States, still less as a portrayal of Latinos as hapless victims. Our purpose is served if we show the ways in which church policies reflected the political premises of the time. We trust that the reader will recall much of what is already known of U.S. history but, like the disciples in the Emmaus account, will discover a new meaning for old events.

Invasions and Transculturation

The United States is not the only country in history to have expanded its borders by imperialist wars. Indeed, the further back one turns the pages of history, the more common this experience has been. The settlers of Teotihúacan eclipsed the Olmecs in Meso-America and then were themselves conquered by the Toltecs, who were later conquered by the Aztecs. This process in our continent is not very much different from the way the Assyrians conquered the Sumerians and later were replaced by Persians, who gave way to the Greeks who were supplanted by the Romans. History's examples of colonial subjugations by force are multiple.

But colonialism is often accompanied by "transculturation," a term explained in the previous chapter. The Greeks under Alexander were changed by contact with the religions of the Persians they conquered. Centuries later, the Greeks Hellenized their Roman conquerors. The disintegrated Roman Empire after the fifth century Latinized the Germanic "barbarians." The romantic novels of Sir Walter Scott paint for us the pain and the glory of this process of merging that took place in medieval England between Saxon and Norman. A less-dramatic side of this tale centers on a host of small struggles over language, symbols, law, and religion, most of which resulted in a new synthesis. Often in history, transculturation has allowed the conquered people a measure of revenge over the invaders by their slow subversion of alien languages and customs. Furthermore, we cannot avoid stressing the economic and social forces that drive such forms of transculturation (Frank, 1978; Hall, 1989).

But if transculturation is the eventual result, is colonialism so bad? What difference does it make to an Irish Catholic in Dublin today that the history of the island mixes conquering waves of Celts, Romans, and Vikings, when the particularities of each of these groups has been lost in the creation of today's Irish cultural identity? At a certain point, the colonial experience is so far removed from everyday reality as to have lost its salience for social science. But then again, the same Irish Catholic is likely to view invasion by the English as a totally different matter. The question should be: At what point can we say that transculturation robs colonialism of an explanatory impact on social behavior? And when must we admit that transculturation has not taken place or is not likely to occur?

We can pose the transculturation question for Latinos more specifically. Are Latinos going to "merge" with the Euro-American population so that both groups leave behind their separate identities and create a new U.S. reality? Will we be able to use the term *"mestizaje"* (Elizondo, 1992) not only to describe the result of Spanish colonialism but also to characterize the end product of U.S. culture? Is U.S. civilization to undergo a gradual hybridization with Latinos comparable to that of the Iberian civilization with the indigenous nations of America? Or is the Latino persistence a herald of the "clash of civilizations" (Huntington, 1996) that will take place within the United States?

Transculturation goes well beyond the superficial incorporation of Latino culture in a world of Taco Bell drive-in restaurants or of a Latino politician into the president's cabinet. And despite some positive signs, we have an overall negative assessment of the potential for a transculturation of U.S. society into a new synthesis with Latino culture. In the United States, the gap between the English-speaking and the Spanish-speaking populations is growing, not shrinking. The present political and social climate at the close of the first Christian millennium seems to be hardening ethnic and linguistic differences. A future like that of a Canada, divided between an English-speaking and a French-speaking population, seems a more likely scenario than that of Ivanhoe in the thirteenth century.

Our interpretation of Latino religion counterpoises two trends: *mestizaje* and Balkanization. Much like the ocean waves that rush onto a sandy beach but disguise an invisible undertow that is forever returning to the depths, Latino religion seems to draw closer and then separate from Euro-American experiences. It seems both forces are at work, pulling in different directions. We offer data here that alternately exhibit one or the other trend, and sometimes both together. In our judgment, neither transculturation nor political separatism are inevitable; much depends on economic and social variables that are difficult to predict. And although we admire the confidence of colleagues who assume one or the other outcome as inevitable, we suspect that this confidence reflects ideological or political bias.

For instance, it could be argued that Latino resistance to assimilation is comparable to the nostalgia immigrant groups have experienced after arriving in the United States from their homelands. In this view, time helps erase attachment to the "old country," until it finally melts into a ritualistic ethnic identity—one that can be "put on or off like a set of clothes" (Greeley, 1977). But this comparison with Euro-American immigrant groups ignores the significant difference between migration and conquest. In the former, individuals choose to leave their homeland and travel to another country; in the latter, military force comes into the homeland and by hoisting a new flag, makes the inhabitants strangers in their own land. To his credit, Nathan Glazer (1983:277–284) recognized this fundamental difference of the Latinos, especially of the Puerto Ricans living under the U.S. flag. He calls attention to the difference in terms of language loyalties. The persistence of Latino identity, especially in the use of the Spanish language, seems to exceed the linguistic loyalty of almost all Euro-American groups to a language other than English.

Once colonialism replaces immigration as the explanation for the Latino presence, the premise of inescapable assimilation can be challenged. Latinos are more like the Irish Catholics in Belfast than the Irish Americans in Boston. We have been subjugated in our own lands, where we were once the masters; we are not voyagers to an adopted country where we are the guests. In our opinion, whether transculturation will prevail over the current centrifugal spin in U.S. society is tied to larger political and economic trends in the twenty-first century (Frank, 1993). It may even be that Latinos will come to view the issue of loyalty in terms of civilization and not citizenship within the nation-state (Huntington, 1996). In any part of the process, religion will very much influence the outcome for Latinos. As this chapter will show, Latinos gradually overcame a similar set of challenges during the hundreds of years of Spanish colonialism, and during those centuries, religion played a major role in transculturation. The new identity emerged as a successful transformation that erased most of the distinctions between the conquered indigenous societies and the Iberian state. A review of the major characteristics of this transculturation in the Latino homelands casts light on how religion influenced the process.

Spanish Colonialism

Although there were always exceptions to the rule, social power in the political centers of Latin America was accessible on the basis of approximation to Spanish identity. European-born whites, called *peninsulares,* or, respectively, *gachupines* or *mojados,* were guaranteed maximum political and social influence by Spain's policies. The children born to these privileged Europeans on the American side of the Atlantic, however, had a lower status as criollos—even though they were white and not of mixed race. In parts of the multiracial Caribbean, "criollo" came to mean simply "a person of the land." Rather early, class divisions in colonial Spanish America assumed fault lines according to color and racial origins. Below the criollos were the predominant mixtures: the mestizo, of Indian and European progeny; the mulatto, of African and European offspring; and the *zambo,* from Indian and African stock. Within these mixed race classifications were a host of variations. Eventually, the mixtures came be to be described in terms of phenotypes, that is, individual appearances. The North American norm that "one drop of African blood makes a person black" did not apply in Latin America. Members of the same family might be called "Negro," "*grifo,*" or "mulatto," depending on the degree of negritude. Below the mixed race people came Africans, with those born free ranked over those who were slaves. Native Americans were generally on the lowest rung, unless they could speak Spanish and wore European clothing, in which case they were "Ladinos," considered to be culturally mixed with the Spaniards, even if biologically they were indigenous peoples (Lockhart and Schwartz, 1983:129–132).

On the eve of the U.S. invasions in the middle of the nineteenth century, the societies of the Latino homelands under Spanish colonialism had important differences from this Latin American pattern of social and racial stratification. The original Spanish settlements in California, New Mexico, Texas, and Florida had been peripheral to the overall colonizing enterprise of Spain. In economic terms, until the dawn of the nineteenth century each of these regions and the island of Puerto Rico were in a dependent position within the economic system of the Spanish colonial world. Dependency in economic matters resulted in an inferior social and political standing as well. Unable to keep its own wealth, or even in some cases to generate any profit, the colonies of the Caribbean and the borderlands north of Mexico were connected only loosely to the Spanish colonial system. These notions are clear to those familiar with dependency and world systems theories (Chilcote and Edelstein, 1974; Frank, 1978), although simpler terminology such as the idea of "fringe" as utilized by James Lockhart and Stuart Schwartz (1983) is adequate to explain the same reality with less ideological baggage. Definitely to be avoided is diffusionist theory, which considers poverty and underdevelopment to have resulted from lack of modernization (see Chilcote and Edelstein, 1974). Rather, we have to view economies and societies as connected to systems that maintain dependency and inferior status as a normal means of exploitation.

Ironically, this marginal status for the Latino homelands allowed for significant transculturation between the Iberian conquerors and the indigenous conquered peoples, because—unlike the population centers in Latin America—there was not much power at risk. In the peripheries of the Caribbean and in Florida, California, and the continental Southwest, these social and racial differences were not as highly demarcated as in the colonial centers (Lockhart and Schwartz, 1983:260–262). From a practical point of view, the dependent economies in the borderlands required every capable person to contribute to the commonweal. There was more of an opportunity at the fringes of the Spanish American colonial system for mestizos, Ladinos, and mulattos to exercise the social role usually reserved in the centers for whites alone. Often enough, successful individuals became "whiter" in social ranking as they acquired wealth and power. Thomas Hall suggests that the U.S. Southwest under Spanish rule was not so much a periphery as a semiperiphery, with its own dynamics of power, race, economy, and prestige (Hall, 1989). Ignoring these Latino differences or subsuming them under notions better suited to Latin America is a perilous course (Hall, 1991:50). In a sense, life in the Latino homelands was more of a meritocracy than in other areas of Spanish America, and this may explain why so many Latinos today have racial attitudes different from those held in both Latin America and the United States.

Inasmuch as the Catholic Church was closely tied to the Spanish colonial apparatus, it suffered the fate of social institutions in the periphery. There were always fewer schools, hospitals, convents, monasteries, and churches in the Latino homelands, just as there were fewer banks, roads, shops, and stores. This does not mean that the religious beliefs of the inhabitants at the frontiers were less fervent than those of people living in the great cities of Spanish America, only that the church institutions had fewer resources and less influence in preserving and developing this faith. Accordingly, the numbers and ability of clergy, the quality of services, and the condition of church buildings and other institutional agencies suffered at the fringes of the Spanish Empire.

Additionally, the practice of religion in a peripheral society was sometimes more racially tolerant than in the class-conscious cities. Indians, Africans, and mixed-race peoples could enjoy a higher level of acceptance from Catholicism at the fringes of colonial power than at its center. After its failure to establish a feudal system in the Caribbean (Stevens-Arroyo, 1993), Spain constructed four agencies of ecclesiastical organization for the Spanish colonies in North America (Borges, 1987). First, there was the parish church in the city, a repetition of European practice and frequently accessible only to Spaniards and white criollos. The city parish was directly under the bishop and staffed by diocesan clergy. Second, there was the mission, directed by religious orders or the "regular" priests. This mission was walled to protect it from marauders and maintain the religious cloister. Inside was a church, however, that was open to the people of the surrounding area. The mission also included industries like leather tanning, toolmaking in forges, and various forms of food processing. Styled on reforms first suggested in 1517, the mission was a *reducción,* or reservation, which allowed the Indians to gradually assimilate both Christian faith and Spanish technology. The mission was not a parish in the strict canonical sense; it enjoyed exemptions from the control of the bishop, on the argument that special privileges and financing were required for the missionary enterprise. The special status of the missions were frequently contested. Third, when the natives were converted, the mission could take down the walls of protection. But it also lost its privileges, becoming a village parish. Although the church may still have stood among the indigenous people of the *reducción,* the parish was subject to the local bishop. Fourth, there was the *ermita,* or local shrine, visited on occasion by priests on horseback. These shrines were built and maintained by lay people, some of whom made *promesas* or joined a *cofradía.* At times, the shrine commemorated a miraculous experience like a sudden healing or a salvation from danger, and not infrequently, it was erected upon a site sacred to the native religion. The *ermita* of Our Lady of Guadalupe on Tepeyac Hill in Mexico demonstrates how a simple *ermita* could be transformed by the baroque religious imagination into one of the world's most important Marian shrines (Stevens-Arroyo, 1997b; Poole, 1995a). These four major agencies of ecclesiastical organization became standard at the beginning of the seventeenth century and endured—albeit with modifications—until the Mexican American War in the middle of the nineteenth century (Weber, 1992:91–121). Shrines continue to exercise considerable influence within Catholicism, even when they no longer follow the strict etiquette of the past. For instance, Cuban Americans in contemporary Miami have built a shrine to Our Lady of Charity because travel to the original *ermita* in Santiago, Cuba, is no longer practical (Tweed, 1996).

Because the peripheral status of the colonies had ecclesiastical and religious effects, Spanish colonial Catholicism in the Latino homelands can be differentiated from Catholicism in much of Latin America. Many of the churches at the fringe at one time were founded as missions and *ermitas*, and they frequently gave voice to the socioeconomic needs of the people. With an eye to satisfying the need for material resources, the churches at the periphery frequently argued for new exemptions or increased contributions on behalf of the poor, who were also the racially mixed population. Hence, the roots of religion among the people who were to become Latinos were often deeper than their loyalties to Spain.

Loyalty to the faith at the periphery also meant that Latino Catholicism depended upon popular religiosity to an extraordinary degree without the nationalistic anticlericalism common in Latin America (Díaz-Stevens, 1991, 1993b). Moreover, the home-centered aspects of Catholicism are very strong among Latinos, assuming a primacy over clerically dominated and institutionally based traditions like attendance at Sunday mass and obedience to the clergy (Díaz-Stevens, 1996a).

Puerto Rico, Cuba, and the Dominican Republic

In spite of a common matrix, the religious transculturation in Latino homelands had marked differences. Puerto Rican, Dominican, and Cuban Catholicisms had special characteristics as Caribbean colonies (Dolan and Vidal, 1994) that make them different from the Mexican and continental experiences (Dolan and Hinojosa, 1994). First, evangelization among the natives had almost ended in the Caribbean even before it began in Meso-America. As has been argued convincingly elsewhere (Stevens-Arroyo, 1989, 1993), the origins of Catholicism in the Caribbean are better understood in the context of a simultaneous evangelization in the Canary Islands at the other end of the Atlantic Ocean rather than by comparison with the Mexican experience (Stevens-Arroyo, 1996b). The second difference is the shift from status as peripheral colony to a source of important exports integrated into the Spanish economic system. This shift for Puerto Rico (and Cuba and the Dominican Republic, as well) occurred after the loss of Spain's Latin American colonies in 1821. Retaining control over the islands became a major concern of successive Spanish governments, and colonial policies became increasingly rigid and repressive. Thus, the Caribbean has the experience of being both periphery and integrated colony in its Spanish history, whereas the continental Latino homelands of Texas, New Mexico, and California were generally only peripheral under their Iberian rulers and during the early Mexican Republic. The third salient difference from the Mexican region is the African presence in the Caribbean. Africans and their descendants contributed new and complex forms to Spanish colonial Catholicism that have no direct counterparts in the continental experiences.

The presence of large numbers of African slaves on Caribbean sugar plantations changed not only the economic, social, and cultural dimensions of life but also the religious aspect. As described in Chapter 2, the Spanish colonial system—at least until the nineteenth century—allowed slave societies certain forms of autonomy that permitted active agency in religious expression. The *fiestas patronales* for Africans in the Caribbean, both slave and free, developed religious music unique to the Americas and redefined the intercession of the saints to fit specifically Afro-Caribbean circumstances (Cros Sandoval, 1995). There is also reason to believe that native indigenous beliefs are also part of the mixture (Stevens-Arroyo, 1995b). Therefore, it is a mistake to discount an active religious imagination among the black peoples in the Caribbean, considering authentic only the purely African elements of their religion in isolation from the dynamic whole. Taíno and European Catholic influences are transculturated with the original African beliefs so that the end product is no longer the same religion as that of the African continent. In the analogy of the string of Christmas tree lights developed in the first chapter, to remove one bulb destroys the connection that animates them all.

Moreover, European theosophy and North American Spiritualism have also had considerable religious impact in the Caribbean (González-Wippler, 1995; Koss, 1972). A syncretism took place between the theosophical beliefs of the Europeanized upper class and the African-influenced religious traditions of the slave blacks, especially as concerns healing rituals (Cros Sandoval, 1995:90). Pérez y Mena also points to the influence of Masonry and the Krausistas, influential in late nineteenth-century Spanish politics, as openings for syncretism of these religious systems (Pérez y Mena, 1991:27, n. 3). But Joan Koss (1972) shows how the establishment of public hospitals after the U.S. invasion provided the major impetus for the syncretism of African-influenced religions with the Spiritism of Puerto Rican elites, a notion Mercedes Cros Sandoval accepts as part of the Cuban experience (1995:91–92). Both scholars suggest that the practitioners of African-derived religions acquired new forms of power by explaining their rituals in terms borrowed from upper-class white Freethinkers. Finally, we need to consider the sophistication of Yoruba religion in Africa before enslavement that gave it a special adaptive power for survival not enjoyed by all the African religions (Cros Sandoval, 1995:83). Without attempting here to determine the complex origins of Afro-Caribbean religions, we take the discussion as evidence that transculturation is at work. We note, for instance, that in Cuba today Santería (or Lucumí) is referred to as a "Cuban" religion, not as an "Afro-Cuban" one (Ramírez Calzadilla, 1996).

The transculturation of African religions into a Caribbean synthesis is related to the character of the sugar economy on those islands. Differences between Cuba, where the transculturated result contained many African elements, and Puerto Rico, where African influence is less strong (González-Wippler, 1995), may be attributed to the smaller role sugar played in the Puerto Rican colony. The process differed still more on the continent, where the basic industry was cattle and sheep raising.

Another factor in transculturation is the reaction of the different indigenous groups. For instance, the Navajo of New Mexico acculturated rapidly to the Spanish presence. They adopted sheep raising as a mode of economic participation and although there was friction under colonial rule, they prospered as Hispanicized natives. The Apaches and Comanches, however, proved to be fiercely resistant, fighting not only the Spaniards but later the U.S. military as well (Hall, 1989).

Florida

Within the present-day United States, there were four major regions of Spanish settlement: Florida, New Mexico-Arizona, Texas, and California. From the Spaniards' perspective, Florida extended almost the entire Atlantic coast of North America, well beyond the borders of the present-day state. But although Florida boasted several successful settlements, notably San Agustín (1565) and Pensacola (1698) (Weber, 1992:64–75), it was a target of cupidity first for the French and English and finally for the United States. Pensacola was invaded and occupied by General Andrew Jackson in 1818. In 1821, President James Monroe demanded that the Spanish surrender Florida forever. Most of the remaining Spanish subjects departed, and the area almost lost its Latino population until the exodus from Cuba after 1960 helped remake southern Florida into a Latino enclave.

New Mexico

What is now New Mexico was systematically colonized by Juan de Oñate from northern Mexico in 1582. The Spaniards sought to establish cattle ranching in this dry and sparse land, which is not unlike parts of the Iberian *meseta* (plains on a plateau). To help ameliorate an economy almost without currency, the native peoples were given social roles similar to those of peasants in feudal Spain. The indigenous groups in New Mexico, principally the Navajo and the Pueblo, offered relatively stable societies that Spanish missionaries and conquistadors alike sought to incorporate into the Spanish system. El Paso, which lies at the entrance to New Mexico on the *camino real*, or King's Highway, and Santa Fe were the largest of the settlements north of the Rio Grande in the seventeenth century, each more than double in population than San Antonio in Texas (Weber, 1992:195).

The revolt of the Pueblo people in 1680 that was interpreted in Chapter 2, dampened the zeal of the Spaniards for intruding upon indigenous ways, as was common in other colonies (Weber, 1992:141). The relaxed supervision of cultural expression also encouraged the maintenance of Jewish practices among a significant sector of the European settlers, so that today, considerable Jewish influence is evident among New Mexico's Latinos (Jacobs, 1996). New Mexico developed an anti-Mexican passion, with an elite group of settlers in Albuquerque calling themselves "Hispanos" to distinguish themselves from the Mexicans, who were viewed as most people of mixed racial ancestry were. Of all the Southwestern regions, New Mexico professed the strongest loyalty to Spanish art and customs after the U.S. invasion (Weber, 1992:346–347).

Texas

The indigenous peoples in what is now Texas were not farmers; they were, rather, nomads (Hall, 1989), and their practices of raiding settlements discouraged Spanish colonization in Texas. Determined to drive out French colonists at the end of the seventeenth century, the Spaniards founded a series of missions, clustered around a river system named after San Antonio. The mission became a town (*villa*) in 1720. The colony in San Antonio desperately sought civilian settlers to build the colony and in 1729–1731, colonists from the Canary Islands were recruited. They were defended from the marauding natives by a presidium that had been established for purely military purposes. The gradual pacification—rather than conversion—of the natives, especially the Comanches, stabilized economic activity. Cattle raising provided a spur to Texan vitality in the band of settled lands that stretched from Corpus Christi on the Gulf Coast and westward through San Antonio to El Paso on the New Mexico border, areas that constituted Texas by the time of Mexican independence in 1821.

Yet the achievement of peace with the indigenous peoples and expulsion of the British did not bring peace to Texas. The United States filibusters, and settlers as well, violated territorial borders with alarming frequency. In search of booty or lands for cotton farming, these people created pressures that were not unlike those that had forced the ceding of Florida by Spain in 1821 (Acuña, 1972:34–54). Eventually, this formed the backdrop for the Texas War of Independence (1835–1836).

Both Texas and New Mexico were characterized by small towns and many outlying villages and ranches. Almost everyone was engaged in some form of subsistence farming, but the cash economy depended on seasonal cattle and sheep drives. The "wide-open spaces" of the Texas range shaped not only the economy and society but religion as well. The practice of the faith depended very much on the missions, sometimes without sufficient clergy and always at great distances. The character of Catholicism in the region was marked by a nearly universal reliance on the practice of popular religiosity by the laity (Matovina, 1995a), much as the economy depended on production from these outlying areas. California was very different: Its economy was more sedentary, more agricultural, and it had numerous indigenous peoples who had been Hispanicized through the missions founded within their traditional communities.

California

By arrangement with the Spanish Crown in 1697, the Jesuit priest Eusebio Kino initiated the evangelization of the natives in California, north of the peninsula of Baja California. He financed the missionary effort with a subsidy called the Pious Fund that was intended to insulate the California settlements from the greed and militarism of the *conquistadores*. The suppression of the Society of Jesus in 1767 meant that the Jesuits had to surrender their missions. The Franciscan priest, now Blessed Junípero Serra, inherited the task of founding missions among the Indians of California. He arrived in San Diego in 1769 and was successful enough to move beyond the *reducción* into the famous string of California missions (Santos, 1983:34–39).

Aided by a Spanish government anxious to prevent Russian advances down the Pacific coast from Alaska, Serra founded twenty-one missions in all, stretching from San Diego in the South to San Francisco in the North. These missions functioned as self-contained economic units, producing food and raw materials for export, as well as manufacturing the basic items of clothing, shoes, and domestic tools internally. Each had its school, where learning was largely by rote, although reading and writing were taught at rudimentary levels. Fray Junípero, who died in 1784, had managed to revive the notion of Indian Republics that had been defended by Bartolomé de las Casas (Weber, 1992:261–263). The Franciscan education of the natives, however, was religious both in purpose and content and was organized around agricultural cycles, permitting long recesses during productive seasons. However one judges these missionary practices today, the California missions added Catholicism and the Spanish language to the new culture.

The Spanish missionaries intentionally undermined and changed the native culture, but it would be a mistake to suppose they only sought to reproduce Iberian society. They envisioned a new synthesis that they believed would be superior in matters of faith to either of the constituent parts. What they established approximates our understanding of transculturation (Weber, 1992:115–121). Ironically, the poorer elements of society often remained more loyal to the transculturated faith preached by the missionaries than did the upper classes of *californios,* or Mexican criollos, who were characteristically more interested in this world than in the next.

California of the nineteenth century had a rich agricultural potential; only the limitations of a weak Mexican state in the aftermath of the War of Independence (1810–1821) had prevented the full development of this region from periphery into an economic center of Mexico. The Franciscan missions, which held land and economic resources, were confronted by the *californios,* who sought private economic advantages. Thus, a class distinction was already present in the colony, dividing it internally on the eve of the conquest by the United States, much as the Hispanos divided New Mexico (Acuña, 1972:101–122).

Popular Catholicism in the Caribbean

After 1850, Cuba and Puerto Rico had witnessed the emergence of political factionalism among the criollo classes. Although most criollos agreed upon Republican ideals and free trade, they were divided over slavery. Wealthy sugar planters wanted to maintain slavery because their plantations depended on it, while coffee and tobacco hacienda owners sought abolition because they scarcely used slaves in their harvests.

Spanish colonial policy no longer treated the region as a periphery, and the Spanish kept careful watch over the clergy and episcopacy. Among the clergy, political loyalty to Spain was often more important than commitment to the ministry. By 1875, institutional Catholicism in Puerto Rico and Cuba was identified with the most conservative elements in an increasingly anticlerical political world and suffered a precipitous decline in the quality of clergy. Popular support for the institutional church was also a casualty (Dolan and Vidal, 1994:38–39, 147–157). Particularly lamentable was the official church opposition to abolition of slavery, which was promulgated in 1872. Thus, on the eve of the U.S. invasion in 1898, the official Catholic churches in Cuba and Puerto Rico had suffered nearly thirty years of continual attacks upon credibility and resources, distancing the institutions from the Catholicism of the people. But when the institutional church suffers corrupting self-interest, the central religious role often shifts to popular religion. That indeed was the case in both islands, where processions, *promesas,* and a host of similar practices kept the Catholic religion vital in its nonclerical manifestations.

The Colonial Difference

The presence of Latinos within the United States is radically different from the position of immigrants who came from Europe to America. Whereas Euro-Americans left Europe by conscious decision, Latinos became foreigners in their own homeland by force of military might. Rather than being characterized by immigration, Latino religion reflects the condition of conquest. Moreover, unlike Euro-American Catholicism, which migrated with the immigrants, Catholicism was already established in parishes and dioceses in America when the lands of Florida (1821), Texas (1847), New Mexico-California (1848), and Puerto Rico (1898) were annexed. The immigrant operates with clear distinctions between the "old country" as the place of origin and the "new country" as the selected homeland. Equal treatment or immediate success can be deferred, because the immigrant is a guest in someone else's country. But inferiorization in one's own homeland constitutes an attack upon cultural identity, social location, and self-worth. It would be impossible to explain the Palestinian and Israeli conflicts without recognizing that neither group considers itself "immigrant" and that both claim the territory as "homeland." Similarly, understanding Latino religion begins with acknowledgment of colonialism.

Colonialism in religion among Latinos is a subject worth pursuing. We think that religious traditions serve as a collective memory for the colonized, preserving a cultural identity that cannot be easily destroyed even by military conquest. In what may seem a paradox to those who have not studied this issue in depth, colonialism denies a nation-state to the conquered, though it does not necessarily deny their nationality. The Latino social cohesiveness via a common language, history, and set of sustaining religious traditions makes it more precise to define Latinos as "peoples" and not as "minority groups." As Latinos, we possess traits that would have entitled us to the establishment of our own nation-state, had there not been intervention from the United States. In fact, military invasion occurred, according to some historians, precisely because some in Washington considered it easier to annex the Latino homelands while they were still Spanish colonies rather than after their independence (Maldonado Denis, 1969/1972:55–56).

As we hope to show, the most important of these traits of peoplehood have endured until the present day. Ours is not easily defined as a vestigial culture derived from the "old country," as might be the case for immigrants. Latinos continue to be vitally connected to the roots of national identity and possess religious traditions as vigorous as they are particular. Perhaps most important, Latino identity responds to cultural patterns that constitute an American transculturation of indigenous and Iberian civilizations. In a certain sense, Latinos march to a drumbeat that does not correspond to the melody of an Anglo-American core but resonates instead with the rhythms of Latin America.

We believe transculturation of indigenous and Iberian civilizations should not be underestimated. It has important consequences for the *mentalité* of Latinos today, particularly in issues of contemporary U.S. politics. For instance, the Spanish state "established" the Catholic Church, whereas the U.S. republic began with a constitutional separation of church and state. Supposedly, Spanish Catholicism was rich and powerful because it was established. But in fact, in crucial matters such as financing and clerical education, Spanish colonial Catholicism suffered disadvantages when compared with the church in the United States (Weber, 1992:174–179, cf. 111–112). Moreover, state subsidy of the church *weakened* institutional Catholicism because in the colonies it served the interests of state to underfund the church in order to keep it weak.

In general, with the church-state separation, relations between government and Protestants have been harmonious in the United States (Bellah, 1975:27–30, 41–46), in contrast with the conflict common in Spanish America, where the church was established. The general distrust of Latinos for government in this country may have its roots in the Ibero-American conflictive tradition, so the imposition upon the conquered Latino territories of the so-called "Protestant separation of church and state" is probably better defined as introducing a collusion between religion and government where Catholicism had often been critical of public officials.

Although Latino Catholicism is similar in some ways to the Latin American experience, it is also significantly different because its incorporation into the United States' political and economic system was the point of separation for Latinos from Latin America. The annexation to the United States as territories with a Spanish-speaking majority occurred before the establishment of independent national governments. Could this be one of the reasons that social and religious identity in Latino homelands was fashioned without many of the traditional trappings of Latin American nationalism such as anticlericalism? We believe that as a consequence, Latino religious identity has a sharply *cultural* dimension and that the maintenance of language and tradition are needs that are quasi-religious rather than the overt affirmation of politically driven patriotism.

The U.S. Invasions

The conquests that placed the Latino homelands under the U.S. flag represented a set of problems that had no exact parallel with Euro-American immigration or the forced importation of slaves from Africa. It is more apt to compare the situation of Latinos as conquered nations to that of indigenous people of the Americas; to Ukraine, Lithuania, Latvia, and Estonia after Russian annexation; and to Palestine after the British mandate took over from the Turkish Empire.

Our focus is on U.S. colonialism as an institution, and we do not wish to pass moral judgment on an entire nation in our use of this word. We have learned this useful distinction from studies of slavery. The institution of slavery was racist, but there was a wide variance among the attitudes of individual slaveholders toward black slaves. Just as some white slaveholders demonstrated a benign attitude toward their slaves despite the vicious nature of nineteenth-century slavery, not every Euro-American who profited from the colonialism imposed on the Latino homelands was an imperialist.

There can be no denying, however, that with the exception of the Texas Republic, the Mexican and Spanish-American Wars transferred the governance of the conquered Latino homelands to the territorial clause of the U.S. constitution (Art. 4, Sec. 3, 2). In a technical sense, this territorial clause constitutes colonialism because it bestows the sovereign power of government upon the U.S. Congress, in which the territories have no voting representative. Residents in a territory—even if they hold U.S. citizenship—are denied the most basic freedom of a democracy: no political power of self-determination in the nation-state. The U.S. Congress was not averse to initiating its rule by placing total governmental power in the hands of the conquering general, ignoring completely any civil governance. Thus, for instance, historians of Puerto Rico accurately speak of 1898 until 1900 as the period of U.S. "military dictatorship" (Silva Gotay, 1995:142–143).

Colonialism is not a matter of uneven application of the law, since the law defines the territory in terms of nonrepresentation and the surrender of sovereignty to the U.S. Congress. Unlike discrimination against civil rights, colonialism is not a domestic legal matter: It is rather, a violation of sovereign rights ensured by the international laws that govern the relations between nations.

The Texas Republic avoided this categorization as a territory, since it surrendered its sovereignty when it was admitted to the federal union as a state in 1845. However, during the interim between the establishment of the Texas Republic and its admission into the United States, the native Spanish-speaking Texan people had been denied equal status with Euro-American settlers. The Texas War of Independence had begun by articulating a vision of a bilingual and bicultural nation, the *mestizaje* of two separate groups, and ended with a society of white, Anglo-Protestant hegemony (Acuña, 1972:13, 35–36). This hegemony was safeguarded by vigilante groups that eventually evolved into the notorious "Texas Rangers"—mercenaries who were often paid bounties to capture or kill Spanish-speaking Texans whenever these natives resisted the usurpation of their lands and mistreatment under U.S.-imposed law (Acuña, 1972:36–41).

So complete has been the alienation of the Spanish-speaking population as cofounders of the Texas Republic that 160 years after the Texas War of Independence, the museum inside the Alamo in San Antonio places the Spanish-speaking defenders with "foreigners" from England, Ireland, Germany, and so on (Matovina, 1995b). The Daughters of the Texas Revolution (who run the museum) apparently continue to believe that natives of San Antonio with Spanish surnames are alien in their own country and not even death in the name of freedom merits the same recognition as "American patriots," a term reserved for those who spoke English.

Although Texas avoided the legality of colonial status under the U.S. flag, it became a model for how to marginalize Latinos. Thus, the effects of colonialism continued even after the continental territories became states. The five effects that have direct relevance to our study of Latino religion are (1) the imposition of the English language for official transactions; (2) the replacement or superseding of existing legal codes with the law of the United States as the supreme law of the land; (3) the declaration of opposition to the above measures as illegal activity, ranging from the political charge of treason to violations of the criminal code; (4) control of the public schools and educational curriculum in order to foster Americanization and inferiorize Latino contributions; and (5) the demographic diminution of the native Spanish-speaking population. In this last instance, the conquering government stimulated Euro-American migration to the Latino homelands so that there would be more English speakers than Spanish speakers. In the case of Puerto Rico, rather than the immigration of English speakers, the native demographics were altered by government-sponsored programs of population control and out migration of Puerto Ricans.

Colonialism and the Demise of the Agricultural Economy

It was stated earlier that Latinos were rooted in agricultural societies until the administration of Franklin D. Roosevelt. This is a general statement meant to include all the Latinos from California to Puerto Rico. Of course, there were regions where the Latino economy was not as dependent on agriculture and the demise of power followed a different trail. Because it was a city, the barrio in Los Angeles was an exception to the rule (Griswold del Castillo, 1979).

But ultimately, our argument is not proven by even the most accurate labor force participation statistics. We know, for instance, that until the twentieth century, upwards of 70 percent of Mexican Americans in California and the Southwest were agricultural laborers (Griswold del Castillo, 1979:54)—which means that nearly 30 percent had jobs as merchants, artisans, or even professionals, figures that are more or less the same as those at the time of the invasions. The U.S. presence did not totally destroy the Latino economy and society; "marginalization" would be a more accurate term. As Griswold del Castillo so aptly expressed it, Latinos were "excluded from a developing economy" and remained merchants only to their own people (1979:30–61). Our conclusion is that the personal and cultural ties Latinos had to the earth remained relatively unchanged for them until the 1950s, even when they no longer lived and worked on farms. Their roots in the agricultural society helped maintain social institutions that had more in common with medieval Christianity than with post-Enlightenment industrialization. But on the premise that agriculture was subordinated to industry and capital, keeping Latinos "down on the farm" was a technique of inferiorization. It succeeded in part because the U.S. economy did not need the immediate industrialization of the former lands of Mexico or the island of Puerto Rico.

These five effects of colonialism upon the Latino peoples in the conquered homelands were sometimes more oppressive than the other legal burden of governance under the territorial clause, at least until the New Deal. The economic impact is particularly noteworthy. Because a U.S. style of capitalism was installed and its operations were controlled so as to benefit English-speaking entrepreneurs, Latinos were rendered the poorest segment of society in Texas, New Mexico, California, and Puerto Rico.

As stated previously, the economic activity in Texas and the Southwest before the U.S. Civil War (1861–1865), for instance, was generally focused on cattle ranching and subsistence farming. The English-speaking residents controlled local courts and agencies and, with the aid of government contracts and monopolies, undermined local control of the economy. In the contracting of loans, for example, they substituted the Anglo-American practice of total liability for interest payment to the renter, whereas the Spanish-based *partido* system had made both the giver and recipient of loans proportionately liable for losses and gains. A drought, diseased cattle, or inability to meet preestablished market quotas made it possible for the newly arrived English-speaking Americans to take over ranches and farms that for centuries had belonged to Spanish-speaking farmers.

Moreover, since the sharing of communal rights to water and pastureland, which were guaranteed in land grants from Spain, did not conform to English common law as used by the United States, the basic ownership rights of ancestral lands were frequently questioned. In the sixty-some years after the takeover of the Southwest by the U.S. government, the ownership of 35,491,020 acres was contested in courts. In these cases, only 2,051,526 acres were retained by Spanish-speaking owners. This means that by 1900, Latinos had lost 83 percent of the disputed lands. And even when they won in court, the lawyer fees often had to be paid in land because Latinos were cash poor and had little choice (Deutsch, 1987:28–29).

The massive dislocations caused by the Mexican Revolution that began in 1910 stimulated migration from Mexico northward to the border states of Texas, New Mexico, and California. Since most of these immigrants were farmers who lacked the resources to buy land, they became part of a growing pool of migrant farmworkers who rented themselves out to growers throughout the region for seasonal work. When the Great Depression and the Dust Bowl days after 1930 also pushed poor whites westward, race and language served to lower the social status of Chicanos, Mexicans, and Mexican Americans still further. Thus, looking back for a century from Roosevelt's election in 1932 to the eve of the Texas Revolution, the agricultural rootedness of the Latino peoples in the West remains constant. What changes is their role from stable landowners to marginal tenant farmers and impoverished migrant workers as U.S. control becomes more complete.

The pattern was not much different in the Caribbean. Despite the beginnings of an agrarian capitalist economy that had developed in the last two decades of Spanish rule, Puerto Rico in 1898 faced economic attack from U.S. businessmen and bankers that was not very different from what had been launched against Texas and New Mexico a half century earlier. Centralization of capital in island banks had brought relative prosperity after 1870 to a ruling elite of Spanish merchants and landowners. But the U.S. government placed all these banks under its regulation and devalued the existing currency. The Puerto Rican economy, which was still in the initial stages of capitalist production in 1898, was vulnerable to foreign control, since that was an aggressive source of expansion capital. Faced with bankruptcy because they had negotiated loans with the Spanish peso, the local plantation owners were frequently forced to sell their holdings to U.S. corporations and banks. In Puerto Rico, 85 percent of all farmland was controlled by a handful of U.S. sugar corporations seventeen years after the 1898 invasion (Maldonado Denis, 1969/1972:74).

With the advent of the Great Depression, the sugar corporations shut down much of their Puerto Rican and Cuban operations, expecting that smaller supply would increase demand and raise the prices for sugar. But Puerto Rican and Cuban families were confronted with the contradiction that the best land lay uncultivated because it belonged to U.S. corporations and military installations, while they were crowded into the most remote regions of the island on tiny plots that provided only enough for subsistence farming. As in the case of other Latino homelands, the process of impoverishment left the Latino natives rooted in agriculture.

Internal Colonialism

The principal difference between what North Americans did in the nineteenth and twentieth centuries and what Spaniards had done in the sixteenth and seventeenth lies in the different purposes of these types of colonialism. Spain had maintained the imbalance of power between the colonies and the mother country as a means of maintaining control, so not only the people but also the political territory were treated as inferior. This is classic colonialism. The United States, however, sought to absorb the conquered lands totally as acquired territory, juridically indistinct from the rest of the country and on the march toward statehood. This policy required equal rights for the inhabitants of the territories. If this norm had been applied fairly, the conquered Latino natives would have been politically strong enough to oppose the incoming North American immigrants who followed the invading troops. Instead, through discriminatory collusion among governmental, economic, and social institutions, the conquered Latinos were effectively denied equality. Barriers were constructed that disenfranchised Latino language, customs, economic systems, educational values, and religious faith, allowing the invaders to usurp social, political, and economic hegemony (Acuña, 1972; Hernández, 1994:20–21).

Mario Barrera is generally considered to have systematically sought to explain Latino experiences with an "internal colonialism" model (1972/1974, 1979). Barrera based his construct on Pablo González Cassanova's (1965) analysis of Mexico and Latin America, incorporating ideas taken from Robert Blauner (1972, 1969) and Robert Allen (1970), both of whom described the African American experience from this perspective. Barrera was interested in shifting the "blame" for Chicano underachievement from models such as the immigrant paradigm back to structural factors (1972/1974:174–202). But, like Blauner, Barrera recognized that a reduction of all discrimination against minorities in the United States to Marxist-defined economic categories would understate the importance of race in producing labor force segmentation (e.g. Bailey and Flores, 1973). Accordingly, Barrera fit the notion of colonialism to the situation of Chicanos, much as Blauner and Allen had for African Americans. Exploitation was seen as a mode of subordinating a class of people not only as cheap labor within a capitalist economy but as a part of hegemonic control over their culture and self-perception as well. The chief difference between this experience in the United States and previous experiences of colonization in Latin America or Africa was the lack of a clear distinction between the country of the colonized and that of the colonizer. Hence, to the notion of colonialism was added the concept of "internal": "Internal colonialism is a form of colonialism in which the dominant and subordinate populations are intermingled, so that there is no geographically distinct 'metropolis' separate from the 'colony'" (Barrera, 1972/1974:194).

Blauner and Allen found it necessary to nuance the notion of colonialism from its classic experience because African Americans had not been colonized in their homelands (Blauner, 1969:396). Instead, slavery was viewed as a sort of "invasion in reverse" that took the native Africans to the land of the oppressor. Although the invasions of Texas, the Southwest, and California fell clearly in line with "classical" colonialism, Barrera had to explain how colonialism could apply when Chicanos were no longer majorities in their former homelands. He countered by stating that majority or minority population statistics were not essential to the condition of powerlessness (Barrera, 1972/1974:195).

Puerto Ricans did not need the internal colonialism model to explain their situation vis-à-vis the United States: Puerto Rico was and remains a classic colony (Bonilla and Campos, 1981). But the situation of Puerto Ricans in the United States cannot be divorced from that of Chicanos, and there was some sympathy with the internal colonialism model among Puerto Rican scholars such as Felix Padilla because the notion helped extend exploitation from the island to the United States (1987:4–20). Interestingly, the so-called "urban enterprise or empowerment zones" introduced as government-sponsored forms of economic development for minorities were viewed as an imitation of colonial economic structures taken from the Puerto Rican Commonwealth's Operation Bootstrap (Bonilla and Campos, 1981:172).

Pious Colonialism

Barrera did not treat the issue of the church extensively in his work during the 1970s. Thus, application of colonialism to an explanation of Catholicism among Latinos is essentially a new step in the analysis of religion, although we recognize an enormous debt to our colleagues. Felix Padilla has applied colonialism to religion in his 1987 study *Puerto Rican Chicago*. Examining the pre–Vatican II experience, Padilla (1987:126–137) suggests that the native Puerto Rican Catholic leadership of the Caballeros of San Juan was unprepared to do much more than repeat the directives of the clergy:

> In the final analysis, Puerto Ricans became just another "immigrant group" for the Catholic Church to accommodate, and this ambivalence disillusioned many Puerto Ricans. The church hierarchy saw the discrimination against Puerto Ricans, but it did not condemn it as part of American society. Instead, it sought to do charity by trying to alleviate suffering by serving as a buffer

without attacking institutionalized racism. The Church could not, due to its own relationship with American society, help Puerto Ricans resist the violation of their culture and personal identity. (Padilla, 1987:136–137)

We extend this paradigm to the ways U.S. churches operated in the Latino homelands from the nineteenth century until the New Deal. Like the Spanish colonialism before it that strove to replace native religions with Catholicism as a means of subjugating the population, the invasion of Latino homelands by the United States during the nineteenth century used North American religious institutions to achieve the subjugation of Latinos. Religion was intended to serve as means of Americanization (Acuña, 1972:147–149; Silva Gotay, 1994), in parallel with other institutions brought in by the U.S. invaders such as civil service, public education, health services, hospitals, and political organizations. These Americanizing religions could not differentiate between the colonized and the colonizer without direct violation of Gospel values, but they could privilege the conqueror's modes of expressing the faith. Thus, the important distinction about "internal colonialism" introduced by Barrera has direct application to the religious institutions established in the conquered Latino homelands (Sunseri, 1979:125–141; Lewis, 1963:103–119). The religious hegemony enjoyed by the invaders stigmatized the ways native Latinos worshiped and lessened the prestige of their local churches, much as had occurred in labor force segmentation, as shown by Barrera's model.

As discussed in Chapter 1, there is a considerable literature on Manifest Destiny and its connection to various Protestant clergymen, such as Josiah Strong (Silva Gotay, 1994:142). Religion supplied legitimation both for the invasion and the colonial treatment of Latinos. The United States and its Protestant religion were exalted as more modern than Catholicism or Hispanic culture:

> Then this [Anglo-Saxon] race of unequaled energy, with all the majesty of numbers and the might of wealth behind it—the representative, let us hope, of the largest liberty, the purest Christianity, the highest civilization—having developed peculiarly aggressive traits calculated to impress its institutions upon mankind, will spread itself over the earth. If I read not amiss, this powerful race will move down upon Mexico, down upon Central and South America, out upon the islands of the sea, over upon Africa and beyond. And can any one doubt that the result of this competition of races will be the "survival of the fittest"? (Josiah Strong, *Our Country*, 1885, cited in Chilcote and Edelstein, 1974:15)

Often enough, U.S. victory in war became evidence for the excellence of Anglo-American Protestantism. The native religion (Catholicism) and native language (Spanish) were made targets for elimination or at least for marginalization. Such was the inevitable and providential result of God's destiny for the United States. Essentially, the English-speaking conquerors were scarcely different from the Spanish Catholics, who centuries before had done the same with the indigenous peoples. They depended not on ill will but on the passionate zeal and noble intentions of missionaries who Americanized as they evangelized. The modes of subjugation, however, were more controlled and complex.

Protestant missionary work in all of the conquered lands assumed three basic patterns. First, there was the work of the missionary board from its headquarters in the United States, which provided personnel and financial support for the work of preaching, teaching, and eventually church building. These funds came mostly from the English-speaking members of the church rather than from the new Spanish-speaking converts in the region.

Second, there was the conversion of natives—even resigned Catholic priests—to the Protestant faith, who often proved themselves to be more effective in ministry than the English-speaking missionaries. Thus, money came from the church mission board controlled by English-speaking people, whereas the preaching and ministration of the new churches came from Spanish-speaking converts. Such arrangements were not contradictory, but they did produce conflicts. Given the gradual impoverishment produced by the U.S. takeovers, the viability of self-financing for the new Latino Protestant congregations found itself diminishing rather than growing larger. Thus, the effective work of the converts was usually subordinated to the control by non-Latino missionaries. Put in other terms, positions of power were given to native English speakers to a degree much greater than to the Spanish-speaking counterparts, even though the churches depended on the Latino preachers and converts for their early effectiveness.

Third, the public school system was used as a vehicle for eliminating the Spanish language, stigmatizing Latino culture and alienating children from their history. This was the consequence of more noble-sounding goals such as "Americanization," "modernization," and "enlightened" education in the spirit of democracy and freedom. The public school system was also a prime employer of English-speaking Protestant missionaries and played a major role in attacking Catholic customs. In Puerto Rico, for instance, teachers and children were penalized for nonattendance at school on January 6, Three Kings' Day, one of the traditional Catholic feast days, which was just another workday for Protestant missionaries (Negrón Montilla, 1970: 121–122). So complete was the identification of the public schools with Protestantism on the island that every superintendent of education was a Protestant from 1900, when the military dictatorship was replaced with civil government, until 1968, sixteen years after Puerto Ricans had acquired the constitutional power to make such appointments themselves.

There can be little doubt that Protestantism legitimated the U.S. conquests and perpetuated the colonialism imposed on Latinos in their homelands. This is a statement of fact that should not be interpreted as impugning the integrity of the missionaries. Doubtless, they viewed the replacement of Catholic tradition as part of their apostolic task and set themselves to preach the faith with intrepid zeal. But in this process, they mixed politics and religion so as to reinforce within the Latino homelands the negative effects of colonialism that were just discussed. English was installed as the official language, local law was supplanted, organized resistance was outlawed, and those who spoke English became the hegemonic majority, even when they were a numerical minority (Besalga, 1970).

U.S. Catholic Colonialism

The U.S. Catholic Church also reinforced colonialism, often producing the same kind of Americanization as U.S. Protestantism. The nurture of the existing Catholic practices of the conquered peoples would have left the church open to charges of fomenting an irredentist nationalism, antagonistic to the Protestant majority in the United States. Rather than serve Latinos in the United States as the church in Poland and Ireland had served its conquered peoples, the Catholic Church fostered an immigrant's view of the Latinos as a substitute for the historical reality. Although Latinos were peoples conquered in war, the U.S. Catholic missionaries undermined this awareness. At times unwittingly and at other times deliberately, the newly imported Catholic clergy told Latinos that they should imitate an immigrant's gratitude for opportunity in a new home rather than nurture resentment against an invading U.S. imperialism.

The historical accounts in the Notre Dame Series on Hispanics and Catholicism (1994) offer many examples of how clergy, particularly the U.S.-appointed bishops of the newly conquered lands, suppressed the existing Latino Catholicism. Some, like Joseph Sadoc Alemany, named bishop of Monterey in 1850 and archbishop of San Francisco in 1853, were benign toward the native Spanish-speaking Californians; others, like his successor in Monterey, Thaddeus Amat (who transferred his residence to Los Angeles, renaming the diocese) were antagonistic to the Spanish-speaking population and to the Mexican clergy who served them (Burns, 1994). But although they differed in attitude, neither bishop opposed U.S. rule over the newly appended lands, and both strove to remake the existing Catholicism into the image and likeness of European immigrant Catholicism on the East Coast.

East Coast Catholicism had used canon law to create national parishes to serve those who did not speak English within an established jurisdiction. National parishes were not located in remote mission territories but were more often found in city neighborhoods that had become ethnic immigrant enclaves. The principle that regulated these national parishes was assimilation. Once the English language was learned, the parishioners of the national parish were expected to join the territorial parish, which conducted services in English (and often only in English) (Fitzpatrick, 1971:123–127; Díaz-Stevens, 1993a:73–83).

Canon law maintained the subordination of the national parish to the local ordinary, or bishop. On the East Coast of the United States, the bishops viewed the national parishes as a temporary measure. In practice, the national parishes were assigned to religious orders, often from a foreign province that could supply clergy from the native land of the immigrants. One of the advantages of this arrangement to the bishop was that the finances of the national parish and the payment of the clergy could be shifted away from the diocese and onto the shoulders of the religious order and the immigrants. Once the immigrant community became established and prosperous, however, the bishop was empowered to reassert his jurisdiction. This was a common occurrence, and when the bishop was viewed as abusing his prerogatives, conflicts frequently arose (Pulido, 1994).

In California, New Mexico, and Texas, the bishops installed with U.S. rule often treated the existing Mexican parishes as national parishes, concentrating diocesan funds and interest on new churches to be built for the English-speaking sector. This inverted the function of the East Coast, where the national parishes were for the newcomers and the existing churches for the English speakers. Yet the application of canon law was used with the same edge that gave financial and legal advantages to the conquerors.

In southern California, Amat's policies were decidedly antagonistic to traditional Latino Catholicism in ways that paralleled the political and economic eclipse of native social status. By the turn of the century in Los Angeles, not only had the original Spanish-speaking population lost political power and economic prosperity, but the diocese was effectively segregated into churches for the poor, who were the Spanish-speaking, and the middle-class English-speaking Catholics. Amat's confiscation of Mexican Franciscan foundations and threats of excommunication added to the alienation of the Spanish-speaking population from institutional Catholicism. Bishop Amat demanded that the already established Spanish speakers adapt to the English-speaking newcomers. Amat and his successors used financial resources to imitate the kind of diocesan and parish structures common to the major East Coast sees of New York, Boston, and Philadelphia. California witnessed the building of Catholic schools, hospitals, convents, and seminaries that provided services for the English speakers. The Spanish speakers were generally expected to raise their own funds, because they were in parishes administered by religious orders (Burns, 1994).

Catholic discrimination toward Latinos was tolerated, even sometimes encouraged by some bishops sent by the U.S. episcopate into the conquered territories. The most outrageous of these prelates may have been Jean-Baptiste Lamy (1850–1885) who became the first archbishop of Santa Fe, New Mexico. French-born, trained in a Gallic Catholicism antagonistic to the spontaneity of popular religiosity, Lamy set about extirpating Latino Catholicism by depriving the native clergy of leadership in New Mexico. Lamy spied on, publicly humiliated, and, in 1857, defrocked the native clergy leader, Father Antonio José Martínez, of Taos, New Mexico.[1]

This conflict is a highly visible example of similar confrontations with native clergy by the hierarchy in Latino homelands after the conquest. The archbishop justified his extreme actions chiefly by citing sexual lapses by Father Martínez, charges that appear to have been true. But did these lapses deserve the punishment of excommunication meted out by Lamy? After all, clergy dalliance with women has been a constant concern throughout the history of Catholicism and not a situation unique to Latinos. Martínez had a high public profile, once serving in the territorial congress, and was admired by the native New Mexican clergy. In plain terms, he was a rival of the archbishop as leader of New Mexico's Catholics, and it would be naive not to impart a political motive to Lamy's actions. Father Martínez had challenged the wisdom of Lamy's policies in a decree of 1854 that imposed a schedule of fees for the sacraments and funeral masses, arguing that this would fuel a charge that Catholics put religious services up for sale. He predicted that blanket restrictions on traditional celebrations of popular religiosity would drive Latino people from the church. He noted that the ban against extradiocesan funding of Spanish-speaking churches was prejudicial (Romero with Sandoval, 1972). In fact, not only Lamy but his successors until 1919—all of French ancestry—impeded special apostolic funding for Spanish-speaking Catholics in New Mexico. In his frequent correspondence with the archbishop, Martínez also complained of incidents when prejudice against native New Mexican priests reared its ugly head in matters like clerical appointments and the assignment of space in rectories. Finally, he questioned the archbishop about hobnobbing with public figures like Kit Carson, who symbolized to the New Mexican people the violent excesses of the U.S. military.

None of the charges of Martínez and other Latino Catholics against Lamy were considered as important to ecclesiastical good order as Martínez's sexual lapses. Thus, although the zeal for personal morality on the part of the archbishop may have been laudable, his insensitivity to public perception of his regulations and personnel policies eroded his credibility with Latinos. Father Juan Romero, who has studied the case carefully, considers Lamy's excommunication of Father Martínez of Taos as part of the archbishop's general disdain for Latinos and their religious traditions

(Romero with Sandoval, 1976). Moreover, the tactic of weakening Latino religion by undermining its defenders within the clergy is not unique to New Mexico or to Catholicism.

The most dramatic confrontations between local culture and U.S. imperialism may have occurred in Puerto Rico. Partially because English-speaking colonists never accounted for more than a fraction of the total island population, favoritism for the English-speaking population has never made much sense in Puerto Rico. Yet when the United States annexed Puerto Rico in 1898, the U.S. episcopate looked upon the island as if it were another New Mexico. One of Lamy's successors in Santa Fe, Placide Chapelle, who had been named archbishop of New Orleans in 1897, used his influence to have a protégé, James Blenck (1898–1907), a naturalized U.S. citizen, appointed bishop of Puerto Rico rather than a native Puerto Rican priest (Vidal, 1994a:39–42). Once again, the premise of Spanish colonialism that no native could be bishop among his own people for fear of inciting rebellion, was echoed by U.S. Catholicism.

Bishop Blenck, who banned the Christmas midnight mass (*misa de gallo*) in the San Juan Cathedral in 1898, considering it too rowdy and offensive to U.S. culture, was greeted with a claim from the island's local government to confiscate all Catholic Church properties: cemeteries, hospitals, schools, rectories, and even the church buildings. The case was settled in an appeal to the U.S. Supreme Court that imposed some limitations on the government's claims to church property. Eventually, Blenck proved less antagonistic to Puerto Rican Catholicism than his successor, Bishop Ambrose Jones (1907–1921). Jones disbanded the centuries-old *cabildo*, or synod of cathedral canons, which could have supplied a native clergy voice in formulating church policy. In his ecclesiastical appointments, the bishop often placed English-speaking pastors over native Puerto Rican priests many years their senior. He actively promoted the massive displacement of local clergy in favor of "missionaries" from New York and Philadelphia who founded parish schools that still teach only in English. Americanizing lay organizations like the Knights of Columbus and the Catholic Daughters of America were established among the wealthy, who became the principal clients of these Catholic schools, seldom affordable for working-class Puerto Ricans (Beirne, 1975:90–97; Silva Gotay, 1994:150–151). These were just some of the measures used to reinforce colonialism.

Native Clergy

The biggest issue confronting Latinos, whether Catholic or Protestant, was native clergy. The social distance between a Catholic priest and his flock was considerable. To be a priest one had to be highly educated, speak English, and live as a celibate outside of family. The Protestant minister was not required to live outside of family, but other demands, especially in formal education, were almost the same. Only in Pentecostalism could one receive the spirit, remain within the family, and, with little formal education or knowledge of English, move into religious leadership.

The dilemma of Protestant and Pentecostal Latinos, however, was that in opting for a religious organization that suited certain social needs of the people, they had to turn their back on centuries of Catholic liturgy and traditions that were interwoven with native Latino culture. Moreover, rather than encourage an accommodation with a Catholic culture, Protestant and Pentecostal churches in the United States adopted a hostility toward Catholicism matched only by the hostility Catholicism held for Protestantism in Catholic countries.

From Puerto Rico to California, church policies depreciated the traditions of Latino Catholicism and subordinated the maintenance or recruitment of native vocations to the goals of using Catholicism as a vehicle for Americanization. This general pattern did not prevent individual Euro-American clerics from identifying with the needs of the Latinos or from fostering the preservation of Latino religious traditions. Priests like Laurence Forristal recognized colonialism. After sixteen years among Latinos in San Diego, the Irish-born Father Forristal emphasized the permanent importance of the Spanish language as the language of the people and warned against Americanization:

> If it means that every Mexican must be recast in a special American mold, the proposal is immense and impossible of accomplishment. . . . There is no more contemptible creature than the Mexican who is ashamed of his blood and race. Invariably he is also ashamed of his religion. (Burns, 1994:150, nn. 10, 11, 12)

There were many clergy, Protestant and Catholic, who responded generously to the call of ministry; they lived among Latinos, often in poverty, learning the language and celebrating the culture (Stevens-Arroyo, 1980/1996). They remained loyal to their ministerial obligations, despite a climate that permitted discrimination against Latinos and their religious traditions. In California, Bishop John J. Cantwell, later archbishop, was a notable advocate of a culturally sensitive ministry to Latinos (Burns, 1994:150–152). But such dedication to apostolic service seldom threatened the structures of colonialism that had been imposed upon the Latinos by force of arms. If there was a certain openness toward incorporating Latino cultural values in the ministry, it usually flowed from the premise that Latinos were an ethnic group on the way to eventual assimilation. We have yet to see evidence that a single Euro-American church leader took any initiative to lift up Latinos as a conquered people with the right to establish their own nation. The dedicated clergy, in effect, sought to lessen the evil effects of colonialism, but they scarcely challenged colonialism itself.

To describe this religious version of internal colonialism, then, we prefer to use the phrase "pious colonialism," which incorporates the word "pious" to describe this participation of the churches. The Latin word *"pius"* means "loyal." In order to fulfill one's religious obligations of the sacraments, liturgy, and prayer, every believer must have recourse to the official church and its clergy and its structures. Put in the terms of Otto Maduro (1982), the "religious production" of Latinos required legitimatization from official religion. For instance, Catholics in the conquered Latino homelands needed the clergy to bless their marriages, baptize their children, bury the dead, and provide everything from holy water to blessed statues for the exercise of traditional Catholic piety. Latinos who did not like the Americanizing cost of the newly installed bishop and clergy could leave Catholicism and become Protestants.

The mainline Protestant churches were no less Americanizing, and perhaps even more so, than the U.S. Catholic Church (Silva Gotay, 1994: 140–146, 153–165; Díaz-Stevens, 1996a). Moreover, as suggested previously, Protestant leaders reserved control over denominational resources even while they encouraged native Latinos to organize and serve in local congregations. Although Protestantism differed from Catholicism in the type of religious production, the pattern of control over the means of religious production was very much the same whether the controls were Protestant supervisors or Catholic bishops. Religion in the conquered Latino homelands was regulated by U.S. administration, much as civil authorities controlled most transactions in the public sphere. Hence, the term "pious colonialism" refers not only to the mind-set of the U.S. missionaries but also to the target of their control.

Of course, all Latinos were not passively submissive to pious colonialism. Some Latino Catholics accepted the stigmatization of their traditional piety and assimilated Euro-American values, but Latinos more frequently rejected this course. However, although some voices were raised against the manipulation of institutional Catholicism for colonial purposes (Stevens-Arroyo, 1980:50–54, 58–63, 85–99), most of those urging resistance to U.S. rule did not turn to religion for support. But we invoke here the notion of "cultural citizenship" that was introduced in Chapter 2. Religion did provide Latinos with a form of unarticulated protest against colonialism. If secular modes of cultural affirmation, such as literature, the arts, and music, can be viewed as inchoate forms of resistance to imperialism (Acuña, 1972:8), then home-centered religion deserves the same classification.

Deprived of native clerical leadership and impoverished by the grinding economic forces of occupation, lay reaction and defense of Catholic values became a defense of Latino culture as well. In New Mexico, the Penitentes became economic and political forces of resistance to U.S. domination. The Penitente Brotherhoods were modeled upon the Iberian *cofradías*, pious lay organizations meant to perform charitable works and motivated by devotion. In New Mexico, Archbishop Lamy suppressed the brotherhood, citing the Holy Week flagellations as superstitious excesses (Sandoval, 1990:37–38). This condemnation of a once-a-year rite, however, could not blind the people to the value of membership in the Penitentes. Often, the Penitente Brotherhood served as a council of town elders, a local board of justice, and even as a *mutualista*, or credit union. There was a plethora of other lay societies, such as the Guadalupanas for women, that provided for continuity with age-old religious traditions in a changing Catholicism (Rodríguez, 1994, in Dolan and Deck).

In Puerto Rico, a lay preaching society called Hermanos Cheos was founded within the first decade of U.S. occupation to counteract the activities of native Spanish-speaking Protestant missionaries. Ironically, the Hermanos's defense of Catholicism and Latino culture was sometimes resented by the Americanizing Catholic clergy as an encroachment upon clerical powers (Vidal, 1982:24–25). Still, the Hermanos have survived as a lay organization, managing to found a house in the Chicago Archdiocese that continues the work of lay preaching today.

Up until the 1950s, the Catholic traditions derived from the Spanish experience tended to thrive most in small towns and remote rural areas. The remoteness of these settings prevented interference with the established Catholicism of centuries. Although the parish church and its sacramental distribution were always a part of such traditional Catholicism, the power of belief in the setting of home altar, local processions, and village customs coexisted with the institutional changes. Social distance, which made Latinos less important to the official churches, had the simultaneous effect of making the official churches less important to Latinos. These patterns were interrupted by mass migrations to urban centers of the United States that occurred after the two world wars, events that will be addressed in the next chapter.

Protestantism had always emphasized a strong role for the laity. That was one of the attractions for Latinos to become Protestants. Protestantism placed great emphasis on individual responsibility to reform one's life. Self-destructive habits of drinking and gambling were special targets of concern. But the denominations more successful among Latinos were those that maintained a family or fictive family support system to confirm the convert in the resolve to live by the Gospel. There is also evidence to suggest that Protestantism did best in towns and cities (Alvarez, 1996).

The Pentecostal Role in Colonialism

However, interpretation of Protestantism among Latinos in the first one-half of the twentieth century must take into account the role of Pentecostalism. Rising from the Holiness movements at the close of the nineteenth century,

Pentecostalism emerged explosively in Los Angeles with the preaching of William Seymour in 1906 and its subsequent move to an old Methodist church on Azusa Street until 1913; Pentecostalism is often traced to these origins (Burgess and McGee, 1988:31–36; Alvarez, 1996). The California beginnings and the multiracial character of this earliest Pentecostalism attracted Latino converts, not only Mexican Americans, as might be expected, but also Puerto Ricans, some of whom had traveled as far as Hawaii in search of work after the U.S. invasion had reduced the island's agricultural production to sugar and almost nothing else (Espinosa, 1995).

Juan L. Lugo (1890–1984), one of the Puerto Ricans converted in Hawaii in 1913, preached in northern California, where a Pentecostal church was founded in 1915, and then was ordained by the General Council of the Assemblies of God in 1916. Lugo was soon to return to his native Caribbean island with several companions to found Pentecostalism in Puerto Rico (Lugo, 1957). Francisco Olazabal (1886–1937) was a Mexican-born convert to Pentecostalism, as notable for his missionary successes as Lugo. Important to the theme of Latino religion, the Puerto Rican–born Lugo and the Mexican-born Olazabal not only preached among their own ethnic groups but helped each other—Lugo in Texas and California, Olazabal in Puerto Rico (Alvarez, 1996).

Another example of early Latino Pentecostalism can be traced to 1916, with the baptism in the name of Jesus of Antonio C. Nava in a Pentecostal congregation in San Diego. Based on a non-Trinitarian Oneness position and considerably smaller than other Latino Pentecostal groupings, the Apostolic Assembly of the Faith in Jesus Christ nonetheless reflects today many of the earliest traditions of Mexican American Pentecostalism (Ramírez, 1996).

Latino Pentecostalism was held in low regard by Protestants and Catholics alike because it was perceived as a religion of shallow theology, excessive emotionalism, and ephemeral importance. Like beliefs of the Jehovah's Witnesses, who have been similarly characterized, through the first one-half of the century, Latino Pentecostalisms were considered marginally important as religions by Catholic and mainline Protestant leaders.

Because Pentecostalism began after the conquests of the Latino homelands, its relationship with pious colonialism is different from that of Catholicism, Evangelicalism, and mainline Protestantism. The early Pentecostals came from the lower social classes, especially those displaced from the traditional agricultural communities, and enjoyed considerable membership from racial and ethnic minorities, both African Americans and Latinos. The intra-Latino character of the membership has already been described, and the openness of early Pentecostalism to Puerto Ricans and Mexican American alike anticipated by nearly half a century a pan-Latino consciousness. The non-Trinitarian Apostolic Assembly certainly qualified as an independent Latino church. Lugo separated the Pentecostal churches in Puerto Rico from the Assemblies of God in 1922, as did Olazabal for his Mexican American congregations in 1923 with the founding of the Latin American Council of Christian Churches. Their leaders complained that the controls of the U.S.-based assemblies threatened the autonomy of the Latino congregations (Alvarez, 1996). They opposed the obligations to speak English or study in Americanizing Bible schools as conditions for membership in Pentecostalism. Puerto Rican Pentecostalism in New York preserved its island roots through the preaching of Lugo, who spent six years from 1931 until 1937 among Puerto Ricans in the city. In sum, Pentecostal Latino congregations were free from the attachments to the establishment usually found in mainline Protestantism (Domínguez, 1990).

But although Pentecostalism was not a source of pious colonialism, that does not mean that it was exempt from its effects. Latino Pentecostalism in the continental United States has had many and frequent interactions with the African American experience. This has permitted considerable Americanization, albeit through the filter of African American experience. Pentecostalism in Puerto Rico, although preserving linguistic and institutional autonomy, shared the premises of American Providentialism of the Protestants (Silva Gotay, 1994). It must also be noted that until the 1950s, this first wave of Latino Pentecostalism was strongly influenced by the anti-Catholicism of Fundamentalist and Evangelical Protestantism. Implicit in conversion to Pentecostalism was a fervent rejection of Catholic culture, beliefs, and traditions. Instead of practicing a home-based religion, Pentecostals transferred almost all their worship to the storefront *templos* that housed the congregations. Often the converts knew no cultural idiom other than the Mexican American or the Puerto Rican, so the first hymnals feature traditional forms of the polka, the mazurka, and the like (Ramírez, 1996). But as Latino Pentecostals rose in social standing, the Americanization implicit in its Protestant origins generated the toxins of alienation from Latino culture. During the 1940s and 1960s, Americanization was preached, if not always followed, in many U.S.-based Pentecostal congregations. Finally, the Latinos who joined non-Latino congregations in the Assemblies of God or the Churches of God, in Foursquare Pentecostalism, and in other like denominations came under the pro-American bias of those denominations. Thus, although there are examples in Latino Pentecostalism at a distance from pious colonialism, for the greater part of the twentieth century, Pentecostalism has offered few impediments to Americanization.

The Consequence of Pious Colonialism

We have suggested that from the sixteenth-century Iberian conquest and evangelization until the New Deal under President Franklin D. Roosevelt, pious colonialism explains most of the policies directed by U.S. churches toward Latinos. We have suggested here the many reasons that lead us to use pious colonialism as the explanation for the contradictions of institutionalized religion among Latinos. Pious colonialism, we contend, partially explains why religious practice of Christianity was simultaneously Hispanization under Spain and Americanization under the United States. Both empires privileged the language of the conqueror (first Spanish, then English), repressed native religious traditions, inferiorized native Latino clergy, and stigmatized the people's culture in the Latino homelands.

Pious colonialism under Spain changed during some three hundred years, however, so that when the Spanish Empire began to break apart, the indigenous peoples and the Spanish conquerors had merged into a new people that was different from either of its components. However, the colonialism of the United States over Latino homelands has lasted only about half as long as the Spanish experience. We do not yet know how or whether there will be a similar transculturation of Euro-Americans and Latinos.

We maintain that under the U.S. flag, the churches—Catholic and Protestant—attended to the religious concerns of Latinos, though almost never in ways that confronted the morally evil institution of colonialism. We have tried to suggest that after the wars of conquest, colonialism—like slavery before abolition—was often viewed as a social reality the church ought to ameliorate rather than challenge. Like slavery, colonialism has persisted in its effects, even after its technical disappearance when statehood was granted to the Mexican territories or, in the case of Puerto Rico, because of the special political status conferred in 1952. Despite laudable efforts to combat the pernicious effects of pious colonialism, Latinos lacked the material resources, the intercommunication, and the leadership necessary to reverse these circumstances. The next chapter describes how the tide was finally turned within the churches.

Notes

1. Lamy's refashioning of New Mexican Catholicism to conform to the values of North American society was described by the novelist Willa Cather in *Death Comes to the Archbishop,* and the image of Martínez, like that of all Latinos, suffered from her bias.

4

Syzygy

$\mathcal{W}$ITH THE U.S. CONQUESTS OF THE HOMELANDS, the internal colonialism practiced by both Catholic and Protestant churches reinforced Latinos' subordination within U.S. society and stigmatized the Latino language and styles of religious expression. For Latinos from California to Puerto Rico, the U.S. invasions brought a dreary landscape of greater socioeconomic impoverishment almost without interruption until the New Deal. The socioeconomic portrait of decline and inferiorization was accompanied by ecclesiastical marginalization, as described in the previous chapter. The initial stages of colonization—during the last one-half of the nineteenth century in California, Texas, and the Southwest and during the first two decades of the twentieth century in Puerto Rico—had witnessed the systematic displacement of most local clergy and traditional Latino Catholicism with the installation of bishops, missionaries, and the institutions of Euro-American denominations: Catholic, Protestant, and Pentecostal. What remained of an identifiably Latino core in religious expression was frowned upon as a superstitious embarrassment when it was not actively repressed (Stevens-Arroyo, 1997c).

One result was the internalization of the colonial premise that Latino religion was inferior to U.S. religious expression. Since the ecclesiastical institutions controlled the mechanisms of church leadership—ordination, assignment to clerical posts, and employment in religious schools—the majority of believers seldom heard or saw anyone in a leadership role challenge the effects of pious colonialism. The Protestant, Pentecostal, and Catholic leaders who disagreed with the premise of colonialism often could do little more than soften the impact of official attitudes by demonstrating affection and understanding for the religious traditions of their congregations. Scarcely, if ever, did these efforts confront the ecclesiastical establishment with reasoned theological or pastoral arguments to protest the continuing discrimination against Latino religion. During the next thirty-five years from 1930 to 1965, however, the stage was set to challenge the effectiveness of pious colonialism by demonstrating that the existing policies were no longer effective (Trinidad, 1988:6–8). This chapter examines these three decades and how they heralded dramatic changes.

Movement to Cities

Unprecedented socioeconomic changes were to reconfigure the Latino reality: A mostly rural, agricultural people became urban and proletarian; educational attainments increased, new class divisions were created, a more complex labor force segmentation appeared, and a wider religious diversity arose among Latinos. Perhaps the changes from 1930 until 1965 did more to alter the everyday life of Latinos than had the political transfer of power from Mexico and Spain to the United States after the wars of conquest. These revolutionary transformations had ecclesiastical aftershocks. As long as Latino religion was itself sheltered within a niche of obscurity within pious colonialism, the establishment ecclesiastical authority was willing to allow the practice of a marginalized form of religion. After all, it did not threaten the legitimacy of total religious control. But as the agricultural base of Latino religion was kicked out from under it, there was a drastic need for rapid adaptation to the new circumstances. Nowhere was this more evident than among the Latino migrants to big cities. Although there was less segregation, a larger number of educated people and a growing middle class, city life brought a host of new problems and challenges, and as the Spanish-speaking urban population swelled in the decade after World War II, many churches adopted policies to attract Latinos to city parishes and congregations.

There was considerable variance in the shape of the outreach. Within Catholicism, for instance, pastoral care and social concerns often competed for hegemony. As explained by Patrick McNamara in his careful study of Catholicism among Mexican Americans at the end of this period (McNamara, 1968), these two categories compete for priority within Catholic ministry even today. They are not mutually exclusive, since both are firmly rooted in Catholic teaching about both faith and the sociopolitical roles for an institution that considers good works essential for salvation. But, as McNamara suggests, in the historical process of deciding priorities, these notions generate different positions, often similar to a conservative-liberal division within a political party. The first approach emphasizes the administration of sacraments, church attendance, and piety; the other views the church's mission in terms of aid in matters like housing, health services, job opportunity, and social organization. In the Mexican American Catholic case, the two emphases can coexist within the same agency. For instance, the interdiocesan initiative of the Bishops'

Committee for the Spanish-Speaking was both pastoral and committed to social work. Established in 1945, this was an effort funded and coordinated at a national level to address the religious and social needs of Mexican American migrant workers who annually traveled in Texas and California or northward toward Illinois, Michigan, and Ohio in search of seasonal work (Sandoval, 1990:46–48). In this program, clergy were trained to speak Spanish and provide services to the workers as they traveled from one place to another. Those who chose pastoral care as their primary duty devoted their energies to administering the sacraments. But alongside them were still others who struggled against poor wages and miserable living conditions by taking political action.

Although ostensibly for all Latinos in the United States, the Bishops' Committee really targeted Mexican Americans, the largest of the Latino groups in the United States and the most widely distributed (Privett, 1988). The existing Bishops' Committee was ill prepared to extend its operations to the Puerto Ricans, a different nationality group with its own particularized experience. That appears to be the reason that Cardinal Spellman of New York inaugurated a similar program with both pastoral and social concerns that linked New York and the Northeast with Puerto Rico, thus providing religious attention to migrants from Puerto Rico (Díaz-Stevens, 1993b; Vidal, 1994). Programs such as these differed from pious colonialism by introducing a more solid institutional commitment by churches to social justice that was backed up with higher levels of economic support, but they shared the essential characteristic of the previous approach that viewed Latinos as another episode of the assimilationist pattern of the Euro-American groups.

Protestantism had its own forms of joining the social and the pastoral. Albeit with denominational differences, the settlement houses and other such Protestant institutions ministered to Latino migrants to the cities. The quality of professionalism among Latino Protestants was noteworthy. Not only were they often trained with seminary or college degrees, but they outnumbered the native Latino Catholic clergy. When Protestant Latino leadership sat at the table in civic and political associations, they were generally treated as equals with the frequently Irish American Catholic clergy, although the number of people they represented was significantly smaller. Thus, if one looked for native Latino clerical leaders after the 1950s, they were more likely to be Protestant than Catholic, even though the majority of Latino people professed Catholicism.

The 1950s saw the end of the "benign neglect" phase of pious colonialism and its replacement by a period of zealous apostolate, a time Saúl Trinidad (1988) characterizes as "pastoral of reproduction." Pastoral policy sought to repeat for Latino religion the familiar patterns of parish and congregational participation that had Americanized Euro-American groups. For instance, Catholicism downgraded the national parishes that had been relatively autonomous precisely because they were colonial. Latinos in New York City, Chicago, and Los Angeles were pushed into "integrated parishes," where they shared facilities with the Euro-American groups (Díaz-Stevens, 1993a:58–63; Fitzpatrick, 1971:123–127; Deck, 1989:58–63; Vidal, 1994a:73–87).

By applying the notion of "basement church" (Tomasi, 1975), *Oxcart Catholicism on Fifth Avenue* studied how these integrated parishes for Latinos easily became two autonomous parishes, sharing the same facilities. The Euro-American congregation continued to assume the lion's share of attention within most New York City parishes, while Puerto Ricans were shunted to the basement church facility. It was a decision that visibly represented the inferior position afforded Latinos within existing church attentions. Yet, with their self-generated creativity, the basement churches often functioned for Puerto Ricans much as a national parish. In many Mexican American migration target cities such as Chicago and Detroit (Badillo, 1994:289–296), a similar pattern took shape, and the "basement church" can be considered a Latino experience nationwide.

Protestantism had a long tradition of its members self-selecting their parishes, and the new urban migration increased the need for more Latino congregations made up almost exclusively of Spanish speakers. But while the Latinos were moving in, Euro-Americans were leaving the neighborhoods. Some urban Protestant churches completely closed down; others followed their congregants to the suburbs. In the 1950s, only a few of the more-progressive congregations anticipated a policy that has become popular in the 1990s, namely, hiring a native Spanish-speaking minister to use the facilities to form new Latino congregations.

The Latino migration forced the churches to reexamine policy (Fitzpatrick, 1987). In Catholicism, integration of the parishes resulted in "parishes within the parishes" where the Spanish-speaking congregation in the basement church enjoyed relative autonomy. For Protestants, the urban migration multiplied the number of pastors and congregations so that they had recourse to buying, renting, or using the buildings of the Euro-American congregations. Pentecostals had much greater flexibility and adaptiveness than mainline Protestant churches. Storefronts could be made into churches, literally overnight. Moreover, Pentecostal congregations were traditionally small—sometimes with no more than fifty to eighty members from four or five extended families. But although Pentecostalism did not rival Catholicism in the number of adherents, the intensity of belief of its adherents—usually coupled with a fierce and antagonistic anti-Catholicism—did not go unnoticed. The 1957 study of Pentecostalism among Puerto Ricans in New York by Renato Poblete and Thomas O'Dea of Fordham University portrayed the anomie of the newly arrived migrants as the principal cause of conversion to Pentecostalism. It was argued that as Puerto Ricans assimilated into U.S. society, the attraction to Pentecostalism would wane along with the anomie that caused conversion. This prediction has not proven to be true: Latino Pentecostals have not moved en masse to Catholicism as economic circumstances have improved.

In a history that is still being researched, Latino Pentecostalism during the 1940s and 1950s suffered from the pressures of assimilation that were generalized throughout second-generation Latinos. Language of worship was a key issue. Does a congregation preserve Spanish and resist Americanization? Or does a church choose English and alienate a wave of newcomers? Puerto Rican Pentecostals did not feel the impact that loss of Spanish presented to Mexican American congregations because Spanish remained the language of Puerto Rico even after the U.S. invasion. But as larger numbers of Puerto Ricans migrated to New York City during the Great Migration (1946–1964), the conflicts described in Chapter 3 at the time of Juan L. Lugo surfaced again. The Spanish-speaking Puerto Rican Pentecostals and English-speaking Pentecostalism wrangled over territorial jurisdiction in the 1950s as they had in the 1920s.

There were also Pentecostal "heresies." Baptism in the name of Jesus, rather than in the name of the Trinity had produced the Oneness position of the Apostolic Assembly of the Faith in Jesus Christ that was described in the previous chapter. In Puerto Rico, there were other "heresies" such as in the congregations founded by Juanita García. Called "La Diosa Mita," she fought Pentecostal ministers for rights to preach and came to the conclusion that she was the living incarnation of the Holy Spirit, much as Jesus was the incarnation of God the Father (Díaz Ramírez, 1975). However unorthodox this preaching might have been to other Pentecostals, her congregation has enjoyed great success in attracting converts and achieving financial stability through a network of profitable church-run industries.

Despite the subordination of Latinos to Euro-Americans that was implicit in the assimilation or integrationist premises of these policies among almost all the denominations, there were important results that bear on the emergence of distinctly Latino religious organizations. For Catholics, the parochial schools began to enroll more Latino pupils, while seminaries and convents experienced a significant increase of Latina and Latino candidates during the 1950s. Within Protestantism and Pentecostalism, a cohort of capable Latino pastors and seminary professors began their journeys to leadership positions.

The Latino Religious Resurgence

The presence of Latinos in small but significant numbers among the clergy ranks and in Catholic sisterhoods was often interpreted as proof that

Americanization would work and that assimilation was a desirable goal. It was expected that missionary work would produce native Latinos anxious to join the Euro-Americans in the apostolate. The pattern among Catholic women and several religious congregations and institutes of sisters merits more systematic and comparative study. But piecing together the accounts from scattered sources discloses some success stories. In New Mexico and California, the Sisters of Victory Knoll provide an example of an order that started among Euro-Americans in the 1920s and by dint of successful catechetical work among Mexican Americans, gradually became a sisterhood with a large Mexican American membership by the 1970s (Burns, 1994: 160–162).

However, religious life for Puerto Rican women has the most impressive history. In an effort to duplicate in Puerto Rico the Catholic school systems of Philadelphia and New York City, the Sisters of Saint Joseph, the School Sisters of Notre Dame, and the Sisters of Saint Dominic were among the most prominent of congregations invited to make foundations on the island. But in 1930, the Misioneras del Buen Pastor were founded because the needs of Puerto Rico required different kinds of apostolate, especially catechetical education and home visitation. This had always been the focus of the Missionary Servants of the Most Blessed Trinity, or Trinitarians, whose presence in Puerto Rico produced a very early and significant influx of Puerto Rican vocations. Similarly, in 1948 a Puerto Rican congregation called Las Hermanas de Fátima was founded by the saintly Madre Dominga Guzmán, who was a member of the Dominican Sisters. The new native order, still nurtured by the Amityville mother house in Long Island, New York, focused on home visitation and catechetical work instead of teaching in parochial schools. As Puerto Rico was rapidly urbanized in the 1950s, the number of vocations to these native congregations increased, helping to solidify these two orders and, eventually, to establish houses outside Puerto Rico. The growing size of the Puerto Rican middle class also brought native vocations to the established orders, not only to those of the United States but to some of the Spanish-based orders as well. By the 1960s, there was a prominent cohort of religious native Puerto Ricans, both men and women, in influential orders like the Dominicans and the Trinitarians, with resources such as the College of the Sacred Heart, run by an order of the same name. The Jesuits from the New York Province had come late to Puerto Rico, but they had also begun to acquire high visibility through their high school, San Ignacio. Similar patterns of "going native" occurred in the Southwest and California: For example, the Sisters of Mercy in San José, California, were successful in attracting Latina members; the Jesuit Province in New Orleans recruited Mexican American members in Texas. It appeared that the work of pious colonialism, begun by the first missionaries, would be completed by native recruits.

Yet abruptly, these trends ended and reversed course after the Second Vatican Council. In what we have chosen to call "the Latino Religious Resurgence," a new role for Latino religion was proclaimed, elaborated, and implemented. Latino Catholic church leaders redefined their ecclesiastical roles. They announced a mission of restoring and redeveloping Latino religion because it was distinct and nonassimilable to the Euro-American experience. The leadership produced many documents that, with considerable theological sophistication, explained the new trend. Latino Protestants saw the changes in Latino Catholicism as a welcome development and took their own initiatives to foster the same process within their denominations. Almost simultaneously, a new theological perspective that had been developed in Latin America entered explosively into U.S. religion. Called the "theology of liberation," and linked to the pastoral planning mandated by the Second Vatican Council, the new theology inoculated the resurgence from ecclesiastical condemnation. How could churches in the United States, which has often argued that it is different from Europe, condemn what Latin American believers had expressed as the particular theology of Spanish-speaking people? Perhaps more important, there was considerable emphasis upon education and leadership formation so that the new vision of Latino religion was rapidly diffused through agencies, organizations, and institutions that had previously served an assimilationist function (Cadena, 1989). In effect, Latino religion, both Catholic and Protestant, dissolved the last bonds to pious colonialism by subverting the very institutions that had been used for Americanization and reconfiguring them into vehicles for Latino reaffirmation.

Finally, these changes were tied to militancy on social justice issues. Parishes and congregations became the core membership, and meeting rooms at the local church became the assembly points for many neighborhood organizations and agencies, many of which received government funds. These new political roles were matched by effective—and sometimes spectacular—ritual celebration in Latino cultural idioms. The liturgy in local churches often assembled musicians and singers who regularly produced worship services that entertained as well as inspired. At times, people came to church because of these services. In other words, the substantial and dramatic changes formulated by leadership were transmitted to Latino churchgoers in ways that were both pragmatically beneficial and culturally popular.

This chapter is about the nature of this Latino Religious Resurgence and offers a theoretical exploration of its historical importance. Our intention is not to write the history of the resurgence but rather to stress the issues that need to be addressed when that history is written. We rely on the important work that has already been done, particularly in the Notre Dame Series on the history of Hispanic Catholics (1994). But the resurgence affected all Latino believers, not just the adherents of Catholicism.

This definition of the Latino Religious Resurgence as a social movement requires further explanation. Everything is always changing, as Heraclitus reminded us when he first stepped into his famous river. Certainly, there is a sense in which the processual concatenation of events represents the flow of time. But social change implies more. As Charles Morazé of *Annales* observes: "[A]ll social change is historical change; but historical changes exist which are not social changes" (Vázquez and Olábarri, 1995:457). As we understand it, the point here is that the intensity and rapidity of change becomes qualitative, making its effects more sweeping than otherwise anticipated. Everyday events of historical change become social change when they produce a new cognitive understanding of self and community to accommodate the intensity and rapidity of the situation. With due genuflections to the works of Eric Voeglin with his "leap in being," to Thomas Kuhn and his study of scientific paradigms, and to Samuel Eisenstadt and his use of "crystallization" as a stage of civilizational development (1987), we propose to link social change to the notions of tradition and colonialism that we developed in the previous chapters.

Periods of sudden and dramatic change are relatively infrequent, but they usually attract the attention of historians and social scientists. Take, for instance, the Great Awakenings of colonial and early U.S. history. Historians have charted a significant and dramatic intensity to religious expression that had profound effects upon society and politics. We chose the word "resurgence" to name the Latino phenomenon because it shares certain characteristics with the nineteenth-century Italian *risorgimento*. The comparison between the two is offered here as an explanatory tool: Both were social, political, and cultural movements that brought unity to disparate regional nationalities and the establishment of an institution to serve them all. Can we not examine the Latino movement with analytical concepts that have helped in understanding the Italian experience? As in the insightful title *The Great Awakening: Event and Exegesis* (Rutman, 1977), the event and its exegesis can be distinguished within the Latino Religious Resurgence. The Italian *risorgimento* and the Latino Religious Resurgence were different historical events, but an analytical exegesis of the two as processes allows for the discovery of similarities.

Although not a religious movement like the Great Awakening, the *risorgimento* has characteristics that seem to resemble those of the Latino experience:

> It [the *risorgimento*] describes a number of different transformations—the collapse of the *ancien régime* and the development of a parliamentary system, the breakdown of traditional rural society and the birth of modern, urban life, the transition from a feudal to a capitalist economy and the replacement of local or regional identities by a single national culture—all of which have been central to present-day understanding of historical change. (Riall, 1994:1)

The Latino Religious Resurgence had similar consequences: It problematized the ability of the churches to practice pious colonialism toward Latinos, and it introduced forms of democratizing self-governance into church disciplines; it transformed the religious practices common under pious colonialism that were dependent on the agricultural cycles of a rural Latino populace into new expressions for religious traditions, social consciousness, and imagination proper to urbanized communities; and it accelerated the process of creating within church usage a transnational label of "Hispanic/Latino" that went beyond the self-contained categories of nationality identity like Puerto Rican, Mexican, Cuban, and so forth. These cultural identities were joined to an ideology that bore resemblance to the unification of the fragmented states and kingdoms of Italy during the *risorgimento*. And, because it occurred in the twentieth century and not the nineteenth, the Latino Religious Resurgence widened the institutional leadership roles of women, a trend currently called "the feminization of religion."

Another similarity between the two phenomena is the relatively short time frame that governed both. The Italian experience admits of various interpretations, but there seems general agreement that the *risorgimento* was closely linked to the abortive attempts by the Republican Young Italy of Giuseppe Mazzini to drive Austria out of the Italian peninsula in the uprisings of 1834–1837, which ended in Mazzini's exile to London. The failure of these early revolutionary attempts fomented the cultural ideal of a united Italy. In 1843, a priest from the Piedmont region suggested the pope as the leader of this drive for Italian unification and the reforms proclaimed in the papal states by a newly elected Pope Pius IX in 1846 offered a reformist path to a new Italy. Thus, in 1847, Camilo Benso di Cavour inaugurated a new publication, *Il Risorgimento*, that properly baptized these diverse impulses from several political segments of Italian society into a single movement (Ghisalberti, 1991:104ff). The movement fed popular culture with images of a common Italian history. Some of the operas of Giuseppe Verdi, for instance, became instruments of awakening nationalism among all the different regional populations of the peninsula. The political goals of the movement were cast as restoration of past glories that would foster a rebirth of cultural richness and economic prosperity, an argument that may be the most lasting legacy of the movement (Riall, 1994:70–74, 80–82). Scarcely fourteen years later, in March 1861, Vittorio Emanuele of Piedmont became the king of Italy. And after intrigues, countermovements and participation in the Austro-Prussian War of 1866, the unification was completed in 1870 with the occupation of Rome. Thus, with a preparation period of about a decade before the appearance of the journal and a concluding decade after the proclamation of the first kingdom, the *risorgimento* took place within about thirty-five years.

The Latino Religious Resurgence developed with a similar rhythm. After a decade of stirrings within the Latino communities, there was an intense period of advocacy and organization between 1967 until 1984, followed by a period of consolidation that is still under way. It is always controversial to make certain dates or events the beginnings of movements, but 1967 is not a totally arbitrary choice. In 1967 the poem "Yo Soy Joaquín" was published by Rudolfo "Corky" González. While much of the turmoil among Chicanos in the 1960s had been in opposition to discrimination and unjust treatment, this literary creation caught the mood of the militants and expressed in positive terms their goals and aspirations, quickly becoming a sort of anthem of Chicano identity. The creation owed a great deal to the narrative form of the Mexican *corrido* and borrowed on popular images used to describe the resistance of Joaquín Murrieta (Stavans, 1995:64–67), who avenged the rape and murder of his wife by Anglos in Fresno County during the Gold Rush in California. Murrieta stole back to Fresno in disguise to kill each of the perpetrators before he was himself murdered in 1853. A Mexican folk hero celebrated in popular *corridos*, the Nobel Prize–winning poet, Pablo Neruda, made him a Chilean in a poetic dramatization "Fulgor y muerte de Joaquín Murrieta."[1] Murrieta was in the spirit of Juan "Cheno" Cortina and Gregorio Cortez, who were unjustly classified as "*bandidos*" by the Texas Rangers in an effort to halt their resistance to injustice against the native Chicanos (Acuña, 1972:38, 47–50). What made Joaquín different from the Texas *bandidos* was his ability to control his rage and the artful stealth of his relentless pursuit of revenge. This quality suggested the Chicano "difference" from the Mexican revolutionary heroes, Pancho Villa and Emiliano Zapata.

When Corky González's poem was distributed to Chicano student leadership groups, it struck a chord responsive to the search for their identity (Muñoz, 1989:60–64). The hunger for knowledge about Chicano history, culture, and art was to be filled in a more academic fashion by the launching of *El Grito: A Journal of Contemporary Mexican-American Thought* by Professor Octavio Romano-V., an anthropologist at the University of California, Berkeley, also in 1967 and by the journal *Aztlán*, emanating from UCLA in 1970 (Muñoz, 1989:143–145). Like Cavour's publication of *Il Risorgimento*, "Yo Soy Joaquín" and journals like *El Grito* and *Aztlán* became visible and effective symbols around which many hitherto diverse Chicano causes could be united.

Significantly, "Yo Soy Joaquín" closed with an affirmation of the religious dimension of Chicano identity. Mixing together the native Mexican religion with Christianity, the poem claimed a composite face for the Chicano:

> *I am the masses of my people and*
> *I refuse to be absorbed.*
> *I am Joaquín*
> *The odds are great*

> *but my spirit is strong*
> *My faith unbreakable*
> *My blood is pure*
> *I am Aztec Prince and Christian Christ*
> *I SHALL ENDURE!*
> *I WILL ENDURE!*
> (cited in Stevens-Arroyo, 1980:20)

Thus, in 1967, a special role for religion was ascribed to the militancy of Chicanos. As will be detailed later on, events of that year in Puerto Rico also wed militancy and religion, so the specifically religious agenda of the resurgence could be viewed as a different facet of the same struggle both among Chicanos and Puerto Ricans. Indeed, the use of the romantic names "Aztlán" and "Borinquén" for their respective homelands suggests that similar cultural processes were operative (Klor de Alva, 1991).

The resurgence, so dependent on the tumultuous changes of the 1960s for its genesis, ends in the early 1980s with Ronald Reagan in the White House and John Paul II in the Vatican. The period of militant expansiveness was finished, as the institutionalization of progressive policies became a major focus for Latino religious leadership. In 1983, the National Council of Catholic Bishops issued a pastoral letter called "The Hispanic Presence: Challenge and Commitment" that repeated in an official ecclesiastical document many of the themes of cultural and religious identity expressed in "Yo Soy Joaquín." One year later, in 1984, the United Methodist Church adopted a pastoral plan that was similar to the policy changes embraced by the Catholic Church. Along with similar documents from other denominations that recognized the legitimacy of Latino religion, by 1983 we have evidence of the capitulation of church institutions and the beginning of a new phase, wherein organizations rather than movements played the major role.

It could be argued that this comparison with the Italian *risorgimento* suffers in disproportion with the goals: The Italian experience created a modern nation-state, whereas the Latino effort merely achieved policy changes within a religious body. But although the scale was much smaller, the Latino Religious Resurgence was analogous to the Italian experience because in both movements, broad cultural and social aspirations were converted into organizations that greatly influenced an institution. For instance, the resurgence leaders made compromises and concessions as they journeyed toward institutionalization in a process similar to the one that made liberals and the Kingdom of Piedmont the principal beneficiaries of the *risorgimento* over the radical Republicans and the Italian South (Riall, 1994:26–28, 77–78). Additionally, although there were antagonisms, in the name of a pan-peninsular identity of *italianità*, there was a trade-off of regional identities (Riall, 1994:74–75), just as "Latino"—despite certain frictions between Mexican Americans and the other groups—has been accepted in most quarters as the term of unity.

Basic Characteristics of
the Latino Religious Resurgence

The intensity of the 1967–1984 period is essential for understanding contemporary Latino religious experience. Like the colonial Great Awakening, the Latino Religious Resurgence was characterized by a revival of religious commitment. The revivals of the Great Awakening called attention to the differences of the colonists from their transatlantic counterparts in order to elicit new religious expressions proper to the American experience. Put in terms that were used in our chapter on tradition, the Great Awakening of colonial America stoked the fires of temporality and social location by asking the Protestant religious imagination to reinterpret life in America within the context of loyalty to Gospel values. According to some interpreters of this period in the preindependence English colonies, when preachers spoke of a special "American" calling they created religious experiences that influenced the process of the political separation from England proclaimed on July 4, 1776 (Hull and Moran, 1989; Lovejoy, 1985). In the insightful terminology of Rhys Williams (1996), "culture and ideology" had united in religion to form a political resource.

The Latino Religious Resurgence had a similar effect that gave grassroots believers a new conception of themselves and their responsibilities as Christian believers in the United States. This new awareness gained its religious legitimacy not by an appeal to its novelty but through its roots in centuries-old Christian experiences and even through the model of apostolic Christianity. Thus, the intense period of new cultural awareness by Latinos about their religious identity was a "resurgence" of something that had previously existed, just as the Great Awakening was portrayed as the rediscovery of old truths. But whereas the colonial Great Awakening depended upon preachers to communicate the new vision, the Latino Religious Resurgence used various forms of leadership formation to accomplish much the same thing. The rest of this book will be necessary to adequately describe and evaluate this educational aspect of the Latino Religious Resurgence.

These comparisons with the Italian *risorgimento,* on the one hand, and with the colonial Great Awakening, on the other, should not be misinterpreted. We are not suggesting that the Latino Religious Resurgence is a carbon copy of the other movements. Still less are we advocating a cyclical notion of history that would rule the flow of history with rigid patterns: In no way do we suggest that issues of leadership, change, politics, and the like correspond in every detail to the Latino Resurgence and these other two events. Our comparisons are a heuristic tool, helping us understand an event that is less clear through reference to better-known events. Nor do we feel comfortable with Karl Mannheim's term "zeitgeist," because that term implies that every social wind was blowing in the same direction: During the Latino Religious Resurgence, the leadership often had to tack against the wind. After all, the greatest gains came during the Nixon presidency, which was not a paragon of liberalism and actively sought to make the "ethnic" Catholic vote (meaning Euro-American) more conservative in its politics.

There are always risks in being bold within academia. We have asked ourselves several hard questions. When is it appropriate to fit social change to a schema, pattern, or periodization? Is not making 1967 the start of the Latino Religious Resurgence as arbitrary as placing the start of the Italian *risorgimento* in 1847 with the publication by Cavour of the paper with the same name? After all, the events and circumstances before 1847 that enabled the publication of *Il Risorgimento* were as important as the publication itself. In the case of the colonial Great Awakening, some sociologists have opined that the increase in church membership during the crucial years of the Great Awakening, 1726–1756, are not attributable to revivalism but rather are general and persistent demographic trends (Hull and Moran, 1989:488). In the contemporary case of the Chicano movement of the late 1960s, Mario García (1989) reminds us that the years 1930–1960 were marked by significant advances and capable Mexican American sociopolitical leadership. He makes the case that too much can be claimed for a movement when the historian does not scrutinize its antecedents. We also recognize that Puerto Rico has a history that is uniquely its own. Although we would emphasize that the resurgence opened up greater lines of communication between the island and the continent after 1967, we acknowledge throughout this book that in Puerto Rico, the linkages between religion and social change developed sooner than 1967 and more explosively than in the states. Finally, our colleagues Rudy V. Busto and Daniel Ramírez have suggested in the two 1996 PARAL symposia that long before the 1960s, Latino Pentecostalism achieved many of the goals of the resurgence, albeit on a smaller scale.

We approach periodization, therefore, with a sobering fear of overemphasizing the importance of individuals. We want to avoid the trap of the "Great Man approach" to social change or to its equivalent that makes a single document or book the sole cause of change. These extremes are as bad as their opposite—a reductionism that makes social forces and economic determinism into factors that are as inexorable as they are impersonal.

Religion and Social Change

At the risk of oversimplification, the golden mean that balances the personal and the ideational, on the one hand, and the economic and social, on the other, seems the best way to understand social change. Aristotelian philosophy describes all living things as the conjunction of matter and form, of matter and spirit. By analogy, social change is created from the infusion of the spirit of ideas and charismatic leadership into material conditions, which themselves come to life as the movement. Ideas without material conditions remain only ideas—not social change. As Christopher Hill puts it: "Steam is essential to driving a railway engine, but neither a locomotive nor a permanent way can be built out of steam" (cited in Vázquez and Olábarri, 1995:283). But material conditions, no matter how open to social change, remain inert without the infusion of the ideal, just as the locomotive remains stationary until the fires produce the steam to turn its wheels.

It is not the ideas and ideology alone but the linkage of these ideas to the collectivity that effects social change. The capacity of ideas to motivate collective action gives them importance. When many individuals view the collectivity as a means of advancing a cause they hold in common, social change becomes more likely. The 1980 book *Prophets Denied Honor* contains sufficient materials drawn from the period of the resurgence to illustrate this process. Clearly, the Latino Religious Resurgence was characterized by the rapid and thoroughgoing diffusion of leadership roles. The democratization within the churches for pastoral initiative was rapidly imparted to the laity in local parishes and congregations. The impact of this democratization was particularly noticeable for its inclusion of women. As was detailed in Chapter 3, Ana María Díaz-Stevens's description of the matriarchal core (1993b) is a departure point for understanding the roles of Latinas. And during the resurgence, these traditional roles were professionalized and established as normal and necessary patterns for Latino religious organization.

We are studying real people in real situations, and although we cannot reproduce here all the detail that a history of the period merits, we were actors in the Latino Religious Resurgence. We lived through that period and know that it differed in intensity, scope, and impact from the periods immediately before and after. But recognizing these individual particulars is not the same as being bewildered by them. Rather, the events are processed as symbols by the movement that agrees upon an interpretation of the events. This creates a collective memory for the movement and reinforces its cohesiveness.

The "history" of the movement is itself the result of the process, rather than its cause. For instance, during the *risorgimento*, the glories of Rome became more glorious because the supporters of the Italian unification found it compelling to compare their cause with a long-ago Golden Age. The Latino resurgence produced an idealized picture of Latino culture to help define Latinos as somehow different from the Euro-American believers, justify a plan of action, and motivate the members for collective action. Without forgetting our Mexican, Puerto Rican, Cuban, or other origins, we began stressing our similarities as Latinos in terms of cultural traits with concepts like "family life," "love of fiesta," and "popular religiosity." In our pastoral centers and theological books, we recovered a legacy that showed we had more in common with one another than with Euro-Americans.

It is not useful to bestow a magical quality upon concepts such as "the people," "the masses," "conscientization" (*conscienzaõ*), "liberation," and "culture." These terms were used by participants within the religious resurgence for ideological purposes that need to be carefully scrutinized. As suggested in *Prophets Denied Honor*, ideological divisions within the resurgence were present from its beginning. Despite these differences within this movement, however, there was also a set of premises that became the core beliefs of the movement's members.

We believe that the documents, position papers, teaching outlines, and grassroots-oriented communications from pamphlets to mimeographed notes express these premises. *Prophets Denied Honor*, published in 1980 by Orbis Books, offered a representative sample of the written production of the resurgence within Catholicism. In order to trace the popularity of these ideas, we can examine the diffusion of such documents generated by a specific group of leaders and imparted to Latino churchgoers, another process outlined in *Prophets Denied Honor*, as also are such practices as attention to hymns (see also Díaz-Stevens, 1993c; Stevens-Arroyo, 1996c), songs, liturgical texts, and preaching. Although more extensive study is certainly needed, there is sufficient evidence to repeat here a previous judgment: Crystallization of a new Latino religious identity took place during the resurgence (Stevens-Arroyo, 1994). The new identity was communicated in parallel fashion among Latinos in many other denominations as well. In sum, the Latino Religious Resurgence provided three of the functions that scholars view as the characteristics of a social movement, as follows:

> identity (definition of the protest group); opposition (a challenge to the repression of certain ideas or interests); and integrity (actions based on universal values and universal realities). Social movements . . . influence the course of historical development taking a leading role in social change. They perform several functions: They *mediate* between individuals and structures or social realities; they serve to *clarify collective beliefs*; and, lastly, they exert *pressure* on public authorities and the elites in power. (Alain Touraine, *Sociologies de l'action*, Paris, 1965, cited in Vázquez and Olábarri, 1995:373)

Generational Change

We can also view the Latino Religious Resurgence as the result of a generational change in Latino leadership. Historian Mario García has adapted this idea in his analysis of Mexican American leaders from 1930 until 1960. He cites a definition from Marvin Rintala (García, 1989:3) to define a political generation: "a group of human beings who have undergone the same basic historical experiences during their formative years." Emphasizing that "a political generation is not a biological generation," García cites Karl Mannheim, who previously developed this idea within social science: "We shall therefore speak of a generation as an actuality only where a concrete bond is created between members of a generation by their being exposed to the social and intellectual symptoms of a process of dynamic destabilization" (García:4, n. 13).

Indeed, Mannheim's term "zeitgeist," literally meaning "the spirit of the times," was frequently employed within Post-Conciliar Catholicism as a standard by which to measure reforms that were expected to conform to new social needs. But as pointed out earlier, zeitgeist is less helpful in analyzing the mind-set of contradictory social forces, for example, civil rights activists, Vietnam War protesters, and Nixon's "Silent Majority," during the same period. In which direction was the wind of social change blowing? Thus, the reason for employing a generational approach to the study of the Latino Religious Resurgence is to better analyze the *mentalité* it created among a cohort of Latino leaders with their own special perspectives on church and society, often in opposition to majority opinions. The interactions among the several forces form an integral part of U.S. religious history.

The Mentalité *of the Resurgence*

The appearance of the Latino *mentalité* was not magical or without contradictions and conflicts. The new paradigm for Latino religion came after a "lag" between the time that the routines of everyday life were altered and leadership was developed. Those who experienced the resurgence often did not recognize the unique importance of the decisions that were made at the time. Frequently, participants were more focused on personal and contingent factors than on historical impact. Dislike of a church official, eagerness to obtain a new position, the size of the meeting place, the effectiveness of the audio hookup, and even the weather on a particular day were all at play in the lived history, even if only the major events are later recalled as "remembered history."

Our analysis places the Latino Religious Resurgence in the context of socioeconomic events taking place in the United States and religious change among its churches, but we have also reserved a role for intellectual leadership. The period of the resurgence produced a heightened intensity that altered the collective understanding of religiously affiliated Latinos. The attainment of a new consciousness stirred religious convictions and redefined responsibilities to God and the community. The religious resurgence was not divorced from the material reality that produced it, but neither was it inevitable. In order to understand how this movement took place, it is necessary to account for both social forces, which plod ever onward, and leadership, which is often mercurial.

We view the Latino Religious Resurgence as a movement that was different from the Chicano Power movement, the United Farm Workers or the Latino Studies' movements, the Puerto Rican Nationalist or Independence movements. Although it was connected to these other realities, it was essentially a religious movement. The Latino Religious Resurgence encountered the dominant Euro-American church *mentalité*. Two worldviews came into conflict in a struggle over who was to set policy for the institution. Thus, there was the *mentalité* or the collective memory of the Latinos, on the one hand, and that of the church establishments, on the other. Certainly, social scientists can explore how the religious resurgence impacted on Latino voting patterns or on the people's view of social issues. But correlations such as these do not sum up the dynamics of the movement and can even distort its achievements by imposing political goals upon a movement with a strikingly different trajectory.

This is one place where we differ from standard Weberian methodology (compare Kniss, 1988). For us, the social action of individuals and groups does not depend so much upon rationality as it does on a "constructed rationality," as Crozier and Friedberg have suggested (Vázquez and Olábarri, 1995:367). In grasping the mind-set of a particular person or group engaged in social action, a social scientist may find that motives for behavior can be supremely elusive. We admit that *mentalité,* collective memory, and other such concepts imply a psychological dimension to each social action. But we think analysis is possible even when hard data on the motives are not available. Much as Neil Smelser does, we tie the social to the cognitive (Vázquez and Olábarri, 1995:471). If individuals inform their actions by perception, institutions can be described as acting in somewhat the same way. After all, boards and committees are made up of individuals acting under psychological motives. Thus, the broad category of cognitive action implicit in any social movement can be applied to religion.

The Leitmotif of the Resurgence

The leitmotif of the Latino Religious Resurgence was equality for Latinos within the churches. During the first half of the 1960s, the Civil Rights movement had offered the United States a vision of a peaceful path toward legislation focused on the demands of African Americans. It produced an attempt at equal protection under the law that was accompanied by new federal programs to make war on poverty in the country. These important events heightened public awareness about race relations between black and white peoples. Soon there were Latino voices saying that the same measures needed to be applied to Latinos. These were mostly college-age voices—often the children of the 1950s generation.

Until the resurgence, Protestants and Pentecostals generally continued in the same trajectory of Americanization that had been initiated with pious colonialism, albeit with more Latino professional leaders than in Catholicism, where non-Latino clergy were the rule rather than the exception. A great contribution of Protestantism and Pentecostalism to Latino religion was and continues to be the rapid inclusion of the ethnic leaders within realms of the ministry. Protestant ministers were perceived by most Latinos as having more in common with the people than the celibate Catholic clergy or the Catholic sisters in religious garb. Even though there were limits to how high a Latino could rise within the more structured establishments of the Protestant churches, there was considerable pride among Latino Protestants in the democratizing traditions of the Reformation, which permitted the people greater control over their official religion than was enjoyed by Catholic Latinos and Latinas in Pre-Conciliar Catholicism. Protestant ministers in mainline denominations were often among the first Latino religious leaders to support the new causes.

The institutional churches frequently gave verbal and financial support to these causes, but until 1965, the churches themselves were not usually the targets of protest (Stevens-Arroyo, 1980/1996). However, when the existing ecclesiastical structures came under fire, not surprisingly, the most vulnerable was Catholicism. The hierarchical nature of Catholic authority depends very much on clerical status that descends from pope to bishops and clergy, who must publicly agree with their superiors. This hierarchical power had been frequently invoked under pious colonialism to control or delegitimate Latino clergy, who raised questions about official policies. Meanwhile, laypersons had little institutional power within Catholicism and were able to control only traditional Latino popular religiosity.

But the hierarchical power, while continually accessible, is not always invoked. In many of the more common decisions about religious practice, Catholicism is not the autocratic monolith it is sometimes perceived to be. There was considerable variation from parish to parish as individual clerics could be more or less interested in developing lay participation in the running of the parish. Thus, for instance, the national parishes and Spanish-language chapels usually conferred considerable status upon the local lay leaders of the various *cofradías, mutualistas,* and community organizations (Burns, 1994:145–146).

Catholicism's Cursillo Movement

The most important new urbanized form of Latino religion preceding the resurgence was the Cursillo movement. Although it appeared almost solely among Catholics, its importance to all Latinos cannot be overstated.

Introduced to the United States from Spain in 1957 and established by
1959, the Cursillo sowed seeds of change because in its affirmation of a
specifically Spanish-rooted Catholicism, it appealed directly to Latinos in
ways that other movements filtered through the existing Catholic structures did not (Vidal, 1994a:109–111; Deck, 1989:67–69; Hinojosa,
1994:114–119).

In pre–Vatican Council Catholicism, the Cursillo provided for liturgies
in Spanish, heavily influenced by folk music and cultural traditions.
Sermons and instruction were provided by the Cursillistas themselves.
They spoke in the Spanish of the people and based their preaching on daily
experiences. The Cursillo movement, and all the pastoral infrastructure
necessary to make it effective, provided a significant sharpening for Latino
Catholic identity and laid the groundwork for much of what was to follow
(Rendón, 1971:323–325).

The recruitment of Latinos into the Cursillo movement was generally
concentrated on the working class and the poor. The island of Puerto Rico,
as the exception to the rule, emphasized contact with the professional
classes, and the movement was correspondingly weaker on the island than
among Puerto Ricans in New York City and the northeastern United
States. Some Latinos who had already been recognized as leaders within
Catholicism, especially those from the professional classes, resisted the
claims that the Cursillo was a necessary badge of Latino Catholicism.
Cursillistas sometimes looked suspiciously upon such professionals, who
seemed to rely more on their social status than on a faith commitment for
prominence in the church. However, more often than not, the professionals
made the Cursillo themselves, so that it can be considered to be class based
but not class biased.

The Catholic Cursillistas had a deep loyalty to Catholic teaching, an experience of community as Latinos, a mode of grassroots organization that
resembled tightly knit kinship groups, and the fervor of Evangelicals in
sharing the faith. The focus of the Cursillo transformed cultural
Catholicism into a practiced and informed faith for most Latinos who took
the three-day exercises. Moreover, the conversion experience that was woven into the Cursillo added a valuable personal dimension to the Catholic
religious experience that was generally unattainable for most Latinos except through the Pentecostal churches. The movement had created a way
of knowing religious truth—testimony or witness—that was new to Latino
Catholicism.

Even the loyalty to ecclesiastical authority preached in the Cursillo was
not a blind loyalty but one based on Gospel criteria. For instance, the
Cursillo empowered laymen and (later) laywomen to be "rectors" for the exercises. Clerics were excluded from decisionmaking roles within the movement until they each made the Cursillo. Moreover, in many cases the clerical

role on the team directing the exercises was subordinated to the authority of the lay rector. The movement cast traditional Catholic clerical authority as one subordinated to communitarian goals. Even before the radical reform of hierarchical authority that was launched by the Vatican Council, the Cursillo movement had begun to push Latino religion away from docility toward the hierarchy that had characterized pious colonialism.

Not everything in the Cursillo was progressive, of course: The movement preserved deep suspicions against Protestantism, Pentecostalism, and Santería. The Cursillo distributed signs for the doors of its members that warned Protestant and Pentecostal evangelizers that a Catholic family resided inside and that no "propaganda of sects" was welcomed. Practices derived from Santería or Spiritism were derided as "witchcraft" (*brujería*) or "devil worship." And the working-class character of the membership often allowed strong leaders to dominate decisionmaking. In sum, the egalitarianism and democratization of the Cursillo was limited mostly to matters of church participation. In official matters, the Cursillo maintained and even strengthened a hierarchical perception of ecclesiastical authority.

An example before the resurgence of how the movement resisted efforts to move it toward a more radical view of church is provided in *Oxcart Catholicism on Fifth Avenue*. Ana María Díaz-Stevens describes how the Cursillistas rejected the efforts of the late Monsignor Robert Fox of the Spanish Apostolate Office to inject political themes into the San Juan Fiesta, New York City's celebration of Catholic Puerto Ricanness. Fox's leadership style was a reminder of pious colonialism. Although he was sincerely committed to the Puerto Ricans and to all of New York's urban poor, Fox's politics were those of the progressive clergy. His progressive vision of political involvement was not cast in the language of the people's experience as preached in the Cursillo. Monsignor Fox and his liberal clergy and "religious" (a Catholic term for men and women living under vows according to a religious rule of life) were unsuccessful in transmitting their political convictions to the Cursillistas, not because the Cursillistas did not support social justice but because Monsignor Fox and his circle did not connect these concerns to the people's religious commitments. Consequently, Summer in the City, Fox's most successful program, was viewed as a paternalistic imposition of "relating to others" (López, 1973:309, 270–275) and a waste of time in terms of organizing Puerto Ricans for political action. We think Monsignor Fox underestimated the central importance of the Cursillo as a religious experience. The failure to rally the people for a political agenda says more about Monsignor Fox and Catholic liberals than it does about the Cursillistas (Díaz-Stevens, 1990, 1993a; see Deck, 1995a). In contrast, César Chávez was very successful in bringing the Cursillo into La Causa in a process that will be described further on.

It is important to be careful not to claim too much for the Cursillo. The movement was democratizing in the sense that it gave new forms of participation in church life to Latinos, regardless of their ability to speak English and their social class. But the movement repeated in popular fashion a traditionalist scholastic theology of sacraments and the church: It did not dethrone the hierarchical authority of bishops and clergy. That was the principal reason that the appearance of the Cursillo movement in 1957 was not enough to launch the resurgence. The Cursillo was effective in helping its members view the faith through Latino experience and the role of Latino leadership. But the Cursillistas were caught with a theological vocabulary that could not capture the élan of empowerment that was articulated by leaders like Monsignor Fox. Until the resurgence supplied a more dynamic theological language, the Latino Cursillistas could only nibble at the edges of the movement's conservatism.

There are many examples within the Cursillo movement of this struggle between a democratizing agenda and a hierarchical theology. For instance, the movement endorsed the male-centered authority of traditional Latino families by requiring that the man of the house should make the Cursillo first. The wife would be allowed to make the Cursillo only after the husband, and the rules imported from Spain stipulated that single women would not be allowed to take part. This last stipulation did not sit well with single Latinas who pushed for and were successful in rewriting the movement's rule to fit Latina expectations. This adaptation to women's roles in the United States is a good example of a potentially radicalizing current running beneath the apparently placid surface of the Cursillo's appeal to tradition. It built upon the foundations of popular religiosity and celebrated the faith with Latino cultural expressions animated by the religious imagination of the people.

The Cursillo proved to be a most effective ministry and by 1962—scarcely five years after being brought to the United States—it had been copied and established in approximately fifty dioceses. Moreover, it was relatively inexpensive in its operating expenses, affirmed the rights of hierarchical authority, was parish based, clerically supervised, produced increasing numbers of Latino Catholics intensely committed to sacramental practice of Catholicism, and encouraged meditation on the scriptures. It transcended the localized role of lay religious leaders of the *cofradías* and other parish organizations and brought together men and women, married and single, clergy, and religious and laity. The Cursillo *ultreyas* (local Cursillo groups) in the basement churches became leadership schools and the *ultreyas de campo* every summer brought together Cursillistas from many parishes within a diocesan region. And because the Cursillistas continually recruited new Cursillistas, the leaders perpetuated themselves and their movement in a supportive religious community. The Cursillo provided grassroots, Spanish-speaking leadership and coordinated all efforts through diocesanwide councils both loyal and ever-watchful of episcopal authority.

In the New York Archdiocese, which includes only part of the city's five boroughs, there were nearly 8,000 Cursillistas by 1967. By multiplying these numbers by the dioceses that had a Spanish-speaking Cursillo movement, the total number of Latino Cursillistas nationally in 1967 can be estimated to have been as high as 150,000. If one includes the families and children of these Cursillistas, by 1967 as much as 10 percent of some 7 million Latino Catholics nationwide may have been practicing their religion under the inspiration of the Cursillo. When one remembers that the Cursillistas were pledged to active church participation, their numbers, large as they were, scarcely match their enormous influence. Almost every Latino lay leader was a Cursillista. Moreover, there seemed to be an expectation that every practicing Latino Catholic would eventually make a Cursillo. More than one-fourth of all Latino Catholics surveyed placed importance on the Cursillo, more than on any other movement and more even than on the Second Vatican Council (González and La Velle, 1985: 133). As it grew in scope and importance, a diocesan and even national role for the Cursillo movement emerged. By 1967, the Cursillo movement had helped to unify Latinos in different episcopal regions in one organization. Cursillistas became the prairie grass that caught fire and spread the flame of resurgence from coast to coast.

Syzygy

The idea of making the resurgence into a special period within the framework of larger changes can be compared to syzygy. The conjunction of several planets is a natural event that can be predicted by observance of the path of the celestial bodies. But although it is normal in this sense, syzygy is also infrequent and uncommon. In somewhat the same way, general socioeconomic forces would have produced change in the practice of Latino religion, but this would not have amounted to the Latino Religious Resurgence without the simultaneous and random coming together of certain individuals and key ideas. Before 1967, the celestial bodies were in their courses but had not yet aligned.

The important political changes that we have outlined in previous chapters altered forever the structures of Latino communities. These changes created the landscape for Latino political militancy and for the religious resurgence as well. The U.S. public was still traumatized by the assassination of John F. Kennedy when legislation proposed by President Lyndon Johnson multiplied Latino opportunities. The War on Poverty, the Civil Rights Bill, the 1965 immigration reforms, and bilingual education thrust

Latino identity into a context wherein there was direct advantage in *not* being white, although being born in the United States rather than south of the border no longer made one automatically into an "American" (Hurtado, 1976; López, 1973). Eventually, new names were found for Latinos in the United States to distinguish them from people from the homeland. "Chicanos" became the new classification for Mexican Americans who sought Atzlán as a native homeland and "Niuricans" described the children of the Puerto Rican migrants who longed for Borinquén (Klor de Alva, 1991). Less than a decade away from the trauma of the Cuban Revolution, young Cuban Americans seemed to generally escape the revolt against existing norms that swept over the nation's Latino youth. But even if it was timid in comparison with the militancy among Chicanos and Niuricans, there was a restlessness among this Cuban generation about what "really" was taking place in Cuba and a desire to participate in the Latino movements.

The domestic changes in the United States were accompanied by national doubt about U.S. foreign involvements. As had been the case with the domestic changes, these concerns about international policy affected the new generation of Latino leadership. The success of the Cuban Revolution in resisting a U.S.-sponsored invasion and intensified attention to involvement in Vietnam gave rise to a militant defense of underdeveloped nations. The continents of Africa, Asia, and South America were lumped together as parts of the world that had not yet known prosperity or development as had the capitalist nations of the West or the socialist countries of the East. There was a Third World, it was said, that needed to assert its own value systems, independently of meddling superpowers.

Third Worldism

This mode of thinking became "Third Worldism" and found root in the new generation of Latino leadership. The literature on Latino student movements fleshes out the dynamics of the time (Acuña, 1972; Barrera, 1988; Flores, 1993; Gómez, 1973; López, 1973; Muñoz, 1989; Rendón, 1971). Spanish speakers had to be instructed in their native language, not only because it was the best way to learn English, but also because it was necessary to preserve their traditional values. Protection of language was a protection of culture. Bilingual education gradually became multicultural education, meant to prevent assimilation into the values of a middle-class America. Moreover, since it was perceived that culture was not transferable from one cultural group to another, making it idiosyncratic, it logically followed that only Latinos should teach Latinos. Instead of assimilation, it was now said that each of the cultures in the United States should remain distinct from each other. If it was imperialistic to invade another country and impose an American economic and political system, so it was also culturally imperialistic to force the Spanish-speaking population already in the United States to sacrifice any of its traditions in order to become assimilated.

This Third Worldism was mightily assisted both by a counterculture that developed in the United States in the middle of the decade and by opposition to the Vietnam War. Latinos, particularly college-age youth, were not slow in accepting these radical reformulations of ethnic and racial identity within the United States. Indeed, the figures of Ché Guevara and Fidel Castro, two leaders of the Cuban Revolution, were prominently hailed as heralds of this Third Worldism, and the fact that more than one-half million Cubans in south Florida and elsewhere had rejected the revolution did not alter this conviction. Fidel Castro, reviled by the Cuban exiles as a dictator, was simultaneously a hero for Mexican Americans and Puerto Ricans in the United States. Leaders from the Mexican and Puerto Rican past who had opposed Yankee imperialism were added to the new pantheon of Latino leaders. Pedro Albizu Campos, who had died in 1965 as a bedridden invalid, was resurrected as a Christlike precursor of Puerto Rican independence. Pancho Villa and Emiliano Zapata enjoyed similar reconstruction among young Mexican Americans who rejected the middle-class aspirations of an older generation (Stevens-Arroyo, 1980, 1994). As described earlier, the 1967 poem "Yo Soy Joaquín" by Rodolfo "Corky" González recast Mexican history as part of the new Chicano identity. Puerto Ricans thrilled to the revolutionary verses of a recording by Lucecita Benítez, who declared, *Soy de una raza, pura y rebelde* ("I belong to a race, pure and rebellious") or to the protest music of Noel Hernández and Roy Brown.

These new identities did not completely replace the existing conceptions of what it meant to be a Mexican American in the United States. In fact, the new identity seemed to be a generational affair, with young people more likely to call themselves Chicanos than their parents. Puerto Ricans in the United States had a similar experience with their identity as Niuricans. Originally coined to describe basketball players who were eligible for the Puerto Rican league even though they had been born in New York, the term quickly became the way to describe a Puerto Rican who did not live on the island.

In 1967, a militant stage of the Civil Rights movement had developed, making the figures of Malcolm X and the Black Panthers rivals with the nonviolent Dr. Martin Luther King. There also appeared a white racist backlash movement that was fueled by the eventual presidential candidacy of Alabama governor George Wallace. Opposition to the war in Vietnam could no longer be dismissed as a fringe movement, and a countercultural movement of "flower children" had forged the outlines of what was to be a

generational mind-set for young people who had been born after the end of
the Korean War. Thus, the *mentalité* of the generation that made the
Latino Religious Resurgence is one of several generational mind-sets that
are part of U.S. history and have made this 1960s generation markedly
skeptical of government. The refrain "I want to live in America" from the
1950s musical *West Side Story* was changed to the "*Amerika imperialista*"
of the 1960s radicals.

The principal area of militant activity among Latinos in 1967 was on the
university campus. Among Chicanos, these groups carried names like the
Mexican American Youth Organization (MAYO), United Mexican
American Students (UMAS), and the Mexican American Student
Organization (MASO) (Muñoz, 1989:58). Chicano Studies departments
and programs were to follow. Puerto Rican students at City College of
New York (CCNY) formulated plans for the Puerto Rican Students'
Union. It supported the strike at Columbia University and played a major
role in a similar strike within CCNY that produced Puerto Rican Studies
departments throughout the university system (López, 1973:317–319).
The university students in New York City founded a chapter of the Young
Lords, which until then had been a neighborhood gang in Chicago. The
Chicago Young Lords had absorbed some of their politics from organiza-
tions like the Black Panthers and Brown Berets. The New York Young
Lords, however, injected the principles of Puerto Rico's independence
movement into the organization, transferring its leadership center to New
York City.

Reies López Tijerina

These student organizations were primarily political, not religious. But
they were not antireligious or anticlerical, either. For example, the Young
Lords in New York chose a Methodist church that had closed its membership to Puerto Ricans as the target for one of their early protests (López,
1973:326–329). Religion was not denounced; rather, attention was directed against the institution that refused to minister to Latino needs.
Chicano students also evaluated religion with this criterion. Their response
ensured that religious issues would not be excluded from the agenda.

On June 5, 1967, in Tierra Amarilla, New Mexico, Reies López Tijerina
led the capture by arms of the county courthouse. The revolt was quickly
put down and its leaders jailed, along with a host of supporters. López
Tijerina's movement, the Alianza Federal de Mercedes, challenged the validity of land distribution in New Mexico in legal arguments based on in-
congruities between the stipulations of the 1848 Treaty of Guadalupe-
Hidalgo and the aftermath of the U.S. occupation. López Tijerina was a
Pentecostal preacher whose premillenarian ideas of a utopian community

are not easily lumped together with the secular goals of Chicanismo. As the important research of Stanford University professor Rudy V. Busto (1991) has shown, López Tijerina's revolt is traceable to his religious convictions. He stated that where the rule of the United States was based on usurpation of the original Spanish land grants, the New Mexican Hispanos had a right to establish their own government. But Tijerina's vision for New Mexico, like his first organizing effort at Valle de Paz in Arizona, was reminiscent of the utopian religious community at Amana or the Mormon one at Salt Lake City rather than the secular society promoted by La Raza Unida Party with which he is sometimes linked. His organization, the Alianza, had no direct ties to the wider goals of Chicano militants in 1967. Carlos Muñoz recognizes that the Alianza was initially supported by the student organizations in solidarity with López Tijerina's bravery rather than because of his ideology. He appeared as a living example of the hero myth spun in "Yo Soy Joaquín." The 1967 takeover of the courthouse by arms resonated with the valiant resistance to U.S. colonialism in Texas and the Southwest and represented a focused and irrefutable example of violence as the legitimate ultimate recourse after legal appeals have been unfairly denied. Puerto Ricans were familiar with this argumentation, which had been the basis of the Nationalist Party under Pedro Albizu Campos (Stevens-Arroyo, 1992, 1996a).

Antulio Parrilla Bonilla

The churches in Puerto Rico, both Catholic and Protestant, had been mobilized in 1967 when the government called for a referendum (popularly but improperly called a "plebiscite") to decide Puerto Rico's status permanently. University groups of Protestant and Catholic students participated in the resistance, asking religious people across the entire political spectrum to boycott the vote because it did not fulfill the basic requisites of international law for its validity. This participation by religious groups in a political cause of electoral abstention was eventually tied to protests against the Reserve Officers' Training Corps (ROTC) on the campus of the University of Puerto Rico and anti–Vietnam War feelings. The 1967 boycott was successful inasmuch as the abstentions—counted together with voters opposing commonwealth status—constituted the majority of Puerto Rico's electorate. Thus, it would be inaccurate to say that in 1967 most Puerto Ricans decided that commonwealth should be a permanent status.

The church leader who inherited much of the public visibility for religious opposition to the vote, the Vietnam War, and the military draft in Puerto Rico was Catholic Bishop Antulio Parrilla Bonilla, a Jesuit priest who had been ordained an auxiliary bishop in the Diocese of Caguas. Bishop Parrilla was the Catholic director on the island of community cooperatives (similar to the *mutualistas* of Chicano experience) and brother to a Baptist minister. He was generally viewed not so much as a Catholic prelate who was preoccupied with his own church but as an independence advocate who brought the prestige of his ecclesiastical office to the cause. He was the first bishop in the United States—not only the first Latino bishop—to denounce the Vietnam War as immoral. He directly counseled students to file conscientious objections to the war on the basis of religious convictions and the illegitimacy of U.S. citizenship for Puerto Ricans.[2]

With the inauguration in 1968 of a pro-statehood governor whose views paralleled in many ways those of the Nixon administration in the United States, a wave of reprisals were launched against all *independentistas*. Around Parrilla, a cohort of newly ordained Puerto Rican priests and Protestant clergy closed a circle of defense as they were driven from seminaries and pastorates by conservative forces within the churches. The cohort of young clergy viewed Parilla's militancy as validation of their own. For Protestants, the vanguard of critical examination of religion in Puerto Rico was found in the Seminario Evangélico and its related agencies for the University of Puerto Rico in Río Piedras; for Catholics, it was the experimental parish of Cristo de la Salud in Comerío that celebrated the liturgy with Puerto Rican folk music and cooperated with Protestant clergy in addressing social needs (Díaz-Stevens, 1993c). From these two groups was to come the progressive vision of the Puerto Rican Ecumenical movement. Earlier, many of the clergy had shared training at Chicago's School of Urban Ministry; now they were to refashion that collaboration in Puerto Rico, and their coming together in 1967 coincided with the Latino Religious Resurgence in the United States.

The Urban Revolts of 1967

Like the smaller-scale protest of Reies López Tijerina in New Mexico, the Puerto Rican religious protests were radical. They went to the heart of the colonial question and challenged in religious and legal terms the legitimacy of the U.S. takeover of these Latino homelands. During that same summer in 1967, riots over police brutality took place in Spanish Harlem, a Puerto Rican neighborhood in New York City. The retaliation against police was justified by some radical leaders as a New York counterpart to the protests in Puerto Rico. This argument had been used by the Puerto Rican Nationalists in the 1950 attack on President Truman and the 1954 shooting in Congress. The Mayor of New York City and Herman Badillo, a Puerto Rican congressman, were unable to quell the anger, and as analyzed by Díaz-Stevens (1993a:164–167), it took a pious procession of lay people, many of them Cursillistas, to restore calm. Jaime Vidal, following Díaz-Stevens (1993a), calls attention to this irony: Monsignor Fox had one of his most significant successes in political terms by appealing to the traditional piety that his apostolate had downplayed (Vidal, 1994b:75–76). But whatever the pastoral implications, public officials took notice. Coming after a similar rebellion among Puerto Ricans in Chicago (Padilla, 1987: 144–148) and after major revolts against injustice in Watts, Detroit, and Philadelphia, this urban unrest alarmed the government. New York City's use of religion as a way toward peace was one of the reasons President Lyndon B. Johnson declared a national day of prayer for racial peace on July 30, 1967.

César Chávez

The cause of the Mexican American migrant farmworkers during the Delano grape strike (1965–1966) was a most important chapter in this process of new Catholic Latino leadership. César Chávez was both a Cursillista and radical labor organizer. In another epoch, these two identities would have been contradictory. Labor organizing among Mexicans had largely been a function of anticlerical Socialists during the 1930s (García, 1989). But the reforms of the Second Vatican Council allowed Chávez to harmonize his piety and devotion to Catholic tradition with his radical labor agenda. His validation within the church as a reliable Catholic was enhanced by his standing within the labor movement as a true leader of his people. The attacks on him as a Communist by the outspoken Redemptorist Bishop Wallinger (former bishop of Ponce, Puerto Rico) rang hollow in the face of Chávez's Catholic piety, his use of Catholic symbols like the banner of Our Lady of Guadalupe, the *peregrinación* (pilgrimage), his fasting, and his appeal for Catholics to support his cause the way Protestants had. When the Kennedy family took up the cause of the Delano strike, considerable national media attention made it impossible for Catholicism to ignore the justice of the cause.

Support for the Delano strikers was generalized throughout the Mexican American community, particularly among those who identified as Chicanos. César Chávez became a symbol for a new kind of Latino—humble and rural in origin but no longer docile before injustice. In the struggle to sign a contract with the largest of California grape growers, the boycott was planned in 1967 to include all table grapes. The response was nationwide and vaulted Chávez into the limelight. When *Time* magazine placed him on the cover of the July 4, 1969, issue, it constituted his anointment as the Latino messiah and identified the farmworkers' struggle as La Causa.

But why did *Time* choose Chávez and not another Latino leader? One suspects that the effort of the United Farm Workers (UFW) was viewed as a struggle to realize the American Dream. This is hinted at in the banner on the *Time* cover, which identified the movement with John Steinbeck's classic book *The Grapes of Wrath*. Chávez was painted as a reformer rather than as a radical, a soothing message to the U.S. conscience. The letter from the publisher on page one compared Chicanos to "their French Canadian cousins in Quebec"—an allusion that in 1969 suggested peaceful coexistence for cultural and linguistic pluralism. The third paragraph in the *Time* article (Anson et al., 1969) called the strike "a holy crusade" and focused on the image of Our Lady of Guadalupe as patroness of the farmworkers. Chávez's reliance on papal social encyclicals such as Rerum Novarum and his Catholic piety were highlighted, including his opposition to abortion. Chávez was given the literary equivalent of a "log cabin" youth and compared to Zapata, Ghandi, Nehru, and Martin Luther King.

Specifically mentioning the Brown Berets Reies López Tijerina and Corky González, *Time* editorialized that Chávez was less "strident" than others. Despite the allusion to French Canadians as "cousins," the Puerto Rican *independentistas* were ignored by a magazine eager to situate the Chicano movement within the safe confines of U.S. reformist liberalism. The magazine article classified lack of English as the "main impediment" to Chicano progress, confusingly classified Chicanos as immigrants, and suggested that Chávez represented pluralism rather than separatism. Ironically, but no doubt intentionally, in the pages immediately following the Chávez story, *Time* asked "Is This Any Way for Nice Jewish Boys to Behave?" in the headline of an article about the Jewish Defense League that had just been organized by Rabbi Meir Kahane. It seems fair to conclude that *Time* had chosen Chávez as the legitimate Latino leader, rejecting both López Tejerina and Bishop Parrilla. Of the three Latino causes that surfaced in 1967 with an identifiable religious connection, the farmworkers' was the safest one. Chávez's goals were contrasted with the separatist aspirations of the Black Panthers (defined as on the Left) and the Jewish Defense League (defined as on the Right).

Resurgence Wildfire

Yet, an icon is an icon, and the movements were handed an opportunity by *Time* magazine that was sorely needed by Latino progressives. César Chávez's cause became a touchstone of solidarity for all Latino militancy, while his connection to the Cursillo brought a traditionalist religious public into the cause. Like an article in Cavour's publication of *Il Risorgimento*, *Time*'s cover with Chávez became a visible and effective symbol of a movement. The radical demands of Latino student militants, the resources of Catholic and Protestant churches, and the piety of Latino Cursillistas had come into syzygy.

Even before the *Time* magazine article, the leaders of Chicano and Puerto Rican movements recognized the symbolic importance of Chávez.

Luis Valdez proclaimed that César was "our first real Mexican American leader ... [the one] we had been waiting for" (cited in Muñoz, 1989:59–60, n. 33). From church headquarters at 475 Riverside Drive in New York, the United Methodist and Presbyterian churches supported Chávez's UFW and opened the way for financial and clergy participation in the 1967 boycott. Important segments of the Episcopal and Catholic churches were to do the same. At Loyola Marymount in Los Angeles, young Chicano Catholics formed what was to become Católicos por la Raza, a group that applied the social justice teachings of the magisterium to the farmworkers' strike. This was a militant Chicano student group that was different from others due to its distinctive Catholic slant.

In Puerto Rico, Bishop Parrilla, as a leader of cooperativism, was immediately supportive of Chávez and the UFW. Eventually, Puerto Rico's progressive clergy would form an ecumenical team to minister to Puerto Rican agricultural workers who annually travel to the United States. Called META (Ministerio Ecuménico de Trabajadores Agrícolas), the group sent the Puerto Rican priest, William Loperena, O.P., to California to establish links between the UFW and the unionization of Puerto Rican tobacco workers in Hartford, Connecticut.

Thus, Chávez's value was symbolic but not artificial. It nurtured the aspirations for national impact among the disparate Latino movements and was interpreted as legitimation of the cause of equality. Because Chávez had been called the "Mexican American Martin Luther King" there was an expectation that every Latino with religious background would identify with this social justice issue as a moral cause just as the black churches of Protestant America had done with the Civil Rights movement. Even for those who were not Mexican American, the general public expected all Spanish-speaking people to view Chávez as *the* leader, because, after all, all Latinos seemed the same.

Generational Leadership

These expectations fell heavily on the shoulders of a Latino cohort of priests, sisters, and lay leaders. A new generation of Latinos was bonded together by national events. It created a new religious identity. This was not an introspective process, however, because the nature of Chávez's recognition required religious leaders to look for networks that were nationwide. The political skills of advocacy, negotiation, and compromise were to be summoned into use by the young generation of religious leaders who had few mentors to guide them. And although Puerto Ricans and Chicanos formed the nucleus of the resurgence, out of the need for unity was to come the all-embracing mission to Latinos. The Chicanos needed Puerto Ricans, especially those in New York, to make the movement truly national; Puerto Ricans, especially those on the island, needed Chicanos to show that Latinos would struggle to preserve their identity even after a century of Americanization; and the other groups of Latin Americans needed the strength of numbers and political clout that the Chicanos and Puerto Ricans generated. Even in the anticommunist atmosphere of the Cuban American enclaves, the cry for social justice found an echo of solidarity that bridged the gap between professional upper-class Cuban Americans in Miami and Mexican migrant workers in the orange groves of central Florida. The movement accommodated all these forces under the rubric of Latino unity.

The Latino Religious Resurgence had two major goals: reform of society and reform of the church. By reason of its numbers and historical role as the majority religion of Latinos, the Roman Catholic Church became the principal battleground. Thus, in a certain measure the resurgence had its launching pad within Catholicism. But the nature of the changes in Latino religion transcended a merely Roman Catholic boundary. Like all movements, it gained impetus by embracing an ever-widening spectrum of issues and interest groups; focus on issues of specifically Catholic organization came in the second phase of institutionalization.

It may be helpful to think of the resurgence in terms of the cliché of the pebble dropped in the lake, causing wider and wider ripples. The initial point of entry makes the biggest splash and most noticeable disturbance. As the ripples spread out, they get larger but less intense. Similarly, the resurgence had its most dramatic impact on Catholicism, but the effects of the new thinking about culture and religion are still being felt well outside the usual ambit of Roman Catholicism.

The Catholic springboard of the resurgence is important for another reason. The rationale for restoring Latino culture as an integral part of religious experience was framed in Catholic theological terminology. Inescapably, the theological reasoning for the resurgence echoed the twin responsibilities of pastoral care and social concerns. But although these goals were simultaneously joined in the enthusiasm of the resurgence's birth, they created a fault line. As first suggested in *Prophets Denied Honor* (Stevens-Arroyo, 1980:175–179), reform of the church was the principal goal of those called the pastoralists, whereas reform of society was the focus of the liberationists. The description of the differences written at the time is still fundamentally sound.

> At times there is little difference between what pastoralists and liberationists say, but the way they go about achieving their involvement is very different. The pastoralists look for a greater visibility—sign value—to the church's presence in social issues. The liberationists evaluate not in terms of presence but of effect. They find no satisfaction in the church's participation in picket of a fac-

tory with discriminatory hiring practices, unless the discrimination is brought to an end. The pastoralists, on the other hand, are apt to say something like this: "Well, the picket was a failure because the people did not organize themselves correctly, but at least the church was present to them in their struggle—sharing, growing, failing, suffering, but always loving." The liberationists respond, "That's the trouble with you: you're always talking about feelings—what the people need is more jobs. You can't eat sentiments. Maybe if you had been more interested in the needs of the people and less in witness and sign value, they would have organized correctly and would have the jobs today, together with all that love." The pastoralists criticize the liberationists for having lost the faith dimension, and the liberationists rejoin that the pastoralists "subjectivize" social action in an effort to control the situation, instead of putting themselves at the service of humankind. The purpose ... is not to justify one model over another, although each believer will have a preference. The process of Hispano church, however, cannot be understood unless it is clear that all Hispano Catholics do not think and act alike. (Stevens-Arroyo, 1980:177–178)

As McNamara (1970) stressed in his description of pastoral care and social concerns, the meshing of these different goals into a single ministry was what gave it power. Pastoralists were not against social concerns; liberationists were not opposed to pastoral care. They differed mainly in the *priority* they assigned to time and resources in the exercise of ministry. As long as both groups saw their agenda advanced by the movement, they had more reason to work together than to clash. Much as in the Italian *risorgimento* where liberals and radical Republicans put aside their differences to topple Austrian domination, pastoralists and liberationists made common cause against an institution chary of sharing power.

The message of the resurgence was for access to church resources. The Catholic leaders found most of their audience among the Cursillistas. Both sets of leaders were to turn to the Cursillistas in order to wean them away from the hierarchical concept of Catholic authority. Because these efforts coincided with the reforms of the Second Vatican Council, the new vision of a Latino Catholicism compared well with the hope for an egalitarian church that formed the "people of God." The process was not always even: Cursillistas generally came from the older generation, and they expressed resistance to the militancy of groups like Católicos por la Raza and were more reluctant to accept the social concerns agenda of the movement than the pastoral care aspects. But if the Cursillistas had not been there to listen to the new generation of leaders and to take up the cause, the resurgence would have been contained within a narrow circle of intellectuals or would have evaporated as university students graduated into a workaday world. Instead, the Cursillistas provided a grassroots public, eager for self-improvement, self-selected by religious commitment, based in cadres organized in each parish but connected to diocesan and national structures that paralleled the hierarchy of Catholicism. As was said before, the Cursillo was the prairie grass that caught fire, carrying the flame of the resurgence across the country.

Latino Protestants were a part of this initial stage because they also supported Chávez and usually did not encounter much opposition within their denominations when rallying the church to this cause. This was similar to the blurring of denominational boundaries that was taking place in Puerto Rico for progressive Protestants and Catholics. And although the Protestant leaders did not have the number of Latino congregants that Catholicism possessed, many of them recognized in the Catholic experiences a model that could be adapted to Protestant needs.

By 1967, the major elements of a new Latino religious identity had been brought into line. This new identity differed from the Latino image of the 1950s and early 1960s. No longer was the burden of change and adaptation laid exclusively on Latinos seeking to be Americanized while conforming to the expectations of religion: Now, North America and its religious institutions were expected to change if they hoped to hold the loyalties of Latinos and Latinas. Most important, the process of change required native Latinos to assume leadership for their own people. A socioreligious syzygy had created an opportunity for Latino leadership, and a powerful national movement was the result. The Latino Religious Resurgence had begun.

Notes

1. See also Richard Rodríguez, *Days of Obligation: An Argument with My Mexican Father* (New York: Viking Press, 1992).

2. Puerto Rico's religious leadership organized several such demonstrations that challenged U.S. treaty rights to the people's lands. These took place to protest the U.S. military and NATO exercises first in Culebra and then, after that issue was resolved by presidential decree in 1971, in Vieques. Arrests of church and political leaders were made in both places; Bishop Parrilla was arrested in the case of the Vieques protest.

5

Agenda

WHY DID THE LATINO RELIGIOUS RESURGENCE succeed after 1967 in dramatically creating a generational mind-set among Latinos toward religion? With the acquisition of Texas and the Mexican territories, the Latino population had been substantial within the United States since as early as the 1840s, and religion was alive and well during the one hundred and twenty-five years that separated the U.S. conquest from the resurgence. But the twentieth-century resurgence differed from earlier manifestations of Latino religiosity in notable ways: (1) it was national in scope, rather than regional; (2) it unified multiple causes and interest groups (UFW strike, liturgical reform, social concern agencies, Cursillo, priest associations, and congregations of religious women) within a single movement; (3) it achieved a high level of effective organization faster than previous efforts; and (4) it developed under new styles of leadership that were collegial, organically connected to local communities and cross-validated by secular politics.

Earlier movements were heralds of the resurgence (Stevens-Arroyo, 1980) but did not enjoy the national and ecumenical scope that made the resurgence after 1967 so remarkable. Nor did earlier social and political movements have a religious counterpart, as occurred in the resurgence. The 1930s offered parallels to the social movements of the 1960s, when Pan-Americanism achieved considerable importance among Spanish speakers in the United States, particularly in El Congreso del Pueblo de Habla Española, which eventually functioned as an organizing committee within the Congress of Industrial Organizations (CIO) (see Stevens-Arroyo, 1994:84ff; García, 1989:145ff). Like other results of the New Deal, it achieved unity between those radical Latinos who identified with the labor movement and the CIO during the 1930s and various reformist groups. As would happen in the 1960s and 1970s, the prewar New Deal unified different ideologies and brought Mexican Americans into collaboration with their Puerto Rican and Cuban counterparts (García, 1989:145–151, 203).

149

However, these secular movements were generally anticlerical, as fit the temper of socialism at the time, and thus provoked, rather than inspired, Latinos who held tightly to their religious identity (Stevens-Arroyo, 1994). The advent of the Cold War eroded the connections of El Congreso with radical Latin American politics, and it ceased to nurture a distinctive Latino identity (García, 1989:163–165). Thus, although there were earlier movements that addressed similar needs, the religious resurgence was a unique experience. According to the measure of its national and institutional impact, it stands without parallel in more than 150 years of Latino presence within the religious history of the United States. The other events served as signposts and voices of the prophets that set "hearts to burning": But it was the resurgence that provided the Emmaus paradigm.

Leadership of the Resurgence

The success of the resurgence is essentially connected to the nature of its leadership. There was no single leader who was promoted because of what Max Weber defined as charisma: "a certain quality of an individual personality by virtue of which he is set apart from ordinary men and treated as endowed with ... specifically exceptional powers or qualities ... [which] are not accessible to the ordinary person" (Weber, 1947:358, 359). César Chávez filled some of those criteria, but he was the leader of the United Farm Workers, not a champion for the religious movement of the resurgence. The term "icon" rather than "leader" best describes his role in the resurgence.

Rather than claiming "exceptional powers or qualities," the leaders of the resurgence emphasized their common roots with the people and stressed the communitarian nature of leadership. The resurgence developed a style of collegial leadership through committees and commissions that developed plans of action and documents outlining pastoral goals. One could say the charisma of the resurgence was derived not from an individual but from these pastoral plans and statements. Leaders did not appeal to themselves but to the documents for authority, arguing that they represented the voice of the people. This was the mechanism that endowed the innovations of the resurgence with a normative character that obligated ordinary Latino believers to follow the stipulations. Thus, the resurgence was protected early on from overdependence upon a single personality and was organically connected to the social-class location of Latino parishes and congregations.

That does not mean that the leaders of the Latino resurgence were dull. In the less-technical sense of the word, many leaders were in fact "charismatic": effective speakers, passionate advocates, inspiring teachers. Such was the case with Antulio Parrilla Bonilla and Patricio Flores, among the first of the Latino bishops. But as bishops, they were tied to the Catholic hierarchy by reason of their office. Thus, despite their often visionary statements, they were expected to serve the institutional church. In the case of Flores, he drew closer to his fellow bishops as years advanced; Parrilla Bonilla continued in a prophetic role almost to the day of his death in 1995, although his passionate commitment to the cause of Puerto Rican independence was often invoked to obscure the value of his many other pronouncements.

Virgilio Elizondo and Justo González

The most enduring role in leadership is often the exposition of the ideas that propel a movement. Virgilio Elizondo and Justo González are theologians whose prolific writings have come to be viewed in the 1990s as charter documents of Latino religion. Elizondo is a Mexican American priest of the Archdiocese of San Antonio, trained in Europe as an educator: González is a Cuban-born Methodist seminary professor. But Elizondo did not play an organizational role in the Catholic segment of the resurgence. In fact, his usage of the term "Mexican American" rather than "Chicano" suggests his distance from the most militant roots of the resurgence. Born and bred in the centuries-old *colonia* (old town) of San Antonio, Elizondo was sent by his bishop to Europe for training in religious education and liturgy. As a priest, his career has been focused upon these pastoral tasks. The militant implications of his writings might be said to have entered by "osmosis" from the Chicano movement. The more vocal spokespersons of the movement had created the need for the larger society to respond to the demands for power. Elizondo's powerful imagery, lucid examples, and effective commonsense language gave a religious dimension to a political and cultural cause. Father Elizondo became a sensible and plausible advocate for cultural preservation and the need for social justice, reflecting the development among his peers of a new sense of Mexican American identity. His theological production interpreted the demands of the Chicano movement in terms acceptable to Catholicism. Without Elizondo, many of the issues raised by the movement might have been "too hot to handle," resulting in a hard line against change. Instead, his theological and pastoral writings offered clear and achievable reforms that rang true to the feelings of Mexican American Catholics.

The Gramscian descriptions of "organic intellectual" and "conjunctural intellectual" fit Elizondo better than the Weberian notion of the charismatic leader. He is a priest who has always stressed his rootedness in the San Antonio experience. For instance, one does not easily find in Elizondo's writings the contention that his ideas apply universally to all Latino reality. That claim comes from others who try to impose *mestizaje* as the defining concept for all Latinos or who huckster devotion to Our Lady of Guadalupe as a benchmark of religion for all Latinos rather than viewing this devotion in its Mexican American context. Never a community organizer or board member of PADRES (Padres Asociados para Derechos Religiosos, Educationales y Sociales), Elizondo's great contribution has been to supply a theological underpinning to the argument that cultural expression is a necessary complement to Christian life. In Elizondo's writings, the theology of culture has become what Rhys Williams (1996) calls a "political resource."

In a similar fashion, Justo González has been the theological figure of magnitude for Latino Protestantism. Unlike Elizondo, González's connectedness to the Latino people comes from his many travels rather than from identity within one specific community. Born in Cuba, educated in an Ivy League U.S. school, faculty member of seminaries in Puerto Rico and Georgia, Justo González has managed to extract from these experiences a comprehensive overview of what Latino groups have in common. Long before rising to prominence as a "Latino theologian," he had produced various textbooks on general trends of scripture and church history. A member of the United Methodist Church, he played roles appropriate to a traditional intellectual and seminary professor for the Latino movements. In both Puerto Rico and Georgia, he demonstrated an enormous capacity for collaboration with pastors in the field. As the movement grew, González turned almost exclusively to theology for Latinos. Like Elizondo, González is a traditional intellectual by training who moved into advocacy for the people by choice. It is a symbol of their shared stature that Elizondo wrote the introduction to González's 1990 groundbreaking book *Mañana: Christian Theology from a Hispanic Perspective.*

But in 1967, neither Elizondo nor González had produced their now-classic works. Elizondo was a part of the seminary faculty in the Archdiocese of San Antonio and had only begun to promote the idea of a separate training facility on seminary grounds to train Mexican Americans for the unique cultural demands of their apostolate. Justo González was on the faculty of the Seminario Evangélico in Puerto Rico, far away from the call to defend the UFW in the fields of California. It was only the following year that González accepted a seminary post in the United States. If he had remained in Puerto Rico, González might never have organized key projects such as the publication of the theological journal *Apuntes,* which injected concern for Latino culture into the Protestant seminary agenda in the United States.

Leadership Through Deroutinization

Elizondo and González are important to the resurgence as intellectuals who supplied theological explanations for the goals of a movement that was organized by others. Crucial leadership often came from unexpected sources. Díaz-Stevens (1993a:182 ff.) calls Father Robert L. Stern, director of the Spanish-Speaking Apostolate of the Archdiocese of New York, a "deroutinizer of the institutional church," because when he incorporated the creative policies of his predecessors into institutional structures, Stern was not just "routinizing the charisma" in a Weberian sense but was also deroutinizing the existing system. In other words, when the leadership of the resurgence set the goal of making the church recognize the various plans and recommendations of the movement, it simultaneously began to undermine the existing *mentalité* that relegated Latinos to a subordinate role in setting ecclesiastical policy.

Deroutinization was first applied systematically to Latino religion by Patrick McNamara (1968:17–18) in order to dramatize the limitations of the priest-or-prophet dichotomy established in Weberian thought. Writing at the dawn of the resurgence, McNamara insightfully diagnosed the importance of linking pastoral care with social concern as twin aspects of ministry. The Catholic priest among Mexican Americans, said McNamara, could be an agent both for ritual expression and a prophet for social change. Separating the two dimensions into dichotomous Weberian categories, wrote McNamara, ran contrary to much of the ministry taking place at the time. McNamara's analysis became the basis for the pastoralist-liberationist descriptions offered earlier.

One could link McNamara's groundbreaking study and the pastoralist-liberationist categories to other important sociological theories. Does not the notion of priestly innovator in ritual and pastoralist leadership approximate the concept of symbolic capital from Pierre Bourdieu (1980/1990:112–121)? Likewise, the apostolate of social concerns borne by liberationists seems to be the mechanism that generates "social capital" (Coleman, 1990). As expounded by Robert D. Putnam (1995a; 1995b) and applied to the 1990s U.S. Catholic experience by John A. Coleman, S.J. (1996b), this becomes a crucial concept. It helps explain how militancy about social concerns evolved into a new generational conviction among clergy and laity alike. The resurgence called upon the church to address the social, economic, and political needs of its people in ways that integrated religious motivations into the experience of neighborhood community. The loyalty built toward the institution by reason of its service to the community is part of its social capital.

Moreover, given the collegial nature of leadership during the resurgence, the generation of both symbolic and social capitals did not have to be the work of a single individual. The resurgence developed specialists in different fields who produced plans for advancing one or other facet of Latino religion, but as a whole, members of the group critiqued and then endorsed each others' suggestions. If presented individually, the demands for reform in ritual or social concern would not have produced ecclesiastical change: Without a skillful bureaucrat, the best pastoral plan does not become policy. The diplomatic skills for forging consensus and advancing these documented plans within church bureaucracy was the motor of deroutinization. People like Father Robert Stern held immense importance in the resurgence.

Of course, the resurgence did not begin with this vision of itself as a movement within the churches. The initial focus was on generating support for Chávez and the UFW as opportunities for religion to address social injustice in the United States. But these initial efforts were swiftly transformed. The leaders of the resurgence adopted reform of ecclesiastical institutions as a goal because of the following principle: The church cannot give what the church does not have. The push toward an egalitarian society was buttressed by the ideology coming from secular movements, and the call for an egalitarian church was strengthened by the theology that evolved as the Latin American theology of liberation. The influences from these contemporary movements engendered the national scope of the resurgence and its call for the unity of diverse nationality groups.

Structuration

But how could a very young cohort of leaders develop a national movement of regional and nationality self-interested groups and organize it so quickly? One answer is structuration. Developed by Anthony Giddens (1984), the concept of structuration impels us to see the incompleteness in the structures of society and, by extension, in organizations like the churches. As we understand it, structuration is a cognitive tendency to attribute more coherence to society than really exists. It may be compared to the way the mind connects dots that are really separate in order to form an image that is satisfying to the eye. In the process, the eye does not play tricks on the mind; rather, the cognitive process makes sense of stimuli, organizing them into a recognizable construct. We often measure intuitive intelligence by how quickly a person can perform this cognitive operation. In the case of the resurgence, we contend its leadership used structuration to "connect the dots" and transform diverse points of energy into a national movement.

The special historical character of the Latino Religious Resurgence can be attributed to the multiplicity of such examples of structuration that occurred almost simultaneously. In the effort to achieve solidarity, each of the different segments and causes incorporated the arguments developed by other groups as part of a single movement. In the example of syzygy, the field of gravity of each of the celestial bodies is magnified by its alignment with all the others. Thus, we would argue, the cumulative force of the resurgence was greater than the sum of the parts because the conjuncture multiplied the power of each cause.

Structuration was also used to deroutinize the prevailing pastoral paradigms. We would argue that according to the principles of structuration, although ideology (in this case, theology) purports to explain and organize every facet of social action, it never does. The establishment often considered itself as built upon theological premises so certain that concessions could be made to Latinos without risk. But the resurgence leadership was better acquainted with the shortcomings of the hegemonic theology than the establishment. Resurgence leaders focused on the anomalies of the reigning system, recasting their functions. Those "unconnected dots" were redefined. For example, a parish program of catechism lessons became for the resurgence "leadership formation"—as soon as the text was changed from the rote catechism to pastoral theological books.

Structuration served the resurgence in both directions: The establishment thought the theology was unshakable; the resurgence leadership knew that it could reconstruct a new theology from bits and pieces of the old. By recasting existing programs as the basis for the new experiences, the movement avoided distancing itself from officialdom. New policies of the resurgence were often adopted by the institution without the implications being clearly understood. The innovations often subverted rather than sustained the system. This process is described in *Oxcart Catholicism*, which demonstrates that many innovations in the apostolate to Puerto Ricans were embraced as long as they were offered as "experiments" (Díaz-Stevens, 1993a:176–198).

The Argument of Representativity

The structuration used in the resurgence can be understood through analysis of certain key premises advanced in the body of documents produced by the collegial leadership (see Stevens-Arroyo, 1980). We will be satisfied here with labeling the sources—describing the bloodlines, so to speak—of each of the arguments that became integral parts of how the resurgence fostered national and intra-Latino unity. These can be grouped under four headings: (1) representativity, (2) cultural idiosyncrasy, (3) poverty as oppression, and (4) democratization. Militants of Chicano and Puerto Rican movements were arguing that representation of minority groups should be quantified to measure an institution's commitment to inclusion. The distribution percentages of Latinos in the general population, it was said, ought to be duplicated by an identical percentage of leaders in official posts. Additionally, it was argued that the government should spend funds for Latinos according to the same formula. Thus, for instance, if Chicanos composed 10 percent of the city's population, any less than 10 percent of mayoral appointments would amount to discrimination. It was to the mutual self-interest of all Latino groups to maximize their numbers by allowing themselves to be lumped together in a single category. The higher the numbers, the greater the argument for representation in decisionmaking positions.

This argument from secular quarters was adapted to the churches, and it was demanded that the appointment of Latino bishops, pastors, and other sorts of ecclesiastical officials match the percentage of Latinos within church membership. Such logic was deftly used by Católicos por la Raza in Los Angeles. Of course, it was less useful among Latino Protestants, since the freer access to ministry often gave them more representation at a national level than was warranted by their numbers within the denominations.

Cultural Idiosyncrasy

In the hands of secular movements, bilingual education had become a defense of biculturalism. Third Worldism tied the authenticity of cultural expression to minority group identity; the message was "If you attack our language, you attack our culture." This became the logic of cultural idiosyncrasy. It was considered that no one but a member of that particular ethnic group could legitimately express that culture or represent that group. Experiential knowledge was privileged above intellectual understanding. In an ecclesiastical context, Latino Catholic leadership interpreted the reforms of the Second Vatican Council requiring liturgies in the language and musical style of the people (the "vernacular") as an ecclesiastical equivalent of bilingual biculturalism (Pérez, 1994). Moreover, as in the "protest music" of general U.S. culture, folk music made a comeback. The Mexican mariachi and Puerto Rican *seis*—folk forms, not popular musical forms—were (re)introduced in a church venue (Stevens-Arroyo, 1996c). The return to folk style in the liturgy can be described as a connection by a new generation with their grandparents. It was an example in musical terms of Gilbert Cadena's *"abuelita* theology" (see Cadena, 1987).

This bilingual-bicultural emphasis was extended to religious education. Although directly opposed to the goal of Americanization espoused under pious colonialism, cultural diversity was presented as a long overdue extension of the American Dream to Latinos. The documents of the First Pastoral Encounter of 1972, for instance, carried the official national motto "E pluribus unum" as the rationale for the entire meeting. Latino Protestants used the bilingual-bicultural argument with great effect to begin a long process of allowing Latino seminary faculty to teach not only the standard topics for which they had been prepared but to begin developing courses focused on the uniqueness of Latino experiences.

Poverty as Oppression

The Latin American theology of liberation addressed social oppression with boldness and direct application to political circumstances. Within Catholicism, it was not so much a break with previous Catholic social justice teaching as its fulfillment. Latinos equated the oppression denounced in Latin American theology with their people's low socioeconomic status. The liberationists tended to stress statistics on economic class in their focus upon remedying society, whereas the pastoralists were likely to emphasize as a major concern the underrepresentation of Latinos in U.S. episcopacy or in the ranks of pastors. With different nuances, both groups demanded cultural integrity and economic advancement for Latinos.

Democratization

The dynamics of *pastoral de conjunto* (team pastoral care) imported from Latin American Catholicism was quickly incorporated by the resurgence in its drive toward democratization. Although this was not as dramatic a change for Latino Protestants as for their Catholic counterparts, the democratization was expanded everywhere from local parishes and congregations to the highest levels of ecclesiastical leadership. Since the Second Vatican Council had stressed a new focus on definition of church as "people of God" rather than in the traditional hierarchical sense, the resurgence had a powerful new theological impetus among Catholic leadership. But it was the success at the local level of *pastoral de conjunto*, and later of the *comunidades de base*, that nourished the drive to reshape Catholicism in the model of egalitarian participation. It is likely that if there had been no experience among the people of the success of these types of organizations, the resurgence would have stalled. Moreover, the Cursillo among Catholics had predisposed them to view the democratization as something Catholic and not as imitation of Protestantism. Pastoralists such as the Cursillistas often saw democratization as a reform of church structures, whereas liberationists grafted the parish organizations onto community mobilization goals such as those derived from Saul Alinsky and the Industrial Areas Foundation (IAF) (see Coleman, 1996a).

However, the resurgence vocabulary of causes did not include those that entailed political separatism. Thus, Puerto Rican independence, the more radical notions of Atzlán as a Chicano nation, the confrontational impulses of the La Raza Unida party, Tijerina's Alianza, the Brown Berets, and the Young Lords found little echo in church circles. The ideals of Puerto Rican independence and nationalism were never embraced nationwide and neither was the anti-Castroism of many Cuban Americans, although in Puerto Rico and Miami church leadership sometimes joined militant groups in demonstrations. Although there was tolerance of these causes within the leadership of the resurgence, they were depicted as too particular to be "Latino" or as threatening the success of the resurgence by associating it with extremist secular elements.

Four arguments—representativity, cultural idiosyncrasy, poverty as oppression, and democratization—set the ideological parameters for the resurgence and provided the general outline of the resurgence's intellectual roots. They were not written in any one place as a manifesto of an organization that set out to create the resurgence. But they emerged rather soon after 1967 as the premises for Latino reform of and through the churches. Fortunately, most have been collected and explained in *Prophets Denied Honor*.

Cross-Validation

The resurgence started with support for Chávez. Many Chicano and Mexican American parishes and congregations had been mobilized early during the Delano strike, starting in 1965. But the boycott in fall 1967 was national in scope and brought Puerto Ricans and Cuban Americans on the Atlantic seaboard into the ranks of supporters. The Chicano cause had become "La Causa" for these other Latinos as well, largely because the boycott, unlike Puerto Rican independence, had been embraced by the Catholic Church and many Protestant denominations.

But in the tenor of times in which ethnic groups were viewed as requiring one of their own as leader, support for Chávez created new sources to legitimate Latino leaders. This process has been described as "cross-validation" (Stevens-Arroyo, 1980:117–118, 198–200). In concrete terms, this meant that the *New York Times* or the *Los Angeles Times* called the young Latino priest for comments about the church's role with a Latino issue rather than an Irish-surnamed chancery official. This logic was based on the principle of cultural idiosyncrasy derived from secular politics that only a member of a minority group could speak for that minority group.

Cross-validation is the achievement of legitimacy from a source outside one's existing community, with the result that one gains power and influence because of a dual source of recognition. Within the Latino experience, cross-validation benefited young clergy and religious because the secular world bestowed on them a leadership function beyond the authority that the church allowed them. With Latinos increasingly restless in politics and neighborhood activism, it was assumed that the Spanish-surnamed clergy or religious sister (a woman consecrated to the religious life) was more the leader of the people than the canonical pastor or superior, who most likely was Euro-American. Church officials often felt compelled to accede to this logic and could only hope that Latino leaders would express loyalty to the institutional church. The Latino clergy, whose members were often very young and had little if any previous claim on church policy, were thrust into the role of spokespersons. Moreover, the process worked not only for male clergy but also for women, most dramatically for Latina religious, that is, the sisters, who could overnight supplant a Euro-American male cleric as the virtual leader of the Latino people in the parish.

A secular political norm had been imported into the ecclesiastical sphere. The institutional churches had to include Latinos and Latinas as leaders and as faithful clients, in order to function credibly in secular eyes. But in this new identification of Latino leadership, institutional Catholicism did not control the bases of legitimacy. Society and the Latino people exercised a role in determining who was a leader and who was not. Title and rank within the church were in themselves not sufficient to make a Latino religious leader; in fact, some leaders in the resurgence gained status among their colleagues and the people in proportion to the opposition they faced from the hierarchy. This fits the dynamics inherent in social movements in the secular arena.

PADRES

The political counterattack against Chávez and the UFW gathered strength during the 1968 presidential campaign. With Nixon at his side, governor of California Ronald Reagan called the Mexican American grape strikers "barbarians." Candidate Nixon claimed the grape strike was illegal and said it should be treated as "any other form of lawbreaking." A year later, as President Nixon, he ordered the Department of Defense to increase its grape purchases in an effort to undercut the farmworkers' boycott. The Teamsters' Union also launched an organizational drive among California lettuce workers in an effort to forestall further UFW incursions into the labor force. But Chávez's struggle came to be viewed as the legitimate voice of Chicano labor because Chávez was himself a Chicano, and according to the argument of representativity, he was a more legitimate spokesperson than any teamster.

The attacks by Nixon and Reagan as well as the teamsters stoked the ardor of Latino leadership, urging them to increased activism to defend La Causa. It became part of a show of solidarity for church leaders to march in picket lines for the UFW, and young clergy from different regions and denominations sometimes met for the first time while rallying in support of the farmworkers' cause. In February 1970, various priests from California and parts of the Southwest met in Tucson, Arizona, to discuss a way of coordinating support for Chávez among the Catholic communities of Mexican Americans that they served. From this meeting came PADRES, an organization for priests in the Mexican American ministry, and later in similar fashion Las Hermanas, the association for religious women. These networks continued even after negotiations bartered by the United States Catholic Conference produced a series of signed contracts with the grape growers over the course of summer 1970. Since the focus for organizing had been to educate parish members about the need to support the boycott as a Christian social justice responsibility, the groundwork that had been laid was easily adapted to more general goals that likewise required education at the grassroots level about issues of social justice.

The organizing meeting for PADRES set two important precedents for leadership roles in these tasks. First, the Catholic Church was targeted for reform on the premise that preaching social justice for the Mexican American farmworkers would be hypocrisy unless there was justice for all Mexican Americans in the Catholic Church. The meaning attached to the acronym PADRES suggests the wide horizon embraced by the organization: Padres Asociados para Derechos Religiosos, Educationales y Sociales translates as "Priests organized for religious, educational, and social rights" (Mosqueda, 1986:146–149; Cadena, 1987). Second, after much passionate debate, the organization excluded anyone not Mexican American from membership. This was later amended so that other Latino clergy could join, but Euro-Americans were still denied full membership. Although this decision about membership reflected the convictions about cultural idiosyncrasy and representativity for the Latino clergy, it deprived PADRES of the goodwill and participation of a large number of sympathetic Euro-American clergy working at the grassroots level.

Las Hermanas was also organized from the beginning for Mexican American sisters or nuns, but because it opened membership to all Latinas, it expanded to other regions of the country and among other nationalities more quickly and more successfully than PADRES (Díaz-Stevens, 1994a). Organized in local chapters that met regularly, Las Hermanas functioned much like a surrogate religious order. It offered a common ground for ministry and training to religious women who otherwise would have been separated from each other. Because it supplied mutual support for an identity as Latina individuals and church professionals, some of the members of Las Hermanas came to feel more loyalty to the organization than to their own congregations. When some of the members left religious life to become laywomen—a step that can be taken with considerably less stigma for Catholic religious sisters than for Catholic priests—Las Hermanas again changed its constitution to allow full membership rights for the former sisters and all laywomen.

Many of the religious women in Las Hermanas belonged to Catholic associations of catechetical teachers and parochial school faculty. They received swift confirmation as the Latina leaders in these professions through the mechanism of cross-validation. Visibility as leaders within Latino Catholicism met a growing need to train workers for ministries. The leaderships of Las Hermanas and PADRES were quick to identify the Mexican American Cultural Center (MACC) in San Antonio, established by Virgilio Elizondo, as the catalyst for this new kind of emphasis. Under the capable administration of Elizondo, MACC obtained funding for this pastoral training, arguing that if the national Catholic Church could fund programs such as the Catholic Interamerican Cooperation Program (CICOOP) to bridge the gap between Latin America and the United States, it made sense that similar financial and institutional support should be given to train people for the sake of Latinos already in the United States (see Stevens-Arroyo, 1980:241–242). This gave a new face to the already accepted notion of pastoral training in the culture and language of Latinos. Since the 1950s, the Bishops' Committee for the Spanish-Speaking under Archbishop Lucey (Privett, 1988) and the Institute for Intercultural Communications, established by Ivan Illich in Puerto Rico for the Northeast (Díaz-Stevens, 1993a:191–193), had provided excellent training programs for the clergy. But with the reforms of the Second Vatican Council, there was now a need for training, not in clerical cultural sensitivity toward Latino groups but in classes of theology and ministry for Latinos and Latinas themselves. The difference between MACC and its predecessors was that it was originated by Latinos and Latinas. The leadership and faculty roles certainly rested frequently, if not exclusively, with the Latinos and Latinas and no longer exclusively with the Euro-Americans alone.

The Encounters

In 1970, the United States Catholic Conference (USCC), the social work branch of the National Council of Catholic Bishops (NCCB) decided to move the Bishops' Committee for the Spanish-Speaking from its Texas office to the Catholic Church headquarters in Washington, D.C. Renamed the Division for the Spanish-Speaking, it immediately developed an agenda for integrating social concerns with pastoral care. This merging of two ministries made the office, later elevated to the rank of secretariat, a mirror of the offices for ministry to the Spanish-speaking population that dotted the country. Bishop Rausch, then administrator of the USCC, named as executive director Pablo Sedillo, a New Mexico native and layman who had started his career as an administrator of social programs. A Puerto Rican priest was invited to take charge of the pastoral issues, which at the USCC was ordinarily a career path to the episcopacy.[1] But instead—at the insistence of Father Robert Stern of the Archdiocese of New York—a Puerto Rican Catholic laywoman who was an experienced professional social worker in New York City, Encarnación Padilla de Armas, went to join Sedillo in Washington. The balancing of a Chicano and a Puerto Rican gave the new office national scope because the two largest of the nation's Latino groups were represented and the absence of a clerical "bishop-in-waiting" on the staff confirmed the message of the resurgence that the laity were ready for leadership.

The first major national event produced by the Latino Religious Resurgence was the Pastoral Encounter held by the Catholic Church in Washington in June 1972. The historical accounts of the events and the documents produced by the three-day deliberations are some of the more available sources for study of the period, and the tale need not be retold here. As suggested earlier in the chapter, the organizers were deroutinizers and deserve major credit for the success of the Pastoral Encounter. There were many deroutinizers during the resurgence who deserve more recognition for making the encounter documents into institutional policy. Robert Stern's role and that of the late Father Joseph Fitzpatrick, S.J. have been explained by Díaz-Stevens (1993a:127–141, 176–243). Edgar Beltrán, a Colombian priest who came to the United States and guided the process for pastoral planning is another such leader, as is Father Juan Romero, who was executive director for PADRES at a critical juncture.

Beltrán and Stern insisted that those attending the encounter needed certification by their dioceses as official delegates. This legalistic requirement for the attendees was crucial to the legitimacy of the deliberative process and was part of the mechanism that had guaranteed the effectiveness of the Latin American documents from Medellín. Perhaps the naming of diocesan delegations was not seen as a radical assertion of lay power but as still another admission of dependency on hierarchical authority. At any rate, given the mind-set of the U.S. episcopacy, once major prelates such as Terence Cardinal Cooke of New York and John Cardinal Krol of Philadelphia, then president of the NCCB, had given their approval, other bishops saw it necessary to get on board the moving train as it left the station.

During the encounter, there were several plenary presentations, including speeches by Father Elizondo and Bishop Flores, followed by workshops that were designed to produce specific policy recommendations. Pragmatic rather than utopian in focus, the suggestions of almost every panel called for the establishment of an officially recognized Latino committee with the power to formulate policy, publish guides, or gain representation equal to standing committees in the bureaucracy of U.S. Catholicism.

For those accustomed to national meetings of Chicano militants and Puerto Rican *independentistas*, the Pastoral Encounter may have been as bland as yesterday's taco. But for an essentially hierarchical institution such as Roman Catholicism, the proceedings were almost revolutionary. Precautions had been taken to exclude "radicals" such as Bishop Parrilla Bonilla of Puerto Rico, who was not invited; nor was Puerto Rican independence given any mention. Partisan political actions were avoided by talking more about all farmworker unionization efforts than about the particular struggle of the UFW in California. Finally, the exact wording of the documents was left to a select committee that had been designated beforehand.

This committee turned these documents produced by a democratic and egalitarian process into church policy. The committee trimmed the proposals so that almost every recommendation was built upon an existing institution or functioning program. By presenting what was truly innovative as "merely" extension of the already tried-and-true, the encounter effectively made successful local "experiments" into models for universal policy. Thus, for instance, in order to establish pastoral training centers in as many dioceses as possible, the documents pointed out the success of MACC in San Antonio. Continuity with current pastoral practice was emphasized over discontinuity, and the threat of further inroads by Protestants and Pentecostals was described as the inevitable result of inaction by the bishops. When the NCCB finally responded, it encouraged the establishment of more pastoral centers such as MACC. NCCB members were far more wary, however, of acceding to recommendations to name more Latino bishops and to placing major funds at the disposal of Latino church organizations.

The first encounter set in motion an intensive period of organization pointed toward the second encounter, but the process was not confined to Catholicism. Protestant denominational leadership recognized that something important was taking place. In retrospect, we see syzygy in the developments that allowed the resurgence to unfold while most of the mainline Protestant churches were headquartered in the same building at 475 Riverside Drive in New York City. The Latino representatives of several denominations frequently came together across denominational lines. Often responding to an invitation to match the Catholic dimensions of the resurgence, this handful of Latino Protestants orchestrated collaborative projects that gave impetus to a vital Protestant presence in the developing national movement. Methodists and Presbyterians, American Baptists and Dutch Reformed needed only to ride the elevator to visit with each other. Whereas PADRES and Las Hermanas had to carefully husband resources to gain a few precious planning hours together once a year, Latino Protestants could have brown-bag lunches almost any day of the week at the "God Box." These talented leaders joined together as Latinos to maximize their otherwise token influence. Once again, the whole was greater than the sum of its parts. Although Latino congregations were not the center of denominational concerns, the Latino Protestant administrators were able to foster unity by making strategic grants that benefited the emerging consciousness of the resurgence. These Latino leaders were usually better placed within the democratic structures of liberal Protestantism than their more numerous Catholic counterparts, who had to look up through many levels of celibate clerical hierarchy.

Theology in the Americas

In addition to many local projects of considerable merit focused on social needs or religious education, the Latino Protestants supported a coordinated effort to bring liberation theology to the United States. Called

"Theology in the Americas," this program was directed by Father Sergio Torres, a priest who had fled the Pinochet regime in his native Chile. He wanted to bring the theologians of Latin America, who had begun writing a corpus of works that emerged as "liberation theology," to lecture in the United States. But Father Torres envisioned the lecture series as a two-way dialogue that would engage U.S. theologians in a response and critique of their colleagues. The program was interdenominational, and the theologians from Latin America, who were mostly Catholic, gave the same talks at the interdenominational Union Theological Seminary in New York as at the Mexican American Cultural Center in San Antonio, Texas.

Eventually Torres's project was funded in 1973 as Theology in the Americas, receiving money from many denominations, including the Catholic Church. The project was located within the offices of Gilberto Marrero at the Presbyterian Church headquarters, then in New York City. After nearly two years of preparation, it held the first of its three conferences in Detroit in 1975. Like all programs, it had both strengths and weaknesses, but it easily dovetailed with the Latino Religious Resurgence, bringing a place at the table for Protestant Latinos. Increasingly accepted as seminary professors or as pastors, some of the Spanish-speaking Latino Protestants were expected by their denominations to become intermediaries between North American theologians and the Latin Americans.

Much in the model of the encounter, Theology in the Americas set about organizing a second conference that would hold a series of smaller assemblies as preparation. Instead of regional or diocesan meetings, however, the project organized itself by denomination and racial, ethnic, or gender caucuses. The first director of the Hispanic project was Anthony M. Stevens-Arroyo, whose connections to Roman Catholicism, the encounter process, and the Puerto Rican Independence movement had lent him considerable visibility.[2] The ensuing process of organization of the theology project and the encounter, however, experienced many of the same pressures that impacted on the specifically Catholic experience. The caucus and denominational organizational pattern proved to be a liability because it emphasized group self-interest without providing institutional or organizational strength. Catholics, for instance, were more likely to see the theology project as subordinate to the encounter preparations than as an autonomous process with different goals.[3]

Yet, on balance, the Theology in the Americas project contributed to the resurgence. The eventual adoption of the principles of liberation theology by a wide spectrum of mainline Protestant seminaries may be traced to the Latino leaders at the Inter-Church Center, who have influenced Protestantism far beyond what their limited numbers might have suggested. The project prepared the way for initiatives directed specifically toward Latino theology in the Hispanic Theology Project, which was a follow-up to the

1975 conference in Detroit and a step toward a second conference.[4] Finally, the momentum generated in Protestant theological circles about the vitality of the Latin American and Latino experience opened the door to creating a scholarship program specifically for Latinos in the Fund for Theological Education (FTE). After extensive reorganization, Theology in the Americas emerged as an association of Third World theologians.

A similar linkage between Latin America and Latinos was provided in the Catholic context by Moisés Sandoval. An experienced New Mexican journalist, he was hired as an editor of *Maryknoll Magazine* and came to Maryknoll headquarters outside New York City. Eventually, Orbis Books, which was related to the Maryknoll missionary association, became a major publisher of books on both liberation theology and the Latino church. Sandoval was well situated to publicize the connections between Latinos and Latin Americans and also to show the differences. He argued successfully that Latinos in the United States should be included in the project of the Commission for the Study of the History of the Church in Latin America (CEHILA). That effort produced in 1983 an important book entitled *Fronteras*, which, until the appearance of the Notre Dame Series in 1994, was the most current collection of historical essays on the church in the Southwest and California. Moreover, Maryknoll's School of Theology, later directed by the distinguished Venezuelan sociologist Otto Maduro, became a conduit for deepening these ties between Latin American and Latino Catholic intellectuals and their ideas.

Weakness of the Institutions

Following Randall Collins's analysis of social movements, it is important to list not only the strengths of the Latino side but the weaknesses of existing church structures, because the Latino resurgence benefited from Euro-American reticence. Collins (1981:71–106) describes the weakness as what he calls "stalemates and vacuums" and "balance of power." He suggests that when the hegemonic institution is lacking leadership or is engaged in a struggle between two or more factions in which none gains an upper hand, a social movement that is well organized and united can interject its own ideological legitimacy. Cervantes says as much when Sancho Panza declares that whether the clay pot hits the stone or the stone hits the clay pot, it is always bad for the pot. Because the post-Vatican Catholic Church had both a vacuum of leadership and a struggle between Euro-American conservatives and liberals (Burns, 1996), the Latino Religious Resurgence had a major impact, which would have been unlikely if the push for egalitarian participation had occurred at another time. The same may be said for mainline Protestantism, which was more vulnerable to the infectious enthusiasm of Latinos at a time when major headquarters were housed together in New York City.

There were roadblocks to the onward march of the movement in its de-routinization of ecclesiastical policy. The work of Ana María Díaz-Stevens in *Oxcart Catholicism* provides a detailed example of the resistance, and Lawrence Mosqueda (1986) offers much the same analysis in his typology. The reaction of church officials tended to focus on individuals in positions of official leadership, apparently believing that once the leader was removed the movement would wither. It was not widely understood that the resurgence had already set down deep roots and was not a creation from the top down, as many other Hispanic ministry programs had been. For instance, Cardinal Cooke of New York, who had supported the encounter at the beginning, had second thoughts after its conclusion. He forbade the promulgation of the encounter documents in the Archdiocese of New York.[5] When the archdiocesan council established by Father Stern met with the cardinal to defend the validity of the encounter and the wisdom of its policies and to question why the recommendations had not been implemented within the archdiocese, the cardinal took offense. Within two years of the fateful meeting, Stern had been dismissed, the Office of the Spanish Apostolate in New York had been shrunk, its programs underfunded and its staff dispersed as subordinates in other church agencies. As detailed in *Oxcart Catholicism*, the office that had done so much to establish a national dimension for Latino Catholicism did not last to enjoy its accomplishments.

But even the installation of a new set of leaders through the mechanism of the Northeast Regional Pastoral Center for Hispanics could not reverse the directions taken toward Latino leadership. Although it was not a grass-roots center—its offices were initially in upscale Park Avenue in downtown Manhattan—the Northeast Pastoral Center ended up being very much of a deroutinizer in liturgical matters. Reforms made though the network of regional centers were packaged in New York for NCCB approval (Pérez, 1994).

A similar process took place in Florida. The South East Pastoral Institute (SEPI) joined together the middle-class Catholics of greater Miami's Cuban exile community with the disparate enclaves of Mexican and Central American migrant workers and the working-class Puerto Rican community of Orlando. Under the able guidance of Father Mario Vizcaino, SEPI has successfully maintained its pastoral outlook and a robust commitment to social concerns and has still preserved Catholic unity among disparate groups divided not only by social class and ethnicity but by the fault line of Democratic and Republican politics in the southern states. SEPI is a direct result of the resurgence and the models for Latino ministry that it advocated. Without the need for a regional center to incorporate both social concerns and pastoral care, Florida's ministry to Latinos might easily have developed two separate approaches, divided along class lines. One might even argue that precisely because SEPI is located in the Latino population where social-class difference is most marked, it is the most successful of the regional centers in deroutinizing the previous *mentalité* and providing a new vision of Latino religion. Overall, deroutinization was most noticeable when pastoral plans were accepted. The transformation of the ideas of the resurgence into policy was the way new ideas displaced established concepts about the subordinate role of Latinos within the churches.

Protestant Leadership

Among Protestants, the Mexican Americans Jorge Lara-Braud, Roy Barton, and Rubén Amendáriz played key roles in converting the charisma of the moment into programs of Latino ministry that formed a generation of Protestant leadership. Much as resulted in the case of Father Robert Stern in Catholicism, these programs begun during the resurgence deroutinized the establishment approach to Latino religion. Nor were the originators of programs the only persons to nibble away at the passivity that Protestant denominations had shown toward Latino culture in ministry. As already described, Gilberto Marrero of the Presbyterian Church shepherded the development of the Theology in the Americas project. Other important contributors to the sense of interdenominational teamwork were the Cuban-born Cecilio Arrastía and the Mexican Americans Joel Martínez, who became a United Methodist bishop, and David Maldonado, who integrated the roles of administrator and innovator at Southern Methodist University. A somewhat different track of development was pursued by the American Baptist Puerto Rican theologians, among them Luis Rivera Pagán and the late Orlando Costas, whose major contributions were as commentators on liberation theology.

It cannot be said that Protestants lagged behind Latino Catholics in transforming the new understanding of Latino religion into programs funded by the institutional churches. The Hispanic-American Institute was originally suggested at the lofty levels of the National Council of Churches in 1968, when two Presbyterian members, Alfonso Rodríguez and John Mackay, urged that support for the cause of the farmworkers should have a solid base among local congregations in Texas and California. The proponents recognized that such a program should be directed by native Latino leaders. Established in Austin, Texas, in 1969, with funding support from the Presbyterian, United Methodist, Episcopalian, and Lutheran churches, the institute began with position papers intended to widen advocacy for the farmworkers and immigrants. But Jorge Lara-Braud, the first director, and Rubén Amendáriz, who succeeded him in 1973, moved beyond the limits of these social concerns into educational programs that included more permanent aspects of pastoral care. Much like the earlier

Catholic programs of Father Ivan Illich at Ponce, Puerto Rico, and later at Cuernavaca, Mexico, the Hispanic-American Institute structured its pedagogy around direct involvement with the people. Thus, ministers among Mexican Americans in the Southwest benefited from an intensive "January experience" of several weeks, during which they were immersed in the lived experience of the people.

PADRES officially supported the institute, responding to its interdenominational scope. But the encounter absorbed the greater part of PADRES's energies toward promoting MACC, the Catholic equivalent of the Hispanic-American Institute. In a sense, the Protestant vision of the institute was *too* successful because the denominations adopted the ideas for their own centers. Lara-Braud moved in 1973 to the Faith and Order Commission of the National Council of Churches with headquarters in New York City and finally to a faculty post at the Graduate Theological Union in Berkeley. In 1976, Amendáriz, who had earlier succeeded Lara-Braud as director of the institute, was invited to join the faculty of McCormick Theological Seminary in Chicago, where he organized a Hispanic ministry program and eventually became a professor of preaching and worship on the faculty of the seminary. After the institute suffered the loss of two visionary directors, it never fully claimed the loyalties or support of the denominations that had participated in its founding. But although the institute was subsequently closed, it cannot be considered to have failed. Its success argued that its programs should be adopted by each of the participating denominations. The institute gave birth to several programs that were permanently attached to established denominational seminaries. Nearly two decades later, the interdenominational approach that had its maximum expression during the resurgence in the institute was to appear again in the Hispanic programs of the Fund for Theological Education.

The Rio Grande Conference of the United Methodist Church was a cosponsor of the Hispanic-American Institute, but the conference—which had a large Mexican American membership—shifted its energies to the Mexican American Ministry Program at the Perkins School of Theology at Southern Methodist University in Dallas. Roy Barton, the son of a Mexican American mother and an Anglo Methodist father, had been named director of the Conference on Ministries of the Rio Grande Conference in 1964, and in January 1974 he became the first director of the ministry program at Perkins. The program was originally focused upon very basic needs of ministry: language skills in Spanish for native English speakers, orientation in Mexican American culture and history for seminary students, and specialized ministerial training for pastors in the Southwest. Eventually, Barton developed a full curriculum track at Perkins that offered a certificate in Mexican American theology and history. In 1980, Barton and his United Methodist colleague, Justo González, began work on *Apuntes*, a journal oriented toward the needs of ministry among Latinos. In both the Hispanic-American Institute at Austin and the more permanent Mexican American Ministry Program at Perkins, Latino Protestants pushed for much the same goals during the resurgence as their Catholic counterparts. Seemingly simple and limited in scope, greater attention to Latino ministry and culture almost always deroutinized the established approach of ecclesiastical institutions.

Women's Leadership

Given the clerical and male focus of the Catholic Church, it is remarkable that some of the more successful deroutinization came from women. Encarnación Padilla de Armas, a Puerto Rican laywoman from Brooklyn, went to Washington to the transplanted office that had previously focused almost exclusively on the needs of Mexican and Mexican American migrant farmworkers.

Her considerable organizational skills were key to achieving a national role for that office. In a story whose outline is known (Díaz-Stevens, 1993a:199–204) but which has not yet been told in full, it was doña Encarnación who steered the Washington office on its journey toward becoming the Spanish-speaking secretariat. With a high profile of work with Father Illich and Bishop Lucey, with experiences in San Antonio in Texas and at Cuernavaca in Mexico, doña Encarnación brought with her to the new national office a political and ecclesiastical sophistication that otherwise would have been lacking. Because she had been educated in Cuba and had worked in San Antonio, she knew far more of the Mexican American reality than Pablo Sedillo knew of the Puerto Rican or Cuban experiences. In effect, she mentored Sedillo, the director of the office during the first encounter, on the wily ways of East Coast Catholicism. She brought wisdom to the task that Sedillo, the New Mexico native, had not yet acquired. This was the woman who had confronted Cardinal Spellman about his neglect of Puerto Ricans (Díaz-Stevens, 1993a:104), had been secretary to Ivan Illich, and was a politically connected member of the Liberal Party in New York's Byzantine world of patronage (Fitzpatrick, 1971:59). With her forced retirement from the secretariat due to age, she returned to Brooklyn, where she administered a government-funded agency for Latino elderly almost up to the time of her death.

Protestant Latinas proved adept at forming caucuses and the like within existing organizations such as the United Methodist Women to accomplish deroutinization for the sake of Latino religion. When the post occupied by Ana María Díaz Ramírez (later Díaz-Stevens) at the Catholic Archdiocese of New York was "terminated" in 1973 (Stevens-Arroyo, 1980:208–213), she was hired by the Board of Global Ministries of the United Methodist

Church in New York to translate the program resources into Spanish. Published annually, the chief function of the program resources of the Women's Division was to serve as a guide to personal spirituality and pastoral formation for the year by providing a written reflection to all the United Methodist Spanish-speaking congregations in the United States and Puerto Rico. In 1974, however, Díaz initiated a new process. Under her leadership, instead of translations of articles already written in English, the United Methodist Latinas began to write original program resources in Spanish. They also contributed to the program resources for the English-speaking women. This was a commonsense change to make United Methodism more representative of its Latina members and give them charge over their own resources. Men were not excluded, either; in fact, Justo González was an early participant in this project. It had significant effects. The Latinas involved in writing the resources by invitation emerged as an autonomous committee that planned and strategized together around a specifically Latina agenda. In a pattern that was becoming familiar, an existing policy had been deroutinized so that the charisma of Latino culture was irreversibly introduced into ecclesiastical organization.

Some of the more well-known Protestant women to represent Latinas at national decisionmaking levels through this and similar processes were the Mexican American Raquel Martínez, the Cuban Consuelo Urquiza, the Puerto Rican Celsa Carrestegui, and the Bolivian Nora Quiroga Boots. Although it is impossible here to list every woman who became a deroutinizer or to explain how each contributed to the process, it should be emphasized that the resurgence depended on women as well as men.

But one did not have to be connected to the church bureaucracy to be a successful deroutinizer. Before the resurgence, a nun like Sister Carmelita Bonilla, M.S.B.T. in Brooklyn, and Pentecostal preachers like Leonicia Rosado and Aimee García Cortese (Sánchez-Korrol, 1988) provided examples of ministries that were driven by the talents of Latinas operating in male-dominated churches. The grassroots women whose leadership roles took on a national character during the resurgence were connected to these pioneers. Olga Villa Parra was herself a migrant worker and joined with Chávez in La Causa in the earliest days of the organizing effort. Her Catholicism was renewed by Chávez's example. Partly because of her connection to the UFW, she was hired by bishops in the Midwest to organize the ministry to migrant workers there. The Midwest Pastoral Office in South Bend, Indiana, was the result of her efforts, and unlike other centers, it did much of its work in the field among the scattered communities rather than in its office facilities. Villa Parra quickly fused her knowledge of social service needs of the farmworkers with the pastoralist goals of the bishops. Thus, she was well placed to assume leadership of the training of clergy and lay leaders when those functions were added to the mission of the center. Later, she was to find a national role for her talents as deroutinizer when in 1990 she was employed by the Lilly Endowment as Hispanic program officer, a post she held for five years.

The Cursillo movement among Latinas nationwide produced a host of grassroots deroutinizers whose targets were individual parishes. For instance, Haydée Borges in New York went from leader of a parish Legion of Mary into the Cursillo movement in 1965, soon becoming one of the woman rectors. As the new ideas of the Vatican Council and then of the encounters entered into Catholicism, Borges grew into a role that articulated women's concerns from the experiences of a working-class laywoman (in Stevens-Arroyo, 1980:290–291). She helped adapt the notion of *comunidades de base* into a form that connected with the Cursillo experience. Borges played an active role in establishing Cristianos Hispano-Americanos pro Justicia (CHAPJ), which conducted a news conference on March 28, 1973, attended by major New York media to denounce the inaction of Cardinal Cooke in the implementation of the encounter's conclusions (Stevens-Arroyo, 1980:278). She continued to press for action by editing a newsletter *El pueblo pide*. Borges was deroutinizer of her parish's Legion of Mary because of her connection to the Cursillo; she helped deroutinize local Cursillo groups (*ultreyas*) through her involvement in the encounter; her righteous wrath at an archdiocesan bureaucracy that refused to implement the pastoral recommendations of the people was based on her concern for the parish leaders whom she had helped train with the new ideas, only to find them thwarted by the chancery's inaction. These frustrations with ecclesiastical administrators never separated her from the church, however, or from her parish-based involvements. She is one among a host of Latinas who lived through the resurgence, learned its lessons, and contributed to its success while still holding a nine-to-five job.

The Latino Religious Resurgence would never have appeared without the organizational talents of these deroutinizers. Their willingness to promote the pastoral plans rather than their own names or denominations imparted a national character to the resurgence. Leadership flowered in a thousand different places with a unified message about *el pueblo* (the people) that institutions could not easily dismiss. Because of the deroutinizers—and they were many more than can be mentioned here—the resurgence acquired the social movement characteristics outlined by Alain Touraine (listed in Chapter 4) and adapted them to the Latino circumstance: (1) It fashioned a new history for the collectivity to help it define itself vis-à-vis the Euro-American churches, (2) it justified a plan of action, and (3) it motivated its members for collective action.

The Encounter Results

In the task of communicating the new understanding of culture and ministry to the parish and the congregation, the resurgence probably had more successes than failures. The Catholic process is the easiest to measure, and because it holds membership of two-thirds of Latinos, it occupies a central role. The Protestant and Pentecostal experiences are analyzed more completely in the next two chapters. These groups learned from the Catholics and fashioned their own place within the resurgence, just as Protestants had done during the Italian *risorgimento* (Spini, 1989). In a sense, just as one has to understand the Evangelical revivals of the American nineteenth century before analyzing their counterpart in Catholic revivalism (Dolan, 1978), the Latino Religious Resurgence has first to be explained in its Catholic dimensions.

After the first encounter, twenty different regions and dioceses held their own encounters from Houston, Texas, in September 1972 to Saginaw, Michigan, in May 1976 (Stevens-Arroyo, 1980:313–315). The process was essentially the same as had been established for the first encounter: elected delegates, specialized committees, written recommendations, climaxed by democratic voting on the resolutions that would become included in a pastoral plan. The secretariat in Washington, under Pablo Sedillo's supervision and Edgar Beltrán's guidance, coordinated the regional process as steps toward a second encounter that was to be held in Washington in August 1977. Each regional encounter reported on the progress of implementation of the recommendations of the first national meeting as part of the preparation for the second one. But certain regions enjoyed more success than others in the implementation of the reforms. Certainly, the openness of the bishops in each of the several regions and the talent of local organizers each played a role. But there were social factors that preconditioned some areas to progress more easily than others. This uneven pace of the resurgence results sowed the seeds for conflict.

Although the secretariat in Washington deserves accolades for the rapid transformation of recommendations from a movement into a national network of Catholic organizations, solidly rooted in local communities, it also deserves some criticism. The strategy of promoting a set of successful programs so that they could become national models became identified, as did the secretariat, with the Mexican American experience. By 1973, doña Encarnación had accepted retirement from Washington, and her eventual successor was Father Frank Ponce from San Bernardino, California. Ponce had no experience with Puerto Ricans and was almost unknown outside of California at the time of his hiring. His appointment violated the principle of representativity—of hiring individuals from diverse Latino groups—that was being advanced in the name of Latinos for the whole church. There were more Mexican Americans in the Latino resurgence than all the other groups put together, so their experience justly deserved its prominence. But it was the way that the dominance was used to obscure the legitimacy of other experiences that proved divisive. Mexican American leaders sometimes lapsed into a pattern of using "Latino" (or "Hispanic") interchangeably with "Mexican American," as if the two were the same.[6] Moreover, the symbols and experiences employed by the Mexican Americans did not stir the collective memory of non-Mexican American Catholics.

But reconciling representativity and group interest afflicted not only the Mexican Americans but the other groups as well, although in different contexts. The numerical dominance of Mexican Americans at the national level was replicated by Puerto Ricans and Cubans within certain regions. For example, Dominicans in New York City did not want to be lumped together with Puerto Ricans; Nicaraguans in Miami did not want to be mistaken for Cuban Americans. These are not bitter conflicts but rather natural affirmations of legitimate cultural pride. It is important, therefore, to examine the causes for such frictions and to assess how they ultimately damaged Latino unity.

Much of the success of MACC had been due to its high concentration of Mexican Americans in the region, a circumstance described as mono-Hispano, in the terminology of the 1970s.

> The mono-Hispano communities have less diversity; hence their cultural homogeneity is likely to produce unity on questions of Hispano identity. . . . The mono-Hispano situation is more cohesive and therefore lends greater strength to the Hispanos when they collectively address an institution like the church or government. (Stevens-Arroyo, 1980:198)

The multi-Hispano region, by contrast, needs to reconcile the disparate groups to a common agenda before the total community can be organized. Thus, in San Antonio a call for Mexican American solidarity reaches about 90 percent of the population. In New York City, a call for a Puerto Rican agenda divides Latinos into segments, with Puerto Ricans composing about 60 percent of the Latino population, while the other 40 percent, composed of Dominicans, Colombians, Central Americans, and other Latin Americans, are likely to feel that they are not included. The same can be said of Miami, where "Cuban" is misapplied as meaning all Latinos.

Other factors first described in the 1980 book *Prophets Denied Honor* merit consideration. The ratio of Latinos to the total population is an important measure of social influence. For instance, there were about 8,000 Mexican Americans in Crystal City, Texas, in 1970, and the total population of the town was only 10,000. These 8,000 Mexican Americans had greater influence in their hometown than the 24,000 Puerto Ricans in Newark, New Jersey, with its total population of 381,930.

A similar sort of analysis needs to measure the ratio of Latino Catholics to the entire Catholic population. For instance, the entire state of Arizona in 1970 had a population of 264,000 Mexican Americans, slightly less than the 289,000 Latinos in New Jersey, "but there are only 414,561 Catholics in Arizona so that Hispanos form a healthy majority of 64 percent, while, in New Jersey, the Hispanos are only 13.5 percent of the total Catholic population of some 2.1 million" (Stevens-Arroyo, 1980:197). The presence of many other ethnic groups also affects the church response to Latinos. If the bishop fears that acceding to Latino demands will open the door for groups of Haitians, Poles, Italians, French Canadians, and so forth to demand equal status in programs, offices, and clerical attention, the diocese is less likely to follow the encounter recommendations than if Latinos are the only significantly large ethnic group.

Thus the emphasis Catholics placed on MACC and San Antonio as "models" imposed unrealizable expectations on other regions. The Northeast, in particular, was faced with the anomaly of a region predominantly Puerto Rican but without an agenda that reflected Puerto Rican cultural patterns. This might have become a strength for the Northeast if its leaders had been able to focus on issues particular to the inter-Latino reality. But the criteria sent out by the Washington secretariat placed a priority on emulation of the Mexican American success story. More important, several leaders in multi-Hispano regions were unjustly characterized as antagonistic to the goals of the resurgence or as interested in career advancement, when in fact they were trying to adapt the policies to their own particular situation. And because the secretariat disproportionately promoted Mexican Americans from MACC as "experts," reliance on this leadership could be used to discredit local leaders attempting to assert the differences of their region from the Southwest and California, as if they were antagonistic to the resurgence.

These dynamics made confrontations between the multi-Hispano regions and the mono-Hispano policies inevitable. For instance, the secretariat sought and obtained special funding for Latino participation in the 1976 Eucharistic Congress that was to be held in Philadelphia. A Mexican American priest from the Archdiocese of Santa Fe was assigned to organize this celebration. But the priest, Lucian Hendren, soon alienated a number of Puerto Rican leaders in the dioceses of New York, Brooklyn, and Philadelphia by his insistence upon Mexican American experience as the matrix for what was "Latino." The tensions came to a head when Hendren and Sedillo attempted to prevent youth groups from the Brooklyn and New York dioceses from marching as representatives of all Latino Catholic youth in one of the processions of the Eucharistic Congress. In essence, it was a trivial matter, but it led to a threat from Juan Amengual, C.M., the priest director of the Brooklyn diocese's youth movement, to demonstrate against the secretariat. A still more difficult confrontation arose with Puerto Rican Cursillistas when the secretariat tried to argue, unsuccessfully, that Archbishop Flores should be the celebrant at the Spanish language liturgy and not Cardinal Archbishop Aponte Martínez of San Juan because "Puerto Rico was not a state" and therefore Aponte Martínez was not "Latino."

The Second Encounter

The conflicts at the Eucharistic Congress were relatively unimportant, but the rivalries of the inter-Latino nationalities became more apparent. A growing number of other Latino groups perceived that the Mexican Americans might become among Latinos what the Irish had been among other ethnic Catholics. Reflecting on the ways that Irish Americans had taken a lion's share of episcopal sees and subordinated other ethnic groups like the Polish and the Italian, there was a fear that Mexican Americans, because of their numbers, were dominating the other Latino groups. To its credit, the secretariat recognized the issue and addressed these difference in the Second Encounter in Washington that adopted the theme "Unity in Diversity" (Stevens-Arroyo, 1980:323–324).

Instead of alleviating these tensions, however, the Second Encounter exacerbated them (Stevens-Arroyo, 1980:324–326; Isasi-Díaz, 1977/1980). The preparations for the Second Encounter adopted a measuring stick that evaluated each region through a Mexican American prism. It may be that this was unavoidable, since the First Encounter had suggested Mexican American pastoralist models for emulation. But unfortunately the diversity proclaimed in the title of the Second Encounter was relegated to a few symbols and rituals. And when these ceremonies suffered from poor organization, there were few substantive issues to rely upon for defense.

For example, in the opening ceremony of the Second Encounter, a parade of all the flags from Latin America omitted the flag of Puerto Rico. When the offended Puerto Ricans complained and demanded an apology, the encounter organizers dismissed the protest. The indifference of the official response was interpreted as a further snub. The situation was not improved when the encounter held two public liturgies, one in a Mexican American cultural mode, with Aztec dance and mariachi music, the other in the National Shrine, organized by Cuban liturgists. There was no celebration that used Puerto Rican culture or music. Finally, in what must surely be the most ironic of comments, journalist Moisés Sandoval, whose job at Maryknoll was partly based on his capacity to translate from Spanish, complained that most of the proceedings at the Second Encounter were conducted in the Spanish language. This measure, he said, "frustrated" Mexican Americans who speak English better than Puerto Ricans and Cubans but are not as proficient in Spanish (Sandoval, 1990:83).

But the frictions among Latinos went both ways. For instance, the mostly Chicano PADRES attempted to embrace non-Mexican American clergy as members or affiliates because the organization wanted to become truly national. On the advice of Anthony M. Stevens-Arroyo, who was vice president of PADRES at the time, the annual meeting for spring 1976 was held in New York City. The leaders of the Northeast's Association of Hispanic Priests (ASH) were invited to attend. There was hope that there was a way ASH could affiliate with PADRES without either group sacrificing its regional roots. Many of the ASH members were not diocesan priests but were so-called "extern clergy," working with a contract for a limited amount of time, or clergy from religious orders dedicated to missionary work. Many of the ASH members were Basques or Spaniards. Significantly, Bishop Parrilla Bonilla from Puerto Rico and Bishop Roque Adames from the Dominican Republic were invited because they represented the native clergy of these two groups in the New York area. Future bishops of the Northeast such as René Valero, David Arias, Alvaro Corrada del Río, and Roberto González also attended. But the members of ASH declined the invitation for affiliation, fearing that PADRES would swallow them up.

Not all of the conflicts were among Latinos: Latin Americans in the United States sometimes resisted the Latino movement. Las Hermanas was rebuffed in its attempt to recruit the large number of Mexican nuns working at many U.S. seminaries in cooking, washing, and cleaning (Herrera, 1994). These congregations had defined their service to the church in terms of such domestic work. Many of their members came from families of modest means in Mexico and Central America, and their preparation for the sisterhood did not include the emphasis on formal education or professional training that was common among U.S. congregations of religious women. For Las Hermanas, it was difficult to accept that most of these Mexican sisters were contented with domestic chores. They had spurned Las Hermanas, sometimes commenting that the Latinas were too much the "feminists" (see Díaz-Stevens, 1994a).

Puerto Rican and Radical Politics

Catholicism was not the only denomination to experience cracks in Latino unity. The Episcopal Church inherited a native Puerto Rican leadership that held to many ideals of the Puerto Rican Nationalist Party. The Hispanic Commission of the church funded several community projects supportive of these ideals. But U.S. intelligence agencies spying on clandestine Puerto Rican liberation groups alleged these projects were connected to terrorists. When the FBI agents came calling, they demanded the commission's records and obliged the Chicana director, María Cueto and her secretary, Raisa Nimitzen, to testify before a grand jury. The two women refused, and both were incarcerated on charges of contempt in 1972. Support for the prisoners from church colleagues was spotty and timid, probably because there was increasing fear of reprisals from the Nixon administration. Certainly, the same sort of rumblings had been raised against Chávez, but in his case, the accusations had been shrugged off. However, supporting underground freedom fighters who wanted separation from the United States was far more threatening than unionizing agricultural workers.

This avoidance of connections to radicals helped Cuban American moderates to join in the centrist goals of the resurgence, but it had negative effects on solidarity with Puerto Rico. The inability to introduce the controversial issue of Puerto Rican independence into the agenda of the Latino Religious Resurgence divorced the movement from its counterparts within the churches of Puerto Rico. For instance, the U.S. Navy had conducted test strafing and bomb attacks on the island of Culebra since the 1940s. Culebra is a small island—scarcely ten square miles in area—and at the time had an impoverished population of less than one thousand, which for many years had fatalistically resigned itself to the situation. But in 1969, an ecumenical group in Puerto Rico participated in the "occupation" of one of the island's public beaches, led by independence militants. The occupation violated a navy ordinance that the beaches were closed during the time of test bombing. Luis Rivera Pagán, an American Baptist professor at the Seminario Evangélico, was jailed for his civil disobedience. To a large crowd outside the prison where Rivera Pagán was held prisoner, Bishop Parrilla Bonilla and Friar William Loperena delivered emotional statements challenging the legitimacy of the navy's actions. In one of history's ironic events, Anthony M. Stevens-Arroyo, who was employed by the Archdiocese of New York at that time, comes from a family that founded the town in Culebra and still owns the land around the beach where the civil disobedience took place. But Stevens-Arroyo was given the task of reporting to Puerto Rican community leaders that the archdiocese had decided that the issue was to be ignored because it was "too political."

This distancing of the resurgence from the 1969 Culebra protest, even though it so clearly resembled the tactics of César Chávez and Martin Luther King, impeded solidarity. The churches in Puerto Rico took reprisals against these leaders, Catholic and Protestant, suspending Loperena, isolating Parrilla, and expelling Luis Rivera Pagán and his colleague Samuel Silva Gotay from seminary posts. But because the basic issues had been avoided at the beginning, the U.S. Puerto Rican leaders involved in the resurgence were unable to elicit statements of Latino support for their island colleagues.

Although leadership continued to show great trepidation about Puerto Rican causes, grassroots Latinos and Latinas occasionally demonstrated a keener sense of fairness. One example came in 1979, after President Carter freed the surviving Puerto Rican Nationalist prisoners. Their release had been requested by a majority of Puerto Rican church leaders, including all of the Catholic bishops, the Episcopal Church, and many of the Protestant denominations on the island. Despite the radical actions of these Nationalists in 1950 and 1954 in the Congress building, their freedom had become a humanitarian issue with bipartisan political support in Puerto Rico. In New York City, where the recently freed prisoners were to stop before returning to the island, Anthony M. Stevens-Arroyo proposed a liturgy at Saint Paul the Apostle church to thank God for their release. It should be remembered that this Paulist church had provided a similar service for César Chávez during the 1960s.

But access to the church was in the hands of the parish council. The Puerto Rican Cursillista leader, Edward Kalbfleish, argued that if Saint Paul's could annually host a liturgy for the survivors of the Cuban exile expedition at the Bay of Pigs, it needed to respect diversity and provide an opportunity to a Puerto Rican cause—in spite of its political implications. One must know that the politics of Kalbfleish are in the direction of statehood, not independence. Yet not only did he make this argument successfully, but Cuban exiles agreed with him. The immense church was filled to capacity and the liturgy was conciliatory, justifying the decision of the parish council. Yet predictably, the media continually asked how the church could support "terrorists."

Thus, with the exception of the Episcopal Church, the question of Puerto Rican independence never became part of the vocabulary of the resurgence. Episcopalian Puerto Ricans, especially in Chicago, have maintained their nationalist commitments and continue to support causes such as freedom for the seventeen Puerto Rican political prisoners still held in federal prisons. But the Episcopal Church as an official body, like many Protestant churches, became much more cautious about the type of projects supported with official funds.

The question of Puerto Rican independence has been an issue "too hot to handle" for the leadership of the resurgence. In similar ways, aspects of the Chicano militancy and the Cuban issues—both for and against the revolution—have been avoided by most national Latino church leaders. But there are signs that the ordinary people are more courageous than their leaders. The most interesting developments may come from the Cuban American religious community. At the Miami airport in 1996, boxes of food and clothing collected from area churches to assist the Cuban hurricane victims became the platform for speeches of political types attempting to stop the shipments. Helping the Cuban people at a time of need was equated with being a Communist lackey of Fidel Castro. But the boxes were delivered, suggesting that the practice of virtue overrides politics for religious believers.

Such conflicts are healthy, in our opinion. Moreover, they were inherited along with the successes of the Latino Religious Resurgence. But while the movement flourished, few were affected by divisions of theology, inter-Latino diversity, and political involvement with radical causes. As long as the resurgence was able to focus on goals that all the diverse interests held in common, the differences did not derail its effectiveness. But within Catholicism, the uneven success of institutionalization in the different regions eventually produced winners and losers. When John Paul II became pope and Ronald Reagan became president of the United States, the time of syzygy came to an end.

Notes

1. This is confirmed by Anthony M. Stevens-Arroyo, who was an assistant to Father Stern at the time.

2. Curiously, in a semidocumentary, semifictional account of the conclave that elected John Paul I, Malachi Martin uses Stevens-Arroyo as the basis for "Father Antonio Arroyo," a character in his novel, which made the *New York Times* bestseller list in 1978. See *The Final Conclave* (New York: Pocket Books, 1978), 186ff.

3. Stevens-Arroyo made this report to Sergio Torres, which ran counter to the expectations of the Chilean priest. An Argentinian Jesuit priest, Santiago O'Farrell, substituted for Stevens-Arroyo in organizing the preparatory meeting at MACC. This was the only activity of the Hispanic Project under O'Farrell, but it produced no document for the second Detroit conference. In fact, Elizondo and Flores, who had insisted that the Hispanic Project meet in San Antonio and that Puerto Rican independence leaders would not be invited, did not attend the second Detroit meeting.

4. Anthony M. Stevens-Arroyo was director of the Hispanic Theology Project and accepted a simultaneous part-time post as the director of the Fund for Theological Education Hispanic Grant program. Thus, his task was to develop a national project of theological reflection and at the same time to recruit new theologians by offering scholarships. He was succeeded in the FTE project by Benjamin Alicea, who became the first full-time director.

5. This is fine point of canon law that denies validity to a policy until it is "promulgated," that is, announced within the ecclesiastical territory. The legal force of this stipulation derives from the Middle Ages, when printing and literacy were so rare that documents were understood by the general public only after they had been read aloud in a public place. This announcement was called "promulgation," and the spoken word rather than the signed document carried the force of law.

6. The Mexican American Cultural Center for a time published a newsletter in which MACC was translated as "Movimiento de Actividades Culturales Católicas" (Movement of Catholic Cultural Activities), identifying the Mexican American agency as the representative of all Latino Catholics. Funds were solicited suggesting MACC served all the nation's Latinos.

6

Ledger

THE LATINO RELIGIOUS RESURGENCE did not achieve all of its goals, but neither can it be said to have failed. Social or religious movements frequently set utopian goals, which by definition can never be fully achieved. In the case of the resurgence, the early successes were largely organizational. Latino leaders wanted to turn a movement, formed by volunteers rallying around a general idea, into an array of organizations with personnel and resources to implement the vision. But creating organizations is easier than maintaining them. Moreover, because most of the organizations were dependent on funding and recognition from larger church institutions, their future was in the hands of the very authority they criticized. The rapid success of the resurgence in establishing church-related organizations financed by the ecclesiastical institutions was therefore a Faustian bargain that insured early acceptance of general goals but spawned long-term ambiguity about particulars.

Moreover, transforming a movement into an organization and then converting an organization into an effective part of the institution are very different processes. The strategies and tactics useful in one stage may prove counterproductive in the next. For instance, the leadership skills essential to heading a movement may not be useful for directing an organizational post that has to navigate through the protocols of an institutional bureaucracy. There is no reason to doubt that the leaders of the resurgence knew all of this, of course, but it is always hard for those involved in a process to draw the lines between phases. Thus, we find different interpretations of the resurgence among our colleagues who struggled with us to bring it to birth. Some still harbor quixotic striving for "impossible dreams" and believe that as long as justice is denied, pursuit of resurgence goals must always use the same confrontational tactics. Others see the resurgence as less important than its results. They point to the appointments of Latino leaders to key institutional posts and now consider it imperative that Latino organizations should defend the larger ecclesiastical institutions instead of attacking them. Finally, there are those who no longer care. Time brings the inevitable "graying" of leadership: As one gets older, energy levels diminish, family and career concerns intrude, and passion for *la lucha* (the struggle) subsides. In the Catholic case, some of the leadership resigned from the active priesthood or religious life, diminishing standing within official Catholicism.

Assessment of the resurgence is much like a bookkeeping task, where success is tallied in black ink and failure in red, with the balance between the two appearing on the bottom line. As suggested in the previous chapter, the resurgence succeeded in fostering a plethora of Latino organizations focused on pressuring ecclesiastical institutions. But these successes often brought conflicts in their wake. Ironically, the disadvantages of diversity in the multi-Hispano regions at the early stages of organization have slowly become advantages in the 1990s because multiculturalism and pluralism have replaced cultural idiosyncrasy as a rallying cause. Thus, it is not always easy to decide what is a plus and what is a minus; indeed, the same result can merit both classifications, depending on the perspective.

The analogy of bookkeeping suggests we add some sophisticated notions of capitalization and privatization, religious marketing, investments for the future, boom and bust, write-offs, downsizing, and franchising to make sense of the resurgence. We hasten to add, however, that use of these metaphors should not be interpreted as an embrace of rational choice theory in the sociology of religion. Moreover, we need to recognize that although the movement phase of the resurgence came to an end by 1984, a second and potentially more important phase is still under way. Thus, if we take stock of achievements of the resurgence now, we could be compared to a Wall Street trader quoting the current stock price, although the long-term payout in cash value is not yet certain.

The Irreversible Changes

It seems evident, however, that as a religious movement, the resurgence has made certain irreversible changes in religion in the United States. This is our appraisal of the key victories. First, the premises of pious colonialism that undermined Latino religion and portrayed it as inferior to the Euro-American experience are now untenable. Second, the confidence that Latinos will be assimilated into the fabric of U.S. society like European immigrant groups has been successfully challenged, creating room for programs that maintain Latino language and culture in the churches and in broader society. Third, the resurgence spelled a change in the *mentalité* of 1960s-generation Latinos and Latinas, so that culture is now afforded a much more positive role in religious believing and ministry. Fourth, this change in thinking has affected not only Latinos and Latinas but other peoples of color and Euro-Americans alike. Fifth, policy formulation in religious institutions is expected to respect the democratic process and premises of diverse representation.

If culture and ministry are now understood differently by non-Latinos, the original arguments of the resurgence have been modified for Latinos also. Among Catholics, for instance, there is less interest in pressing for representativity in episcopal nominations in the 1990s than during the resurgence. The militant stridency of cultural idiosyncrasy that almost defined ethnic identity as a requisite for leadership has been supplanted with a more tolerant message of mutual respect in the embrace of multiculturalism. Although the appointment of a Latino bishop is still welcomed, the bishop's policies are considered more important than his ethnicity.

In all denominations, poverty is still viewed as oppression, but the tendency toward viewing it as victimization seems lessened now. Obviously, someone is to blame for poverty. The movement witnessed sweeping generalizations about how the white race, Anglo culture, U.S. imperialism, and the church had shackled Latinos to inescapable passivity. Diagnosis of social ills today has moved toward a more critical stance that considers worldwide trends and is not afraid to examine Latino deficiencies. The most important achievement of the resurgence, however, may prove to be the way it has embedded the process of democratization into church life. This has occurred at almost every level of religious experience and in almost all denominations. Pride in Latino culture, expressiveness of the Latino religious imagination, and an admirable competence in grassroots leadership have enabled this democratization process to prosper.

The identity of Latinos as a protest group began during the resurgence and endures today in the general acceptance of multiculturalism. Reliance on organic intellectuals as part of a process of empowerment of the people established a standard by which to judge Latino church organizations. Do these agencies and associations function as guardians of the integrity of Latino religion? Or are they more concerned about the preservation of the institutional church than about the people's needs? A sense of high moral purpose enabled the resurgence to almost end pious colonialism. It was impossible to claim that the policies of pious colonialism were geared toward the benefit of Latinos, when Latinos and Latinas themselves argued otherwise in the name of the faith. This impulse within the resurgence also fixed certain criteria by which ecclesiastical institutions could be judged for their responsiveness to Latino religion. Representation of Latinos in decision-making positions, the commitment of institutional resources, and such measures became expectations that if not fulfilled to some degree, exposed an institution to criticism as prejudiced against Latinos. Put in other terms, the resurgence created "symbolic capital" for Latino religion that could be used vis-à-vis any religious institution. Latino organizations, departments, commissions, caucuses, and the like could appeal to this symbolic capital as armament for opposing prejudicial policies. Thus, the resurgence not only affected Latinos but simultaneously impacted on all institutionalized religion in the United States. We still do not know if transculturation will take place, that is, if the cultures of Latinos and Euro-Americans will form a new hybrid. Nor can we predict how African-American and Asian American interests will fit into the picture as Latinos become the country's largest minority. We can be sure, however, that the Latino and Euro-American views of faith and culture are now connected within the life of church institutions.

Latino Franchising

Latino religion is not some amorphous fabrication. Nor are we claiming that it is a labeling device, meaning that wherever there is a Latino, there is also Latino religion. Rather, we insist that coupled to a generational *mentalité*, Latino religion consists of specific organizations, most of which have been franchised by the larger church to service Latino members. Found within almost every U.S. denominational structure, these organizations are also connected to each other in advocating the three goals described above: maintenance of Latino cultural identity, critique of existing policy, and accountability to the Latino people.

Because it has always been the church of most Latinos, Catholicism is the most affected of institutionalized denominations. The resurgence has restructured U.S. Catholicism so that the Catholic Church in the United States is different today that it would have been if the Latino Religious Resurgence had never taken place. Of course, history and socioeconomic changes always work to restructure religious institutions, thus not every change in Catholicism can be attributed to Latinos. The careful analysis of the interplay of social changes and the restructuring of American religion provided by Robert Wuthnow in a book of the same name (*The Restructuring of American Religion: Society and Faith Since World War II,* 1988) needs to be invoked here. But Latinos (or Hispanics) are not featured in his exposition. We feel it useful, therefore, to apply Wuthnow's approach to the Latino resurgence for its contribution to the restructuring of U.S. Catholicism.

Catholic structures depend in large measure upon the collective decisions of the bishops. With its hierarchical ranking of ordained clergy, Catholicism has a command structure almost unique in major world religions. As already suggested, the Catholic leadership of the resurgence appealed directly to the bishops for approval of the pastoral plan democratically developed through the encounters. The U.S. bishops take collective action through the National Conference of Catholic Bishops, the council for official national policy of U.S. Catholicism, in accord with the decrees of the Second Vatican Council. The NCCB has approved and often funded organizations that advocate Latino cultural awareness in every aspect of the ministry. Moreover, a wide spectrum of church activities have been sponsored in order to implement the vision.

But the proposals that came through the encounters during the resurgence were not the first suggestions to U.S. bishops for a turnabout in how culture was incorporated into ministry. In fact, the history of U.S. Catholicism provides us with a nineteenth-century document that anticipated many of the encounter recommendations. A detailed comparison is offered here to measure how official Catholicism responded to the challenge. Much like the "before-and-after" photographs that compare the ninety-seven-pound weakling to the muscular Charles Atlas, the strength of the Latino Religious Resurgence in effecting structural change stands in sharp contrast to the feebleness of the nineteenth-century attempt (Stevens-Arroyo, 1987).

The Lucerne Memorial and the First Encounter Document

Peter Paul Cahensly, a nineteenth-century German Catholic layman of means, was appalled by the deficiencies of the spiritual attention to Germans who had migrated to the United States. Adopting the patronage of Saint Raphael, protector of travelers, the society he helped found in 1871 provided both information and services to emigrants to better prepare them for the difficulties they would encounter upon arrival in America. The idea was not completely new, with precedents in proposals to Cardinal Gibbons from Father Abbelen, vicar general of the Diocese of Milwaukee (Tomasi, 1975:82–84), but Cahensly's group became an effective advocate of a more culturally sensitive ministry and the St. Raphaelsverein eventually had branches in Italy, Spain, and Belgium.

The national leaders of the St. Raphaelsverein met at Lucerne, Switzerland, December 9–10, 1890, and drafted proposals for better pastoral care of immigrants in the United States, which Cahensly was to forward to the Vatican. This is the basic context for the Lucerne Memorial, presented by Cahensly to Pope Leo XIII on April 16, 1891. With characteristic diplomacy, the Vatican made no direct pronouncement on the suggestions that had come from the St. Raphaelsverein. The Holy See sought first to consult with bishops in the United States, since many of the recommendations dealt with pastoral practice shown the migrants in America. Although separated by more than seventy years of history, the similarities of the memorial with the encounter recommendations are thought provoking.

The Lucerne Memorial has eight basic points. The first states that there should be a "distinct parish, congregation or mission" for each different group of immigrants of a particular nationality. The document of the encounter (no. 21) recognizes the type of national parishes referred to by Cahensly as "personal parishes (worshiping communities canonically established not on the basis of a certain territory, but rather on the basis of a certain group of people who have something in common)." But whereas in 1891 the emphasis was on separation, in 1972, the encounter called for inclusion "with traditional national parishes and territorial parishes as recommended forms of local pastoral organization" and concluded: "The linguistic, cultural, and religious expression of the Spanish speaking should be respected at the local parish level; integration should not be confused with assimilation" (no. 22).

In effect, the Latinos at the encounter advanced the same goal as the Lucerne Memorial of 1890: culturally distinct parishes. In fact, the encounter document was even more sweeping, since it included territorial as well as national parishes.

The second of the Lucerne principles stresses that "the administration of such a parish should be assigned to a priest of that nationality to which the faithful belong." There is no comparable conclusion from the Hispanic encounter, although number 29 does suggest that "[m]ore positions of responsibility and authority should be given to Spanish speaking priests in local dioceses." The reason for this omission in the 1972 document can be attributed to the focus by the participants at the encounter on national and diocesan structures. The encounter's conclusions do describe in detail the role of deacons (nos. 30–37) and suggest grassroots ecclesial communities (*comunidades eclesiales de base*) rather than parishes as the basic unit of local worshiping assemblies (nos. 19–22).

The third of the Lucerne principles stresses that at the very least a priest should be assigned to the pastoral care of immigrants when it is impossible to found a parish. For its part, the encounter suggests that a deacon be assigned if no priest is available (no. 37). Both documents emphasize, however, the importance of culture and its preservation in the ministry. The wording of this principle in the Lucerne Memorial is less elaborate than in the encounter document. Cahensly merely stated that "the sweet and dear memory of one country" by immigrants has always "gained for the Church certain benefits." The wording of the Spanish-speaking leaders is in different context. The cultural principle is framed differently, not in reference to the homeland left behind but as a basis of insertion into U.S. society. The preface and introduction to the conclusions state:

[E]very people has a right to self-determination and . . . the most effective instrumentality of development of a people is an indigenous leadership. . . . In education and formation, a harmonious and organic development of each person demands a respect for, understanding of, and realization of the potentialities of the culture and society in which he lives and from which he has sprung.

Yet the document nuances this statement in favor of cultural difference by suggesting that it is a form of integration, one that "is achieved when diverse groups are at positions of relatively equal strength and prestige and have mutual respect." To attempt integration without this relative equality of institutional power would lead to "an undesirable assimilation," which, according to the Hispanics, "means cultural absorption or, from the other point of view, cultural domination and replaces the mutual enrichment which is the fruit of true integration."

The fourth point of the Lucerne Memorial stressed the appropriateness of opening Catholic schools to the immigrant groups and teaching the native language. The encounter made similar points in a separate section of the conclusion (nos. 61–68). Likewise, the attention in Point 6 of the memorial about membership in lay church societies was addressed in the encounter document sections on the liturgy (nos. 49–54), catechetics (nos. 55–59) and the lay apostolate (nos. 69–70). Both documents view culture as an organizing principle, so parish organizations as diverse as the Holy Name Society or the Charismatic movement would have separate branches based on language and culture.

In almost identical language, the fifth point of the memorial and number 45 of the Hispanic conclusion requested a status for the clergy serving immigrants that was equal to that of priests working with the English speaking. Moreover, the call for special seminary training that was articulated in the eighth point of the memorial is elaborated in various ways in the encounter's conclusions (nos. 8, 9, 24, 41, 43, 44, 46).

The most controversial point of the Lucerne Memorial and the one most frequently cited by its critics was the seventh principle, which dealt with episcopal authority.

It seems very desirable that the Catholics of each nationality, wherever it is deemed possible, have in the episcopacy of the country where they immigrate, several bishops who are of the same origin. It seems that in this way the organization of the Church would be perfect, for in the assemblies of the bishops, every immigrant race would be represented and its interest and needs would be protected.

This recommendation is almost the same as the 1972 encounter's articulation (no. 23): "The number of native Spanish speaking bishops in the United States should be increased so that the proportion of Spanish speaking in the hierarchy is similar to the proportion of Spanish speaking in the total Catholic population."

However, the recommendations of the encounter are even more detailed than those of Cahensly and introduce mathematical quotas, stating that there should be a Spanish-speaking auxiliary bishop "in those dioceses of the United States whose Catholic population is more than one-third Spanish speaking" (no. 14).

Moreover, in other encounter recommendations (nos. 12–13) the canonical powers of a bishop, that is, an episcopal vicar, are to be given to a person designated as a director of the Spanish-speaking apostolate and would be "preferably, native Spanish speaking." The encounter goes as far as to suggest that the Spanish-speaking leaders—including the laity—should have the opportunity "to present nominations to the diocesan bishop for the vicar for Spanish speaking" (no. 15) and that such a bishop should share responsibility with "a collegial group" (no. 16). The encounter also called for a special committee within the NCCB to be headed by a native Spanish-speaking bishop (no. 3) and to have Hispanic bishops on "each of the committees of the National Conference of Catholic Bishops" (no. 4). In order to realize this goal, the encounter participants stated (no. 5): "A first priority of the American hierarchy should be the recruitment and ordination of Spanish speaking bishops in such numbers that the percentage of Spanish speaking ordinaries in the Catholic Church in the United States is in proportion to the percentage of Spanish speaking Catholics in the American Church."

Since the document had specified that "the Spanish speaking constitute as much as one quarter of the Catholic population of the United States" (*Proceedings*, J1, 2), this would mean that the Hispanics expected 25 percent of the U.S. hierarchy to be of Spanish-speaking national origin. Moreover, they stated that "a special and major portion of the funds, facilities and properties of the USCC and the NCCB should be deployed in the service of the Spanish speaking" (no. 6).

Such expansive goals about the episcopate in 1972 certainly went beyond the simple request of the Lucerne Memorial. Yet almost every provision of the encounter document was embraced by the U.S. hierarchy, whereas the Lucerne Memorial was denounced as "Cahenslyism" by Bishop John Ireland and many of his fellow bishops. The Lucerne Memorial was characterized as a step away from American values (Tomasi, 1975:87–92; Dolan, 1992:298–300). The encounter inverts that argument, making cultural sensitivity the "true" American value and Americanization the false one: "'E pluribus unum' and 'In God we trust' mark the spirit of the people of the United States of America and of the Church of Christ. The strength of the unity of our country and our Church is proportionate to the respect for the individual persons, families and ethnic groups that compose them."

The focus on integration and the inversion of the arguments about the nature of American pluralism are the principal differences between the

Lucerne Memorial and the conclusions of the Hispanic encounter. The encounter conclusions suggest that it would be un-American *not* to respond favorably to the recommendations in favor of cultural persistence. The surprising reversal of fortunes for two documents that are essentially similar testifies to a restructuring of American Catholicism that took place between 1891 and 1972.

This extended comparison of the two documents does not "prove" that the Latino Religious Resurgence by itself changed the attitude of U.S. Catholicism toward ethnic assimilation. After all, more than two-thirds of the twentieth century separated the two documents historically, and myriad other factors beyond the Latino Religious Resurgence were at work. But the old Charles Atlas advertisements always made it seem that the transformation of the ninety-seven-pound weakling into a muscle man was easy. The "before-and-after" effect may not disclose the hard work involved in effecting change, but it surely dramatizes the end result. This is our perspective in demonstrating how radically different the response of U.S. bishops was to these two different documents, both requesting a multicultural church and ministry.

We would argue that although the resurgence did not produce the restructuring by itself, it made an essential contribution and was the catalyst for finally restructuring Catholic response to cultural ministry. Throughout this book, we stress the important role of Latino leadership that complemented and maximized the flow of social forces. Such is the context for making a distinction between historical change and social change. The Lucerne Memorial emerged as a part of historical, that is, incremental change, but it failed to achieve its major goals because it was perceived as a plan of foreigners imposed on the U.S. bishops. This perception as something "foreign" was a crucial issue, for as Silvio Tomasi has shown in his history of the Italian apostolate at that time, several U.S. prelates were inclined to follow the pastoral methods suggested in the memorial until the issue became hopelessly politicized (Tomasi, 1975:74–80). It may even be surmised that Cahensly's pious devotion to the Holy See undermined his efforts. His eighth point requested that the society of Saint Raphael and its work be placed directly under the supervision of the Holy See by naming a cardinal protector. Such a petition placed him so far outside the structures of the U.S. hierarchy as to constitute the kind of threat to episcopal authority that provoked John Ireland and his fellow prelates. By contrast, the Latinos at the First Encounter in 1972 stressed their desire to be under the U.S. bishops' conference. They requested an upgrading of the Spanish-speaking secretariat and emphasized the role of pastoral centers (nos. 1, 3, 9, 10). The Hispanic Pastoral Encounter was "Cahensly revisited," but the leadership of the resurgence had turned "outside in" the complaints first articulated at Lucerne in 1890. Just as the Lucerne document had done, the encounter rejected ethnic assimilation as the price for church attention. However, the Latinos proposed to achieve their goals by preserving cultural ministry from within the institution already serving the people.

Thus, the restructuring of Catholic practice toward ethnic assimilation was rejected vehemently by prelates such as Ireland and Gibbons in the 1890s, but it was embraced by their successors in the 1970s. The strategy of the resurgence was to present its recommendations as the fruit of an already successful ministry and to ask for its continuance. When criticism was delivered, it was accompanied by an appeal for adjustments, portraying the Latino recommendations as consistent with extending the status quo to changing circumstances. Catholic officialdom was presented with proposals to restore to preeminence a Catholicism that had always been in existence. The proposals of Latino Catholicism were written with vocabulary that made them appear less dramatic than they really were. The organizations created by the resurgence became adept at deroutinization from within. Without such leadership, it might have remained a movement that could only stand on the outside and shout for change. Thus, when contrasted with the Lucerne Memorial, it was not only the proposals but the effective leadership of the resurgence that defined this moment as one of significant socioreligious change in the history of U.S. Catholicism.

The Bottom Line for the Latino Catholic Church

Today, a culturally determined Latino Catholicism has official standing because the U.S. bishops have formally created church-sponsored agencies specifically charged with developing alternatives for the practice of Latino Catholicism. Chief among these is the Secretariat for Hispanic Affairs which was established by the USCC, which was upgraded from its place as a program within one of the divisions of the USCC (Sandoval, 1990: 70–71). As secretariat, the office was given the mission of influencing all U.S. Catholic agencies and not just those in the social work arena. Irrespective of its daily operations or its rise or fall in influence, the placement of the secretariat within the bureaucratic flow chart of U.S. Catholicism constitutes structural change.

In terms of policy, the secretariat and its predecessor office organized pastoral encounters in 1972, 1977, and 1985, each of which produced pastoral plans specifically designed to minister in the Spanish language and within Latino cultures. In response to an invitation from the secretariat, Pope Paul VI delivered a taped message to the Latinos at the Second Encounter, which encouraged their work and—not incidentally—demonstrated to the U.S. bishops that Rome was protecting Latino Catholicism (Stevens-Arroyo, 1980:322). In 1987, the NCCB approved a pastoral plan for Hispanics (the National Pastoral Plan), thus indicating a separate and special dimension to

Latino Catholicism as compared to Euro-American Catholicism. One may criticize the secretariat for not being powerful enough to compel compliance with all of the provisions of the pastoral plan, but the existence of both stands as a significant alteration of U.S. Catholicism.

From the bookkeeper's perspective, "the bottom line" shows that the encounters successfully instituted alternative ministries and structures that utilize an ecclesiology different from the Euro-American church (Stevens-Arroyo, 1980:197–201). For example, as implementation of encounter reforms, on December 3, 1989, the U.S. bishops made mandatory a Spanish text for the Ordinary of the Mass that had been developed by the Institute for Hispanic Liturgy. The Spanish-language version of the Proper of the Mass texts were authorized on March 12, 1990. An approved version for the Rite for the Christian Initiation of Adults was published in 1991.

The reforms of the encounters and these episcopal approvals that preserve and legitimate the use of the Spanish language among Latinos in the United States are significant. Because they differ from the church's treatment of Euro-American cultural diversity, they constitute a historically new stance toward maintenance within the church of native cultures and languages other than English, breaking with previous strategies (Gleason, 1987:46–54; Dolan, 1992:204–208). Maintaining linguistic and cultural difference alters Catholicism's role in fostering assimilation and reverses the policies that imposed U.S. nationalism upon the faithful (Fitzpatrick, 1987:99–115; O'Brien, 1990:19–23; Doyle et al., 1982, 2:61–85).

The issues of Spanish language and cultural maintenance within Catholicism deserve some mention because they are matters that currently influence the definitions of U.S. nationalism. The decisions of U.S. Catholicism run in a diametrically different direction from the seventeen state legislatures that have made English the only official language in their jurisdiction or from those that call for a constitutional amendment to do the same for the entire United States. The liturgical books are intended to prevent Latino assimilation into a monolingual, monocultural Catholicism (Division for the Spanish Speaking, 1974 F:2–3, conclusions:2, 10). Moreover, following the encounter's suggestion (Division for the Spanish Speaking, 1974 F:6–8), liturgical texts for Latinos are not simply translations of existing English versions. Rather than presuming that liturgical books produced in Latin America are sufficient, the encounter calls for new translations to reflect Latino culture and linguistic usage proper to the United States.

Thus, the U.S. NCCB has made the Catholic Church in this country as officially bilingual as it is in Canada and Belgium. Furthermore, the use of languages other than English in the United States has risen rapidly in the past ten years. According to 1990 U.S. Census Bureau numbers, there are more than 17 million people in the United States who speak Spanish in the home, a 50 percent increase from 1980 (April 1993). This makes highly question-able the conclusion that unless Hispanics or Latinos learn English, they will be likely to leave the Catholic Church (Budde, 1992a:94, citing Greeley).

Moreover, in 1995, a new ritual was issued for *la quinceañera*, the reli-gious ceremony that celebrates a young woman's coming of age. As dis-cussed in Chapter 2, it belongs to the matriarchal core of Latino religion (Díaz-Stevens, 1993b). Significantly, this is a ritual that is officially pub-lished by a recognized agency of the U.S. Catholic Church, not a text im-ported from Latin America or a translation of some preexisting English text. Latinos in Catholicism have now taken a modest step toward creating official liturgies that express a unique dimension of their religion, thus end-ing the premise that Spanish is used only as a translation of something al-ready possessed by Euro-American Catholics.

These structural changes in U.S. Catholicism are unlikely to be swept away by ecclesiastical fiat. In his 1996 visit to the United States, Pope John Paul II spoke in Spanish on the Great Lawn in New York City's Central Park, urging Latino and Latina youth to hold fast to the cultural awareness first advocated by the resurgence: "The pope also loves the sons and daughters of the church who speak Spanish. Many of you have been born here or have lived here for a long time. Others are more recent arrivals. But you all bear the mark of your cultural heritage, deeply rooted in the Catholic tradition. Keep alive that faith and culture" (Pope John Paul II, October 8, 1996).

Only days before at the United Nations, this same principle had been ex-pounded as a integral part of international justice:

> Its [a nation's] right to exist naturally implies that every nation also enjoys the right to its own language and culture, through which a people expresses and promotes that which we would call its fundamental spiritual sovereignty. History shows that in extreme circumstances (such as those which occurred in the land where I was born) it is precisely its culture that enables a nation to survive the loss of political and economic independence. (Pope John Paul II, October 5, 1996)

Thus, in order to reject the cultural autonomy gained by Latino Catholicism, one would have to go against a papal statement, attempting the improbable trick of being "more Catholic" than the pope.

Social Forces of Cultural Affirmation

As described in the treatment afforded syzygy in Chapter 4, social forces in the 1960s drove cultural affirmation. In the secular sphere, cultural idio-syncrasy created opportunities for Spanish-speaking public services and created Latino political constituencies. But these legislative changes, although political, were not artificial. They responded to a real and growing community of Spanish-speaking people nationwide. The neoconservative accusation that liberalism created "Latinos" by preventing assimilation is gainsaid by the private sector. Commerce and enterprise have swiftly moved into the Latino market. The constituency supports two national television systems and hundreds of local radio stations, newspapers, and magazines; a bilingual school system that includes a national university research network; a congressional caucus that defines legislative goals, along with several lobbying agencies that research policy; and a growing number of banks, commercial and professional organizations, and community groups that periodically consult about coordinating their activities.

Will the Latino cultural presence within the churches translate into social justice commitments by parishes and congregations to Latinos in the way that the cultural recognition by government sparked the explosion of public services? There are encouraging signs that this is happening in many churches and denominations. Latino parishes and congregations, in concert with each other, often participate in social action programs. The cross-validation that was first experienced in terms of individual Latino church leaders has now developed the capability to legitimate neighborhood causes such as better housing, improved public schools, and anticrime measures. The church communities morally validate the community organization as truly interested in the welfare of the people, and the parish or congregation is validated politically as an agency actively helping the people. Cross-denominational Latino cooperation operates autonomously within its cultural and linguistic parameters, interpreting general church policy, setting its own special goals, and taking its own initiatives (Stevens-Arroyo, 1997a). Without mediation by these congregations between church and Latino neighborhoods, many U.S. religious institutions would not be connected with a large segment of the U.S. population (Sandoval, 1990:61–87; Stevens-Arroyo, 1980:153–213).

Cross-Validation of Organizations as Social Capitalization

We view cross-validation as a concept useful for evaluating the performance of Latino organizations. In Chapters 4 and 5, it was explained that during the resurgence, cross-validation was applied to individuals. Leadership fell upon the shoulders of those who had a standing both among the people and within the institutional church. The more influence the leaders had with the people, the more likely it was for the institution to recognize that individual as a spokesperson. Simultaneously, leaders with such newly acquired institutional credentials gained even more credibility with the people. And so the process escalated, rapidly creating Latino religious leaders.

We think the process of cross-validation helps explain how organizations function in the present context. Leadership in the Latino religious experience has been diffused; there are now many trained leaders, whereas before there was only a handful of professionals. Moreover, the new leadership often corresponds to the organic intellectuals of Gramscian description, and they are firmly loyal to the organizations that have given them an opportunity of service to the people. Some further questions include these: Which Latino religious organizations have a solid base with the community? Are they likely to be awarded status by the larger institutions?

Bases of Power: Religious Marketing

In order to assess the importance of organizations that emerged from the Latino Religious Resurgence, it is useful to analyze the bases of power in an institutional context. A similar analysis has been applied to the secular realm. Carlos Muñoz observes, for instance, that the campus radicals of the 1960s became the bilingual teachers, social workers, legal defense lawyers, and cultural community artists of the 1970s and 1980s, with a few moving into university departments of Chicano, Puerto Rican, and Latino Studies (Muñoz, 1989:183–188). However, the cutbacks in education, social, and community services since the 1980s have devastated these bases of secular power, leaving as perhaps the most faithful voice of this militancy today the writers and poets of Chicano, Puerto Rican, and Latino experience.

In terms of the churches, a similar analysis of the bases of power is necessary to understand why some elements of the resurgence became weaker while others grew strong and acquired institutional status. It has already been shown how categories like mono-Hispano and multi-Hispano, ratio, percentage, and the like affected the implementation of encounter recommendations within Catholicism. Similar criteria can be applied to organizations. The Catholic Cursillo, for instance, lost its primacy after the encounter, largely because so many other new programs were begun. The three-day Cursillo was designed as a once-in-a-lifetime affair, much like a Christian rebirth revival experience. It was then given continuity through weekly meetings or the *ultreyas* and required the group to report periodically on participation in regular parish activities. When the Cursillo was the only act in town, its training and educational follow-up programs flourished. But with the encounter came the pastoral centers, each with educational programs that competed with the Cursillo's offerings. Also, new movements appeared in the 1970s and 1980s that competed for membership. The Catholic Charismatic movement, for instance, was often a parish-level rival to the Cursillo, and conflicts between both groups for resources, membership, and ecclesiastical recognition were common. The Cursillo is now one among many Catholic movements. In Evangelical and Pentecostal circles, Promise Keepers, a movement for Christian men, has assumed a prominent role, perhaps analogous to the Catholic Cursillo movement of the 1960s. It will be important to examine how Promise Keepers among Latinos affects issues of cultural idiosyncrasy and whether the personal, salvific focus will open out into a wider social agenda.

For analysis of the bases of power of Latino religious organizations, the ideological or (theological) distinctions between pastoralists and liberationists continue to be useful. In the analogy of the bookkeeper, these are the "markets" and the "brand names" for religious products. We described the meaning of these terms in Chapter 4, and we believe they are applicable across denominational and ethnic lines. The priorities for the pastoralist are on change in the church, whereas the liberationist is more focused on society. Pastoralists, both Catholic and Protestant, as could be expected, developed strengths in agencies that administered or educated people for locally based ministries, such as teaching the faith, instructing the young, or providing liturgical or prayer services. Pastoralist education is specifically for church ministry and is often coordinated out of a pastoral center, located near Latino neighborhoods. Some of these pastoral centers are parish- or congregation-based; others are sponsored by a diocese or district; a few are regional. They produce what we have called "symbolic capital," that is, the "honor and prestige" within a social order for believers (see Bourdieu, 1980/1990:116–118; Maduro, 1982:95–102). Most are run by Latinos, but ecclesiastical institutions frequently hold the purse strings. Frictions have developed between Latino directors of such centers and bishops or district supervisors when the pastoralist focus-on-the-church teaching is perceived to foster political action in the public sphere or to adopt an overly critical attitude toward "the hand that feeds" the center. Thus, although pastoralists have established a firm footing in pastoral centers, as long as funding comes from church institutions, autonomy is never guaranteed.

Liberationists have access to funds from government and foundations in order to deliver their services to the people. A priest who is director of a governmentally funded program has autonomy from his ecclesiastical superior when he acts as employee of the community organization. As clergyman, however, he is obliged to obey his bishop. Many denominations have begun to prohibit local clergy from such direct involvement because of the many conflicts of interest it generates. Within the Catholic Church in particular, this has opened the door for many Latino laypersons to assume official directorship of community-based programs with outside funding. In our understanding, it is often these programs that earn social capital for the parish or congregation.

The different sources of symbolic capital (pastoralist) and social capital (liberationist) set up a necessary connection between the two perspectives. Both need each other to successfully market their religious production, much like supermarkets or department stores add profitability by stocking so many items that clients come in for "one-stop shopping." But is it likely that we can expect closer collaboration between Latino organizations of the resurgence that have inherited different bases of power? What are the chances that pastoralist and liberationist organizations will find common cause as did the leaders of the resurgence? We analyze below the principal successes of the pastoralist initiatives—music, education, and theology— and we then compare these with the special characteristics of Catholicism and Pentecostalism before examining contemporary liberationist struggles. In the final chapter, we move to some judgment on future directions.

Music: A Bonus Payoff

Among Catholics, a late and perhaps unexpected success of the resurgence was in liturgical reform. The Instituto de Liturgia Hispana was founded at MACC in 1979 and has since become an important base of power for a national Latino agenda. As described by Father Arturo Pérez in his informed account of music and liturgy (Pérez, 1994), the reforms of the Second Vatican Council had created a need for missalettes in Spanish. From the publication of *Misal del pueblo* in New York by Bernard Benziger in 1971, such missalettes strove to embrace all Latinos in order to maximize their market appeal. In concert with the printing of lectionary and ordinary texts, popular hymns were usually included.

Thus began an important process of preserving traditional hymns, developing new ones, and professionalizing the arrangements and musical sophistication of the music sung by Latinos. Pérez believes that the 1989 publication by the Oregon Catholic Press of the hymnal *Flor y Canto* is a most significant event that demonstrates the maturity of Latino liturgical expression (1994:392). *Flor y Canto* was developed in large measure by Mary Frances Reza, a Catholic laywoman of New Mexico, who sought to include a wide ethnic, regional diversity in the collection. Musical composer and educator herself, Reza attuned the collection to both musicality (ease and beauty in singing) and theological expression in the words of the hymns. The collection ranges from Puerto Rican, Cuban, and Mexican folk styles to traditional Spanish hymns to new Latino creations with elements of popular music. The outreach and the diversity of *Flor y Canto* would have been impossible if the same model had not been employed by the Instituto de Liturgia Hispana, which built on regional efforts such as that of Sister Rosa María Icaza, C.C.V.I. at MACC and Rogelio Zelada at

SEPI in Florida and maintained a sensitivity to the need to alternate its presidency among representatives of the various Latino groups.

Latino Protestants have long created liturgy by writing and rewriting hymnals, often across denominational lines. Two United Methodist women who have exercised leadership in this regard are the Cuban-born, California-based Raquel Gutiérrez Achón and the Mexican American Raquel Martínez. William Loperena, O.P., the Dominican friar who composed the *Misa Jíbara* in the Puerto Rican folk idiom in 1964, worked with the United Church of Christ from 1993 to 1995 to prepare a hymnal for that denomination. Along with *Flor y Canto*, all of these collections minimize denominational and ethnic boundaries. As the cliché puts it, music is a universal language. Parishes and congregations of many different denominations today sing the same hymns, including a large number that were originally composed in the Spanish language and have no English equivalents. In a sense, in liturgical music as in the use of the spoken Spanish language, Latinos are growing closer to each other across denominational lines, leaving a greater distance in worship between Latinos and non-Latinos in the same denomination.

As the Latino liturgical resources wax richer, the place of folkloric style grows more celebrated. Obviously, folk music played with traditional instruments is found in many liturgical settings, not only those of Latinos. Part of the appeal of the folk style is that new immigrants from rural areas know this musical style best. But there is a much larger public of urbanized Latinos who recognize a striking difference between popular music and folk music, in terms of class status, ethnic identity, and nationalism (Stevens-Arroyo, 1996c). In the case of Puerto Rico, Díaz-Stevens (1993c) has shown that the folk style of Loperena's *Misa Jíbara* represents an affirmation of Puerto Rican nationalism and hence of the independence cause. Once outside the political context of Puerto Rico, Loperena's compositions become used more widely on the basis of their aesthetic and liturgical value. Similarly, the mariachi mass of Carlos Rosa and the *danza* used in the Cathedral of San Fernando in San Antonio, Texas, represent an affirmation of Mexican identity.

Protestants and Pentecostals have a tradition in which hymns and hymnals have a major role. Much liturgical music has tended to be hymns written originally in English (or German) but translated into Spanish. Latino Pentecostalism also has direct links to popular U.S. music, through the connections with gospel singers in the African American traditions. One can find drums, saxophones, electric pianos, and the other instruments of jazz and rock bands used in Pentecostal worship. Lead singers often croon a romantic ballad, singing to Jesus instead of to a sweetheart. In some instances, such music is as important in attracting people to church as the preacher.

Musical and liturgical development affords Latinos a unique creative and artistic edge. The cultural idiosyncrasy of Latino music erects a wall of autonomy around these composers and performers, isolating them from Euro-American control. Much like the composition of liturgical texts and rituals, these have become bases of power within ecclesiastical institutions that depend on Latino organizations for input. The warmth of the service, the vibrancy of the music, the emotional ties evoked with the homeland and one's family, the religious feelings stimulated by the ritual—all of these are the symbolic capital accumulated in parishes and congregations where liturgy in the Latino cultural style is celebrated. In the ledger of the resurgence, this is a booming market and has produced a huge dividend from past investments.

Education, the Reliable Investment

Protestantism's strong emphasis on education has strengthened the pastoralist vision within the various denominations. There is ample anecdotal evidence that many Latino Protestants in local congregations were more reluctant than the national caucuses and commissions to declare support for national causes like that of the UFW in the 1960s. But Protestant grassroots congregants have been very open to Bible schools, pastoral institutes, and ministerial training programs that added a Latino dimension to these solidly traditional aspects of the faith. Although the Hispanic-American Institute in Austin, Texas, was established with much the same goals, it did not attain the stature of MACC in the 1970s. The efforts of denominations, usually in concert with seminaries, to create ministry programs were more successful. Programs such as those at Perkins School of Theology at SMU, at the New York Theological Seminary, at Andover-Newton Seminary and Gordon-Cromwell Seminary in Massachusetts, and in Chicago at the Lutheran School of Theology, McCormick Seminary, and Northern Baptist Theological Seminary have each developed within the a range of general types (González, 1988:81–107).

In the "continuing education" model but with a national, interdenominational and intra-Latino dimension is the Hispanic Summer Program at the Fund for Theological Education, which was first organized by the Puerto Rican Benjamin Alicea and the Cuban Justo González for summer 1986. It has provided an ecumenical forum that condenses courses on Bible, theology, and issues such as popular religiosity into a two-week format. Since it was reorganized under the Associación para la Educación Teológica Hispana (AETH), the Hispanic Summer Program selects its students from a wide pool of Catholics, Protestants, Evangelicals, and Pentecostals. Based on the needs voiced by pastoralists, the Hispanic Summer Program has been able to introduce into its yearly curriculum themes of liberationist concern. Meanwhile, the juxtaposition of Latinos of different denominations generally offers the opportunity to critically examine narrow denominational beliefs and to explore cultural similarities.

The Latino component of the FTE moved its program from one region to another, cementing its national outreach. Eventually, under Benjamin Alicea, the summer program became more effective than its year-round scholarship program for Latino candidates for degrees in theology and related studies of religion. When the entire FTE was phased out of existence in 1995 by decision of the funding agencies, most of the Latino educational programs were absorbed by AETH at Columbia Theological Seminary in Georgia. The scholarship program was reconstituted through funding from the Pew Charitable Trusts under an exclusively Latino leadership as the Hispanic Theological Initiative (HTI). Affiliated with Emory University and with ties to the Chandler School of Theology in Atlanta, the HTI is designed along the same interdenominational, interregional, and intra-Latino model of the Hispanic Summer Program, but with a focus on high-quality academic achievement for prospective Latino and Latina seminary and university faculty members.

Despite these successes, seminaries remain a battleground for Latino religion. In 1988, Justo González reviewed theological education in a report for the FTE. That document dramatically registered the high interest in ministry but the disappointment with curriculum on the part of Latinos enrolled in seminaries. Moreover, the report showed that there were more Latino and Latina Protestants and Pentecostals studying for the ordained ministry than Latino Catholics, even though Catholic adherents outnumber the others two to one (González, 1988:73–75). Certainly, the requirement for priestly celibacy and the exclusion of women from the Catholic priesthood are the obstacles that prevent Catholicism from attaining a proportionate number of seminarians, but Latino presence in Catholic seminaries is rising. Moreover, as the attendance at the Hispanic Summer Program has shown, Latino Catholics prepare increasingly for ministries outside of ordination as priests. Ten years later, another survey of U.S. seminaries was conducted by PARAL sociologist Edwin Hernández (1995) for AETH. This second report showed that the absolute number of Latinos preparing for ministry in seminary programs had continued to rise, particularly in the specialized programs where pastoral techniques, language training, and the like are communicated. But the 1995 report recorded the dearth of Latinos in the theological faculties of seminaries. In effect, seminaries apparently believe Latinos can train lay people and run training programs in the "practical" fields but offer few faculty appointments in the departments of systematic theology, scripture, or ethics, the most prestigious of seminary departments. Latinos with theological degrees have a slightly better chance in departments of religious studies located in universities, but in those positions, they do not have direct roles in training future ministers or priests.

Theology as a Spin-Off Industry

Latino theologians have attempted to address this disparity through two scholarly journals, both interdenominational but with roots in different theological traditions. The publication *Apuntes,* mentioned earlier, is edited at the Perkins School of Theology at Southern Methodist University and has addressed theological issues related to ministry since 1980. Its base of support and subscriptions are with the ministry programs, particularly those that are run by Protestants, Evangelicals, and Pentecostals, although it has always been open to Catholic writers. *Apuntes* reflects the mind-set of the generation that launched the resurgence. It has generated an interest in forming an ecumenical theological caucus, called La Comunidad, but this group has had only sporadic success in common theological projects.

More successful has been the Academy of Catholic Hispanic Theologians in the United States (ACHTUS). The academy has about fifty members and meets annually to discuss a particular topic, although it does not represent all of the varied Latino Catholic theologians (Medina, 1994). ACHTUS has acknowledged its debt to Elizondo's theology of mestizo culture by naming its annual achievement award after him; however, it has gravitated toward more restricted academic fields of interest. Publication of the *Journal of Hispanic/Latino Catholic Theology* began in 1993. The journal has assumed the style of a blind peer-review journal with a board of international correspondents and has published articles dealing with academic and speculative issues. Published in English by the Liturgical Press, its base and target audience lie outside Latino religion and its focus on academic theology distances it from Latino Catholics preparing for nonordained ministry. This journal is crafted for the libraries of seminary and theological schools, which is a welcome development. Judged with the criteria of support base, however, it is unclear how the *Journal of Hispanic/Latino Catholic Theology* will contribute to the training of Catholic lay ministers, which is the major concern today of Latino Catholicism, or if it has a mechanism that will tie it to the kind of accountability to *el pueblo* that was ushered in by the resurgence.

Catholic Downsizing

When Latino Catholics moved their institutions toward the funding of educational and pastoral centers, the role of the many coordinating offices and commissions within diocesan structures was diminished. Before the resurgence, these offices of the Spanish-speaking apostolate served as official arms of ecclesiastical attention. Today, the pastoral centers have absorbed almost all but the bureaucratic functions of most of these directors and their apostolate offices. Many of the directors welcomed this change because they often belong to the sponsoring or advisory boards of the centers, when they are not also its director. The centers take the clergy out of a chancery office and bring them closer to the people.

Pastoralists achieved considerable influence in Catholicism by staffing most of the pastoral centers erected in response to the encounter's recommendations. Each area of the country, even each large (arch)diocese, was expected to open a Latino pastoral center. Thus, the more centers at the regional and local levels, the less the national importance of any one of them. This applies to MACC as well. The national stature of MACC in San Antonio derived from its role as model for other centers. People came from all over the country to be taught how to set up their own training programs. But the success of MACC in fostering a brood of pastoral centers everywhere meant that it gradually eroded the national role that had been assigned to it by the First Encounter.

Moreover, as institutions began to make concessions by naming bishops, funding commissions, changing seminary curricula, and the like, Latino pastoralists were the most likely to be satisfied with the gains. They suggested that the need for militancy was at an end, since the goals of the resurgence (as they understood them) had now been achieved. The base of power of these Catholic institutions and the pastoralists who headed them has already been described as dependent upon institutional funding. Thus, whenever there was need for downsizing of church programs, for trimming or paring budgets, the Latino pastoralists were caught in a bind. They could not bargain for new expensive programs with diminishing funds; they had to defend their own organizations, often accepting reduced budgets that severely hampered their best intentions. The election of Ronald Reagan in 1980 and the ascendancy of conservative challenges to the liberal agenda that had benefited Latinos dramatically changed the climate of social and political opinion. Often, pastoralist leadership discovered that without the pressure on the institution generated by the liberationists, ecclesiastical authority no longer felt compelled to accede to Latino requests for programs and funding.

The general acquiescence of the pastoralists to the downsizing often antagonized liberationists. They had generally supported pastoralist goals such as more Latino bishops and the funding of pastoral centers, although they had maintained the priority of more direct community action with social and political results. Many of them felt that the pastoralists on the inside of the institution who held posts such as bishop or director of diocesan programs had simply shut the door. But complaints against "your own" often divide the movement and bring greater frustrations. For instance, when

Roberto Peña, O.M.I., who was president of PADRES in 1977, wanted to issue a document holding the Latino bishops accountable to the goals of liberation, pastoralists opposed the measure, saying that it would weaken the standing of Latino bishops before the Euro-American episcopacy. Peña argued that without such a strong affirmation, the bishops would forfeit their base of support with the people and liberationist clergy in the parishes. This division between pastoralists and liberationists proved insurmountable for PADRES, as it has for other sectors of Catholicism worldwide since the election of John Paul II to the papacy.

One casualty was the secretariat in Washington. The Washington office did help the Latino Catholic bishops who had a window on the ecclesiastical intrigues and funding decisions of the USCC—more or less a church equivalent of a Washington lobby for Latino Catholics. But this did not serve the agenda of Latino liberationists, who were focusing on the multiple problems caused by the Reagan regime's wholesale attack on affirmative action, antipoverty agencies, civil rights legislation, public education, bilingualism, and other essential pillars of Latino social progress.

The conservative tide of the Reagan years accelerated the merger of Latino liberationists into larger, cross-ethnic and interracial movements. For example, Latinos and non-Latinos joined together in the Sanctuary movement (González, 1990:41–42). This was a network of church people around the country who invoked the medieval custom of exemption from civil authority while under protection of the church as a means of saving from deportation refugees from Central America. The ideological thrust of the movement was to protest against U.S. support for military regimes in Central America and Washington's orchestrated attacks upon the Sandinista government of Nicaragua. The Sanctuary movement was a religious cause shamelessly attacked by the U.S. justice system (Yarnold, 1991:34ff). Appeals to Latino religious leaders for solidarity from the Sanctuary people were often answered at a local level. Moreover, various official statements were to come from ruling church bodies, such as the NCCB. But as in the case with Puerto Rican independence and Cuban American campaigns against the revolution, the protection of political refugees from Central America and denunciation of U.S. foreign policy was not always embraced by pastoralist leadership. Barbara Yarnold's (1991:28–46) characterization of the Sanctuary movement as a "fringe" cause may be applied to how the movement was viewed by the pastoralists of the resurgence, who now perceived themselves to be one of the "entrenched" church organizations. The Latino Catholic bishops' 1983 pastoral letter, entitled "The Hispanic Presence," never mentioned the Sanctuary movement or the refugees it sheltered as one of the Latino challenges or commitments.

The liberationists intensified their commitment to local community organizations. Some of these urban organizations started as mostly Latino organizations: Communities Organized for Public Service (COPS) in San Antonio, United Neighborhood Organizations (UNO) in Los Angeles, and the multiple organizations of the South Bronx clergy and laity in New York City. Others, such as Pacific Institute for Community Organizing (PICO)—which rapidly outgrew its West Coast origins—and Brooklyn's Nehemiah Houses never claimed to be specifically Latino. In Puerto Rico—where almost everyone is Latino—the community organizations such as those in Comerío and the agency that was created from it in 1968 by the island's ecumenical movement, Proyecto de Renovación e Investigación Social para el Adiestramiento en la Misión Cristiana (PRISA), point directly to the issues without recourse to the argument for minority representation. Misión Industrial, created by the Episcopal Church to focus on industrial safety and public health when there were few governmental agencies operative on the island, has adapted to the concerns of today and focuses on protection of the environment.

The longevity of COPS makes it worth examining as an example of the relationship between church and community (Stevens-Arroyo, 1980: 229–231). It seems safe to say that without COPS, Henry Cisneros would never have become mayor of San Antonio. The organization successfully ended at-large representation on the San Antonio municipal council, making it possible for heavily Mexican American districts to elect their own council members. Previously, citywide districts allowed Euro-Americans to designate an entire slate of officials, often excluding any Mexican American representatives. But the success of COPS required an adaptation of general principles of community organizing to the specific problems of San Antonio.

Each of the community organizations may be linked to national associations or to a specific model of organizing, but effectiveness is rooted in response to local conditions. They are excellent examples of the need to follow the dictum "Think globally, act locally." Moreover, Latinos must continually relate to non-Latino groups to maintain the effectiveness of such organizations. Liberationist-type organizations have a focus different from the cultural and linguistic emphasis of the pastoralist Latino organizations that cater only to Latinos. Finally, these organizations secure funding from sources outside the church; they are not Latino versions of Catholic charities, that is, institutional agencies serving the public. They are rather community organizations made up of religious people providing for a better life in their neighborhoods.

Cultural Idiosyncrasy as a Write-Off

One of the "red ink" items in the resurgence ledger is the issue of cultural idiosyncrasy. The painful lesson learned is that the ability to speak Spanish does not of itself make one Latino. The need to import clergy from overseas or to train Euro-Americans to speak Spanish is particularly acute in denominations like Roman Catholicism, where celibacy is required of the ordained clergy. In the Catholic Church, priests from Spain are often contracted to work among Latinos. Spaniards usually identify themselves with the Latino populations by emphasizing the Hispanic heritage of Latinos. The Spanish Catholic clergy used cultural idiosyncrasy themselves, with the result that the New York and Newark Archdioceses, for example, chose Spaniards as bishops in response to the call for a native Latino hierarchy. In other cases, priests with a Latino surname and an establishment mentality were elevated to the episcopacy. We do not suggest here that every Spaniard failed the Latino community or that every conservative is not a true Latino, only that cultural idiosyncrasy by itself is no longer an adequate argument for Latino leadership selection.

The reaction of Euro-American clergy to cultural idiosyncrasy was more complex. Most of these clergy ministered to Latinos because they had chosen an apostolate to the poor. These priests and pastors were often among the most progressive clergy in their respective dioceses or districts, and they did not feel vulnerable to charges of racism or discrimination against Latinos as did many church bureaucrats. These Euro-American clergy agreed with the resurgence that the church institution should deliver more resources to Latino ministries, but they viewed themselves as integral parts of those ministries. This claim was weaker in areas of the apostolate that were pastoralist, that is, concerned with injecting culture into church concerns, than in the area of local community needs where the liberationist goals were most in evidence. Moreover, although few objected to developing Latino lay leaders, cultural idiosyncrasy did not always seem sufficient reason to surrender to Latino clergy all claim for community leadership.

When PADRES excluded them from membership, the non-Latino clergy did not cease their service to the social and pastoral needs of Latino parishes. The liberationists, both Latino and non-Latino, were content to be effective at the local level and avoided, when not actually discouraging, the attention of bishops and chancery offices that was such a part of the pastoralist agenda. Life in the parishes continued, at times indifferent to and at other times skeptical of the pastoralist struggles with the institution. Eventually, the focus on cultural idiosyncrasy by Latino pastoralist spokespersons generated ill will because their constant harping on representation in the hierarchy and diocesan chanceries was viewed as selfish pursuit of an episcopal appointment.

Cultural idiosyncrasy has not been a compelling force in community organizing. On the contrary, many of the Euro-American clergy argue, as had New York's Monsignor Fox in the early 1960s, that cross-ethnic and interracial solidarity was necessary for neighborhood survival (Díaz-Stevens,

1993a:171–175). Division of communities into Latino, black, Euro-American, and the like, they said, was a threat to overall success. The pastoralist argument that only Latinos could be culturally sensitive to Latino culture was often interpreted by this activist Euro-American clergy as an inverse form of Orientalism (Said, 1978:328). The call from Latino leaders for native leadership was often viewed as an effort to reserve institutional positions of leadership for themselves. The activist Euro-American clergy saw this aspect of cultural idiosyncrasy as a direction that would isolate Latino grassroots people from their neighbors.

There certainly have been Latinos in many denominations who received their positions through some sort of ecclesiastical "affirmative action," although they were not always without the talent or the vision to make them worthy of leadership. In any movement, there are always members more interested in personal advancement than in the cause. But this is not a problem peculiar to Latinos. Many church institutions suffer from an inadequate selection process for bishops or church administrators, whether Latino or not. We think that belonging to a particular cultural group does not automatically make one an organic leader of a community. However, if barriers of discrimination are removed, the Latino community will produce native leadership as frequently as other communities. The growing number of Latinos among the Protestant, Evangelical, and Pentecostal leaders is an argument that the same should be expected for Catholicism. In other words, when Latino religion has its fair share of pastors and priests, cultural idiosyncrasy, like affirmative action, is less important.

Whereas at the beginning of the resurgence, Latino leaders defined their organization by excluding Euro-Americans on the basis of ethnic identity, in the 1990s this approach has lost much of its cogency. The more important issue is how to reconnect local leaders and the community organizations in which they work with the need for Latino participation. The liberationists are producing the social capital, on the one hand, while the pastoralists have generated the symbolic capital, on the other. But Latino religion depends upon both resources.

Sadly, some of the sharpest criticism of the achievements of Latino Catholicism has come from Latino liberationist Catholics. In a sense, the Latino Religious Resurgence has created its own "Black Legend." Much as complaints against Spanish policy in the sixteenth century by heroes like Bartolomé de las Casas were used to argue that "Catholicism accomplished nothing worthwhile," it is easy to cite current criticism by Catholics impatient with the church to suggest that Catholicism has failed Latinos. But such analysis often ignores that las Casas in the past and the loudest critics of the church today are themselves Catholics. Their efforts at reform necessarily entail attacking the status quo, but the criticism is itself a product of Catholic concern. Ironically, the downsizing of Catholicism that split apart the alliance between pastoralists and liberationists may become an instrument of reunion. With the diffusion of leadership to the Latino Catholic laity and their organizations, the natural flow in Catholic life between social concern and pastoral care is restored at the pragmatic, daily level (see O'Brien, 1971). As at Emmaus, when the disciples find failure in the events, they sometimes realize that their own expectations were exaggerated.

New Movements and the Privatization of Religious Production

Latino Catholic leadership has begun to devise alternatives. For instance, Latino Catholics no longer rely on the national secretariat in Washington for creating a national agenda, recognizing that the larger Catholic institution no longer permits the secretariat the latitude it once enjoyed. But what is impossible to an official agency of U.S. Catholicism is permissible to a voluntary association with a base outside of the bureaucracy. This is the importance of a new initiative called the National Catholic Council for Hispanic Ministry (NCCHM). With funding from the Lilly Endowment, NCCHM is emerging as a network to unite Latino ministry as conducted in parishes and by organizations. Under the leadership of its first president, Jesuit Father Alan Figueroa Deck, the NCCHM has held several conferences that have assumed many functions of the encounters. The language of the NCCHM is loyal to Catholic doctrine and hierarchy, but it is not controlled by institutional funds. This makes it autonomous and distinctively Latino in its leadership and agenda. In sum, reports of the demise of Catholicism as the major religion of Latinos are premature.

Latino Pentecostals as a Growth Industry

Pentecostals have a long tradition of Bible schools as the central part of their educational programs. Corresponding Evangelical institutions have generally achieved a somewhat more professional standing as accredited religious colleges. And because there is not as marked a difference between laity and clergy in the Pentecostal and Evangelical traditions as in other denominations, many church-related colleges also serve as seminaries. Thus, such institutions address both educational and ministerial aspirations for Latinos and unlike the Catholic-sponsored pastoral centers, often train people who become ordained.

But the emergence of these educational institutions as resources for Latino religion developed more slowly than in Catholicism. Pentecostals and Evangelicals were not prominent players in the Latino Religious Resurgence that began in 1967. Almost by definition, Pentecostals and

Evangelicals are pastoralists, since the millennial vision often precludes concerns for social and political change. By examining the autocephalous nature of Pentecostal-Evangelical organization and the theological reluctance to be involved with political causes, one can see the structural impediments to cooperation with the Catholic and Protestant leaders during much of the 1970s. But the resurgence made some Latino Pentecostal and Evangelical leaders reexamine the church's role in the struggle for social justice.

During that decade, sporadic efforts of individual Pentecostal leaders raised the consciousness of the fellow congregants. Raymond Rivera, a Puerto Rican Pentecostal from New York's Spanish Harlem, provided a charter for a liberationist understanding of Pentecostalism (Stevens-Arroyo, 1980:339–340) before most of his fellow Pentecostals considered it important. Speaking from an important administrative position within the Dutch Reformed Church during the resurgence, Rivera argued that the concern for the poor that has characterized Pentecostalism from its beginnings was compatible with an apostolic involvement in social justice projects. He was farsighted in connecting the Pentecostal spirit to the themes of liberation theology, then quite new outside of Latin America. He directed funding from his church to the Theology in the Americas project in the 1970s. Rivera eventually moved to a Latino outreach program at the New York Mission Society and now directs a Latino Pastoral Action Center in the Bronx. This has become an Evangelical and Pentecostalist interdenominational training center that specializes in what he calls "holistic ministry," or social concerns. It attracts not only Protestants from similar backgrounds but a growing number of Catholics. An important theological voice from the Pentecostal experience is that of Eldín Villafañe, now at Gordon-Cromwell Seminary in Massachusetts. Author of an important book titled *The Liberating Spirit: Toward an Hispanic American Pentecostal Social Ethic* (1993), Villafañe is the best published of a small, but important circle of scholars who enrich Latino Pentecostalism with theological reflection.

It was the mobilization of the religious Right during the Reagan years, however, that most effectively moved Latino Pentecostal and Evangelical congregations toward direct political engagement. Part of this movement was enlightened self-interest. Congregants had a huge investment in stabilizing neighborhoods against urban rot, crime, and drug addiction. The money made available to church groups for a variety of neighborhood preservation programs did not compromise the religious goals sought by Latino Pentecostals and Evangelicals but instead offered needed assistance in working toward such goals. Latino ministers also came to understand that by assuming dual roles as pastor and director of a funded program, they could work full-time at ministry, instead of working at a nine-to-five job and moonlighting the apostolate. At times, Pentecostals and Evangelicals committed to social action joined other Protestant denominations that were more open to these kinds of ministry. Today, Methodist, Baptist, and Lutheran Latino congregations often share elements of the Pentecostal-Evangelical traditions.

Another type of Pentecostal-Evangelical organization is the neighborhood association of ministers. Forming not-for-profit corporations and community service organizations, such associations secure governmental and private funding to bring religious commitment and social concerns together. The association Nueva Esperanza in Philadelphia, founded by the Reverend Louis Cortés, has been very effective in fostering a Latino agenda. In 1995, Nueva Esperanza was one of several Latino organizations that successfully included the largely Puerto Rican Hunting Park neighborhood in a Philadelphia-Camden empowerment zone that otherwise would have been dominated by exclusively African American concerns. The Reverend David Anglada, now minister of a Lutheran church in Brooklyn, is another leader from the same cohort of New York–born Puerto Rican Pentecostals. And a Brooklyn College professor, Union Theological Seminary graduate Hector Carrasquillo, has developed a Pentecostal children's choir into a government-funded youth services agency in the Sunset Park neighborhood of Brooklyn.

At a national level, the Alianza de Ministerios Evangélicos Nacionales (AMEN) has become a confederation of local associations like Nueva Esperanza. AMEN was funded in 1992 by a grant from the Pew Charitable Trusts and established headquarters in Los Angeles after the first national meeting, held in 1994. The Reverend Jesse Miranda, a director of Hispanic ministry at Azusa Pacific College, was elected the first president and executive director. The national stature of AMEN will probably strengthen local organizations by providing leadership training and access to technical help and funding. In some ways, these functions serve Latinos in Pentecostal and Evangelical congregations much as did PADRES and the encounters for Catholics. Chief among these functions is cross-validation. Raymond Rivera and Louis Cortés, for instance, gave important presentations at the AMEN conference in Long Beach, California, in November 1995. Recognition of progressive ministers by a national evangelical association enhances the leadership of these ministers with their own congregations, but it also makes AMEN more influential because the success in local projects represented by people like Rivera and Cortés becomes AMEN's success as well. Such visibility for successful leaders fosters a progressive social agenda of holistic ministry, and AMEN will likely assist Latino Pentecostals and Evangelicals to minimize the effects of a breach between pastoralists and liberationists such as developed in Latino Catholicism.

Similarly, AETH, the educational and pastoralist organization, frequently includes liberationist theologians in its summer faculty. The success at the grassroots level of AMEN and AETH also impacts upon institutions, and several important Evangelical seminaries have embraced this progressive side of Latino Pentecostal and Evangelical traditions. At Gordon-Cromwell, for instance, Elizabeth Conde-Frazier and Samuel Solivan have joined with Villafañe in faculty and administrative posts. On the West Coast among Mexican Americans, Claremont School of Theology has invited the Reverend Miguel Mata to launch a similar effort. Rudy V. Busto and Daniel Ramírez at Stanford University and Luis León and Gastón Espinosa at the University of California at Santa Barbara have produced cogent historical and anthropological materials on Evangelicals and Pentecostals.

If AMEN and AETH bring success and visibility to their member congregations and bring professionalism and better education to their adherents, these organizations will experience the positive effects of cross-validation. We can expect them to expand their national bases and become the leading organizations of Latino Pentecostalism and Evangelical Christianity. However,, it will be surprising if both can altogether avoid the conflicts of regional and ethnic interests or the stress fracture between pastoralist and liberationist orientations.

Structural Changes in Latino Pentecostalism

These changes beg for systematic analysis, but even our panoramic summary suggests considerable vitality in Latino Pentecostalism. Luis León's study (1994) of Victory Outreach—a California church founded by a Puerto Rican—demonstrates the adaptation to the 1990s of the message against sin and in favor of repentance. Salvation is no longer as narrow and individualistic a concern as might have been considered before the resurgence. Latino Pentecostalism has enjoyed remarkable success in reforming drug abusers and gang members and reinserting them into society as Latinos with a mission to return to their original communities and prevent others from repeating their mistakes. But this conversion is often coupled with an astute ability to attract government funds to weave together social services with the message of the Gospel. Such congregations combine the traditional message of personal accountability with current awareness of social and economic factors.

Much as with Latino Catholicism, there is a restructuring at work within Latino Pentecostalism and Evangelicalism. These denominations have been celebrated for their capacity to "go with the Spirit." It now appears that the Spirit is moving Latino Pentecostalism and Evangelicalism toward some of the traditions that come from their Catholic cultural legacy. For instance, as Pentecostal and Evangelical ministers move toward larger ecclesiastical associations, they have also adopted elements of mainline

Protestantism and Catholicism. It is not uncommon now to see Evangelical ministers wear black and a clerical collar. In some places, the title "bishop" has gained favor for leaders of other Pentecostal clergy. There are still traditional Pentecostals who scorn Catholics because—supposedly— "Catholics never read the Bible" or "worship idols." But such ignorance about other faiths is doomed by the tendencies toward openness and ecumenism. In fact, some Catholic Pentecostals, or Charismatics, are classified as "Catholic Evangélicos" by Reverend Rivera of the Latino Pastoral Council in the Bronx. At the same time, Catholic converts to Pentecostalism often bring into their new congregations some of their "Catholic" heritage (Deck, 1994).

Of course, there is always danger in any denomination for a clergy leader who goes too far or too fast for the congregation, and more than one progressive Pentecostal minister has sought refuge from fundamentalist furor by joining a more accepting denomination. One notes the large exodus of bright, educated Latino Pentecostals away from their original beliefs and into Protestant churches, which have a less rigid theology. However, the migration of Latino Pentecostals into Evangelical and mainline denominations makes it important to distinguish between "Pentecostalism" and "Pentecostal influence." Many of those who leave behind the Pentecostal churches for mainline Protestant denominations seem to take with them the Pentecostal traditions of prayer and spirit-filled spontaneity. Thus, just as there are Pentecostalist Catholics, there seem to be Pentecostalist Methodists, Lutherans, and Presbyterians.

Pentecostal Latinas

We should not pretend that Latino Pentecostalism is without its difficulties. Attention to the matriarchal core of Latino religion helps diagnose both the problem and also its possible remedy. Women have always been a vital presence in Pentecostalism. Professor María Pérez y González of PARAL has studied these and other Latinas in ministry, gathering extensive data on the types of church commitment (1994). She suggested upon reviewing the data (Pérez y González, 1995) that Pentecostal women are willing to initiate programs of self-help and social concerns outside the umbrella of Pentecostal churches, though very much in the Pentecostal spirit. For instance, in New York City, Angels Unaware counsels parents of retarded children and supports them and their families. This contradicts the strict theological teaching of Pentecostalism that retarded children are possessed by the devil and need exorcisms, not counseling. Pérez y González reports that many of these Pentecostal women have grown impatient with Pentecostal traditions of authoritarian leadership and rigid fundamentalism. She interprets their role as one of "prophets," suggesting that by openly embracing what can be considered a Pentecostal "heresy," these women are generating a new theological understanding of their faith (Pérez y González, 1995). Thus, the movement toward national associations and networks among Latino Pentecostals and Evangelicals suggests that a simultaneous transformation of theological beliefs is occurring.

The Bottom Line

Our analysis of the base of support for each Latino organization makes possible an assessment founded on sociological factors instead of breast-beating. The criteria for judgment of effectiveness of the resurgence are similar to those for evaluating social movements (Hart, 1996; Williams, 1996). How do they perform their functions: Do they *mediate* between individuals and structures or social realities? How do they serve to *clarify collective beliefs*? And how do they exert *pressure* on public authorities and the elites in power? It remains for a new generation of case studies on Latino religious organizations to spell out the responses to such questions.

Even without such detailed research, we think it is possible to provide an accurate general opinion about the Latino Religious Resurgence. We have witnessed the creation of symbolic capital and the mobilization of church-related resources at the service of a new conceptualization of being religious and Latino. But the success ended the movement. Much as the Italian *risorgimento* sacrificed the passionate unity among its various segments to the concerns for stabilizing the nation-state, when the resurgence established a host of Latino church organizations, it ceased to be a movement. As in syzygy, where the alignment of celestial bodies is never permanent, the unique combination of forces that came together with spectacular intensity is now over. A new Latino generation must build its consciousness upon the successes of the generation of the resurgence and replace it in the process. But rather than judge the Latino Religious Resurgence negatively because it did not achieve its utopian goals, one should take stock of its solid achievements. The *mentalité* of this generation of leaders has changed the nature of how Latinos think about religion. The resurgence created a need for institutional churches to reach out to Latinos on terms derived from the secular and cultural changes of the 1960s and 1970s. Then the resurgence supplied the leaders and the organizations to satisfy those needs. As a result, a movement advanced to an organizational stage in which it has restructured the organs of pastoral and ecclesiastical organization that relate to U.S. Latinos.

One might compare the resurgence to a company that patented the formula of a home-cooking recipe and bottled it for general consumption. The products of the resurgence blend culture and ministry together in recipes to Latino taste. The leadership of the resurgence markets these

Latino foods to supermarkets, arguing that there should be a special section for just Latino foods. The largest religious supermarket (the Catholic Church) now offers this special section for Latinos as a matter of policy, and other supermarket chains (mainline Protestant churches) do the same. The products need not be relabeled as the store's own brand (Catholic or Protestant); just being authentically religious and authentically Latino is sufficient trademark. The local corner grocery stores (Pentecostal and Evangelical congregations) generally sold the homemade products, but little else. Now they are moving into more sophisticated systems of management, production, and delivery. Some of their products are also available in the larger supermarkets, while in their own stores, they freely use products manufactured originally for their competitors.

In the search for the "bottom line" of this Latino Religious Resurgence, we can see movement toward "privatization," wherein the subsidy of Latino organizations by the institution is replaced with independent suppliers. This analogy would fit the NCCHM, which now provides a national leadership process that was once supplied in Catholicism by the national secretariat. The eclipse of the secretariat is a form of "downsizing," wherein there is a reduction of redundant bureaucracy for the sake of efficiency. The book-keeper evaluating the resurgence would also tell us that it is now time to take our "write-offs," such as with the narrowness of cultural idiosyncrasy. There are organizations that had their time of maximum efficiency but no longer fit the situation and need not consume additional resources to merit their place in history. Might we classify Theology in the Americas, PADRES, and Las Hermanas in this way? We would also need to balance such cutbacks with some "investments for the future" such as liturgical renewal, youth apostolate, and theological education. These are areas that require general agreement and special consideration, because while not yet cost-efficient, they will provide the areas for future growth (Hayes Bautista, 1992).

Above all, we would stress the strength of the resurgence in providing "models" for pastoral and theological commerce. This has been the source of the symbolic and social capital for the resurgence. One might compare the resurgence to a company that has based itself on "franchising." Through documents like those of the encounters and the pastoral centers, the resurgence has empowered local agencies to adapt a nationally packaged idea to regional market needs. It has trained the personnel for these operations and provided the advertising and technical assistance necessary to multiply itself wherever there are Latinos who practice religion. Assessment of the likely future of Latino religion follows in the next and final chapter.

7

Options

$\mathcal{H}$OW CAN THE CHURCH CHANGE the world if the church is itself in need of reform? But if we wait until the church is perfect, will we ever have time to address the problems of the world? This is the dilemma of pastoralists and liberationists, and it is the catch-22 that confronts Latino religion at the approach of the millennium. During the resurgence, this issue was not divisive. Meetings such as the encounters and national offices like the secretariat in Washington for Catholics and various Protestant commissions provided common ground for both pastoralists and liberationists. In essence, any ideological division was subordinated to larger questions of unity as a movement on behalf of the Latino people. With few exceptions, church institutions had not placed Latino leaders in important positions of administration, so those who placed priority on pastoral care saw themselves just as much in need of recognition as those who viewed social concerns as the more urgent need. The resurgence's appeal to theological ideas of liberation reconciled these visions. The unity gave the movement phase of the resurgence its vitality and spectacular hold on the religious imagination of Latinos. But as the pastoralists rose more rapidly in institutional ranks than the liberationists, the balance between these interests was upset, and agencies with a pastoralist orientation generally fared better in terms of institutional resources than those groups focused on Latino material needs. As a result, different sets of liberationist and pastoralist organizations compete for Latino loyalties today.

Although viewing religious movements through a social science perspective is useful for understanding political dynamics, it ought not to become a form of reductionism that obliterates the religious purpose and motivations that animate such movements. If liberationists and pastoralists were political parties competing for control of the resurgence, then the victory of one would also be the defeat of the other. For one side to gain advantage, it would be necessary to attack the other. But liberationists and pastoralists are not political partisans, and the division between the two approaches—although real—is also reconcilable.

Organizations and Multiple Identities

The reconciliation is easier if we define organizations rather than individuals. Most organizations can be classified by their stated goals: Those focused *primarily* on the internal needs of religion are pastoralist; those that give priority to the social and material needs of a community are liberationist. In our opinion, it would be a mistake to suppose that the pastoralist achieves a higher state of perfection than the liberationist, or vice versa. They are, rather, two of the multiple identities available to Latino believers today. One obviously makes a commitment to either a liberationist organization or a pastoralist one at a given time by evaluating need and personal talents; but this does not automatically reject the work and worth of the other approach. In fact, parishioners often belong to several organizations, each of which may have a different purpose. Thus, a Latino active in congregational life may simultaneously be a member of the Bible study group, which would be a pastoralist organization, but may also belong to the social action committee, with its liberationist goal, and to the parents' association of the school, which is a little bit of both.

Because both tendencies feed into religious commitment, an analogy could be drawn to the AC current in an electric system: The alternation between charges generates the power, and if there were no alternation, the current would not turn on the motors plugged to the source. We recognize that there are ecclesiastical and political forces that find advantage in separating pastoralist and liberationist organizations from each other, but we remain optimistic that the future will bring them together with important results. In other words, even though pastoralist and liberationist organizations each have different spheres of interest, they frequently include the same individuals in their membership. We think the reconciliation of these visions of Latino religion will come from multiple commitments on the part of individuals, as they learn to mix and manage both dimensions of religious commitment by choosing how and when to participate in the organizations.

The passage from the movement phase of the resurgence to an organizational focus sharpened the differentiation of goals. A movement proposes to change everything, whereas an organization limits itself to specific programs. Latino organizations have separated the generic impetus of a movement into differing spheres of pastoralist and liberationist activity. Organizations with tasks in liturgy and pastoral education spin in orbits different from those that address such problems as lack of housing or public services. But there are signs of convergence beyond institutional and denominational boundaries. Liberationist and pastoralist organizations meet in the Hispanic Summer Program of AETH and in national associations like the National Catholic Council for Hispanic Ministry and the Alianza de Ministerios Evangélicos Nacionales.

Our thinking on the future of the liberationist and pastoralist convergence owes much to the work of Father John Coleman, S.J., who has examined several religiously motivated organizations that work toward material improvement.[1] Coleman chose to study six organizations: Habitat for Humanity, the Pacific Institute for Community Organizing, Bread for the World, Pax Christi USA, Focus on the Family, and, for reasons of racial diversity, two African Methodist Episcopal Church congregations, one in Baltimore and the other in Los Angeles. The first three organizations focus on social concerns; Pax Christi and Focus on the Family are more pastoralist but have strong political profiles; the congregations are a combination of both at the local level. Based on the premise that such organizations generate social capital, Coleman's study provides a window on the religious motivations, or symbolic capital, that is also present.

Although Coleman does not employ our terminology of pastoralist and liberationist, he understands the inevitable tension that arises from these divergent concepts. Approximating the distinction between social concerns and pastoral care, he calls it "the dilemma of the twin vocations" and "the ingenious dual structure of paradenominational group and congregation, their mutual autonomy and symbiosis" (Coleman, 1996b:18–19). He is especially interested in PICO, founded by a fellow Jesuit. He states that PICO modifies the confrontational tactics of the Industrial Areas Foundation, founded by the radical community organizer, Saul Alinsky. While IAF and other organizations rely heavily on self-interest and confrontation to secure gains for the community, PICO's religious motivation has separated the conflicts necessary to secure material improvement and policy changes from personal attacks intended to humiliate opponents. PICO's strategies fit better into a religious culture (Coleman, 1996b:22–23, 44–47). Discarded from the armory of tactics are noisy picketing of an alderman's house or "the intentional consumption of huge quantities of beans for a flatulent stink-out at a local city council meeting" (Coleman, 1996b:27). Judy Reyes-Ortiz recognizes the centrality of religious motivation for her PICO group, referring to "the grounding in faith [that] keeps us from getting too wild or too way out there. In other words, it keeps us from trashing people, our opponents. We have to respect their dignity, and that comes from the faith base" (Coleman, 1996a:12).

Such networks of church-based community organizing groups are now large enough to command a national role. Citing sociologist Sidney Verba's collaborative research, Coleman says the most viable of present-day social movements are the paradenominational organizations (Verba, Schlozman, and Brady, 1995). They provide training in transferable skills, establish networks for civil activity, confirm a sense of worth in a local setting, and cue people about politics. With testimony that secular alternatives such as neighborhood poverty organizations and civil rights and labor advocacy groups are on the wane (Gittell, 1981:43–47), it seems that the religious-based organizations are to be the most likely route for community mobilization in the next century. Coleman reports that the *Nation* found that two-thirds of those active in social movements in the United States "draw principally on religious motivation for their involvement." He also notes that "from soup kitchens to non-profit, low-cost housing alternatives, from AIDS hospices to shelters for the homeless and services to immigrants, the religious sector takes up the slack where government programs fall down" (Coleman, 1996a:9).

Princeton sociologist Robert Wuthnow is another scholar who has written extensively about the exercise of compassion through church organizations (1991). From a Protestant perspective, Wuthnow has described in considerable detail how these paradenominational groups provide religious believers with a public role in U.S. society. Such statements confirm for us that contemporary religion encourages believers to participate actively in different organizations that address the needs of both church and society. Far from considering them as antagonistic, Denise Collazo, a PICO organizer, views the bonds of church community as fundamental for social involvement:

> If someone you've been going to church with for 15 years comes up to you and says, hey, we're working on this project with the Oakland Community Organization [PICO's original name] and it's something that would really interest you, you're going to take that much more seriously than if some organizer comes knocking on your door. (Coleman, 1996a:10)

Certainly, such sentiments are likely to be found in any religious community, but they have particular importance for urban Latinos, most of whom live in poor, segregated neighborhoods. Latinos are an important presence in many community organizations. For instance, PICO reported that Latinos accounted for 31.8 percent of the total PICO membership of 852,000 (Coleman, 1996b:7), or about one out of every three PICO members. About one-half the Catholic membership of PICO is Latino, which may indicate that Latinos and Latinas are more involved in community organizations than are Euro-American Catholics.

In these emerging religious-based community organizations, we see the reflection of the public role for Latino religion promoted by the leaders of the Latino Religious Resurgence. We would not claim that each of these organizations today draws its inspiration from the resurgence, since the myriad forces that have shaped them come from a variety of social and religious events. But we think it fair to say that the resurgence organized Latinos around the ideal of merging pastoral care and social concerns as integral parts of religious commitment. It did so early, efficiently, and with national scope. The resurgence prepared Latinos for paradenominational religious organization, and without the resurgence, groups like PICO would have had a rockier road to community organizing among Latinos. Indeed, this was the assessment made by Monsignor Fox of New York's Summer in the City two decades ago (Díaz-Stevens, 1993a:172). We do not have sufficient data at present to make this more than a hypothesis, but the issue is worth exploring not only for what it may tell us about the past but also for what light it may shed on the future.

Denominational Belonging and Multiple Identities

The concept of multiple identities is particularly important to U.S. Catholicism in the twenty-first century. With an insightful turn of phrase, Professor Catherine Albanese describes the Latino religious experience as "a Catholic bolt of cloth, with Protestant embroidery around the edges," just the opposite, she said, of what is generally expected in the study of religion in the United States where Protestantism dominates.[2] Considering past slights, insults, and attacks directed at Latino tradition, language, and religious practices, it is truly remarkable that 63 percent of young Latino Catholics responded in a recent survey that "they could not imagine any circumstances under which they would leave the Catholic Church," whereas less than one-half of their Euro-American counterparts were that thoroughly committed to Catholicism (D'Antonio et al., 1996:155). But can these findings be squared with others (Deck, 1994) that suggest extensive conversions away from Catholicism to Protestantism and Pentecostalism?

Some preliminary research on the conversion of Latinos (Pantoja, 1996) points to a greater likelihood of dormant or nonpracticing Catholics converting to other denominations than those actively engaged in the practice of their faith. In other words, Catholic "losses" are not coming at the expense of Catholic parish membership. We have seen some parishes turn against the theological doctrine that sacraments work *ex opere operato* and deny baptism to an infant if the parents and godparents do not attend extended classes of instruction. This strategy, whose probable intention is to use the desire for the sacrament as leverage for increasing the number of active Catholics, is an aspect of a general trend in the pontificate of John Paul II to promote a smaller Catholic Church, where the members are "few but good." And the restrictive policies extend to matrimony, the Eucharist, and Confession. No doubt as a result, some Latinos who were refused the sacraments and who spurned the conditions imposed of active Catholic membership are now in Protestant, Evangelical, and Pentecostal congregations that provide welcome. There are no reliable empirical data, however, that suggest that the exodus is large enough to threaten the majoritarian status of Catholicism among Latinos. Nor is it complimentary to the other denominations to view their new members as "disgruntled Catholics."

Significantly, Catholicism is not the biggest "loser" in the matter of conversions. One study, conducted by Edwin Hernández and Roger Dudley among Seventh-Day Adventists (1990), found that only about one-half of the converts to this denomination came from Roman Catholicism, with the other one-half coming from Protestant or Pentecostal churches. Since the pool of non-Catholic Latinos is much smaller than the Catholic one, conversion to Seventh-Day Adventism represents a larger proportional drain on Protestant and Pentecostal Latino congregations than on Catholic parishes.

It is more useful to pursue the notion that among the factors producing a change in denominational affiliation is the Latino proclivity toward multiple identities. In *Old Masks, New Faces* (Stevens-Arroyo and Cadena, 1995), it was suggested that Latino Protestants have come to think about *el pueblo* like Catholics do (Rosado, 1995), and that Latino Catholics can find solace in a church service celebrated by an Episcopal priest in a United Methodist congregation (Goris, 1995). The collaboration of Latino congregations through community organizations blurs the differences that were once thought to clearly define these denominations. In our opinion, Catholicism remains the religion of the Latino majority, not because of some imagined doctrinal triumphalism but because Latino Catholicism has itself been changed. It now develops Latino leaders, promotes Latino cultural expression, and fosters organizations committed to social justice issues important to all Latinos. These goals, articulated during the encounters, form the official policy of the Catholic bishops as a collective body.

In this sense, the policy toward Latinos within the Catholic Church is far from being conservative or anti-Latino. Latinos who are upset with special attention can attend all-English services, if they wish, of course, choosing to assimilate into the mainstream, but we have seen nothing to suggest that significant numbers of Latino Catholics are upset with the progressive policies of their church. Actively practicing Latino Catholics are most likely to leave the church if individual prelates and pastors refuse to implement these national policies. In other words in "ideological conversion" to other denominations, the source of discontent is often not Catholicism's stance toward Latinos but the recalcitrance of individual parishes or dioceses to follow the national directives. In the Archdiocese of Philadelphia, for instance, Catholic clergy were discouraged at one time from joining in the citywide association for Latino ministers that inspired the community organizing of Nueva Esperanza. This restriction diminished participation in a highly successful project that injects religious values into the public arena.

Although the restriction has since been lifted, its effects are still being felt in the low profile Latino Catholics have in this vital community organization. Had Latino Catholics in Philadelphia been permitted to exercise "multiple identities" when the community organizing project was still being shaped, they might have had fuller participation in establishing Nueva Esperanza without having to sacrifice their Catholic loyalty. Now that the project has been successful, it has an identity as a Protestant organization, and the inclusion of Catholics has become more difficult.

The shoe fits the other foot. The desire for multiple identities can also be found among Pentecostals and Evangelicals who may want to cooperate with Catholics in community organizations or who wish to send their children to parochial schools. The Pentecostal pastor who thwarts such willingness to engage in interdenominational sharing may find it as hard as a Catholic counterpart to control the ecumenical mind-set of the congregation.

Control of Organizations

Of course, few institutional leaders state that they oppose official national policies or the social programs of their church. The more common pattern of ecclesiastical disapproval is censure of the individual leader of the social program. Authority often believes that if it "cuts off the head" of a community organization, it can then control the membership. This happens in all denominations, although in different ways. Roger Finke (1994) offers an analysis of Southern Baptist congregations, where the disapproval results in the firing of the pastor by the local church members. In Catholicism and other hierarchical churches, the disapproval may be exercised through a decision of the bishop to transfer the committed leader to another, less visible post.

One of the more dramatic of such episcopal transfers occurred in the San Bernardino Diocese of California, where the transferee was not a cleric but a religious woman. In 1986, with the momentum of the resurgence passing to organizations, the bishop ordered the removal of Sister Rosa Marta Zárate from her position in the evangelization and catechetical program for Latinos. Sister Rosa Marta was a member of a Mexico-based congregation of religious women that had come north of the border to teach in elementary school. But she was among a handful of these Mexican sisters to change her view of the ministry after contact with Las Hermanas. At the time of the bishop's order, Sister Rosa Marta had directed a successful youth ministry that featured music as a vehicle for religious education and had established a diocesanwide network of *comunidades de base*. The reason given to dismiss Sister Rosa Marta was a somewhat vague assertion that her work did not "preach Christ." Believing that the command stemmed from the bishop's personal political inclinations, Sister Rosa took the extreme step of suing the bishop in civil court for violation of her civil rights and for discrimination against her as Mexican. No one wins in such confrontations, and the courts tend to avoid intervening in internal church decisions about how to deploy personnel. Sister Rosa Marta has been forced to "start over again" in an autonomous, nonchurch community organizing project called Calpulli, from the Nahuatl word for "ours." At the beginning, she relied on the sale of various records and cassette recordings of her music and singing to help sustain the effort, which now has grown in ten years to provide a wide range of community services, is staffed by fourteen full-time employees, and receives funding from several sources.

The pattern of such dismissals is for the transferred leader to continue the same work in another place, though usually at considerable personal cost both to the leader and the people affected. Sister Rosa Marta's tale is not unlike those of other ministers and leaders such as the Puerto Rican priest the late William Loperena, O.P., who "get too far ahead" of their superiors. Happily for Sister Rosa Marta, she has been supported by the people and some colleagues, for example, Father Pat Guillen, a cofounder of PADRES, who upon reaching retirement age established a theological training center within Calpulli. Her struggles have given her national visibility, and she was featured in a documentary special on Catholic women, prepared for the *Frontline* program on public television in 1994.

Father William Loperena, O.P., used music at the very beginning of his ministry to gather the people in Comerío, Puerto Rico. His *Misa Jíbara* (1968) was the first such composition to use the Spanish language and folk music for the Catholic liturgy. But Father William was more than just a composer; he had graduated summa cum laude from the Dominican seminary in Holland after studies under Edward Schillebeeckx, one of the Second Vatican Council's *periti* (experts). Upon return to his native Puerto Rico, it became clear that Fray William possessed an ecclesiological vision that was very progressive. The liturgical compositions were created by dialogue with the members of the parish, in one of the most impoverished sectors of the island (Rodríguez León, 1996). Under William's direction, verses of the entrance song at the Sunday mass often described the particular concerns of the congregation, and the weekly improvisation tied together the social or liberationist needs with the liturgy.

The Comerío parish administered by the Dutch Dominicans in Puerto Rico exemplified the harmonious blending of pastoralist and liberationist goals in the same ministry (Díaz-Stevens, 1993c). Thus, Comerío not only had a progressive liturgy, it also enjoyed a program for the aged, continuing education for adults and teenagers, and an art center that cultivated the beauty of Puerto Rico's national culture. In Puerto Rico, parishes usually embrace the entire rural and town population, hence the entire town participated in these programs, including the United Methodist minister,

Alberto González. The progressive parish generated political controversy from more conservative church officials, who objected to the connection between Comerío's clergy and the cause of Puerto Rican independence. Eventually, the Puerto Rican hierarchy removed the Dominican priests from the parish. Unable to directly impugn any violation of liturgical rules or doctrinal deviance, the bishops simply invoked their prerogatives to act without cause, as stated in canon law. But the ire was not limited to the Dominican priests or to the social programs they directed: The *Misa Jíbara* also became a target. Its performance was discouraged on grounds that Puerto Rican folk music was too "undignified" for worship. As pointed out by Ana María Díaz-Stevens (1993c), the *Misa Jíbara* was an ideological battleground for the war between those who view Puerto Rico as a nation and those who do not. Separated from his parish, Father William again tied his music to his liberationist vision of ministry in Rochester, New York, and the South Bronx in New York City. The *Misa Jíbara* is accepted today, despite episcopal disdain in Puerto Rico; it is well known among both Catholics and Protestants, not only in Puerto Rico but in Cuba and the Dominican Republic as well.

We see a pattern of antagonisms when the pastoralist and liberationist agenda are forced apart. But there are also more encouraging examples of harmony when they are blended. Coleman cites "Father Joe" of Saint Ann's parish in Orange County in California, who views his role as maintaining a balance between faith and action for the Latinos of his parish. Speaking about PICO's community organizing, he says:

> My whole goal is that we are trying to get the lay people involved in this [community organizing]. My role in it is to keep the faith orientation going, [making sure] that we have a reason why we are doing this. This is not disconnected from everything else we do. All this time we spend at Mass and at prayer, at catechism classes and all of those things, somewhere it has to be expressed. And this is one of the important ways of expressing it. . . . I think we would be deficient without community organizing because it seems to me this is very much what so many of our church documents talk about. And it does it in a respectful, healthy, good way. I think for some pastors the temptation would be to take it over and impose their agendas as well. And I think that is a dangerous thing as well, because that basically is taking away people's authority and power. (Coleman, 1996b:18)

We would have liked to report in this book that most Latinos encounter such a balance between pastoralist and liberationist goals in their parishes and congregations, but such data are not available. We know only that *some* parishes and congregations successfully manage such a balance and that *some* do not. But is the balance achieved in 30 percent, 50 percent, or

80 percent of the cases? We need survey data to count the number of local churches employing this strategy and to establish a baseline from which to measure future patterns. Absent survey data, the most certain fact is that the balance between pastoralist and liberationist goals that was articulated during the Latino Religious Resurgence has been established as a model or paradigm. Convergence of pastoralist and liberationist commitments was incorporated into many pastoral training programs established as a result of the resurgence. Reconciliation of pastoral care and social concerns was taught as a model for organizations, much like a technique for individual self-betterment.

Status as a "model" is doubly important within religion because of the important role that codification plays. Once a particular method or approach is approved within a church, it is repeated step by step, adapted to local circumstances, and improved upon. Manuals and books are used in the instruction, and theology is frequently employed to legitimate the goals. We would say that the array of liberationist and pastoralist organizations in Latino religious communities ought to be counted as one of the resurgence's results. Put into more technical terms, the resurgence accelerated for Latinos the process of religious differentiation, allowing greater specialization in choosing organizations to achieve religious goals. Thus, in Gramscian terms, Latino religion embraces both culture and ideology (Williams, 1996:373).

As we outlined in the previous two chapters, pastoralist organizations generally get a larger share of institutional resources than liberationist ones. But because the movement projected multiple goals, the friction among Latino religious organizations was more often over institutional relationships than over the legitimacy of their agenda. Most of the organizations maintained a common appeal to liberation theology. Latino parishes or congregations, like individuals, can support several organizations simultaneously, each with its own specialized agenda, while preserving a unifying theological vision. In this way, the resurgence continues to shape community action among Latinos while simultaneously developing additional vehicles for Latino religious identity. In all cases, the reconciliation of goals requires a democratization of the governance apparatus at the local level and a pluralistic tolerance for different goals and priorities within the same community.

Cultural Citizenship as an Identity

The notion of multiple Latino religious identities that we have used resonates to the concept of multiple citizenships employed by Coleman in his interpretation of community organizations. Modifying the explanations offered in José Casanova's prize-winning book *Public Religions in the*

Modern World (1994), Coleman suggests that loyalty and participation are summoned to four different poles: the world community or humanity, the nation-state, civil society, and the partisan political party. The paradenominational groups he studied feel that their world and civic citizenships supersede loyalties to either nation-state or political party. We would suggest that there is a fifth form of citizenship, a cultural one that complements rather than impedes Latino participation in the larger society. In that cultural citizenship, Latinos feel loyalty to language, religious customs, and family traditions. We described the functions of cultural citizenship as developed by anthropologist Renato Rosaldo (1989) in Chapter 1. As Gilbert Cadena (1987) has pointed out, Latino identity during the resurgence created "*abuelita* theology." Much as Hansen suggested for the general population, Latinos have looked to their grandparents' values to affirm continuity with the past. The components of Latino ethnicity, culture, language, and traditions, have been reimaged as solutions to contemporary problems. As suggested in Chapter 2, tradition provides an inoculation against the fragmentation of group identity for those experiencing modernization.

We need to understand better, however, how insistence on Latino ethnicity as a requisite for leadership during the resurgence affected locally based projects from which emerged today's paradenominational community organizations. In Chapter 6, we described how the insistence on Latino leadership for Latino projects has generally benefited Protestant, Evangelical, and Pentecostal congregations, most of which have numerous native clergy drawn from the ranks of married men and women. But the resurgence has also had an effect on Latino Catholicism, in spite of the celibacy requirement and restriction of the priesthood to men alone. For example, the late Luis Olivares, C.M.F., who was president of PADRES in 1979, used the annual meeting of the association to provide training in community organizing. Based on his own experiences in UNO in Los Angeles, Olivares saw the importance of the paradenominationals and of cross-ethnic, interracial organizations to Latino religion. By the time of his presidency, however, PADRES as national organization was in decline and could not halt the growing perception that the Latino organizations produced by the resurgence were focused principally on pastoralist goals. Although Olivares never produced a book, he was an eloquent spokesperson on the need for lay leadership. He also had an internationalist vision that pushed hard against the mono-Hispano emphasis on Chicanos in California. Before his tragic death as the result of one of his many trips of mercy to Central America, he converted the historic church in the heart of the Los Angeles barrio into a home for Salvadoreans and other Central Americans, adding their madonnas and devotions to that of the Mexican Our Lady of Guadalupe. Until his sudden death, Olivares had the potential to be a deroutinizer for Latino organizations *after* the resurgence.

The legacy of Father Luis Olivares was to challenge the encounter documents to adapt to new circumstances. As stated in the previous chapter, cultural idiosyncrasy may need to be "written off" the resurgence ledger and a substitute found. Cultural idiosyncrasy is exclusionary because it promotes the notion that only a person from a particular group can understand that group. It had a positive effect when it represented a large constituency such as "Latinos." But cultural idiosyncrasy can become reductionist, to the extent, for example, that only a left-handed, brown-eyed, Mexican American woman born in San Diego to a Korean War veteran can speak for the left-handed, brown-eyed, Mexican American women of San Diego from military families. In short, cultural idiosyncrasy becomes a Latino version of Bellah's "Sheilaism," in which Sheila's religious preference was uniquely her own and belonged to almost no one else (Bellah et al., 1985). Eventually, this kind of thinking leads to an excessive deference to particularity or a polite trivialization of deeply felt convictions. Allan Deck has pointed out, with characteristic insights, that multiculturalism may easily be manipulated into a folkloristic whitewash of fundamental differences in worldview (Deck, 1990).

We prefer to view Latino loyalties to culture and language as multiple religious identities. With the proper appeals, cultural citizenship in a religious context may contribute rather than hinder commitment to civic causes and community mobilization. The optimism we express for the future comes from our confidence that this reconciliation of multiple loyalties is a positive trend. We think the paradenominationals and religiously supported community organizations represent a new stage and a new generation of leadership for Latinos in religion that will influence the future of religion in the United States. In Catholicism, the inexorable force of demographic increase will prove compelling. In Protestantism, Evangelicalism, and Pentecostalism, spectacular Latino growth has become a major phenomenon of urban ministry. We do not think that Catholicism will fail to recognize that the Latinos—and not the Irish or the Italians—are the "most typical" of Catholics; we just wonder what changes this admission will bring to Catholic practice. Likewise, we do not think that U.S. Protestantism is anxious to be the religion of only the suburbs and the middle class; we are not sure, however, what mechanisms will be developed to ensure that Latinos, along with blacks and Asians, are viewed as equal coreligionists.

We also know that paradenominational organizations are vulnerable to manipulation. The direction of the Christian Coalition under Ralph Reed provides an example of how the faith commitment and local focus of action groups can be chained to partisan political purposes, a trend that is often inimical to Latino needs. Coleman criticized his six organizations for a strangely unquestioning acceptance of capitalism. Likewise, in evaluating the mistrust of the existing political structure in the United States that was present among many of his respondents, he called such attitudes "excessively localist, anti-Federalist sympathies" (Coleman, 1996a:13).

Not all antiestablishment sentiment is necessarily bad, however. Our previous study, "Latino Churches and Schools as Urban Battlegrounds," (Stevens-Arroyo and Díaz-Stevens, 1993b) reviewed the suspicions religious people harbor about public education. Skepticism about public institutions has induced Latino religious believers to seek their own programs of leadership formation, which more or less correspond to "adult" or "continuing education" programs. The paradenominationals exercise a positive role in providing leadership formation. But a more difficult topic is how cultural autonomy and mistrust of secular institutions affects the education of Latino children.

Latino Youth and Religious Schools

Only about 10 percent of Latino youth attend religious schools in the United States today. That means that the overwhelming number of Latino youth are in the public school system. But in Latino neighborhoods, it is not uncommon for the parochial school to have a nearly 100 percent enrollment of Latinos. Increasingly, the remaining slots in these neighborhood schools are often occupied by African American students. Thus, while religious schools in general and Catholic schools in particular can be criticized for not including more Latinos as students, there are schools at the local level that are for all practical purposes dedicated to Latino youth (Hall and Reck, 1987:39–46; Yeager et al., 1985).

The moral training imparted within religious schools and the discipline and the parental involvement at every level are compelling characteristics of their success, usually producing students with high grades. At the level of secondary education in the high schools, Catholic school education is the most remarkable. Whereas the national level of drop-outs for Latinos from public education fluctuates between 40 and 50 percent, the success rate of Catholic schools is over 90 percent (Moore and Pachón, 1985:68–69; Doyle et al., 1983:3–4). The study by the State Department of Education in New York (1993) for the governor's Blue Ribbon Panel on Catholic Schools found that Hispanics who attended Catholic schools had significantly higher proficiency than public school Hispanics in each academic category. Correspondingly, the graduation rates for Latinos from Catholic high schools and entrance rates into four-year colleges were significantly higher than among their Latino public-school peers. In fact, nearly 95 percent of Latino high-school graduates from Catholic schools obtain a university degree, whereas only about 20 percent of Latino public high-school graduates do so. Based on these numbers, it has been suggested that about one-half of all Latinos educated in New York state who obtain university degrees have gone to Catholic school at some time. This remarkable success rate of

Catholic schools is sometimes attributed solely to selective admissions policies. Catholic schools can throw out students who are at risk, it is argued, whereas public schools must accept whoever is sent there. But the study of the Blue Ribbon committee found that in New York City there was less than a 5 percent variance between the proportion of students at risk in Catholic school and those of the same type in public schools. In the rest of New York state, there were proportionately more students at risk in the Catholic schools than in the public schools. The findings suggest that of Latinos, those with religious conviction are among the most likely to succeed in higher education, regardless of socioeconomic status.

In most cases, religious affiliation sharply increases the educational achievement levels for women. Barry Kosmin and Ariela Keysar (1995) found that religious practice was a constant predictor of attainment in higher education for all women. There were higher rates of educational participation for women members of religious denominations than for the general female population. In one denomination, the Seventh-Day Adventists, both Latinos and Latinas had higher levels of educational achievement than the general membership of the church. The exceptions were among Pentecostal and Southern Baptist women, whose rates were lower than the average.

It is from the pool of college graduates that the professional leaders of the Latino communities will come. Doctors, lawyers, and successful business and community leaders are much influenced by the value system of their education, even if they cease to practice their religion in a regular way. Catholic and other religious schools ought to be criticized for how well they inject elements of Latino cultural awareness into their curriculum. Are Latino students provided with civic or history texts that enhance cultural citizenship to help them develop simultaneous personal pride in their heritage and stimulate religious commitment? Negative answers to this question can be found in the autobiographical accounts of the Catholic school experience offered by literary writers such as the Puerto Rican Edwin Rivera in *Family Installments: Memories of Growing Up Hispanic* (1982) and the Mexican American Richard Rodríguez in *Hunger of Memory: The Education of Richard Rodriguez* (1982).

Whatever the eventual outcomes of these cultural issues, religious Latino parents often choose education with moral values over secular education without such values (Stevens-Arroyo and Díaz-Stevens, 1993b). This also explains the popularity of Bible institutes, leadership formation programs, and catechetical and other continuing education programs for youth and adults sponsored by church institutions. Believers living in the barrio want education that is built upon life choices they have made or are in the process of making.

The phenomenon Paul Ricoeur called the "hermeneutics of suspicion" is found not only in the paradenominational groups studied by Coleman but also in the attitudes Latinos have toward the public schools. Religious individuals often presume that secularity is dangerous. This suspicion, it must be added, does not challenge the legitimation that secular education brings to a professional career; rather, people question the motives that undergird society's outreach to Latinos. Believers want an education, and whenever possible, a degree—but they want it to benefit their community. This skepticism toward secular and political authority is a trend in many parts of the world and in the United States in particular (Kavolis, 1988; Casanova, 1994). Although it is not confined just to Latinos, it does have some consequences special to the Latino circumstance.

Public-school education is currently groping to discover how to introduce morality into its curriculum without violating the U.S. constitution. One way has been to change the environment for learning. President Bill Clinton, a Baptist who attended Catholic elementary school and graduated from a Catholic university, in 1996 proposed uniforms for public schools for just such a purpose. There are also programmatic modifications proposed to counter low performance levels, high absenteeism, drop-out rates, and lack of discipline in many public schools. Through the mechanism of target schools and specialized programs, discipline is imposed at the threat of expulsion—if not from schooling, from the chosen school. Moreover, faced with draconian cuts in funding due to a lost tax base, urban public schools often seek donations and fund-raising activities from parents, much as characterize the "cookie sales" familiar in Catholic school experience.

In these circumstances, support for school choice, including a voucher system that would help finance a Catholic school education, is widening among segments of the Latino urban community, as reported in a poll released March 2, 1997, by Hart-Hanks Communications and the University of Texas. Whereas 57 percent of Euro-Americans in Texas supported vouchers for religious schools, Latino support was higher, at 77 percent. The issue is not viewed in the traditional terms of the separation of church and state but rather as a question of how best to provide a quality education in the face of a deteriorating public-school system. It should be emphasized that in what is clearly a complicated political debate, religious schools and the Catholic parochial schools in particular are hugely successful with the Latino cohort they serve. The question of how best to build upon these successes will likely shape future debate about educational reforms in the twenty-first century.

Latino Youth and Religious Formation

But all education does not take place in schools. The traditional, that is, rural, experience of many Latinos creates a problematic understanding of family participation in education. In many Latino households, one is considered a child until marriage prompts one to move out of the parents' household. The idea of teenagers—no longer children, but still only young adults—did not fit a pre-1950 Latino society because schooling generally ended at high school when Latinos were more or less limited to the marginal farming lives of their parents and grandparents. Migration to the cities in the 1950s and the consequent explosion of educational and career opportunities for Latinos began to change attitudes toward youth. Within Latino Catholicism, for instance, teenage girls were segregated into an association called Hijas de María, which provided social activities and participation in church affairs apart from young men. A function of the Hijas de María and their Protestant and Pentecostal counterparts such as the child choirs was to combat sexual sin by inculcating piety. In a sense, such organizations served the purpose of the chaperone system of Mediterranean culture, in which young men and women were never left alone without supervision by an adult (Fitzpatrick, 1971:97–98). Even after the encounter, however, church organizations, both Catholic and Protestant, have been slow to incorporate the special needs of teenagers into their ministries.[3]

Today, much of church supplemental schooling for youth has been focused on the need to find ways to counter the appeal of juvenile gangs. The old pious organizations have generally been eclipsed as the principal means of addressing the needs of teenagers. In their place, we have movements dedicated to moral training. Through a host of programs with different names—Crusade for Youth, Jornada, Youth Retreats—the churches have attempted to create the environment for a conversion experience. Thus, the commitment to Christ involves renunciation of drug use, abandonment of gang membership, avoidance of sexual promiscuity, and even rejection of fad clothing and hairstyles.

Rather than emphasize the limitations of such emotion-based conversion experiences, however, it seems more appropriate here to stress their *effectiveness*. Just as Alcoholics Anonymous offers evidence that quasi-religious faith is essentially required for rehabilitation of alcoholics, these youth movements have enjoyed marked success in reforming youth surrounded by the drug culture.[4] Religious programs of moral training for young people have entered into the public consciousness and have provided elements that are repeatable even by government. The blurring of the lines between what is religious and what is secular is addressed by scholars such as David Hayes Bautista (1992) of the University of California at Los Angeles, who views ethos as a vital dimension of Latino cultural identity. In sum, it appears that through many doors of entry, moral training influences public education. Moreover, its importance to religious Latinos can be expected to continue.[5]

But if Latino youth are attracted to church membership, to what kind of church do they belong? Are parishes and congregations that encourage multiple forms of religious commitment to both pastoralist and liberationist needs preferred? Or are conservative denominations sought? This is an important issue, not only for Latino youth already in the United States, but also for the youth emigrating from Latin America. Adolescents are extremely sensitive to questions of group identity and, not being adults, have little personal experience to guide them. From dress, choice of music, sense of humor, and food preference to types and forms of social activities, adolescents are vulnerable to peer pressures. These differences complicate outreach to youth in Latino communities, because these communities include not only the Latinos who have born here but also those arriving from Latin America.[6] For both Latinos and newly arrived Latin American youth, church-based Latino youth movements, then, are boiling stew kettles, into which notions of cultural identity, group loyalty, linguistic preference, and social consciousness are tossed, along with religious values (Díaz-Stevens, 1994b).

In 1974, we both organized the youth group Naborí, named after the native Taínos of Puerto Rico. The experience taught us some lessons about the integration of these various Latino identities.[7] Using cultural identity as the matrix for organization, Naborí's members came to view their social identity as based on a Catholic ethos. Moreover, because it was a grassroots community rather than a parish activity club, Naborí drew a distinction between service to the church as institution, on the one hand, and commitment to Catholic social justice, on the other. Naborí fostered the creation in the Northeast of the Concilio Pastoral Juvenil (CPJ) in the years 1974–1977 between the First and Second Encounters. It created training programs specifically for Latino youth that combined a week of education in aspects of Chicano, Puerto Rican, and Cuban history and culture with a week of service in the labor organizing of migrant workers. Hosted first at the Passionist Retreat House in West Hartford, Connecticut, and later at Saint Joseph's College in Hartford, these training programs were not the first efforts at creating programs specifically focused on Latino youth. But as with the regional convocation at San Isidro, California, organized by Teresita Basso and Rosa Marta Zárate in 1971, Latino culture and identity were integral parts of the project. Naborí was able to secure resources to make their training programs representative of not only East Coast Puerto Ricans, Dominicans, and Cubans but also Mexican Americans and Chicanos from California. Working together through the mechanisms of the Catholic encounters, groups like these achieved the establishment in 1977 of a national committee on Latino youth ministry sponsored by the secretariat in Washington.

Although this national youth committee became inactive after 1980 as the influence of the secretariat waned, the efforts serve as precursors of more recent Catholic efforts. In July 1995, a national symposium was held at Saint Mary's University of Minnesota that drew delegates from twenty-six Catholic dioceses for what was named the Prophets of Hope Project. Under the editorship of Carmen Cervantes, director of the Instituto Fe y Vida in Stockton, California, Saint Mary's Press publishes a bilingual newsletter titled *Building Our Hope*, in order to advance the work of the youth ministry through the formation of youth *comunidades de base*. Although these projects are more pastoralist than the efforts of Naborí, such efforts nonetheless break with the older model for Latino youth. The written manuals and leadership techniques also reinforce Latino cultural identities. The various crusades, rallies, and Christian music concerts for young Latino Evangelicals and Pentecostals represent the potential for organizations similar to those that have been formed for young Latino Catholics.

The emergence of new approaches for Protestant, Evangelical, and Pentecostal denominations to Latino youth represents an effective adaptation of traditional cultural norms to new circumstances. In our experience, Latino religion succeeds most when it creates fictive family. The constant use of kin terms like *"hermano/a"* in these youth groups are indications that family is a metaphor for religion. But such terminology is not artificial "feel-good" euphoria; Latino youths are frequently committed to community service projects, which are often linked to the sacrament of confirmation or some other step toward Christian maturity. We have only incomplete data, but almost all religious youth groups report regular engagement in service projects such as visiting hospitals, caring for the elderly, repairing homes, and the like.

Latino youth are called to community service by secular programs such as Aspira, a Puerto Rican educational program begun in the early 1970s, and AmeriCorps, which is a government-sponsored program. But much as in the discussion of the paradenominational organizations, Latino religion predisposes Latino youth to see this community service as a responsibility in service to their own people as identified by class, racial, and ethnic characteristics. This last is an important consideration. Because Latino youth frequently receive from religious-based education a heightened awareness that faith must be a lived experience, redress of social inequities becomes an aspect of religious commitment. Latino identity with this sort of religious origin is rooted in a concern for others and stands in contrast to the elitist and self-absorbed Latino identity promoted by some in academia (see Stavans, 1995).

The Ensemble

Our analysis of the different currents, groups, and theologies in Latino religion is not meant to divorce them from each other. They function organically as interacting parts of a single body. Along with Paul of Tarsus, we question whether the eye can separate itself from the hand or the heart from the head (I Corinthians 12:12–26). In our opinion, Latino religion should not be reduced to the merely political, social, or economic dimension. If we recall Dan Merkur's insight (1994) cited in Chapter 1, after analyzing all the elements of Latino religion synchronically, we must then recognize that Latinos know themselves and their history diachronically.

As Stephen Carter (1993) has done for U.S. religion in general, so Jesuit Father John Coleman has stressed the importance of a religious interpretation of the paradenominationals (1996a:13–14). We find Coleman's summary conclusions particularly telling. It is naive to assume, he says, "that we can easily find secular warrants that will compel universal or large-scale assent in our pluralistic society" or to assume that one can argue "that religious people must give up their deepest selves, motivation and language whenever they enter the common arena of citizenship and be obliged to talk in someone else's language, motivation and motifs" (Coleman, 1996a:14).

We hope that in this book we have provided an interpretation of Latino religion that can be connected to other religious experiences that have produced movements and organizations. This is new ground, because scholarly work on social movements and new religious movements has been carried on "largely in mutual disregard" (Mauss, 1993:127). Despite the absence of specifically religious movements in these studies, Professor Armand Mauss suggests that important theories have emerged: resource mobilization, rational choice, and marketplace theory. Along with Mauss, we note that such theoretical speculations "have tended to ignore the importance of ethnic, gender and other special demographic categories in movement rise and development" (Mauss, 1993:127). Unfortunately, despite the significantly larger numbers of Latinos practicing Latino religion when compared, for instance, to the followers of the Reverend Moon, Latino religions have not been included in the fashioning of most theories that study religious movements.

This inattention may be providential, however. Although he did not write on Latino religions per se, we think Professor Mauss was correct in challenging his colleagues to define better the meaning of "success" for religious movements. Clearly, a cult operates differently from the Latino Religious Resurgence, although we consider both to be types of religious movements.[8] Whereas in cults, the symbols spell conflictive protest against dominant values, the principal thrust of the Latino Religious Resurgence was to emphasize heritage without denying pluralism. Thus, we hope that some of the concepts offered here about Latino religion may tempt theorists of religious movements to widen the scope of study as they refine their work.

The Production of Symbolic Capital

We view the pastoralist tendency in Latino religion as the production of symbolic capital. As Pierre Bourdieu points out (1980/1990:140), symbolic capital is more important to many of the people who possess it than other forms of capital. And unlike its economic counterpart, symbolic capital increases in value the more it is given freely to others. Thus, the more Euro-Americans borrow from Latinos—even in seemingly trivial matters like a hymn at a worship service—the more value is added to the symbol. The paradenominationals, for their part, provide the liberationists with an opportunity of accumulating social capital. Community organizing has become a facet of Latino religion because it addresses the daily needs of people: maintaining the family, securing a decent wage, establishing a peaceful neighborhood, and a host of other basic preoccupations. Moreover, through the prism of a liberationist commitment, the procurement of these local needs is linked to global economic concerns. The measures for the success of Latino religion as a movement revolve around the accumulation of both the symbolic and the social forms of capital. Congregations move with different rhythms to collect first one, then the other—but the movements are in the same religious experience. Much like the beat and the melody in a song, the pastoralist and liberationist tendencies complement each other. Admittedly, the Afro-Latin religions like Santería have generally avoided what Pérez y Mena calls "Homeric duality," wherein actions are either morally good or morally bad (Pérez y Mena, 1991:36–38, 1995a:142–143). But the impetus of the favorable Supreme Court decision in 1992 (Campo, 1995) began a movement within these religions to establish themselves independently, much as might a storefront church (Pérez y Mena, 1995b). Almost simultaneously, changes in the Cuban Constitution at the Fourth Communist Party Congress sparked new openness in the practice of Santería in Cuba (Ramírez Calzadilla, 1996), including a more independent form of organization resembling that of Christian denominations. It is problematic if Santería, so successful in producing its own form of symbolic capital, will develop vehicles for generating social capital through involvement in community organizing. However, this is a prospect worthy of future research attentions.

Social Capital

It has been observed that social capital is more easily derived from religious organizations such as the black churches and Protestant congregations than from Catholicism (Verba et al., as cited in Coleman, 1996a:11). We would add that social capital in the Catholic experience may be more commonly produced by the Latinos in their parishes than by churches where Euro-Americans are the majority. This possibility was explored in an essay on barrio religion (Stevens-Arroyo, 1995e; see also Stevens-Arroyo, 1997a). It was argued that the poverty and the need to struggle against political and social exploitation are conditions more favorable to an authentic practice of religion than middle-class prosperity. In this line of thinking, Latino experience in the barrio is the model for what Christianity requires in order to preserve its Gospel authenticity. Reversing the specious argument that assimilation occurs in only one direction so that Latino Catholics must necessarily move within the middle-class ranks of most Euro-American Catholics (Budde, 1992a), we see Euro-American Catholicism gradually assuming many of the salient characteristics of Latino Catholicism, which is appreciated for its richness in terms of social capital.

This was the argument advanced in *Oxcart Catholicism* on the matter of Catholic practice in the midst of a permanent priest shortage. Latino Catholics, said Ana María Díaz-Stevens, are already prepared for a Catholicism without clergy, and Euro-Americans have something to learn from Latinos in this matter. A recent survey of U.S. Catholics (D'Antonio et al., 1996:156) found that fewer Latinos felt the lack of clergy would damage Catholicism than Euro-Americans. Although predicted by Díaz-Stevens in 1993, this finding apparently surprised the authors of the 1996 research.

But to understand the tendency for the economically better off to learn from people of lesser prosperity, certain premises need to be challenged. As described in the treatment of tradition in Chapter 2, one need not be secular to act rationally. Vital Latino parishes and congregations bring modernity to community action while still upholding religious beliefs. Along with other scholars, we consider these grassroots groups to be efficient vehicles for producing the sacred within the daily lives of millions of people (Wuthnow, 1994). The successful Latino parish today shares power among the people and clergy, fosters communal responsibility, and promotes democratization, thus creating social capital. Simultaneously, ritual and fictive kinship relations engender symbolic capital. Moreover, the pastoral documents provided by meetings and commissions beginning with the 1972 Catholic encounter, offer the "conceptual lenses" that Williams (1996) finds crucial to formulating how religious movements approximate social ones.

Norms such as mass attendance or strict adherence to the pronouncements of ecclesiastical authorities such as the bishops and the pope are imperfect measures of Latino religion. Probably because these survey categories are derived from bourgeois, liberal conceptions of religion, they have become standard in contemporary sociology of religion. When extended beyond the cultural boundaries of religion, however, they introduce an ethnocentric bias to social science (Marín and Van Oss Marín, 1991). For instance, from a Latino religious perspective, a person who prays daily and extensively in the home is more religious than another who merely spends one hour a week in church. But those who employ only a Euro-American perspective in interpreting the data see the substitution for mass attendance by Latino home-based piety as anomalous (see D'Antonio et al., 1996:154–155).

Civilizational Difference

In underscoring our departure from a few principles generally held in social science, we do not imply that the Latino experience is normative. Our argument here is for pluralism, not hegemony. Father Allan Deck (1995a) has noted that the traditional notions of "liberal" and "conservative" do not apply to Latino religion. We heartily endorse that position, while adding a different historical rationale.[9] Latino religion is connected to Ibero-American civilization and produces a *mentalité* different from the northern European civilization that was generated by Protestantism, the Reformation, and the Enlightenment (Stevens-Arroyo, 1997b). Our differences are not based on a lack of education or inferior levels of intellectual sophistication: The Ibero-American civilization we share is based on notions developed by thinkers as different as Jaime Balmes and José Ortega y Gasset or Francisco Suárez, S.J., and José Vasconcelos (Stevens-Arroyo, 1996a). In terms of contemporary Latino religion, it means that our symbolic capital derives from sources that northern European civilization often ignores. Much like the traveling tourist who finds it impossible to plug an electric razor into the outlet in a European hotel bathroom, Euro-Americans often find that Latino religion flows from a power source that is incompatible with theirs. The inverse is also true, though it does not preclude other modes of adaptation. As R. Stephen Warner succinctly states from the Euro-American perspective: "The reluctance to show emotions does not mean that we do not have them" (Warner, 1996).

We think that the evolution of the Latino future will be influenced considerably by religion, because unlike in Latin America, there is no apparatus of a nation-state to sculpt the features of Latino nationalism. In contemporary Puerto Rico, the churches and the religious movements within them have taken on some of the functions that were previously exercised by political parties. Religion has united Puerto Ricans across class and denominational boundaries for causes such as language, civil rights, and protection of the environment that are seen as moral issues. Organizations like the PRISA and Misión Industrial, founded by the Episcopal Church, have provided a platform for this kind of apostolate among leaders of different denominations. We think that within the continental United States, Latino religion is assuming a similar role. Religion is capable of producing both the symbolic and social capitals crucial to a successful passage for the urban centers of the United States into the twenty-first century. There are inklings of how such a role emerges from within religion by examining the recent history of a country like Brazil (Mainwaring and Viola, 1964), where the democratization of church-based groups provided the impetus to criticize the government. Puerto Rico has also had similar types of church mobilization, first under *Cristianos por el Socialismo* (Stevens-Arroyo, 1980:295–302) and later with the successful defeat in 1994 of constitutional amendments that would have made Puerto Rican law more like that of the United States. Will such antistatist trends be duplicated among religious Latinos in the United States?

We would welcome survey data that explore these differences. We also are eager to test whether the enhanced importance of barrio religion and a more intense commitment to it from Latinos produces more satisfying participation in parish and congregational life. In the case of Catholics, there is some indication of a significant difference between Latino and Euro-American parish experiences. Researchers in a 1993 survey of the laity asked if "the Catholic Church should have more democratic decision-making in Church affairs that do not involve matters of faith than it has at the present time." The survey allowed for a different response to this question by referring to the parish, diocesan, and Vatican levels (D'Antonio et al., 1996:152). When replying about a diocese (59 percent for Latinos, 61 percent for Euro-Americans) and about the Vatican (54 percent to 58 percent, respectively), Latinos and Euro-Americans were within 4 percentage points of agreement; but at the parish level, 64 percent of Euro-Americans expressed a desire for more democracy, whereas only 47 percent of Latinos responded that their parishes needed more democratization. Thus, if our premise about more satisfying lay participation in Catholic Latino parishes is correct, Latinos would be more content with their parishes than Euro-Americans with theirs.

We are puzzled by the researchers' conclusion to the effect that Latinos are less inclined to favor democratic procedures than Euro-Americans. It does not logically follow that people satisfied with the level of democratization in their parish favor authoritarianism. Could it not be that Latinos find more democracy in their parishes than Euro-Americans do in theirs? The possibility that Latinos, who are poorer and less professionally educated, could be more advanced than Euro-Americans in securing democratic parish governance did not seem to occur to the authors of this survey. We roundly reject the intimation that "the values of democracy, freedom and autonomy" are creations of American society rather than aspirations of all humanity.[10]

Global Relations

In concluding this book, we would like to connect our study of Latino religion to studies of religion worldwide. In our judgment, Latino religion is not becoming more secular or Americanized when it stresses education, community organizing, training of lay leaders, and communal attention to problems such as improved housing and public services. Nor do the maintenance of the Spanish language and injection of Latino cultural expression into ritual constitute a rejection of modernization. Latino religion is the product of contemporary trends of religious differentiation and the worldwide empowerment of colonized nationalities in the last one-half of the

twentieth century. For those accustomed to conceptualizing "modernization" and "Americanization" as inseparable aspects of social progress,
Latino religion might represent a pathological anomaly because it modern-
izes without Americanizing. For others, "Americanization" in a pluralistic
world represents close to a denial of one's own Latino culture and timid
obsequiousness to economic power.

We hope that the dynamics of Latino religion as we have explained them
will encourage those studying religion from a social science perspective to
reexamine some general premises current in the field. We are satisfied to
conclude this book suggesting that Latino religion exposes some of the fallacies of secularization. As pointed out by José Casanova (1994), the term
"secularization" comes from the political process that confiscated church
properties. It is extended by analogy to the state and civil society's assumption of the functions of religion in the wake of the disestablishment of religion after the Protestant Reformation, the Enlightenment, the Industrial
Revolution, and atheistic communism. We agree with Casanova's summary
analysis that Christianity before the Reformation had constructed a sacramental dimension for religion that mediated between secular and profane
aspects of life. Ana María Díaz-Stevens has called this buffer zone between
the officially sacred and the daily experience of the mundane the place for
"communitarian spirituality" (Díaz-Stevens, 1996c). This spirituality is related to the material religion of Christianity, protected by Catholic teaching on the efficacy of the sacramentals. The Reformation and its aftermath
was "corrosive" on the sacramentals so vital to Christianity. But whereas
most of northern Europe experienced a meltdown of religious functions,
the relative isolation of the Latino homelands from these influences ex-
empted Latino religion from some of these trends.

Casanova has summarized the basic tenets of secularization theory: A religion in retreat from public life becomes "invisible" (Luckman, 1967) or a
"canopy" (Berger, 1967) and explains the fallacies in both. Accordingly, he
does not agree with the systems view of Niklas Luhmann (1984) that
posits privatization as the process that will reduce religion to irrelevance.
Casanova cites two questions about public religion that follow Weber's notions of secularism.

   (1) Is there a legitimate religious resistance to secular world views that is
   more than a refusal to accept the consequences of the Enlightenment?
   (2) Is there a legitimate religious resistance to de-politicization, a resistance
   that is more than clinging to inherited privileges? (Casanova, 1994:38, citing
   Wolfgang Schluchter, 1989).

Casanova answers yes to both of these questions and provides precise
measures for analysis. Society is moving toward functional differentiation,

but, he argues, institutional religion is capable of strategies to minimize the negative impact of such a trend. Among Casanova's examples of the adaptive capacity of religion are the Solidarity movement in Poland and development of liberation theology in Brazil. These movements helped religion recover functions that had supposedly been irretrievably conceded to secularism:

> In this respect, both concepts, that of civil society and that of "the people" were not so much principles of mediation between state and society as principles of self-organization of society without mediation and without the state, principles of direct communitarian democracy. (Casanova, 1994:131)

Much in this description resonates with what we witnessed in the Latino Religious Resurgence when it utilized the concept *el pueblo*, "the people," as a principle of self-organization, although of course on a smaller scale. But as in Casanova's examples, "the people" represent a moral force. Political circumstances in the United States are not those of Poland or Brazil, and there has not yet been a need for Latino religion to assume anti-state functions. But in the current climate of Puerto Rico, antigovernment attitudes may grow into a mind-set that challenges not just local authority but the role of the nation-state.

Thus, we believe that Latino religion, like the mostly Catholic examples offered by Casanova, challenge three Eurocentric prejudices: Protestant bias, liberal bias, and nation-state bias (Casanova, 1994:39). We have a view of the contemporary Western world as undergoing mostly centrifugal forces that have substantially weakened nation-states and conformist notions of national culture and language. Whatever one's political opinions of Spain's autonomous governments, Quebec's separatism, Yugoslavia's and the Soviet Union's fragmentation, these are undeniable events. Ignoring such trends in expounding a paradigm for religion is to spit into the wind.

Moreover, the resurgence does not fit the theory of a revitalization movement suggested by Rodney Stark and William Bainbridge (1985). As pointed out by Casanova:

> If the assumption [of supernatural compensation] were correct, the sacred should have returned and religious revivals or the birth of new religions should have occurred ... where secularization had gone the furthest and the absence of religion created the greatest need. (Casanova, 1994:234–235)

But the Latino Religious Resurgence took place among a sector of U.S. religion that had been little affected by secularization. Casanova adds an analysis of globalization theory as developed by Roland Robertson (and Chirico, 1985) to arrive at a conclusion that we think applies to the resurgence: "The national churches stopped viewing themselves as integrative community cults of the national state and adopted a new transnational, global identity which permitted them to confront prophetically both the national state and the given social order" (Casanova, 1994:225–226).

Casanova's critique runs so closely with ours that it is tempting to think that we have offered a sixth example for his 1994 book *Public Religions in the Modern World.* His framing of this new role for religion, although lengthy, is worth citing here because it summarizes the many connections of Latino religion to theoretical issues about religion.

> Against those evolutionary theories which prefer to interpret what I call the "deprivatization" of modern religion as antimodern fundamentalist reactions to inevitable processes of modern differentiation, I argue that at least some forms of "public religion" may also be understood as counterfactual normative critiques of dominant historical trends, in many respects similar to the classical, republican, and feminist critiques. The public impact of those religious critiques should not be measured solely in terms of the ability of any religion to impose its agenda upon society or to press its global normative claims upon the autonomous spheres. In modern differentiated societies it is both unlikely and undesirable that religion should again play the role of systemic normative integration. But by crossing boundaries, by raising questions publicly about the autonomous pretensions of the differentiated spheres to function without regard to moral norms or human considerations, public religions may help to mobilize people against such pretensions, they may contribute to a redrawing of the boundaries, or, at the very least, they may force or contribute to a public debate about such issues. Irrespective of the outcome or the historical impact of such a debate, religions will have played an important public role. Like feminist critiques or like republican virtue critiques of modern developments, they will have functioned as counterfactual normative critiques. Besides, one does not need to accept the normative premises of such religious critiques in order to recognize that they may help to reveal the particular and contingent historical character of modern developments and to question the normativity of modern facticity. (Casanova, 1994:43)

As with many contemporary views of religion, we draw upon the theory of public space developed by Jürgen Habermas (1990), although we prefer the U.S. contours suggested by Robert Wuthnow (1994). Latino religion contributes to the "unfinished project of modernity" and ought to be afforded a permanent place in the study of U.S. religion, especially since it gives every indication of growing in size and importance within contemporary society. A review of U.S. religion that includes the Latino and Latina experiences, we think, will "set hearts burning," as the disciples claimed on the road to Emmaus. Our description has covered many years, projected bold comparisons, offered new interpretations, introduced important personages, and outlined the future. We hope that those who took the journey that we have traced through these pages have found satisfaction in sharing knowledge with us, much as do friends at a table breaking bread together.

Notes

1. Father Coleman's research was funded by the Lilly Endowment, 1992–1995. In 1996, as a fellow at the Center for Theological Inquiry in Princeton, New Jersey, he was preparing a book manuscript reporting on these findings. We eagerly await its publication. In preparing our book, however, we were obliged to use references to drafts from his manuscripts and to an overview of his work that was published in *America Magazine* (May 11, 1996) as an edited version of the John Courtney Murray Forum lecture presented at Fordham University on May 1, 1996.

2. Plenary session response at the PARAL Symposium, University of California, Santa Barbara, April 11, 1996.

3. When there were programs for youth, they were usually intended to prevent involvement with gangs. See Fitzpatrick, 1971:96–97, n. 19.

4. Doyle et al., 1983:40–42. The list of former-addicts-turned-minister/preacher is a long one among Latinos and includes Nicky Cruz, Piri Thomas, and Harold Recinos.

5. Hayes Bautista's survey studies only California, but the theoretical basis of his analysis is applicable to all Latinos.

6. Hurtado (1976) studied Mexicans and Mexican Americans, but the data seem applicable to most Latino groups, except for Puerto Ricans, who have a special political arrangement with the United States that makes citizens of people both in the homeland and in the United States. For this last point, see Stevens-Arroyo, 1994.

7. For one of the documents from Naborí, see Stevens-Arroyo, 1980:341–343. The history is analyzed in Díaz-Stevens, 1994b.

8. The exception to this premise about Latino religion is Santería and other Afro-Latin expressions of religion, which are often both Latino and cult. However, as discussed previously in the historical portion of Chapter 3 and further on in this chapter, Santería has functioned from within Catholicism until very recently and is not easily compared to the new religious movements in the Euro-American literature.

9. Repeating Orlando Espín, Deck alleges a "medieval," pre-Tridentine Christianity as the basis for Latino popular religiosity. We see no historical or empirical data to support this assertion that would contradict the widely documented reliance of Ibero-American culture on devotional and doctrinal beliefs concurrent with the decrees of the Council of Trent and the Baroque epoch during which this occurred (Stevens-Arroyo, 1997b).

10. This is the impression imparted in D'Antonio et al. (1996:153), which was derived by "Deck, 1989" without a page reference. In our reading, Deck described the experience only of recent immigrants from Mexico before the wave of neo-liberalism and not all Latinos. The Puerto Rican experience stands in stark contrast, against which the U.S. system of politics is viewed as less democratic. This explains, for instance, why Puerto Rican electoral participation averages over 80 percent on the island but drops dramatically in the United States.

Bibliography

Documents and Reports

Baugher, Eleanor, and Leatha Lamison-White. 1996. *Poverty in the United States: 1995.* Current Population Reports, P60-194. Washington, D.C.: U.S. Department of Commerce, Bureau of the Census.

Division for the Spanish Speaking. 1974. *Proceedings of the Primer Encuentro Hispano de Pastoral, June 1972, Washington, D.C.* Washington, D.C.: United States Catholic Conference.

Enchautegui, María E. 1995. *Policy Implications of Latino Poverty.* Washington, D.C.: The Urban Institute.

Gallup Organization, Inc. 1978. *A Gallup Study of Religious and Social Attitudes of Hispanic Americans.* Princeton: Gallup Organization.

Journal of the American Medical Association. January 1991. *Report on Hispanics.*

National Conference of Catholic Bishops. 1987. *National Pastoral Plan for Hispanic Ministry.* Washington, D.C.: National Conference of Catholic Bishops.

Primus, Wendall E., Kathryn Porter, Margery Ditto, and Mitchell Kent. 1996. *The Safety Net Delivers: The Effects of Government Benefit Programs in Reducing Poverty.* Washington, D.C.: The Center for Budget and Policy Priorities.

Puente, Sylvia. 1996. "Selected Demographics." *Latino Urban Policy Agenda Project.* Chicago: Latino Institute.

State Department of Education. 1993. *Roman Catholic Schools in New York State.* Albany, N.Y.: Report of the Office for Planning, Research and Support Services.

U.S. Bureau of the Census. April 1991. *Hispanic Population Report,* series PPL-41. Washington, D.C.: Government Printing Office.

_____. December 1992. *Estimates of the Population of the United States.* Population Estimates and Projections, series PPL-57. Washington, D.C.: Government Printing Office.

_____. April 1993. *Foreign Language Use at Home,* series CPH-L-133. Washington, D.C.: Government Printing Office.

_____. February 1996. *Population Projections of the U.S. by Age, Sex, Race and Hispanic Origin, 1995 to 2050,* series P25-1130. Washington, D.C.: Government Printing Office.

_____. March 1997. *Demographic State of the Nation: 1997,* series P23-193. Washington, D.C.: Government Printing Office.

U.S. Commission on Civil Rights. 1974. *Counting the Forgotten.* Washington, D.C.: Government Printing Office.

Books and Articles

Abalos, David. 1986. *Latinos in the United States: The Sacred and the Political.* Notre Dame, Ind.: University of Notre Dame Press.

Acuña, Rodolfo. 1972. *Occupied America.* San Francisco: Canfield Press.

Aguilar, Louis. 1997. "Hyphenated-Generation: Youth Reclaim Roots." *Hispanic Link* (June 21) 15:25.

Allen, Robert. 1970. *Black Awakening in Capitalist America.* Garden City, N.Y.: Doubleday Anchor.

Alvarez, Carmelo E. 1996. "Panorama Histórico de los Pentecostalismos Latinoamericanos y Caribeños." In Benjamin E. Gutiérrez, ed., *En La Fuerza Del Espíritu: Los Pentecostales en América Latina: Un Desafío a Las Iglesias Históricas,* 35–56. Santiago, Chile: CELEP.

Anson, Robert, Marshall Berges, Sandra Burton, and Susan J. Diamond. 1969. "The Little Strike That Grew to La Causa." *Time,* July 4, 16–21.

Arenal, Electa, and Stacey Schlau. 1989. *Untold Sisters: Hispanic Nuns in Their Own Works.* Albuquerque: University of New Mexico Press.

Badillo, David A. 1994. "The Catholic Church and the Making of Mexican-American Parish Communities in the Midwest." In Jay P. Dolan and Gilberto M. Hinojosa, eds., *Mexican Americans and the Catholic Church, 1900–1965,* vol. 1 of Notre Dame Series on Hispanic Catholics in the U.S., 9–125, 237-308. Notre Dame, Ind.: University of Notre Dame Press, 1994.

Bailey, Ronald, and Guillermo V. Flores. 1973. "Internal Colonialism and Racial Minorities." In Frank Bonilla and Robert Girling, eds., *Structures of Dependency,* 149–160. Palo Alto, Calif.: Nairobi Press.

Barrera, Mario Carlos Muñoz, and Charles Ornelas. 1972/1974. "The Barrio as an Internal Colony." In F. Chris Garcia, ed., *La Causa Política: A Chicano Politics Reader,* 281–301. Notre Dame, Ind.: University of Notre Dame Press. Reprinted from Harlan Han, ed., *Urban Affairs Annual Reviews,* Sage Publications 6 (1972):465–498.

_____. 1988. *Beyond Aztlán.* Notre Dame, Ind.: University of Notre Dame Press.

Beirne, Charles J., S.J. 1975. *The Problem of Americanization in the Catholic Schools of Puerto Rico.* Río Piedras: Editorial Universitaria de la Universidad de Puerto Rico.

Bellah, Robert N. 1975. *The Broken Covenant: American Civil Religion in a Time of Trial.* New York: Seabury Press.

Bellah, Robert N., Richard Madsen, Ann Swidler, William M. Sullivan, and Steven M. Tipton. 1985. *Habits of the Heart: Individualism and Commitment in American Life.* Berkeley: University of California Press.

Benavides, Gustavo. 1994. "Resistance and Accommodation in Latin American Popular Religiosity." In Anthony M. Stevens-Arroyo and Ana María Díaz-Stevens, eds., *An Enduring Flame: Studies of Latino Popular Religiosity,* vol. 1 of the PARAL Series, 37–68. New York: Bildner Center Books.

_____. 1995. "Syncretism and Legitimacy in Latin American Religion." In Anthony M. Stevens-Arroyo and Andrés Pérez y Mena, eds., *Enigmatic Powers,* 19–46. New York: Bildner Center Books.

Benavides, Gustavo, and M. W. Daly, eds. 1993. *Religion and Political Power.* Albany: State University of New York Press.

Benko, Stephen. 1993. *The Virgin Goddess*. Leiden: Brill.

Benmayor, Rina, Rosa M. Torruella, and Ana L. Jurabe. 1992. "Responses to Poverty Among Puerto Rican Women: Identity, Community and Cultural Citizenship." New York: Centro de Estudios Puertorriqueños, Hunter College.

Bennett, Spencer. 1993. "Civil Religion in a New Context: The Mexican-American Faith of César Chávez." In Gustavo Benavides and M. W. Daly, eds., *Religion and Political Power*, 151–166. Albany: State University of New York Press.

Berger, Peter. 1967. *The Sacred Canopy*. Garden City, N.Y.: Doubleday.

Besalga, Edward, S.J. 1970. "Cultural Change and Protestantism in Puerto Rico: 1945–1966." Ph.D. diss., New York University.

Blasi, Anthony J. 1978. Review of *The American Catholic*, by Andrew Greeley. *Sociological Analysis* 39 (2) (Summer 1978):171–173.

_____. 1988. *Early Christianity as a Social Movement*. Bern and New York: Peter Lang.

Blauner, Robert. 1969. "Internal Colonialism and Ghetto Revolt." *Social Problems* (Spring):393–408.

Blauner, Robert, ed. 1972. *On Racial Oppression in America*. New York: Harper and Row.

Blaut, J. M. 1983. "Assimilation vs. Ghettoization," *Antipode* 15 (1):35–41.

Bonilla, Frank, and Ricardo Campos. 1981. "A Wealth of Poor: Puerto Ricans in the New Economic Order." *Daedalus* 110 (2) (Spring):133–176.

Borges, Pedro. 1987. *Misión y civilización en América*. Madrid: Editorial Alhambra.

Bourdieu, Pierre. 1980/1990. *The Logic of Practice*. Translation of *Le Sens Pratique* by Richard Nice. Cambridge: Polity Press.

Budde, Michael. 1992a. *The Two Churches: Catholicism and Capitalism in the World System*. Durham, N.C.: Duke University Press.

_____. 1992b. "The Changing Face of American Catholic Nationalism." *Sociological Analysis* 53 (3) (Fall):245–255.

Burns, Gene. 1996. "Studying the Political Culture of American Catholicism." *Sociology of Religion* 57 (1) (Spring):37–54.

Burns, Jeffrey M. 1994. "Mexican Americans and the Catholic Church in California, 1910–1965." In Jay P. Dolan and Gilberto M. Hinojosa, eds., *Mexican Americans and the Catholic Church, 1900–1965*, vol. 1 of Notre Dame Series on Hispanic Catholics in the U.S., 9–125. Notre Dame, Ind.: University of Notre Dame Press, 1994.

Burgess, Stanley M., and Gary B. McGee, eds. 1988. *Dictionary of Pentecostal and Charismatic Movements*. Grand Rapids, Mich.: Zondervan.

Busto, Rudy V. 1991. "Like a Mighty Rushing Wind: The Religious Impulse in the Life and Writing of Reies López Tijerina (Chicano Pentecostalism)." Ph.D. diss., University of California, Berkeley.

Buxó i Rey, María Jesús. 1989. Introduction to C. Alvarez Santaló, María Jesús Buxó and S. Rodríguez Becerra, eds., *Vida y muerte: La imaginación religiosa*, vol. 2 of *La Religiosidad Popular*, 7–10. Barcelona: Anthropos.

Cadena, Gilbert R. 1987. "Chicanos and the Catholic Church: Liberation Theology as a Form of Empowerment." Ph.D. diss., University of California, Riverside.

_____. 1989. "Chicano Clergy and the Emergence of Liberation Theology." *Hispanic Journal of Behavioral Sciences* 11 (2) (May):107–121.

_____. 1992. "Gramsci, Maduro and the Sociology of the Chicano/Latino Religious Experience." Paper presented at the Conference of the Society for the Scientific Study of Religion, November 8, 1992, Washington, D.C.

_____. 1995. "Religious Ethnic Identity: A Socio-Religious Protrait of Latinos and Latinas in the Catholic Church." In Anthony M. Stevens-Arroyo and Gilbert R. Cadena, eds., *Old Masks, New Faces: Religion and Latino Identities*, 33–60. New York: Bildner Center Books.

Cahill, David. 1996. "Popular Religion and Appropriation: The Example of Corpus Christi in Eighteenth-Century Cuzco." *Latin American Research Review* 31 (2):67–110.

Campo, Orlando do. 1995. "The Supreme Court and the Practice of Santería." In Anthony M. Stevens-Arroyo and Andrés I. Pérez y Mena, eds., *Enigmatic Powers: Syncretism with African and Indigenous Peoples' Religions Among Latinos*, vol. 3 of the PARAL Series, 159–180. Bildner Center Books: New York.

Carnoy, Martin, Hugh Daley, and Raúl Hinojosa Ojeda. 1990. *Latinos in a Changing U.S. Economy: Comparative Perspectives on the U.S. Labor Market Since 1939*. New York: Research Foundation of the City University of New York.

Carter, Stephen. 1993. *Culture of Disbelief: How American Law and Politics Trivialize Religious Devotion*. New York: Basic Books.

Casanova, José. 1994. *Public Religions in the Modern World*. Chicago: University of Chicago Press.

Chavez, Linda. 1991. *Out of the Barrio: Towards a New Politics of Hispanic Assimilation*. New York: Basic Books.

Chilcote, Ronald H., and Joel C. Edelstein, eds. 1974. *Latin America: The Struggle with Dependency and Beyond*. New York: John Wiley and Sons.

Clark, Margaret. 1970. *Health in the Mexican-American Community: A Community Study*. Berkeley: University of California Press.

Coleman, James. 1990. *Foundations of Social Theory*. Cambridge:Harvard University Press.

Coleman, John A., S.J. 1996a. "Under the Cross and the Flag," John Courtney Murray Lecture, May 11, 1996, Fordham University, New York. *America*, May 11, 6–14.

_____. 1996b. "PICO-Church-Based Community Organizing." Paper presented at seminar forum, The Center for the Study of American Religion, Princeton University.

Collins, Randall. 1981. *Sociology Since Midcentury*. New York: Academic Press.

Colpe, Carsten. 1975/1980. *Theologie, Ideologie, Religionswissenshaft*. München: N.p.

Cros Sandoval, Mercedes. 1995. "Afro-Cuban Religion in Perspective." In Anthony M. Stevens-Arroyo and Andrés I. Pérez y Mena, eds., *Enigmatic Powers: Syncretism with African and Indigenous Peoples' Religions Among Latinos*, vol. 3 of the PARAL Series, 81–98. New York: Bildner Center Books.

Davidman, Lynn. 1991. *Tradition in a Rootless World: Women Turn to Orthodox Judaism*. Berkeley: University of California Press.

D'Antonio, William, James Davidson, Dean Hoge, and Ruth Wallace. 1989. *American Catholic Laity in a Changing Church.* Kansas City, Mo.: Sheed and Ward.

_____. 1996. *Laity American and Catholic: Transforming the Church.* Kansas City, Mo.: Sheed and Ward.

Deck, Allan Figueroa, S.J. 1989. *The Second Wave.* Mahwah, N.J.: Paulist Press.

_____. 1990. "The Crisis of Hispanic Ministry: Multiculturalism as an Ideology." *America,* July 14–21, 33–36.

_____. 1994. "The Challenge of Evangelical/Pentecostal Christianity to Hispanic Catholicism." In Jay Dolan and Allan Figueroa Deck, eds., *Hispanic Catholic Culture in the U.S.: Issues and Concerns,* 409–439. Notre Dame, Ind.: University of Notre Dame Press.

_____. 1995a. "A Pox on Both Your Houses: Liberal-Conservative Polarizations from the Hispanic Margin." In Mary Jo Weaver and R. Scott Appelby, eds., *Being Right: American Catholic Conservatives,* 88–106. Bloomington: University of Indiana Press.

_____. 1995b. Review of *Our Lady of Guadalupe: The Origins and Sources of a Mexican National Symbol, 1531–1797,* by Stafford Poole, C.M. *America,* September 30, 25–26.

De la Garza, Rudolfo O., Louis DeSipio, F. Chris Garcia, John Carcia, and Angelo Falcón. 1992. *Latino Voices: Mexican, Puerto Rican, and Cuban Perspectives on American Politics.* Boulder: Westview Press.

Delumeau, Jean. 1971/1977. *Catholicism Between Luther and Voltaire: A New View of the Counter-Reformation.* London: Burns and Oates. First published in French, 1971.

Deutsch, Sarah. 1987. *No Separate Refuge: Culture, Class, and Gender on an Anglo-Hispanic Frontier in the American Southwest, 1880–1940.* New York: Oxford University Press.

Díaz Ramírez, Ana María. 1975. "Religion in the Melting Pot of the Caribbean: San Juan, Puerto Rico." *New World Outlook* (May):8–15.

Díaz-Stevens, Ana María. 1990. "From Puerto Rican to Hispanic: The Politics of the *Fiestas Patronales* in New York." *Latinos Studies Journal* 1 (1) (January 1990):28–47.

_____. 1991. "Social Distance and Religious Conflict in the Pre-Vatican Catholicism of Puerto Rico." *MACLAS* 4:291–299.

_____. 1993a. *Oxcart Catholicism on Fifth Avenue.* Notre Dame, Ind.: University of Notre Dame Press.

_____. 1993b. "The Saving Grace: The Matriarchal Core of Latino Catholicism." *Latino Studies Journal* 4 (3) (September):60–78.

_____. 1993c. "La misa jíbara como campo de batalla sociopolítica en Puerto Rico." *Revista de Ciéncias Sociales* 30 (1–2) (enero-junio):139–162.

_____. 1994a. "Latinas and the Church." In Jay Dolan and Allan Figueroa Deck, eds., *Hispanic Catholic Culture in the U.S.: Issues and Concerns,* 240–277. Notre Dame, Ind.: University of Notre Dame Press.

_____. 1994b. "Latino Youth and the Church." In Jay Dolan and Allan Figueroa Deck, eds., *Hispanic Catholic Culture in the U.S.: Issues and Concerns,* 278–307. Notre Dame, Ind.: University of Notre Dame Press.

244   *Bibliography*

_____. 1994c. "Analyzing Popular Religiosity for Socio-Religious Meaning." In Anthony M. Stevens-Arroyo and Ana María Díaz-Stevens, eds., *An Enduring Flame: Studies of Latino Popular Religiosity*, vol. 1 of the PARAL Series, 17–36.

_____. 1995. "La religiosidad popular y el sincretismo: Dónde comienza una y dónde termina el otro." Presentation at the Seventeenth Congress of the International Association of the History of Religions, Convento de Sor Juana, Mexico City, August.

_____. 1996a. "Aspects of the Puerto Rican Religious Experience: A Sociohistorical Overview." In Gabriel Haslip-Viera and Sherrie L. Baver, eds., *Latinos in New York*, 147–188. Notre Dame, Ind.: University of Notre Dame Press.

_____. 1996b. "In the Image and Likeness of God: Literature as Theological Reflection." In Ada María Isasi-Díaz and Fernando F. Segovia, eds., *Hispanic/Latino Theology: Challenge and Promise*, 86–103. Minneapolis: Fortress Press.

_____. 1996c. "Latino Popular Religiosity and Communitarian Spirituality." Occasional Paper presented at the PARAL Symposium, Catholic Theological Union, Chicago, October.

_____. 1996d. "Ethnoreligious Identity as Locus for Dialogue Between Puerto Rican Catholics and American Jews." *Religious Education* 91 (4) (Fall):473–479.

Dolan, Jay P. 1978. *Catholic Revivalism*. Notre Dame, Ind.: University of Notre Dame Press.

_____. 1992. *The American Catholic Experience*. Notre Dame, Ind.: Notre Dame University Press.

Dolan, Jay P., and Allan Figueroa Deck, S.J., eds. 1994. *Hispanic Catholic Culture in the U.S.: Issues and Concerns*, vol. 3 of Notre Dame Series on Hispanic Catholics in the U.S. Notre Dame, Ind.: University of Notre Dame Press.

Dolan, Jay P., and Gilberto M. Hinojosa, eds. 1994. *Mexican Americans and the Catholic Church, 1900–1965*, vol. 1 of Notre Dame Series on Hispanic Catholics in the U.S. Notre Dame, Ind.: University of Notre Dame Press.

Dolan, Jay P., and Jaime R. Vidal, eds. 1994. *Puerto Rican and Cuban Catholics in the U.S., 1900–1965*, vol. 2 of Notre Dame Series on Hispanic Catholics in the U.S. Notre Dame, Ind.: University of Notre Dame Press.

Domínguez, Roberto. 1990. *Pioneros de Pentecostés: Norteamerica y las Antillas*. Barcelona: Talleres Gráficas de la MCE Horeb.

Doyle, Ruth, John Kuzloski, Thomas M. McDonald, and Olga Scarpetta. 1983. *Church-Related Hispanic Youth in New York: An Exploratory Study*. New York: Office of Pastoral Research, Archdiocese of New York.

Doyle, Ruth, Olga Scarpetta, Thomas M. McDonald, and Norman Simmons. 1982. *Hispanics in New York: Religious, Cultural and Social Experiences*. 2 vols. New York: Office of Pastoral Research, Roman Catholic Archdiocese of New York.

Early, Gerald. 1997. "Dreaming of a Black Christmas." *Harper's Magazine*, January, 55–61.

Eisenstadt, Samuel N. 1987. "Introduction: Historical Traditions, Modernization and Development." In Samuel N. Eisenstadt, ed., *Patterns of Modernity*, vol. 1, *The West*, 1–11. London: Frances Pinter.

Elizondo, Virgil. 1975. *Christianity and Culture.* Huntington, Ind.: Our Sunday Visitor Press.
_____. 1992. *The Future Is Mestizo.* New York: Crossroad Publishing Co.
Entwistle, Harold. 1979. *Antonio Gramsci: Conservative Schooling for Radical Politics.* London: Routledge and Kegan Paul.
Espín, Orlando. 1994. "Popular Catholicism Among Latinos." In Jay Dolan and Allan Figueroa Deck, eds., *Hispanic Catholic Culture in the U.S.: Issues and Concerns,* 308–359. Notre Dame, Ind.: University of Notre Dame Press.
Espinosa, Gaston. 1995. "Azusa Street and the Origins of Puerto Rican Pentecostalism, 1912–1940." Paper presented at the Annual Meeting of the Society for the Scientific Study of Religion, St. Louis, Mo., October 27.
Finke, Roger. 1994. "The Quiet Transformation: Changes in Size and Leadership of Southern Baptist Churches." *Review of Religious Research* 36 (1) (September):3–22.
Fitzpatrick, Joseph P., S.J. 1971. *Puerto Rican Americans: The Meaning of Migration to the Mainland.* Englewood Cliffs, N.J.: Prentice Hall.
_____. 1987. *One Church, Many Cultures.* Kansas City, Mo.: Sheed and Ward.
Flint, Valerie. 1991. *The Rise of Magic in Early Medieval Europe.* Princeton: Princeton University Press.
Flores, Juan. 1993. *Divided Borders: Essays on Puerto Rican Identity.* Houston: Arte Público Press.
Flores, Richard R. 1995. *Los Pastores: History and Performance in the Mexican Shepherd's Play of South Texas.* Washington, D.C.: Smithsonian Institution Press.
_____. 1996. "Gender and the Politics of Location in Popular Religion." Occasional Paper presented at the PARAL Symposium, Catholic Theological Union, Chicago, October.
Foster, George W. 1960. *Culture and Conquest: America's Spanish Heritage.* New York: Wenner-Gren Foundation.
Frank, André Gunder. 1978. *Dependent Accumulation and Development.* New York: Monthly Review Press/London: Macmillan.
_____. 1993. "Latin America at the Margin of World System History: East-West Hegemonial Shifts (992–1492–1992)." *Comparative Civilizations Review* 28 (Spring):1–40.
Fulton, John. 1987. "Religion as Politics in Gramsci: An Introduction." *Sociological Analysis* 48 (3) (Fall):197–216.
García, Mario T. 1989. *Mexican Americans: Leadership, Ideology, and Identity, 1930–1960.* New Haven: Yale University Press.
Ghisalberti, Carlo. 1991. *Istituzioni e risorgimento: Idee e protagonisti.* Firenze: Felice le Monnier.
Giddens, Anthony. 1984. *The Constitution of Society: Outline of a Theory of Stucturation.* Berkeley: University of California Press.
Gittell, Marilyn, with Bruce Hoffacker, Eleanor Rollins, Samuel Foster, and Mark Hoffacker. 1981. *Limits to Citizen Participation: The Decline of Community Organizations.* Beverly Hills, Calif.: Sage Publications.
Glazer, Nathan. 1983. *Ethnic Dilemmas, 1964–1982.* Cambridge: Harvard University Press.

Gleason, Phillip. 1987. *Keeping the Faith: American Catholicism, Past and Present.* Notre Dame, Ind.: University of Notre Dame Press.

Goldberg, Carey. 1997. "Hispanic Households Struggle as Poorest of the Poor in U.S." *New York Times,* January 30.

Gómez, David F. 1973. *Somos Chicanos: Strangers in Our Own Land.* Boston: Beacon Press.

González, Justo. 1988. "The Theological Education of Hispanics." Report to the Fund for Theological Education, New York.

———. 1990. *Mañana: Christian Theology from a Hispanic Perspective.* Nashville, Tenn.: Abingdon.

González, Robert O., and Michael La Velle. 1985. *The Hispanic Catholic in the U.S.: A Socio-Cultural and Religious Profile.* New York: Northeast Hispanic Pastoral Center.

González, Rudolfo "Corky." 1972. *I Am Joaquín.* New York: Bantam Books. (Copyright of poem, 1967. Reproduced with permission in Antonio M. Stevens-Arroyo, ed., *Prophets Denied Honor,* 15–20. Maryknoll, N.Y.: Orbis Books, 1980).

González-Wippler, Migene. 1995. "Santería: Its Dynamics and Multiple Roots." In Anthony M. Stevens-Arroyo and Andrés I. Pérez y Mena, eds., *Enigmatic Powers: Syncretism with African and Indigenous Peoples' Religions Among Latinos,* vol. 3 in the PARAL Series, 99–112. Bildner Center Books: New York.

Gordon, Milton. 1974. *Assimilation in American Life: The Role of Race, Religion, and National Origins.* New York: Oxford University Press.

Goris, Anneris. 1995. "Rites for a Rising Nationalism: Religous Meaning and Dominican Community Identity in New York City." In Anthony M. Stevens-Arroyo and Gilbert R. Cadena, eds., *Old Masks, New Faces: Religion and Latino Identities,* 117–142. New York: Bildner Center Books.

Greeley, Andrew. 1977. *The American Catholic.* New York: Basic Books.

———. 1982. *Catholic High Schools and Minority Students.* New Brunswick, N.J.: Transaction Books.

Griswold del Castillo, Richard. 1979. *The Los Angeles Barrio, 1850–1890: A Social History.* Berkeley: University of California Press.

Gutiérrez, Ramón. 1991. *When Jesus Came, the Corn Flower Mothers Went Away.* Stanford: Stanford University Press.

Habermas, Jürgen. 1990. *The Structural Transformation of the Public Sphere.* Cambridge: MIT Press.

Hall, Suzanne S.N.D. de N., and Carleen Reck, S.S.N.D., eds. 1987. *Integral Education: A Response to the Hispanic Presence.* Washington, D.C.: National Catholic Educational Association.

Hall, Thomas. 1989. *Social Change in the Southwest, 1350–1880.* Lawrence: University of Kansas Press.

———. 1991. "Civilizational Change: The Role of Nomads." *Comparative Civilizations Review* 24 (Spring):35–57.

Hamington, Maurice. 1995. *Hail Mary? The Struggle for the Ultimate Womanhood in Catholicism.* London: Routledge.

Hammond, Phillip E. 1993. "Religion and Nationalism in the United States." In Gustavo Benavides and M. W. Daly, eds., *Religion and Political Power,* 167–172. Albany: State University of New York Press.

Hanegraaf, Wouter J. 1995. "Empirical Method in the Study of Esotericism." *Method and Theory in the Study of Religion* 7 (2):99–129.

Hart, Stephen. 1996. "The Cultural Dimension of Social Movements: A Theoretical Reassessment and Literature Review." *Sociology of Religion* 57 (1) (Spring):87–100.

Haslip-Viera, Gabriel, and Sherie Baver, eds. 1996. *Hispanic New York.* Notre Dame, Ind.: University of Notre Dame Press.

Haveman, Robert H., ed. 1997. *A Decade of Federal Antipoverty Programs: Achievements, Failures, and Lessons.* New York: Academic Press.

Hayes Bautista, David. 1992. *No Longer a Minority: Latinos and Social Policy in California.* Los Angeles: Chicano Studies Research Center, University of California at Los Angeles.

Hernández, Edwin. 1995. "The National Survey of Hispanic Graduate Theological Education." Report of the Association for Hispanic Theological Education (AETH), Decatur, Georgia.

Hernández, Edwin, and Roger L. Dudley. 1990. "The Persistence of Religious Thought and Primary Group Ties Among Hispanic Seventh Day Adventist Youth." *Review for Religious Research* 32 (2) (December).

Hernández, José. 1994. "Hispanics Blend Diversity." In Felix Padilla, ed., *Handbook of Hispanic Cultures in the United States: Sociology,* 17–34. Houston: Arte Público Press.

Herrera, Marina. 1994. "The Context and Development of Hispanic Ecclesial Leadership." In Jay P. Dolan and Allan Figueroa Deck, S.J., eds., *Hispanic Catholic Culture in the U.S.: Issues and Concerns,* vol. 3 of Notre Dame Series on Hispanic Catholics in the U.S., 166–205. Notre Dame, Ind.: University of Notre Dame Press, 1994.

Hinojosa, Gilberto. 1994. "Mexican-American Faith Communities in Texas and the South West." In Jay P. Dolan and Gilberto M. Hinojosa, eds., *Mexican Americans and the Catholic Church, 1900–1965,* vol. 1 of Notre Dame Series on Hispanic Catholics in the U.S., 9–125. Notre Dame, Ind.: University of Notre Dame Press, 1994.

Hobsbawm, Eric, and Terence Ranger, eds. 1983. *The Invention of Tradition.* Cambridge: Cambridge University Press.

Hull, Brooks B., and Gerald F. Moran. 1989. "A Preliminary Time Series Analysis of Church Activity in Colonial Woodbury, Connecticut." *Journal for the Scientific Study of Religion* 28 (4) (December 1989):478–492.

Hunter, James Davison. 1991. *Culture Wars: The Struggle to Define America.* New York: Basic Books.

Huntington, Samuel P. 1996. *The Clash of Civilization and the Remaking of World Order.* New York: Simon and Schuster.

Hurtado, Juan. 1976. *An Attitudinal Study of the Social Distance Between the Mexican-American and the Church.* San Antonio, Tex.: Mexican American Cultural Center.

Isasi-Díaz, Ada María. 1977/1980. "The People of God on the Move—Chronicle of a History." Published in Spanish in *El Visitante Dominical,* September 18, 1977. Translated and reprinted in Antonio M. Stevens-Arroyo, ed., *Prophets Denied Honor,* 329–333. Maryknoll, N.Y.: Orbis Books, 1980..

Isasi-Díaz, Ada María, and Yolanda Tarango. 1988. *Hispanic Women: Prophetic Voice in the Church.* San Francisco: Harper and Row.

Jacobs, Janet. 1996. "Women, Ritual, and Secrecy: The Creation of Crypto-Jewish Culture." *Journal for the Scientific Study of Religion* 35 (2) (June):97–108.

Jameson, Frederic. 1981. *The Political Unconscious: Narative as a Socially Symbolic Act.* Ithaca: Cornell University Press.

Jorge, Antonio, Jaime Suchlicki, Adolfo Legiva de Varona, eds. 1991. *Cuban Exiles in Florida: Their Presence and Contributions.* Coral Gables, Fla: North-South Center Publications for the Research Institute for Cuban Studies.

Kammen, Michael. 1991. *Mystic Cords of Memory: The Transformation of Tradition in American Culture.* New York: Alfred Knopf.

Kavolis, Vytautas. 1988. "Contemporary Moral Cultures and the 'Return of the Sacred.'" *Sociological Analysis* 49 (3) (Fall):203–216.

Klor de Alva, J. Jorge. 1991. "Aztlán, Borinquen and Hispanic Nationalism in the United States." In Francisco Anaya and Rodolfo Lomeli, eds., *Aztlán: Essays on the Chicano Homeland,* 135–177. Albuquerque: University of New Mexico Press.

Kniss, Fred. 1988. "Toward a Theory of Ideological Change: The Case of the Radical Reformation." *Sociological Analysis* 49 (1) (Spring):29–38.

Kosmin, Barry A. 1991. *The National Survey of Religious Identification, 1989–1990.* New York: City University of New York.

Kosmin, Barry A., and Ariela Keysar. 1995. "The Impact of Religious Identification on Differences in Educational Attainment Among American Women in 1990." *Journal for the Scientific Study of Religion* 34 (1) (March):49–62.

Kosman, Barry A., and Seymour P. Lachman. 1993. *One Nation Under God: Religion in Contemporary American Society.* Harmony Books: New York.

Koss, Joan D. 1972. "Why Cults Are Born: The Case of *Espiritismo* in Puerto Rico." In Basil Ince, ed., *Race, Society, and Politics in the Caribbean,* 37–54. San Juan: Benzal Publishing Company.

Lafaye, Jacques. 1974/1976. *Quetzalcoatl and Guadalupe: The Formation of Mexican National Consciousness, 1531–1813.* Translated by Benjamin Keen. Chicago: University of Chicago Press.

León, Luis. 1994. "*Somos un Cuerpo en Cristo*: Notes on Power and the Body in an East Los Angeles Chicano/Mexicano Pentecostal Community." *Latino Studies Journal* 5 (3)(September):60–86.

Lewis, Gordon K. 1963. *Puerto Rico: Freedom and Power in the Caribbean.* New York: Monthly Review Press.

Llanes, José. 1982. *Cuban Americans: Masters of Survival.* Cambridge: ABT Books.

Lockhart, James, and Stuart B. Schwartz. 1983. *Early Latin America: A History of Colonial Spanish America and Brazil.* Cambridge: Cambridge University Press.

López, Alfredo. 1973. *The Puerto Rican Papers: Notes on the Re-Emergence of a Nation.* Indianapolis, Ind.: Bobbs-Merrill.

Lovejoy, David S. 1985. *Religious Enthusiasm in the New World: Heresy to Revolution.* Cambridge: Harvard University Press.

Luckmann, Thomas. 1967. *The Invisible Religion.* New York: Macmillan.

Lugo, Juan L. 1957. *Pentecostés en Puerto Rico o la vida de un misionero.* San Juan: Puerto Rico Gospel Press.

Luhmann, Niklas. 1984. *Religious Dogmatics and the Evolution of Societies.* Lewiston, N.Y.: Edwin Mellen Press.

Maduro, Otto A. 1982. *Religion and Social Conflicts.* Maryknoll, N.Y.: Orbis Books.

Mainwaring, Scott, and Eduardo Viola. 1984. "New Social Movements, Political Culture and Democracy: Brazil and Argentina in the 1980s." *Telos* 61 (Fall):17–52.

Maldonado, Lionel A. 1991. "Latino Ethnicity: Increasing Diversity." *Latino Studies Journal* 2 (3) (September):49–57.

Maldonado, Luis. 1975. *Religiosidad popular: Nostalgia de lo mágico.* Madrid: Ediciones Cristiandad.

Maldonado Denis, Manuel. 1969/1972. *Puerto Rico: Una interpretación histórico-social.* Mexico: Siglo Ventiuno. Translated as *Puerto Rico: A Socio-Historic Interpretation.* New York: Vintage Books.

Malley, Brian E. 1995. "Explaining Order in Religious Systems." *Method and Theory in the Study of Religion* 7 (1):5–22.

Maravall, José Antonio. 1975/1986. *Culture of the Baroque: Analysis of a Historical Structure.* English translation of *Cultura del barroco* by Terry Cochran. Minneapolis: University of Minnesota Press.

Marín, Gerardo, and Barbara Van Oss Marín. 1991. *Research with Hispanic Populations.* Newbury Park, Calif.: Sage Publications.

Matovina, Timothy. 1995a. *Tejano Religion and Ethnicity: San Antonio, 1821–1860.* Austin: University of Texas Press.

_____. 1995b. *The Alamo Remembered: Tejano Accounts and Perspectives.* Austin: University of Texas Press.

Mauss, Armand. 1993. "Research in Social Movements and in New Religious Movements: The Prospects for Convergence." In David G. Bromley and Jeffery K. Hadden, eds., *Religion and the Social Order,* vol. 3a, 127–151. Greenwich, Conn.: JAI Press.

McDannell, Colleen. 1995. *Material Christianity: Religion and Popular Culture in America.* New Haven: Yale University Press.

McGuire, Meredith. 1992. *Religion: The Social Context.* Belmont, Calif.: Wadsworth.

McNamara, Patrick Hayes. 1968. "Bishops, Priests and Prophecy: A Study in the Sociology of Religious Protest." Ph.D. diss., University of California.

_____. 1970. "Dynamics of the Catholic Church from Pastoral to Social Concerns." In Leo Grebler, Joan Moore, and Ralph Guzmán, eds., *The Mexican-American People,* 449–485. New York: Macmillan Free Press.

_____. 1973. "Catholicism, Assimilation and the Chicano Movement: Los Angeles as a Case Study." In Rudolfo de la Garza, Z. Anthony Kruszewski, and Tomás A. Arciniega, eds., *Chicanos and Native Americans,* 124–130. Englewood Cliffs, N.J.: Prentice Hall.

_____. 1995. "Assumptions, Theories and Methods in the Study of Latino Religion After 25 Years." In Anthony M. Stevens-Arroyo and Gilbert R. Cadena, eds., *Old Masks, New Faces: Religion and Latino Identities,* 23–32. New York: Bildner Center Books.

Medina, Lara. 1994. "Broadening the Discourse at the Theological Table: An Overview of Latino Theology, 1968–1993." *Latino Studies Journal* 5 (3) (September):10–36.

Merkur, Dan. 1994. "Reductions of a Working Historian." In Thomas A. Idinopulos and Edward A. Yonan, eds., *Religion and Reductionism: Essays on Eliade, Segal, and the Challenge of the Social Sciences in the Study of Religion,* 220–229. Leiden: Brill.

Mészáros, Istvan, ed. 1972. *Aspects of History and Class Consciousness.* New York: Herder and Herder.

Mills, C. Wright, Clarence Senior, and Rose Kohn Goldsen. 1950. *The Puerto Rican Journey.* New York: Harper and Row.

Moore, Joan. 1990. "'Hispanic/Latino': Imposed Label or Real Identity?" *Latino Studies Journal* 1 (2) (May):33–47.

_____. 1994. "The Social Fabric of the Hispanic Community Since 1965." In Jay Dolan and Allan Figueroa Deck, eds., *Hispanic Catholic Culture in the U.S.: Issues and Concerns,* 6–49. Notre Dame, Ind.: University of Notre Dame Press.

Moore, Joan, and Harry Pachón. 1985. *Hispanics in the United States.* Englewood Cliffs, N.J.: Prentice Hall.

Moore, Joan, and Raquel Pinderhughes. 1993. *In the Barrios: Latinos and the Underclass Debate.* New York: Russell Sage.

Mosqueda, Lawrence J. 1986. *Chicanos, Catholicism, and Political Ideology.* Boston: University Press of America.

Muñoz, Carlos, Jr. 1989. *Youth, Identity, Power: The Chicano Movement,* Verso Haymarket Series on North American Politics and Culture. New York: New Left Books.

Negrón Montilla, Aida. 1970. *Americanization in Puerto Rico and the Public School System, 1900–1930.* Río Piedras: Editorial Edil.

O'Brien, David J. 1971. *The Renewal of American Catholicism.* New York: Paulist Press.

_____. 1990. "The Catholic Church and American Culture During Our Nation's Lifetime, 1787–1987." In Cassian Yuhas, C.P., ed., *The Catholic Church and American Culture,* 1–23. Mahwah, N.J.: Paulist Press.

Orsi, Robert. 1985. *The Madonna of 101st Street: Faith and Community in Italian Harlem, 1880–1950.* New Haven: Yale University Press.

_____. 1996. *Thank You, St. Jude: Women's Devotion to the Patron Saint of Hopeless Causes.* New Haven: Yale University Press.

Ortíz, Fernando. 1947/1963. *Cuban Counterpoint: Tobacco and Sugar.* New York: Knopf. Spanish translation published by Editora Nacional de la Cultura, La Havana.

Ortíz Cofer, Judith. 1990. *Silent Dancing: A Partial Remembrance of a Puerto Rican Childhood.* Houston: Arte Público Press.

Padilla, Felix. 1985. *Latino Ethnic Consciousness: The Case of Mexican Americans and Puerto Ricans in Chicago.* Notre Dame, Ind.: University of Notre Dame Press.

_____. 1987. *Puerto Rican Chicago*. Notre Dame, Ind.: University of Notre Dame Press.

Pantoja, Segundo, 1996. "Religious Switching and Conversion Among Latinos." Paper presented at the Annual Meeting of the Society for the Scientific Study of Religion, Nashville, Tenn., November 9.

Peña, Milagros. 1996. "Sociology and the Clergy: Progress Report on an Experiment in Collaborative Research." Paper presented at the Annual Meeting of the Society for the Scientific Study of Religion, Nashville, Tenn., November 9.

Pérez, Arturo. 1994. "The History of Hispanic Liturgy Since 1965." In Jay Dolan and Allan Figueroa Deck, eds., *Hispanic Catholic Culture in the U.S.: Issues and Concerns*, 360–408. Notre Dame, Ind.: University of Notre Dame Press.

Pérez y González, María Elizabeth. 1994. *Latinas in Ministry: A Pioneering Study on Women Ministers, Educators, and Students of Theology*. New York: New York City Mission Society.

_____. 1995. "The Heresy of Social Justice: Latinas in the Barrio." Paper presented at the Annual Meeting of the Latin American Studies Association, Washington, D.C., September 29.

Pérez y Mena, Andrés I. 1991. *Speaking with the Dead: Development of Afro-Latin Religion Among Puerto Ricans in the United States*. New York: AMS Press.

_____. 1995a. "Puerto Rican Spiritism as a Transfeature of Afro-Latin Religion." In Anthony M. Stevens-Arroyo and Andrés I. Pérez y Mena, eds., *Enigmatic Powers: Syncretism with African and Indigenous Peoples' Religions Among Latinos*, 137–156. New York: Bildner Center Books.

_____. 1995b. "Transculturación de las religiones Afro-Latinas entre las comunidades de Latinos en los EE. UU." Presentation at the Seventeenth Congress of the International Association of the History of Religions, Convento de Sor Juana, Mexico City, August.

Poblete, Renato, and Thomas O'Dea. 1960. "Anomie and the 'Quest for Community': The Formation of Sects Among the Puerto Ricans of New York." *American Catholic Sociological Review* 21 (Spring):18–36.

Portes, Alejandro, and Robert L. Bach. 1985. *Latin Journey: Cuban and Mexican Immigrants in the United States*. Berkeley: University of California Press.

Poole, Stafford, C.M. 1995a. *Our Lady of Guadalupe: The Origins and Sources of a Mexican National Symbol, 1531–1797*. Tucson: University of Arizona Press.

_____. 1995b. "Our Lady of Guadalupe: An Ambiguous Symbol." *Catholic Historical Review* 81 (4) (Winter):588–599.

Privett, Stephen A., S.J. 1988. *The United States Catholic Church and Its Hispanic Members: The Pastoral Vision of Archbishop Robert E. Lucey*. San Antonio, Tex.: Trinity University Press.

Pulido, Alberto López. 1994. "Searching for the Sacred: Conflict and Struggle for Mexican Catholics in the Roman Catholic Diocese of San Diego, 1936–1941." *Latino Studies Journal* 5 (3) (September):37–59.

Putnam, Robert D. 1993. "The Prosperous Community: Social Capital and Economic growth." *American Prospect* 354 (Spring):35–42.

_____. 1995a. "Bowling Alone: America's Declining Social Capital." *Journal of Democracy* 6 (January):65–78.

_____. 1995b. "Bowling Alone, Revisted." *Responsive Community* (Spring):18–33.

_____. 1995c. "Tuning In, Tuning Out: The Strange Disappearance of Social Capital in America." 1995 Ithiel de Sola Pool Lecture, American Political Science Association Conference, New Haven, Conn. September.

Ramírez, Daniel. 1996. *"Flor y Canto Apostólico*: Preliminary Inquiries into Latino Pentecostal Hymnody." Paper presented at the Annual Meeting of the Society for the Scientific Study of Religion, Nashville, Tenn., November 9.

Ramírez Calzadilla, Jorge. 1996. "Religion and Culture: Socioreligious Research in Cuba." Paper presented at the Annual Meeting of the Society for the Scientific Study of Religion, Nashville, Tenn., November 9.

Ramírez de Arellano, Annette B., and Conrad Seipp. 1983. *Colonialism, Catholicism, and Contraception: A History of Birth Control in Puerto Rico.* Chapel Hill: University of North Carolina Press.

Ramos, Marcos Antonio, and Agustin A. Román. 1991. "The Cubans, Religion, and South Florida." In Antonio Jorge, Jaime Suchlicki, and Adolfo Leyva de Varona, eds., *Cuban Exiles in Florida: Their Presence and Contribution,* 111–143. Miami, Fla.: University of Miami.

Rendón, Armando. 1971. *Chicano Manifesto.* New York: Collier Books.

Riall, Lucy. 1994. *The Italian Risorgimento: State, Society, and National Unification.* London: Routledge.

Rivera, Edward. 1982. *Family Installments: Memories of Growing Up Hispanic.* New York: William Morrow and Company.

Robertson, Roland, and JoAnn Chirico. 1985. "Humanity, Globalization and Worldwide Religious Resurgence: A Theoretical Explanation." *Sociological Analysis* 46 (3) (Fall):219–242.

Rodríguez, Clara E. 1989. *Puerto Ricans Born in the U.S.A.* Boston: Unwin Hyman.

Rodríguez, Clara E., and Virginia Sánchez-Korrol, eds. 1980/1996. *Historical Perspectives on Puerto Rican Survival in the United States.* 3d ed. Princeton: Marcus Weiner.

Rodríguez, Edmundo, S.J. 1994. "The Hispanic Community and Church Movements: Schools of Leadership." In Jay Dolan and Allan Figueroa Deck, eds., *Hispanic Catholic Culture in the U.S.: Issues and Concerns,* 206–239. Notre Dame, Ind.: University of Notre Dame Press.

Rodríguez, Jeanette. 1994. *Our Lady of Guadalupe: Faith and Empowerment Among Mexican-American Women.* Austin: University of Texas Press.

Rodríguez, Olga. 1977. *The Politics of Chicano Liberation.* New York: Pathfinder Press.

Rodriguez, Richard. 1982. *Hunger of Memory: The Education of Richard Rodriguez.* Boston: David R. Godine.

Rodríguez León, Mario A., O.P. ed. 1996. *Homenaje al P. William Loperena, O.P., 1935–1996.* Bayamón, Puerto Rico: Instituto Histórico Juan Alejo Arizmendi.

Romero, Juan, with Moises Sandoval. 1976. *Reluctant Dawn.* San Antonio, Tex.: Mexican American Cultural Center.

Roof, Wade Clark. 1994. *A Generation of Seekers: The Spiritual Journeys of the Baby-Boomer Generation.* San Francisco: HarperCollins.

Roof, Wade Clark, and William McKinney. 1987. *American Mainline Religion: Its Changing Shape and Future.* New Brunswick, N.J.: Rutgers University Press.

Roof, Wade Clark, and Karen Walsh. 1993. "Life Cycle, Generation, and Participation in Religious Groups." In David G. Bromley and Jeffrey K. Haden, eds., *The Handbook on Cults and Sects in America*, vol. 3b, 157–171. Greenwich, Conn.: JAI Press.

Rosado, Caleb. 1995. "The Concept of Pueblo as a Paradigm for Explaining the Religious Experience of Latinos." In Anthony M. Stevens-Arroyo and Gilbert R. Cadena, eds., *Old Masks, New Faces: Religion and Latino Identities*, 77–92. New York: Bildner Center Books.

Rosaldo, Renato. 1989. *Culture and Truth: The Remaking of Social Analysis.* Boston: Beacon.

Rouse, Irving. 1992. *The Taínos: Rise and Decline of the People Who Greeted Columbus.* New Haven: Yale University Press.

Rudolf, Kurt. 1979. "Synkretismus—vom theologischen Scheltwort zum religionswissenschaftlichen Begriff." In *Humanitas religiosa*, Festschrift für Haralds Biezais zu seinem 70 Geburtstag, 194–212. Stockholm.

Rutman, Darret B., ed. 1977. *The Great Awakening: Event and Exegesis.* Huntington, N.Y.: Robert E. Krieger Publishing.

Said, Edward. 1978. *Orientalism.* New York: Pantheon.

Saldigloria, Romeo F. 1980. "Religious Problems of the Hispanos in the City of New York." In Antonio M. Stevens-Arroyo, ed., *Prophets Denied Honor*, 166–169. Maryknoll, N.Y.: Orbis Books.

Salvo, Joseph. 1996. "A Critical Time for the 2000 Diennial Census Process." *Analysis and Commentary,* APOU Newsletter, vol. 20 (5) (June):1–12.

Sánchez-Korrol, Virginia E. 1983. *From Colonia to Community: The History of Puerto Ricans in New York City, 1917–1948.* Westport, Conn.: Greenwood Press.

Sandoval, Moises, ed. 1983. *Fronteras: A History of the Latin American Church in the U.S.A. Since 1513*, vol. 10 of *General History of the Church in Latin America,* Commission on Studies for Church History in Latin America (CEHILA). San Antonio, Tex.: Mexican American Cultural Center.

_____. 1990. *On the Move.* Maryknoll, N.Y.: Orbis Books.

Santos, Richard. 1983. "Missionary Beginnings in Spanish Florida, the Southwest and California." In Moises Sandoval, ed. *Fronteras: A History of the Latin American Church in the U.S.A. Since 1513.* Vol. X of the General History of the Church in Latin America, Commission on Studies for Church History in Latin America (CEHILA). San Antonio, Tex.: Mexican American Cultural Center, 3–54.

Sassoon, Anne Showstack. 1980. *Gramsci's Politics.* New York: St. Martin's Press.

Schluchter, Wolfgang. 1980. *Rationalism, Religion, and Domination: A Weberian Perspective.* Berkeley: University of California Press.

Schmidt, Leigh Eric. 1995. *Consumer Rites: The Buying and Selling of American Holidays.* Princeton: Princeton University Press.

Seda Bonilla, Eduardo. 1967/1973. *Interacción social y personalidad en una comunidad de Puerto Rico.* San Juan: Ediciones Juan Ponce de León. Published in English as *Social Change and Personality in a Puerto Rican Agrarian Reform Community.* Evanston, Ill.: Northwestern University Press.

Seelye, Katherine Q. 1997. "The New U.S.: Grayer and More Hispanic," *New York Times*, March 27.

Shils, Edward. 1981. *Tradition*. Chicago: University of Chicago Press.

Silva Gotay, Samuel. 1994. "The Ideological Dimensions of Popular Religiosity and Cultural Identity in Puerto Rico." In Anthony M. Stevens-Arroyo and Ana María Díaz-Stevens, eds., *An Enduring Flame: Studies of Latino Popular Religiosity*, vol. 1 of the PARAL Series, 133–170. New York: Bildner Center Books.

Spini, Giorgio. 1989. *Risorgimento e Protestanti*. Milano: Arnaldo Mondadori Editore.

Stark, Rodney, and William Bainbridge. 1985. *The Future of Religion: Secularization, Revival, and Cult Formation*. Berkeley: University of California Press.

Stavans, Ilan. 1995. *The Hispanic Condition: Reflections on Culture and Identity in America*. New York: HarperCollins.

Stevens-Arroyo, Antonio M. 1980/1996. "Puerto Rican Struggles in the Catholic Church." In Clara E. Rodríguez and Virginia Sánchez-Korrol, eds., *Historical Perspectives on Puerto Rican Survival in the United States*, 3d ed., 153–166. Princeton: Marcus Weiner.

Stevens-Arroyo, Anthony M., 1989. "The Radical Shift in the Spanish Approach to Intercivilizational Encounter." *Comparative Civilizations Review* 21:80–101.

_____. 1990. "Puerto Rico's Future Status: Prisoners of Many Myths." *Nation*, January 22, 86–90.

_____. 1992. "Catholic Ethos as Politics: The Puerto Rican Nationalists." In William Swatos, ed., *Twentieth Century World Religious Movements in Neo-Weberian Perspective*, 175–193. Lewiston, N.Y.: Edwin Mellen Press.

_____. 1993. "The Inter-Atlantic Paradigm: The Failure of Spanish Medieval Colonialism of the Canary and Caribbean Islands." *Comparative Studies in Society and History* 35 (3) (July):515–543.

_____. 1994. "The Emergence of a Social Identity Among Latino Catholics: An Appraisal." In Jay Dolan and Allan Figueroa Deck, eds., *Hispanic Catholic Culture in the U.S.: Issues and Concerns*, 77–130. Notre Dame, Ind.: University of Notre Dame Press.

_____. 1995a. "Latino Catholicism and the Eye of the Beholder: Notes Towards a New Sociological Paradigm." *Latino Studies Journal* 6 (2) (May):22–55.

_____. 1995b. "The Persistence of Religious Cosmovision in an Alien World." In Anthony M. Stevens-Arroyo and Andrés I. Pérez y Mena, eds., *Enigmatic Powers: Syncretism with African and Indigenous Peoples' Religions Among Latinos*, vol. 3 in the PARAL Series, 113–135. New York: Bildner Center Books.

_____. 1995c. "Discovering Latino Religion." In *Discovering Latino Religion*, with Segundo Pantoja, vol. 4 in the PARAL Series, 13–40. New York: Bildner Center Books.

_____. 1995d. "Il programma Latino: Deamericanizzare e recattolicizzare il Cattolicesimo Americano." *Religioni e Società: Rivista di Scienze Sociali Della Religione* 21 (10) (gennaio-aprile):10–29.

_____. 1995e. "The Counterhegemonic Role of Barrio Religion." Paper presented at the Annual Meeting of the Latin American Studies Association, Washington, D.C., September 29.

_____. 1996a. "Jaime Balmes Redux: Catholicism as Civilization in the Political Philosophy of Pedro Albizu Campos." In Marina Pérez de Mendiola, ed., *Bridging the Atlantic: Iberian and Latin American Thought in Historical Perspective*, 129–151. Albany: State University of New York Press.

_____. 1996b. "Juan Mateo Guaticabanú, September 21, 1496: Evangelization and Martyrdom in the Time of Columbus." *Catholic Historical Review* 82 (4) (October):614–637.

_____. 1996c. "Liturgical Music as Collective Memory." Paper presented at the Annual Meeting of the Society for the Scientific Study of Religion, Nashville, Tenn., November 9.

_____. 1997a. "Building a New Public Realm: Moral Responsibility and Religious Commitment in the City." In Alberto Vourvoulias-Bush and Margaret Crahan, eds., *The City and the World*. New York: Council on Foreign Relations Press.

_____. 1997b (forthcoming). "The Evolution of Marian Devotionalism Within Christianity and the Ibero-Mediterranean Polity." *Journal for the Scientific Study of Religion*.

_____. 1997c (forthcoming). "Understanding Pious Colonialism: How the Churches Replaced National Identity with Ethnicity." In Mario García and Gastón Espinosa, eds., *New Directions in Chicano Religion*. Berkeley: University of California Press..

Stevens-Arroyo, Anthony M., ed. 1980. *Prophets Denied Honor*. Maryknoll, N.Y.: Orbis Books.

Stevens-Arroyo, Anthony M. 1987. "Cahensly Revisted?: The National Pastoral Encounter of America's Hispanic Catholics." *Migration World* 15 (3) (Fall): 16–19.

Stevens-Arroyo, Anthony M., and Ana María Díaz Ramírez. 1982. "Puerto Ricans in the United States." In Gary and Rosalind Dworkin, eds., *The Minority Report*, 2d ed., 196–232. New York: Holt Rinehart and Winston.

Stevens-Arroyo, Anthony M., and Ana María Díaz-Stevens. 1993a. "Religious Faith and Institutions in the Forging of Latino Identities." In Felix Padilla, ed., *Handbook for Hispanic Cultures in the United States*, 257–291. Houston: Arte Publico Press.

_____. 1993b. "Latino Church and Schools as Urban Battlegrounds." In Stanley Rothstein, ed., *Urban Schooling in America*, 245–270. Westport, Conn.: Greenwood Press.

_____. 1994. *An Enduring Flame: Studies in Latino Popular Religiosity*. Vol. 1 of the PARAL Series. New York: Bildner Center Books.

Stevens-Arroyo, Anthony M., and Gilbert R. Cadena, eds. 1995. *Old Masks, New Faces: Religion and Latino Identities*. Vol. 2 of the PARAL Series. New York: Bildner Center Books.

Stevens-Arroyo, Anthony M., and Andrés I. Pérez y Mena, eds. 1995. *Enigmatic Powers: Syncretism with African and Indigenous Peoples' Religions Among Latinos*. Vol. 3 in the PARAL Series. New York: Bildner Center Books.

Stolzenberg, Ross M., Mary Blair-Loy, and Linda J. Waite. 1995. "Religious Participation in Early Adulthood: Age and Family Life Cycle Effects on Church Membership." *American Sociological Review* 60 (February):84–103.

Sullivan, Kathleen. 1997. "Religious Conversion and the Recreation of Community in an Urban Setting Among the Tzotzil Maya of Highland Chiapas, Mexico." Ph.D. diss., City University of New York.

Sunseri, Alvin R. 1979. *Seeds of Discord: New Mexico in the Aftermath of the American Conquest, 1846–1861.* Chicago: Nelson Hall.

Tatum, Charles A. 1987. "Geographic Displacement as Spiritual Desolation in Puerto Rican and Chicano Prose Fiction." In Asela Rodríguez de Laguna, ed., *Images and Identities: The Puerto Rican in Two World Contexts,* 254–264. New Brunswick, N.J.: Transaction Books.

Taves, Ann. 1986. *The Household of Faith: Roman Catholic Devotions in Mid-Nineteenth Century America.* Notre Dame, Ind.: University of Notre Dame Press.

Thernstrom, Stephan T., ed. 1980. *The Harvard Encyclopedia of American Ethnic Groups.* Cambridge: Belknap Press.

Tomasi, Silvio. 1975. *Piety and Power: The Role of Italian Parishes in the New York Metropolitan Areas, 1880-1930.* New York: Center for Migration Studies.

Torres, Joseph. 1996. "Report Says Combining Race and Ethnicity in Census Lowers Latino Response." *Hispanic Link Weekly Report,* June 3.

Trinidad, Saúl. 1988. "Apuntes hacia una pastoral Hispana." *Apuntes* 8 (1) (Spring):3–17.

Tweed, Thomas A. 1996. "Identity and Authority at a Cuban Shrine in Miami: Sanería, Catholicism, and Struggles for Religious Identity." *Journal of Hispanic/Latino Theology* 4 (1) (August):27–48.

Vázquez de Prada, Valentín, and Ignacio Olábarri. 1995. *Understanding Social Change in the Nineties: Theoretical Approaches and Historiographical Perspectives.* Aldershot, England: Variorum.

Verba, Sidney, Kay Schlozman, and Henry Brady. 1995. *Voice and Equality.* Cambridge: Harvard University Press.

Vidal, Jaime R. 1982. "Popular Religion in the Lands of Origin of New York's Hispanic Population." In Ruth Doyle, Olga Scarpetta, Thomas M. McDonald, and Norman Simmons, *Hispanics in New York: Religious, Cultural, and Social Experiences,* vol. 2, 1–48. New York: Office of Pastoral Research, Roman Catholic Archdiocese of New York.

_____. 1988. "Popular Religion Among the Hispanics in the General Area of the Archdiocese of Newark." Pt. 4 of *Nueva Presencia,* 235–348. Newark: Archdiocesan Office of Pastoral Planning.

_____. 1994a. "Puerto Rican Catholicism." In *Puerto Rican and Cuban Catholics in the U.S., 1900–1965,* vol. 2 of Notre Dame Series on Hispanic Catholics in the U.S., 11–134. Notre Dame, Ind.: University of Notre Dame Press.

_____. 1994b. "Towards an Understanding of Synthesis in Iberian and Hispanic American Popular Religiosity." In Anthony M. Stevens-Arroyo and Ana María Díaz-Stevens, eds., *An Enduring Flame: Studies of Latino Popular Religiosity,* vol. 1 of the PARAL Series, 69–96.

Villafañe, Eldín. 1993. *The Liberating Spirit: Toward an Hispanic American Pentecostal Social Ethic.* Grand Rapids, Mich.: William B. Eerdmans.

Vovelle, Michel. 1990. *Ideologies and Mentalities.* Chicago: University of Chicago Press.

Wakefield, Dan. 1959. *Island in the Sun*. Boston: Houghton Mifflin.

Warner, Stephen J. 1996. "Religion, Boundaries and Bridges." Furfey Lecture at the Annual Meeting for the Association for the Sociology of Religion, New York, August 16. Forthcoming in *Sociology of Religion*.

Weber, David J. 1992. *The Spanish Frontier in North America*. New Haven: Yale University Press.

Weber, Max. 1947. *The Theory of Social and Economic Organizations*. Edited with an introduction by Talcott Parsons. New York: Free Press.

Wellmeier, Nancy. 1995. "Marimbas for the Saints: Culture and Religion in a Maya Refugee Association." Paper presented at the Society for the Scientific Study of Religion Conference, St. Louis, Mo., October 28.

Williams, Rhys H. 1996. "Religion as Political Resource: Culture or Ideology?" *Journal for the Scientific Study of Religion* 35 (4) (December):368–378.

Wuthnow, Robert. 1987. *Meaning and Moral Order*. Berkeley: University of California Press.

_____. 1988. *The Restructuring of American Religion: Society and Faith Since World War II*. Princeton: Princeton University Press.

_____. 1991. *Acts of Compassion: Caring for Others and Helping Ourselves*. Princeton: Princeton University Press.

_____. 1994. *Producing the Sacred*. Urbana: University of Illinois Press.

Yarnold, Barbara M., ed. 1991. *The Role of Religious Organizations in Social Movements*. Westport, Conn.: Praeger.

Yeager, Robert J., Peter L. Benson, Michael J. Guerra, and Bruno V. Manno. 1985. *The Catholic High School: A National Portrait*. Washington, D.C.: National Catholic Educational Association.

Index

Abbelen (vicar), 184

Abuelita theology, 51, 156, 222

Academy of Catholic Hispanic Theologians in the United States (ACHTUS), 199

Acculturation, 39, 79

ACHTUS. *See* Academy of Catholic Hispanic Theologians in the United States

Adames, Roque (bishop of Dominican Republic)

AETH. *See* Associacíon para la Educación Teológica Hispana

Affirmative action, 15, 19

African Americans, 18, 113, 114, 196
demographic comparisons, 21, 22, 23(table, fig.), 24, 25, 26, 29

Africans, under colonial rule, 75–76, 91–92

Afro-Latin religion, 76, 77

Agricultural cycle, 58, 60–61, 62, 64–65

Agricultural labor, 100, 101. *See also* Farm workers

Aguinaldos, 66–67

Albanese, Catherine, 216

Albizu Campos, Pedro, 78, 139, 141

Alianza de Ministerios Evangélicos Nacionales (AMEN), 207, 208, 214

Alianza Federal de Mercedes, 140, 141

Alicea, Benjamin, 197

Alinsky, Saul, 157, 214

Allen, Robert, 102, 103

All Saints' Day, 61, 65

All Souls' Day, 61, 65

Amat, Thaddeus (bishop of Monterrey), 106, 107

AMEN. *See* Alianza de Ministerios Evangélicos Nacionales

Amendáriz, Rubén, 167, 168

Amengual, Juan, C.M., 174

America, 56

American Catholic, The (Greeley), 2–3, 4, 42, 47(n9)

Americanization, 38, 58–59, 99, 104–106, 110, 114, 187, 235
in Puerto Rico, 77, 109

AmeriCorps, 229

Angels Unaware, 209

Anglada, Rev. David, 207

Annales (Morazé), 123

Anointing of the Sick, 73

Anticlericalism, 77, 90, 95

Antojos, 71

Apostolic Assembly of the Faith in Jesus Christ, 113, 120

Apuntes, 152, 169, 199

Arenal, Electa, 80

Arias, David, 176

Arras, las, 71

Arrastía, Cecilio, 167

ASH. *See* Association of Hispanic Priests

Aspira, 229

Assimilation, 3, 19, 31, 38–39, 40, 46(n4), 86–87, 107, 110, 118, 181, 185, 186, 189, 190, 192, 232
individual, 41–42
See also Transculturation

Assimilation in American Life (Gordon), 38–39

Associacíon para la Educación Teológica Hispana (AETH), 197, 198, 207, 208, 214

270

Index